Southern News, Southern Politics

Southern News, Southern Politics

HOW A NEWSPAPER DEFINED
A STATE FOR A CENTURY

Rob Christensen

THE UNIVERSITY OF NORTH CAROLINA PRESS

Chapel Hill

*This book was published with the assistance of the
Fred W. Morrison Fund of the University of North Carolina Press.*

© 2025 Rob Christensen

All rights reserved

Designed by Jamison Cockerham
Set in Scala Pro, Scala Sans Pro, ITC Franklin Gothic Std, and BodoniSevITC
by Jamie McKee, MacKey Composition

Cover art: Newspapers © BillionPhotos.com / Adobe Stock.

Manufactured in the United States of America

LIBRARY OF CONGRESS CATALOGING-IN-PUBLICATION DATA
Names: Christensen, Rob, author.
Title: Southern news, southern politics : how a newspaper
   defined a state for a century / Rob Christensen.
Description: Chapel Hill : The University of North Carolina Press,
   [2025] | Includes bibliographical references and index.
Identifiers: LCCN 2024044989 | ISBN 9781469685243 (cloth) |
   ISBN 9781469685250 (epub) | ISBN 9781469685267 (pdf)
Subjects: LCSH: Daniels family. | News & observer (Raleigh, N.C. : 1894)—
   History. | American newspapers—North Carolina—Raleigh—History. |
   North Carolina—Politics and government. | BISAC: HISTORY / United
   States / State & Local / South (AL, AR, FL, GA, KY, LA, MS, NC, SC, TN, VA,
   WV) | BIOGRAPHY & AUTOBIOGRAPHY / Editors, Journalists, Publishers
Classification: LCC PN4899.R355 N49 2025 | DDC
   071/.75655—dc23/eng/20241030
LC record available at https://lccn.loc.gov/2024044989

This book is dedicated to the men and women

who worked long hours, often under high stress,

for modest pay to produce the *News and Observer*

for generations of North Carolinians.

Contents

List of Illustrations ix

Introduction 1

1. White Supremacy 6
2. Beginnings 30
3. War to the Knife 39
4. Crusader 47
5. Wilson 60
6. Cup of Joe 66
7. Between the Wars 97
8. Mexico 112
9. Jonathan 120
10. Washington and Josephus's Last Days 137
11. Triumph and Despair 155
12. Civil Rights and Integration 164
13. Frank Sr. and Frank Jr. 183

14 Claude Sitton, the Outsider *197*

15 The Neighbors' War *226*

16 Frank III, the Fourth and Last Generation *235*

17 The Decline of Newspapers *248*

Conclusion *265*

Acknowledgments 271

Notes 273

Bibliography 301

Index 313

Illustrations

Frank Daniels Sr. and Frank Daniels Jr. 2

Josephus Daniels 7

Racist cartoon 14

Martin Street offices 52

Josephus Daniels with William Jennings Bryan, Woodrow Wilson, and Franklin Roosevelt 67

Josephus Daniels and Franklin Roosevelt 82

Jonathan Daniels 147

McDowell Street offices 185

Claude Sitton 203

Bob Brooks 205

Frank Daniels III 237

Pulitzer Prize announcement 241

Anders Gyllhenhaal 250

John Drescher 254

The removal of the Josephus Daniels statue 266

Introduction

On September 24, 1985, the *News and Observer* celebrated its success as one of the South's most powerful and respected media companies with a gala dinner attended by 1,550 guests at the Raleigh Civic Center. The North Carolina Symphony provided music as guests ate roast duckling with orange sauce, wild rice, green beans, and chocolate mousse pie.

One of the day's highlights was the unveiling of a seven-foot statue of one of the paper's founders, Josephus Daniels, in a city park across the street from the newspaper's offices. Offering an invocation at the unveiling, the Reverend Arthur Calloway, an African American pastor serving on the Raleigh City Council, called Daniels an example of "public concern and human enlightenment" and added, "May this statue remind us of the greatness of the human spirit within us." In accepting the statue, Raleigh mayor Avery Upchurch said the sculpture would be "an enduring remembrance of a citizen whose legacy should be an example to us all." William C. Friday, president of the University of North Carolina and one of the nation's most widely respected academic leaders, told the dinner guests that if Josephus Daniels were alive today, he would be indignant about the "poverty, greed, illiteracy, hunger, poor health, neglected senior citizens, unemployment."[1]

But the verdict of history would change thirty-five years later, as the Daniels family paid to have the statue carted away for storage before it received a more ignominious fate at the hands of protesters. There were no speeches or hoopla as contractors pulled the statue down. "Josephus Daniels' legacy of service to North Carolina and our country does not transcend his reprehensible stand on race and his active support of racist activities," said a statement by his grandson Frank Daniels Jr., the last family member to serve as publisher.[2]

Frank Daniels Sr. and Frank Daniels Jr., the son and grandson of Josephus Daniels, unveil a statue of the family patriarch in 1985. (Reprinted with permission of the News and Observer.)

In the age of racial reckoning, Josephus Daniels's bigoted past had caught up with him.

Josephus Daniels was the preeminent figure in a publishing family that would play an outsize role in the political, civic, and cultural life of North Carolina for more than a century. Josephus Daniels and his son Jonathan would help shape the twentieth-century rise of the national Democratic Party, serving as political lieutenants to the likes of William Jennings Bryan, Woodrow Wilson, Franklin D. Roosevelt, and Harry Truman and to a lesser extent aiding the careers of Adlai Stevenson, John F. Kennedy, and Lyndon Johnson.

The story of the Daniels family and the *News and Observer* reflects a turbulent period in the South.

Josephus Daniels was a forceful advocate for the underdog throughout his career—for hardscrabble farmers, labor unions, suffragettes, Jews, navy swabbies, and Mexican peasants, among others. Few people fought longer or harder to expand educational opportunities in North Carolina than did Daniels.

But Daniels's reputation has cratered as his darker side has caught up with him in recent years. His name was ripped from school and other public buildings, his statue torn down, and his home stripped of its historic designation and demolished.

He used his Raleigh newspaper to help initiate the era of Jim Crow, which sharply defined the political, economic, and social limits of Black people. He fueled the vicious and sometimes deadly white supremacy campaigns of 1896, 1898, and 1900 and worked to impose and uphold the state's segregation laws throughout his life.

Several generations of Black North Carolinians would have little voice in their government—in the laws, taxes, and regulations that governed their lives. They would be restricted regarding where they could eat, sleep, and learn; what jobs they could hold; and where they were treated during medical emergencies. If they ran afoul of the law, they were arrested by white law enforcement officers, tried by white judges, and at the mercy of racist white juries. They sometimes were sentenced to Black chain gangs or worse.

Leading Black journalists viewed Daniels with contempt. "What we need on the race question is free and open discussion," wrote T. Thomas Fortune in the *New York Age*. "And this cannot be had as long as Josephus Daniels and the likes of him are allowed to patrol the highway of opinion loaded with a gun."[3]

Daniels, of course, did not invent the Jim Crow system, which was rigidly enforced by law across the South and by custom in the North. But he was one of the architects of Jim Crow and helped maintain it throughout his life.

Prominent southern editors such as Daniels were more than just chroniclers of their time and place. "More than mere peddlers of racist tropes and stories, many white editors and publishers in the Jim Crow South were straight-out political actors, deeply entrenched in Democratic Party campaigns, machines, and policy making," wrote historians Sid Bedingfield and Kathy Roberts Forde.[4]

Few southern editors had more political clout than Daniels. It is one of the great paradoxes of North Carolina history that Daniels—a racist—helped shape North Carolina's twentieth-century image as one of the more progressive states in the South. He was widely viewed by his white contemporaries—from William Jennings Bryan to Henry Wallace—as one of the South's most notable progressives. When he died, Eleanor Roosevelt wrote in her nationally syndicated column that Daniels was one "of the hardest working liberals in the South."[5]

But it was a curious brand of liberalism. He was part of a group that conservative columnist Westbrook Pegler dubbed "Jim Crow liberals." That may be a difficult concept for some twenty-first-century readers to grasp, because ideas of social and racial justice have become entwined with the idea of liberalism. But Daniels saw little contradiction between his liberalism on a broad range of issues and his ardently held segregationist beliefs.

Daniels was not alone. Many progressive reformers at the turn of the last century misguidedly believed that removing poorly educated and, in some cases, illiterate Black voters was necessary to achieve progress in other areas. As historian C. Vann Woodward has written, "The typical progressive reformer rode to power in the South on a disfranchising or white-supremacy movement." Writing in his landmark study, *The Strange Career of Jim Crow*, Woodward added, "Racism was conceived of by some as the very foundation of Southern progressivism."[6]

The *News and Observer* evolved over time, although it would always be regarded as liberal in its editorial policies. By the 1930s, under the direction of Josephus's son Jonathan Daniels, the Raleigh paper was at the forefront of the South's efforts to renegotiate the racial code, pushing for incremental change that would provide a fairer deal for African Americans. But it still supported segregation.

So changed was the *News and Observer*'s mid-twentieth-century reputation on race that future senator Jesse Helms, a segregationist, declared in 1953 that the paper had been "selling out the South [for] at least two generations."[7]

That journey—from the voice of white supremacy to charges of selling out the South—is one of the storylines of this book. This work also examines how the newspaper and the Daniels family influenced the state's politics and its cultural and civic life.

This book contains several narrative threads—it is a story of a family dynasty, four generations of the Danielses who controlled the paper. It explores the rise of newspapers in the late nineteenth century and their fall in the twenty-first century. It is a chronicle of the state's political life—the constant tension between its conservative, racist roots and its progressive impulses.

For more than a century, the paper performed a watchdog function, monitoring local and state government, college athletics, businesses, labor unions, and other institutions. For most of its history it was applauded by the political Left and cursed by the political Right. It also acted as a cultural arbiter, encouraging and organizing events to promote poetry and literature. It was the community crier announcing the marriages and deaths of citizens.

This work is a timely story today because the *News and Observer*—or "Nuisance and Disturber," as critics called it—is like many newspapers in the Internet age, struggling to survive.

CHAPTER ONE

White Supremacy

In January 1895, Josephus Daniels returned from a top federal job in Washington to take command of the *News and Observer*, a paper he had purchased six months earlier.

Daniels left little doubt how he would use his newly acquired business. He immediately launched white supremacy campaigns that covered six years and reshaped North Carolina politics, resulting in the rise of a rigid Jim Crow system of segregation and sixty years of one-party Democratic control of the state.

In announcing his arrival in Raleigh, the thirty-two-year-old Daniels wrote that North Carolina had fallen upon "evil days," like those of Reconstruction following the Civil War, and it was time for regime change. "In this crisis that confronts the patriotic people of my state," Daniels declared, "I could not feel that I was doing my whole duty, as a loyal son, in any other way than by becoming an active member of the army that must needs band together to redeem the state from the rule of prejudice and revolution."[1]

Prompting Daniels's declaration was a political revolution the previous November that pushed the Democrats out of power for the first time in a generation, replacing them with a Republican/Populist biracial coalition government. The insurgency was part of what historian Lawrence Goodwyn called "the largest democratic mass movement in American history." In the 1880s and 1890s a pitchfork revolt swept much of the country. In the South, it was a reaction to the system of tenancy, which tied many farmers to indebtedness to local merchants, sentencing them to a perpetual cycle of poverty.[2]

The movement started in Texas with the Farmers' Alliance but quickly spread across the country—with North Carolina a hotbed of alliance activity.

Josephus Daniels at his newspaper desk around the
time of the white supremacy campaigns.
(Courtesy of the State Archives of North Carolina.)

The movement first focused on creating cooperatives to provide farmers with credit and a place to sell their crops but soon moved into politics. Dissatisfied with the conservative tilt of the Democratic Party, many alliance members formed the Populist Party, the most powerful third party in American history. It achieved success by forming a coalition—or Fusion—with a Republican Party dominated in North Carolina by African Americans in the east and white farmers in the west. The populists won control of many southern states, including North Carolina, where in 1894 they captured the legislature and in 1896 gained the governorship.

The Fusion government was a progressive force, capping interest rates on loans at 6 percent, levying new taxes on railroads and other businesses, increasing spending on public education, and overseeing the fairest elections in the South. But it created powerful enemies: Democrats lost power, prestige, and patronage; business interests worried that the state was being run by antibusiness radicals; and many whites were dismayed to see growing Black political influence.

In other circumstances, Daniels might have joined the Fusionists, with whom he shared many views. Like them, he distrusted the railroads, Wall Street, and corporate trusts, and he saw himself as a Jefferson-inspired spokesman for the small farmer. But Daniels's economic populism was countered by his partisanship and racial views.

Daniels was tightly bound to the Democratic Party. Democrats bankrolled his paper's purchase with his promise that it would be a party organ. Daniels profited from Democratic political patronage, winning the state printing contract and landing a top job in the Cleveland administration. The following year, in 1896, Daniels was elected the state's Democratic National Committeeman, making him one of the most influential figures in party councils.

Just as crucial as Democratic loyalty was Daniels's segregationist worldview. Daniels, who had been born during the waning days of slavery, raised in the cotton culture of the coastal plain, and spoon-fed tales of the Lost Cause and who had interacted with a partially illiterate Black population still emerging from generations of shackles, had views that were firmly rooted by the time he reached adulthood. Eighteen eastern counties had Black majorities in the years before the twentieth century's great African American migration north. African Americans composed 38 percent of North Carolina's population in the late 1800s, compared with 22 percent today.

The rise of Black Republicanism was personal to Daniels, who was infuriated when his mother lost her patronage job as postmistress by order of a Black Republican congressman, James O'Hara—most likely because of Daniels's editorials attacking him. Daniels traveled to Washington, DC, in an unsuccessful effort to save his mother's job. Even as a teenage newspaper editor in Wilson, Daniels declared that Black people were not fit for self-government.[3]

Daniels fashioned the *News and Observer* into a rabid opposition publication, finding fault in everything the Fusion government did. His goal was to split the Populist-Republican biracial coalition by using racial prejudice as a wedge. In Daniels's telling, the Populists were not the champion of the small farmer but the allies of Blacks, who had unleashed a "reign of terror, lust and incompetency" in the state.[4]

No target was too small for Daniels if it touched the raw nerve of racial prejudice. In 1895 the state House adjourned for the day in honor of Frederick Douglass, the famous Black abolitionist. The paper started referring to the Fusionist General Assembly as "the Fred Douglass Legislature," falsely claiming it failed to adjourn in honor of Confederate hero Robert E. Lee. "The essence of Fusion is to break down all barriers and solve the negro question by inter marriage between the races," the paper dishonestly asserted.[5]

The paper repeatedly targeted Black Republican appointee Abe Middleton, an assistant House doorkeeper, who replaced a one-armed Confederate veteran. "We warn the colored people that they are being used to kindle a fire that cannot easily be extinguished, and we warn the White men who are using them that a day of reckoning is coming," the paper declared in 1895.[6]

It took three elections for the Democrats to regain political control of the state, and the *News and Observer* was heavily involved in all of them.

Whites Shall Rule

The first attempt, in the 1896 elections, was unsuccessful. But the Raleigh paper conducted a rehearsal of the race-baiting efforts it would use to help retake control of the state during the 1898 and 1900 elections. The paper attacked Daniel Russell, the GOP gubernatorial candidate, claiming his election would result in Black domination in rural Eastern North Carolina towns. And the paper published racist editorial cartoons. Among Russell's election-year promises was never to allow Daniels inside the governor's mansion.[7]

James Young, a Black newspaper editor and Raleigh politician, wrote in 1896, "It is apparent to all observers of political events that the Democratic machine, in its desperation, goaded on by the *News and Observer*, its malicious and vindictive negro-baiting organ, is going to attempt to carry the coming election by force and violence prior to and on election day."[8]

It is hard to overstate Daniels's political influence. As the state's Democratic National Committeeman, Daniels was a pivotal figure for the out-of-power party that had no governor or US senator. It is hard to decide whether Daniels was a newspaperman heavily involved in politics or a politician who owned a newspaper. He was the printed voice of the white supremacy campaign, his old ally Furnifold Simmons was the chief strategist, and his boyhood friend Charles Brantley Aycock was the chief stump speaker. All three men were products of the state's Black Belt, the eastern section of the state most like the Deep South.

The Democratic establishment widely supported white supremacy campaigns—from the courthouse politicians, bankers, textile mill owners, tobacco manufacturers, railroad executives, and others in the business community who financed the campaign. The campaign had a conservative tilt, with much of the business community worried about the economic populism of the Fusion government. Backing the campaign were both the *News and Observer*, the leading progressive newspaper, and the *Charlotte Observer*, the leading conservative voice. To help whip up support at white supremacy rallies, the railroads provided free passes and textile mills gave their employees time off to attend the events. Daniels later expressed shock at some of the secret deals made by Simmons to gain conservative support, promising corporations that the Democrats would not raise their taxes and telling church leaders—many of whom sponsored private colleges—that Democrats would not increase funding for the University of North Carolina.

After the 1898 election, the *Charlotte Observer* credited the Democrats' victory to "the bank men, the millmen, and the businessmen in general—the backbone of the property interests of the state."[9]

The Democrats regained power through two white supremacy campaigns—in 1898 to elect a new legislature and in 1900 to elect a new governor and decide a referendum to require a literacy test for voting. These were campaigns of raw intimidation. Besides the standard fare of rallies, speeches, and handbills, the campaign included roving gangs of white vigilantes called Red Shirts—a group started in South Carolina as a successor to the Reconstruction-era Klan—who rode through the Black sections of towns brandishing Winchester rifles to discourage voting. The campaign of terror included night riding, beatings, and even murder. Republican governor Daniel Russell avoided an assassination attempt in 1898 by hiding in a train's baggage car. During the campaign's final days, state Republicans asked for federal troops to restore order.

"In 1898 North Carolina people were engaged in two wars," Daniels wrote years later, "each waged with such fury as to make it sometimes difficult for the readers of the *News and Observer* to tell which was bloodier, the war against Spain or the war to drive the Fusionists from power."[10]

Yellow journalism was at its height in 1898, a period featuring screaming headlines and fact-bending stories. Earlier that year, a newspaper war between Joseph Pulitzer's *New York World* and William Randolph Hearst's *New York Journal* helped ignite the Spanish-American War with a stream of falsehoods about Spaniards raping women, the roasting of twenty-five priests, and attacks on hospitals. The newspaper campaign led to 379 American deaths in the war, 4,234 American deaths in the Philippine insurrection that followed, and at least 200,000 Filipino deaths.

The first journalism school did not open in America until 1908, and there was little tradition of journalistic ethics. In the 1920s, influential newspaper columnist Walter Lippmann called for newspapers to discard yellow journalism and print only carefully gathered facts. "Most newspapers were unabashed advocates of a political party; the creed of 'objectivity' made few converts until the 20th century," writes historian Michael Kazin.[11]

Although the *News and Observer* under Daniels had used racist tactics since 1895, the race-baiting reached a fever pitch in the 1898 campaign. Even forty-three years later, Daniels did not disavow the campaign. As he wrote in his 1941 memoir, "The *News and Observer* was the printed voice of the campaign. The *News and Observer* was relied upon to carry the Democratic message and to be the militant voice of white supremacy, and it did not fail in what was expected, sometimes going to extremes in its partisanship."[12]

Daniels made the paper a propaganda tool—filled with a toxic mix of manufactured stories, unproven rumors, gross distortions, and outright lies. The paper "led in a campaign of prejudice, bitterness, vilification, misrepresentation, and exaggeration to influence the emotions of the whites against the Negro," wrote historian Helen Edmonds.[13]

The *News and Observer* used two main devices to stir racial prejudice. Starting on August 12, 1898, the paper began running racist cartoons on the front page most days. Beginning on September 21 it also ran front-page stories highlighted with black borders—usually two daily—outlining some purported "outrage" by African Americans.

If one believed the Raleigh paper's news stories, Black people were preparing for a race war against whites, were planning to turn North Carolina into an independent territory for African Americans, and were engaged in a Black-on-white crime spree—none of which was true.

No incident was too small to be sensationalized. The headlines alone tell the story: "Negro Brute Slapped a White Girl in the Face," "New Bern's Plight; An Orgie of Crime under Negro Magistrates," "Inspected by a Negro. White School at Maysville Visited by a Negro Committeeman." (Then there were the editorials "All the N——s in Office We Want," "The Negro the Aggressor," and "Why We Cry N——r.")[14]

The stories dripped with outrage about any sign of Black equality: a white Republican kissing a Black baby in Charlotte, a Black deputy sheriff taking an insane white man to an asylum, inmates of both races at the state prison farm at Caledonia eating together, a Black deputy sheriff in Wake County serving subpoenas on white men.[15]

"No man who loves his state can read the daily occurrences without trembling for the future of the State," read a Daniels editorial. "There have been more assaults upon white women by Negro brutes in one year and a half of Republican rule than in twenty years of Democratic rule. There have been more insults to white girls, more wrongs to white men, more lawlessness and more crime committed by negros in North Carolina during the last twenty months than during the previous twenty years."[16]

These statements were false. As historian Glenda Elizabeth Gilmore has noted, there was no appreciable increase in rapes or attempted rapes in North Carolina in either 1897 or 1898. "The rape scare was a politically driven wedge powered by the sledgehammer of white supremacy," wrote Gilmore.[17]

Not only did Daniels dispatch correspondents to towns across Eastern North Carolina to gather information to form another story about supposed Black "outrages," but every day three or four county Democratic chairmen would visit Daniels to relay some anecdote or a rumor that Daniels published as fact. Daniels later acknowledged in his memoirs that "we were never very careful about winnowing out the stories or running them down."[18]

These were fabrications. As the *People's Paper*, a Charlotte Populist weekly, noted, the reports of Black domination didn't exist six months before the election and would soon vanish. "One more week and the Big Headlines about 'N——r Domination' will disappear from the Democratic papers until the next campaign opens," it declared.[19]

A particular target was Second District Republican congressman George White, the only African American serving in Congress, representing the northeast part of the state. White was responsible for numerous patronage appointments in his district, often appointing Black postmasters, forcing whites to go into Black neighborhoods to pick up their mail.

The *News and Observer* twisted White's every move and utterance out of context. The most egregious example was a front-page story alleging that the congressman's wife, an Oberlin-educated schoolteacher, had received an express package containing rifles. The paper also asserted that White's daughter, a twenty-year-old teacher, had circulated a petition asking Black people to refuse to work for white people. The health of White's wife suffered during the attacks, and she died six years later at age forty—for which White blamed Daniels.[20]

When White introduced an anti-lynching bill in 1900, he said that only 15 percent of lynchings grew out of rape allegations and added that "there are more outrages against colored women by white men than there are by colored men against white women." His remarks angered Daniels, who complained that "it is bad enough that North Carolina should have the only n———r congressman" and said White's remarks demonstrated that he was a "menace to the peace of the commonwealth and a danger to the safety of both races." He added, "White is typical of his kind. Venomous, forward, slanderous of whites, appealing to the worst passions of his own race, he emphasizes anew the need of making an end to him and his kind. That is what the white people of this state propose to do," referring to the proposed literacy test.[21]

White asked that the *News and Observer* editorial be read on the US House floor, saying he wanted to "give the vile, slanderous publication the widest possible circulation . . . that the world may see what the poor colored man in the Southland had to undergo from a certain class."[22]

The paper hired the state's first editorial cartoonist to drive home its racist message in a population that still had high rates of illiteracy. Starting as a mail clerk for the paper in 1895, Sampson County native Norman E. Jennett began drawing editorial cartoons for the paper during the 1896 election, pumping the presidential candidacy of William Jennings Bryan and attacking Republican gubernatorial candidate Daniel Russell. But that was just a warm-up for the white supremacy campaigns of 1898 and 1900, where he specialized in drawing threatening-looking Black men—often juxtaposed with young white women.

Nearly every day from mid-August until the November 1898 election, a Jennett cartoon ran at the top of the front page. The seventy-three editorial cartoons depicted such scenes as a white man crushed under the giant foot of a "Negro." Whites were portrayed as subservient to African Americans, whether it was a white woman appearing before a Black deputy chief clerk or white road workers toiling under the supervision of a Black overseer. One particularly gruesome cartoon included a terrifying Black vampire—titled "Negro Rule"—reaching out and grabbing white people. Another showed a Black giant dressed in expensive clothes, wearing a top hat, and smoking a cigar while a small white man is on his knees begging. The man is identified as a "fusion office seeker." The caption is "The New Slavery."[23]

The facts were irrelevant. The *News and Observer*, for example, ran at least two editorial cartoons showing a Black official from Raleigh, James Young, inspecting blind white women at a state institution—the implications, of

"The Vampire That Hovers Over North Carolina." One of the
racist cartoons that the *News and Observer* published
during the 1898 white supremacy campaigns.
(Courtesy of Wilson Special Collections Library,
University of North Carolina at Chapel Hill.)

course, were lurid. Young had been appointed to the board of overseers to provide token Black representation at a white-run institution that served both races. Not only did he not inspect white quarters, but he was no longer even on the board when the cartoons ran. "Any man who will persist in such political rot as this, should be regarded as a low down, mean, dirty scoundrel, and the party he represents should be repudiated by all decent men who have the interest of the institution at heart," opined the *Homefront*, a populist weekly published in Raleigh.[24]

Blacks were routinely portrayed as sexual predators, feeding white paranoia. "Daniels worked to portray black men as sexually insatiable and, at the same time, weak willed and easily duped," wrote journalist David Zucchino in his history of the Wilmington violence of 1898. "Even in situations where a white woman was merely in the presence of a black man, the *News and Observer* found cause for alarm. In May, it published an article about a white woman who spotted a black man crossing her yard while she was using her outhouse. The woman screamed. The man fled. That was all. But the *News and Observer* headline suggested a narrow escape for the terrified woman: NO RAPE COMMITTED; BUT A LADY BADLY FRIGHTENED BY A WORTHLESS NEGRO."[25]

The Democratic Party subsidized Jennett's salary and fronted the costs of sending 100,000 copies of his work in a supplement to the western part of the state where the Raleigh paper did not circulate—an early version of attack ads. In 1898, the *News and Observer* had a paid circulation of 6,200 in a state with 1.8 million people, so the Democratic Party worked to increase the reach of the paper's propaganda campaign. In all, the Democratic Party may have financed 2 million pieces of literature statewide.[26]

After the campaign, Daniels arranged with industrialist Julian Carr to finance Jennett's art studies in New York. The state Democratic Party paid for him to return and continue drawing his cartoons for the 1900 suffrage amendment campaign. "Your work two years ago helped us to carry the state, the people of the state looked upon you and Aycock as the great leaders," Daniels wrote to Jennett, successfully urging him to return from New York. "They are going to make him governor and you will earn the lasting gratitude of the state if you can come back and help us carry the Amendment this year."[27] Jennett had a successful career, working for several prominent New York papers and creating his own nationally syndicated comic strip before retiring to California to paint oils and watercolors.

The cries of Black domination were baseless—there were only ten Black lawmakers who served in the 170-member General Assembly from 1895 to 1899, and North Carolina never had more than one Black congressman at any one time and a total of four in the 1800s. Even so, North Carolina in 1898 probably had more Black public officials than anywhere in the country—and the only African American to serve in Congress for thirty years, from 1897 to 1927. Many counties had Black deputy sheriffs, and there were 300 Black magistrates.[28]

Not only did Daniels and the *News and Observer* invent the narrative of Black domination, but he suppressed news of white-on-Black violence. Only after the votes had been cast in the 1898 election did the paper tell its readers that two Black men had been lynched in the days leading up to the election—information that might have raised doubts about the false story of Black domination. One lynching involved an eighteen-year-old Black farmhand who eloped with the twenty-eight-year-old wife of a white Orange County farmer. The couple was caught in Jonesboro, with the white woman returned to her father and the Black man lynched.[29]

Two days before the 1898 election, the paper ran a poem by William Gaston, titled "The Whites Shall Rule."

> The whites shall rule the land or die!
> The purpose grows in the hearts of steel;
> With burning cheek and flashing eye
> We wait what waiting will reveal.
> But, come what may, the whites must hold
> What white men's patriot valor bought;
> Our grandsire's ashes not yet cold,
> Hallow the soil for which they fought.[30]

All of the state's daily newspapers were Democratic and supported the white supremacy effort; the only Republican papers were weeklies. The Democrats "managed and controlled all of the daily newspapers in the state," wrote historian Jeffrey Crow. "Whereas the Populists and Republicans had to rely on weekly papers to spread their message and to respond to a continuous barrage of Democratic propaganda, the Democrats could publish their own views every day with little or no accountability."[31]

Much of the *News and Observer*'s coverage of supposed Black outrages were reprints from other papers—the *Charlotte Observer, Winston Free Press, Kinston Free Press, Atlanta Constitution, Greenville Reflector, Wilmington Star, Wilmington Messenger, Alamance Gleaner, Apex News, Winston Journal, Richmond Dispatch, Manufacturer's Record, Nashville Argonaut,* and *Asheboro Courier.*[32]

On the Sunday before the election, Daniels penned an editorial that seemed to sanction violence. "The white man shall rule, and he will rule," Daniels wrote. "He will rule peacefully if he can, he will rule forcibly if he must."[33] Concluded Crow and Robert F. Durden, "Cynically manipulated by Simmons and urged on by Daniels's *News and Observer*, the white supremacy campaign placed North Carolina on the verge of a race war."[34]

The northern press was hardly better. The two lead 1898 Election Day stories in the *News and Observer* were reprints of racist editorials that appeared in the *Washington Post* and the *Baltimore Sun*. The *Washington Post* described Craven County (New Bern) as "negro ridden." It added that "no county in Massachusetts or Pennsylvania would have permitted the calamity to attain such a sinister development." The *Baltimore Sun* opined that Fusion governance in North Carolina "has been a rule of the unfit, of the unclean, of the barbarous—the rule of the savage over the civilized, of the lowest elements over the best."[35]

A large crowd gathered outside the *News and Observer*'s office on Fayetteville Street on election eve. As the returns were posted on a large screen, the crowd cheered, blew on tin horns, and beat on pans.

With the propaganda barrage, physical beatings, voter intimidation, and fraud, Democrats swept the 1898 election, winning 134 of 170 legislative seats and 5 congressional seats. The Republicans did not regain control of the legislature until 2011. By then the GOP had become the more conservative party, benefiting from a white backlash.

Miraculously in the days after the election, the so-called Black crime wave that the Raleigh paper had conjured up for political purposes disappeared from its pages.

Daniels had promised "the assurance of peace and good government" if the Democrats regained control. But a day after the election, a mob of 400 in the mountain town of Dillsboro lynched a young Black man accused of forcing his way into two houses, scaring two white women. The sheriff had simply handed the keys to the cell he was detained in to the mob.[36]

Worse was yet to come.

Wilmington

The white supremacy campaign of 1898 had a bloody coda—the massacre in Wilmington that occurred two days after the election. In another context, it might be called a pogrom.

Wilmington was North Carolina's largest city, with African Americans outnumbering whites 11,324 to 8,731. Regarded as one of the best cities in the South for African Americans, it had a substantial Black middle class. With the election of a Fusion legislature and the return of local control, a biracial Fusionist coalition ran the city in 1898. Of Wilmington's thirty-two-member police force, eleven were Black officers. Of the city's five aldermen, two were Black.[37]

The white backlash was already gathering force when Alex Manly, editor of the *Wilmington Daily Record*, the only African American daily in the state, wrote a provocative editorial in August 1898 that touched on deeply held racial taboos and fears. The editorial responded to a prominent Georgia woman who argued that whites should "lynch a thousand times a week if necessary" to protect white women from Black rape. Manly wrote that Black rape was not widespread, but there had been plenty of rapes of Black women by white men. Furthermore, there were many white women attracted to Black men.

Sensing imminent violence, newspapers from across the country dispatched correspondents to Wilmington in the days leading up to the election. As a committee of leading white Wilmington citizens formed a secret society to plot a governmental takeover, the two Wilmington papers fanned the flames.

Election Day was relatively peaceful. But two days later, armed whites issued a set of demands to Wilmington's Black community. The whites then proceeded to burn the offices of Manly's newspaper—although Manly had already fled town in fear for his life. The mob degenerated into a manhunt in Black neighborhoods, where African Americans were shot indiscriminately. The *News and Observer* reported that eleven Black men were killed, but a Black Virginia newspaper, the *Richmond Planet*, was nearer the mark, reporting twenty-five deaths. A state study published in 2006 numbered the deaths at sixty. It is likely we will never know the true count.[38]

After the shooting, the mob marched on Wilmington city hall and demanded the government's resignation, forcing the officials on a northbound train with instructions to never return. It was one of the few coups d'état in American history, although there had been similar actions by white mobs in Mississippi during Reconstruction.[39]

Wilmington was not the primary focus of the *News and Observer's* coverage—despite accounts that conflate the white supremacy campaigns with the Wilmington massacre. None of Jennett's seventy-three racist cartoons—the focal point of the propaganda campaign—mentions Wilmington. Nor did Wilmington dominate front-page news coverage of the *News and Observer* during the white supremacy campaign. Of the fifty-seven racist front-page stories highlighted by black borders, seven were related to Wilmington, and most of those were not particularly incendiary by the standards of that vile campaign season.

Josephus Daniels used Wilmington as one of several examples of the dangers of Black political agency. The Raleigh paper ran stories about Wilmington's supposed lawlessness and disrespectful Black population and stories dripping with outrage that there were Blacks on the police force. Daniels later boasted that his paper's Wilmington reports "sealed the doom of Fusion."[40]

The Manly editorial might have been only a Wilmington controversy if Daniels had not helped bring it to statewide attention. In August, three months before the massacre, the *News and Observer* reprinted Manly's editorial under the headline "Vile and Villainous."[41]

Two days before the election, the paper reprinted—deep in the paper—a speech by former congressman Alfred Waddell, threatening mass killings of Blacks in Wilmington if they voted. The paper called it "the boldest and most remarkable speech in the most wonderful campaign in the state's history."[42]

Daniels used the situation in Wilmington—and Manly's editorials—as kindling for the racial wildfire he was attempting to ignite across the state. But it was Wilmington's white-owned newspapers that lit the fuse to the massacre. The *Wilmington Messenger* turned its office into what was described "as a veritable arsenal."[43]

After the bloodshed, Daniels expressed disappointment but no outrage. He wrote, "There is not a good citizen of Wilmington or the State who does not regret that the change from no government by incompetents to good government by competent men was attended by a riot that resulted in the loss of human life." The *News and Observer*'s coverage of the Wilmington massacre was filled with falsehoods—stating that eleven had been killed, that Blacks had started the shooting, and that there had been a legal change in the government. But the national press was hardly better. The *New York Times* falsely claimed that the Wilmington deaths occurred after 200 to 300 Blacks opened fire.[44]

To celebrate their victory in the white supremacy campaign, the Democrats held an ironically named "good will jubilee." It was a three-hour torchlight parade in Raleigh that included 150 horsemen, carriages, bicyclists, and men carrying pitchforks, brooms, banners, and 2,000 torches lit by 500 barrels of tar. The *News and Observer*'s office was illuminated with electric lights and decorated with brooms, symbolic of a sweeping victory, and a rooster, a symbol of the Democratic Party. The parade ended in Nash Square, with Daniels presiding—hoisted to the platform in the arms of Wake County Democrats.

The role of the news media in the Wilmington massacre was a stain on the profession. Most newspapers did not question white supremacy, appeared to make no effort to talk to African Americans, and raised few qualms about a newspaper office torched with the editor chased out of town for voicing an unpopular position. National newspaper accounts leading up to the massacre all but predicted a violent revolution. In this case, the public watchdog was more like the fox in the henhouse.

There were exceptions. The *Washington Evening Star* condemned the white citizens for resorting "to the most radical measures without necessity," and T. Thomas Fortune in his *New York Press* described the state's leadership as "degenerate."[45]

The *News and Observer* pushed for Jim Crow cars just two weeks after the election. "The people of North Carolina prefer to ride as they vote, as they go to church, and as they send their children to school," Daniels wrote. As they retook control of the legislature in 1899, the Democrats began enacting Jim Crow laws, starting with a measure to require segregated railroad cars—an initiative opposed by the railroads, which cited the expense of maintaining a dual system. Segregation soon spread to every aspect of life, including separate entrances and exits at theaters and separate boardinghouses, toilets, water fountains, waiting rooms, ticket windows, hospitals, mental institutions, public parks, schools, textbooks, residential neighborhoods, cemeteries, employment, and homes for the aged, the blind, and hearing impaired.[46]

Democratic leaders moved in 1900 to make permanent their political gains by disenfranchising Black voters using a literacy test and a poll tax—devices already used in three states. Daniels traveled to Louisiana to examine how such voting restrictions worked there, a trip suggested by Furnifold Simmons and paid for by the Democratic Party. Daniels returned with a plan protecting white voters with a grandfather clause that allowed anybody to vote if their grandfathers had—thereby shielding whites from the literacy test. An estimated 40 percent of Black males were illiterate compared with 20 percent of white males.[47]

"The Democrats propose a constitutional amendment by which the great mass of negroes, notoriously unfit for suffrage, may be eliminated from the ballot box, thus putting an end to negro rule and the jeopardy of it," Daniels wrote. "This proposition is based on the same fundamental principles that have actuated the State of South Carolina, Mississippi, Louisiana and other Southern states in dealing with the ignorant negro voters, that Massachusetts adopted to prevent rule of the foreign voters who had recently landed and that was put in practice by the Pacific States and the federal Congress to put an end to the wholesale importation of Chinamen who threatened the occupation of the laborers of California and adjacent states on the Pacific slope."[48]

In a front-page story, the *News and Observer* made plain its racist assumptions. "He [the Black man] is on a different plane and level intellectually and morally, from the white man. Nature has taken account of the fact, and by nature the lower organism is repulsive to the higher man."[49]

Daniels put his newspaper's full might behind a ballot amendment in 1900 to impose the literacy test. This third white supremacy campaign was a repeat of 1898, complete with heavily armed roving Red Shirts, voter fraud, and Jennett returning from New York to draw dozens of racially loaded political cartoons that were featured on the front page. Once again, the paper was filled with scare stories with such headlines as "Fiendish Crime of a Negro Brute" and "Negroes Threaten to Apply the Torch."[50]

The election results were so corrupt that the eighteen counties with Black majorities voted overwhelmingly for a literacy test that barred most Black people from voting. The literacy test results were quickly evident: In 1896 there were 126,000 Black North Carolinians registered to vote, but by 1902 there were only 6,100, eliminating more than 95 percent of African Americans from the voting rolls.[51]

Although Daniels had promised that disenfranchisement would remove race from North Carolina politics, the passage of the literacy amendment would not come until July 1902. Daniels waved the flag of white supremacy, urging the election in November 1900 of Democrat William Jennings Bryan and the defeat of Republican William McKinley. "A vote for Mr. McKinley is a vote to continue in office in North Carolina a negro Collector of Customs in the state's metropolis; twenty-seven negro postmasters and many negro revenue and other federal officials."[52]

As the Jim Crow barriers went up, Black voices in the North expressed outrage. In the South, Black voices were often intimidated or suppressed by white pressure with some African American editors driven from the South such as Alex Manly in North Carolina, Ida B. Wells in Tennessee, and J. Max Barber in Georgia. The New York–based T. Thomas Fortune, perhaps the most influential Black journalist of the late nineteenth century, wrote, "We know to our sorrow that a voteless citizen is a pariah, to be victimized by mobs and by legislators, and that he must put up with injustice that makes the blood boil with indignation. A body of citizens so large as that of the African American people in the Southern states would never with the ballot in their hands be subject to separate car laws, separate school laws, separate penal institutional regulations—separate everything that arrogance and insolence, uncurbed by the fear of retaliation at the ballot box, are disposed to heap upon the defenseless."[53]

Maintaining Jim Crow

Daniels personally enforced the literacy test. During a 1903 referendum involving liquor dispensaries, Daniels manned his polling place, an unpainted plank building in Raleigh's Fourth Ward, personally challenging every Black voter who was not a teacher or minister or otherwise known to be educated.

As a white crowd of hundreds gathered around, Black people trying to register were asked whether they knew what ex post facto law was or whether they could correctly pronounce "lieutenant governor." Daniels later acknowledged that many whites would have failed the test. "It was cruel," Daniels wrote in 1941 of his challenge to Black voters. "When they failed, they were disqualified and had to stand aside. After a dozen had made the attempt and failed, the other uneducated negroes did not seek to vote."[54]

Worried that the North Carolina Supreme Court might overturn their actions, Democratic lawmakers in 1901 impeached two Republican justices on trumped-up charges. The House passed the impeachment measure in a party-line vote, but the Senate voted narrowly to acquit. While the *Charlotte Observer* called the impeachment trial a "scandalous and shameful" effort to pack the court, the *News and Observer* remained neutral during the two-month debate. Afterward, the Raleigh paper declared that even though the judges were legally acquitted, "they were morally convicted of high crimes and misdemeanors."[55]

Over the years, Daniels argued that Democratic primaries should be for white voters only—even though North Carolina never passed a whites-only primary law as had several southern states. By 1932 there was a push by African Americans to register as Democrats, particularly in Wake County, the home of Raleigh. There were several factors: the US Supreme Court striking down Texas's all-white primary law, support for Democratic presidential candidate Franklin Roosevelt, and the creation of several Black voter registration groups.

Objecting to Black voters registering as Democrats in Wake Country, Daniels wrote, "The Democratic Party in North Carolina is a white man's party" and that African Americans had "no more right to vote in a Democratic primary than a Baptist had to vote in the selection of a bishop in an Episcopal convention." Daniels warned that the voter registration effort was "trying to destroy the great victory won under the leadership of Aycock and Simmons in 1898 and 1900." During the first two decades of the twentieth century, the Black southern press was often too intimidated by the white power structure to push back against such racism. But by the 1930s, things were beginning to change. Backing the voter registration effort were Black editors such as Hugo I. Fontellio-Nanton, editor of the Raleigh-based *Carolina Tribune* (later called the *Carolinian*), and Louis Austin of the Durham-based *Carolina Times*. A team of four Black attorneys won that fight to restore the registration of 210 Black Democrats in a Wake County superior court.[56]

Black people's move to the Democratic Party was made easier by the Republican Party's abandonment of them soon after the white supremacy campaigns. The GOP barred African Americans from participating in its state executive committee in 1901 and its state convention in 1902.

Josephus Daniels never apologized for his actions during the white supremacy campaigns, although in his 1941 memoir, he acknowledged that "in the perspective of time, I think it [the paper's actions] was too cruel."[57]

During his lifetime, Daniels steadfastly manned the segregation battlements. There could be no exceptions, not even for Booker T. Washington, an Alabama educator and a leading Black figure, whom Daniels admired for his advice that Black people should focus on vocational education rather than on challenging Jim Crow laws.

Like many southern editors, Daniels was offended when Washington dined with President Theodore Roosevelt at the White House in 1901. While Roosevelt could invite whomever he wanted to his home, he wrote, it was an affront to southerners. "Call it what you please—prejudice, provincialism, a relic of the war or what not—it is deeply rooted in the minds of the Southern people that the only true position for the races is one of absolute social separation," he said in an editorial. "Break down that barrier—and then the deluge."[58]

In 1903, Daniels was at it again, complaining that Washington got preferential treatment at a North Carolina restaurant. Washington headed a group of Black travelers who stopped for a prearranged breakfast in the main dining room at a railroad hotel in Hamlet. The hotel proprietors, through a misunderstanding, then required the white passengers to eat in a separate improvised white dining room. The incident received sensational front-page coverage as another example of a southern custom being violated—a repeat of Washington dining at the White House. The result of Washington eating at the White House, Daniels thundered, was worse behavior by Blacks and more lynchings. "Instead of letting the barrier down, every effort should be made to raise it higher," Daniels wrote.[59]

Booker T. Washington was the topic again in November 1903 when Daniels demanded the firing of John Spencer Bassett, a historian at Trinity College (what is now Duke University). In an article in a scholarly journal he edited, Bassett wrote that Jim Crow and the white supremacy campaigns were toxic and discriminatory, worsening race relations—the very opposite of what

Daniels and his colleagues argued. What especially set Daniels off was that Bassett wrote that Washington was "the greatest man, save General Lee, born in the South in a hundred years." Daniels fumed that no Black man—no matter how accomplished or educated—could ever be judged higher than the lowliest illiterate white farmhand. Caste was everything. "He is of a race superior to the negro race, even if he is uneducated."[60]

Daniels led a monthlong campaign to pressure the school to fire Bassett, who was identified in news stories as "bAsset." But the fight was about more than one professor's job or even academic freedom—it was about the interpretation of history.

"What ought a North Carolina college to teach a North Carolina boy?" Daniels asked. "Should he be taught that his father and his people are a race of men guilty of the basest crimes toward a weaker race when he knows the contrary to be true? . . . Should he be taught that the negro race is not inferior to the white race? Should he be taught that the negro will win equality? Should he be taught that the Southern idea is false and wrong, and the New England idea is right?"[61]

The Bassett affair drew national attention. Although many North Carolina papers joined Daniels in his campaign, Trinity president John C. Kilgo stood his ground, and the school's trustees refused to fire Bassett by an 18–7 vote. After the vote, students hanged Daniels in effigy.

Daniels did not mellow in his upholding the battlements of segregation. He accused Republican Herbert Hoover of selling out the South in 1929, when the First Lady included Jessie De Priest, the wife of Oscar De Priest, the first Black man to serve in Congress since George White, at a White House event for congressional wives. But by that time, there were some brave Black voices in North Carolina voicing dissent. Louis Austin, editor of the *Carolina Times* in Durham, wrote, "Mrs. Hoover's action met with the approval of the majority of Blacks North and South."[62]

While Daniels was obsessing over a college professor's writing, the paper virtually ignored one of the biggest stories of the century in its backyard, the first flight by the Wright brothers at Kitty Hawk, North Carolina, in December 1903.

Daniels championed Jim Crow for the rest of his life. But the South was not monolithic, and Daniels's views did not neatly align with many other leading southern editors. Daniels opposed the resurgence of the Ku Klux Klan, fought lynching, and criticized convict leasing and the mistreatment of Black inmates.

Daniels fit into what historians David S. Cecelski and Timothy B. Tyson called North Carolina's "paternalist ethos." They wrote that North Carolina's "new social order combined a commitment to white domination with measured but unequal support for black education, a posture of 'moderate' white supremacy, and a constraining civility in race relations."[63]

Daniels argued that the white caste had certain obligations to those they ruled. A couple of days after the 1898 white supremacy campaign, Daniels spoke to the Negro State Fair in Raleigh seeking to "voice to them the genuine friendship which leaders of white supremacy felt for them."[64]

As early as 1899, Daniels sought to stamp out lynching. "What is wanted is a public sentiment . . . so stern in its condemnation that it will beget a few clean-cut jury convictions," he wrote. "Then, and not before, lynchings will cease. The lyncher is no legitimate product of our civilization." Daniels repeatedly returned to the subject, writing in that same year that lynching presented a choice "between law and order and anarchy."[65]

Daniels's views were like those of other North Carolina white supremacist leaders who did not hesitate to use intimidation and violence to disenfranchise Black voters but who saw lynching as barbaric. Furnifold Simmons, as a senator, rushed back to his Jones County farm to prevent the lynching of a Black farmhand accused of murdering his father in 1903. Charles Aycock, as governor (1901–5), repeatedly mobilized the militia to prevent lynchings and personally offered rewards for the conviction of those who participated in such killings. Daniels's financial benefactor Julian Carr urged that "the pulpit, the pew and the press" be mobilized to "stamp out lynch law." As historian W. Fitzhugh Brundage has noted, "The nascent campaign against lynching posed no threat to the preservation of white supremacy; indeed, many editors believed that the eradication of lynching would strengthen the claims of white Southerners that Jim Crow was humane and in the interest of Blacks themselves."[66]

Whether the pleadings of white leaders were effective or not, North Carolina and Virginia had by far the fewest lynchings in the South—more akin to Montana than the Deep South states. North Carolina had 101 lynchings between 1882 and 1968 compared with the 531 lynchings in Georgia.[67]

Another blight on the southern landscape was the convict leasing system, widely used in states such as Texas, Florida, Georgia, and Alabama. In many cases, the practice smacked of a form of slavery, with sheriff's deputies arresting Black men for loitering and assigning them to dangerous work. North Carolina practiced convict leasing, hiring out inmates for road building, railroads, farms, mines, and manufacturing. Inmate leasing was most often used during the administration of Daniels's friend Aycock.

Daniels's record is mixed on this issue. The paper called for an end to the practice of leasing inmates for road construction in 1913 but apparently had no problem with county road gangs. In 1928 a *News and Observer* ran an editorial headlined "Relic of Barbarism" when Alabama ended its convict leasing system. "In North Carolina convicts are still being subjected to the leasing system that will continue until aroused public sentiment forces the enlightenment that has come to Alabama," the paper said.[68]

Daniels never made convict leasing a crusade, although the paper would denounce mistreatment of inmates. The paper in 1899 accused the superintendent of a Northampton County prison farm of brutal treatment of inmates while leasing them out to help rich planters harvest their cotton. It called for the superintendent's firing. The superintendent both sued the *News and Observer* and threatened to shoot Daniels. When the superintendent spotted Daniels at a Weldon railroad station, the armed prison official went from car to car searching for the unarmed Daniels, who escaped harm by locking himself in a lavatory.[69]

In a 1930 incident, Willie Bellamy, a nineteen-year-old serving a six-month sentence on a Wake Country road gang for a Prohibition violation, became involved in a short-lived food strike. He was beaten and thrown into a sweatbox, where he died in the 110-degree heat. The prison official responsible was acquitted. Daniels called it "a piece of barbarity that has no place in our penal system."[70]

The 1920s saw the revival of the Ku Klux Klan. It had died out after Reconstruction, but fueled by the movie *The Birth of a Nation* and growing antipathy toward Blacks, Asians, Jews, Catholics, and the foreign-born, as many as 4 million people joined the new Klan, which, unlike the Reconstruction version, was national in scope. Daniels fought the resurgence of the Klan, arguing that such extralegal vigilantism may have been necessary during Reconstruction but not now. "The danger is that wherever disguised men take the law into their own hands they will not only punish the guilty but the innocent also," Daniels wrote in 1923. "Who is safe if a few disguised men may with impunity punish whoever they decide in secret gatherings is deserving of punishment?" When three Black men were lynched in Salisbury in 1906, Daniels published a grisly photograph of the bodies of the men hanging from a tree at the top of the front page and urged authorities to vigorously prosecute the mob.[71]

The paper helped defeat Klan-inspired legislation in 1927 outlawing sex between the races and adding restrictions on religious education, banishing the Knights of Columbus, and establishing speech codes involving Catholics. Daniels sought to split the Klan by accusing the national organization of dictating to local organizations. The paper highlighted Klan activity such as the flogging of an African American postman and of a white Wake County couple seeking separation. Daniels also broke with many southerners when he voted for an anti-Klan plank at the 1924 Democratic National Convention in New York that bitterly divided the Democrats.[72]

Like many white segregationists, Daniels's relationship with African Americans was complex. While decrying any form of Black political engagement, Daniels elevated Black voices that accepted the Jim Crow message of racial inequality. When Robert Moton, head of the Black Tuskegee Institute in Alabama, spoke in Raleigh in 1921, Daniels not only published his speech on the front page but introduced the speaker to a large, racially mixed audience. The next year, Daniels spoke at Tuskegee, at the unveiling of a statue of Booker T. Washington.[73]

He took a paternalistic interest in Black people, as long they were politically powerless and subservient; served his meals but did not join him at his table; and used the back door. He rewarded Black people who stayed within their caste-assigned role. One of his last acts as navy secretary was to make sure his servant, Bob Gaines, obtained civil service status to work as a navy messenger. Even during the 1898 white supremacy campaign, one of his neighbors, Wesley Hoover, a Black saloon owner, secretly shadowed Daniels home each evening to make sure he was not attacked, according to his son Jonathan.[74]

He lived much of his adult life in a Black-majority neighborhood in South Raleigh with a gardener, a maid, two nurses, and a cook, all of them African Americans. At the back door, the Daniels family operated a part-time medical dispensary and soup kitchen, mainly for needy Black residents.

Daniels's paternalism did not fool many African Americans. But the criticism of Daniels was muffled in North Carolina's Black press, which was cautious after the white violence in the early years of Jim Crow.

T. Thomas Fortune was free to offer his opinions from his perch as editor of his paper, the *New York Age*. In 1904, Fortune wrote that Daniels was "one of the mildest spoken and meekest-appearing men who ever fomented riot and revolution and reveled in the slaughter of unarmed men guiltless of crime or other offense other than being Black or yellow."[75]

Daniels was a racist operating in a racist age. That does not diminish his racism, nor does it excuse it. That does not mean that Daniels did not have choices or that he was simply riding along with the times. But historical context is vital in understanding the motivations and actions of people.

Not only did racial segregation become the law across the South, but there was widespread de facto segregation across the nation in housing, jobs, neighborhoods, clubs, public beaches, and many other aspects of life. Thirty states had miscegenation laws, making it a crime for white and Black people to marry or even have sex. The nation passed laws forbidding Chinese immigration, and Japanese were forbidden from owning land in California, becoming a voting citizen, or serving on a jury. Biological racism, the social Darwinism belief that people are organized hierarchically by race, was widely accepted as "cutting age science," wrote historian David S. Reynolds, a leading interpreter of nineteenth-century American culture.[76]

C. Vann Woodward, perhaps the preeminent southern historian, wrote that a "doctrine of racism reached a crest of acceptability and popularity among respectable scholarly and intellectual circles. At home and abroad, biologists, sociologists, anthropologists, and historians, as well as journalists and novelists, gave support to the doctrine that races were discrete entities and that the 'Anglo-Saxon' or 'Caucasian' was the superior of them all."[77]

Daniels remained a segregationist until he died in 1948. Just months before his end, he railed against the findings of the Committee on Civil Rights appointed by President Harry Truman. Daniels argued that its recommendations were an intrusion on states' rights and unfairly singled out the South and said that the plight of southern Blacks had markedly improved. "The remedy proposed would prove worse than the disease, a disease that needs healing rather than the proposed surgeon's knife," he wrote.[78]

"Of all the blasts against the anti-Southern implications of the President's civil rights committee's report last fall, the most thunderous and widely quoted, and to some the most amazing, was Josephus Daniels in his Raleigh *News and Observer*," wrote John Temple Graves, a Birmingham, Alabama–based syndicated columnist, at the time of Daniels's death. "And he meant what he wrote, for he took pains to have his tear-sheets sent to fellow editors. Great American, world citizen, he was also a Southerner."[79]

A decade after the Daniels family sold the paper, the *News and Observer* under Melanie Sill's editorship sought to come to grips with its white supremacist legacy. In 2006, the paper hired historian Timothy Tyson to write a special sixteen-page section on the white supremacy campaigns and the Wilmington massacre, published by both the Raleigh paper and the *Charlotte Observer*. The General Assembly passed a law requiring the teaching of the tragedy in the public schools. The special section won the Excellence Award from the National Association of Black Journalists. The *News and Observer*'s special section—and its apology—followed the release of a 500-page report on the massacre by the state Office of Archives and History earlier that year headed by historian LeRae Umfleet.

The Wilmington massacre story was first told by Black writers, most notably by historian Helen Edmonds in her 1951 book, *The Negro and Fusion Politics in North Carolina*, and by scholar Leon Prather in his 1984 book, *We Have Taken A City*. It was later examined by white scholars, including in a 1998 book, *Democracy Betrayed*, a collection of essays by eleven scholars edited by Cecelski and Tyson with a foreword by John Hope Franklin. Although well known in North Carolina circles, the Wilmington massacre reached a broader national audience in 2020, with journalist David Zucchino's masterful retelling in *Wilmington's Lie*, which won a Pulitzer Prize. The events were also the subject of a film documentary and at least six novels, the first by Black author Charles W. Chesnutt, whose 1901 novel, *The Marrow of Truth*, is considered among the most important works of African American realist fiction.

Frank Daniels Jr., Josephus's grandson and the last Daniels to be the paper's publisher, resented the paper's apology for its role, saying it lacked perspective. "I still think that was a political activity and not a racial activity, and yet in all the presentations, it's been racial," Daniels said in a 2007 interview. "I thought the rioting stuff was just a flat-out mistake. It was something that got started, and they couldn't stop it. And it irritated me that the *News and Observer* apologized for their role." By the time his grandfather's statue was pulled down, Frank Jr. seemed more aware of his forebear's faults.[80]

CHAPTER TWO

Beginnings

Josephus Daniels was born a war refugee on May 18, 1862, his family fleeing from the Union bombardment of Washington, North Carolina, a coastal town along the Pamlico River that changed hands several times during the Civil War. Many buildings were destroyed, including two Daniels homes. To escape the carnage, his mother, Mary Cleaves Daniels, fled to the safety of Ocracoke Island with her three children. Her husband, Jody Daniels, was not so lucky.

A ship's carpenter, Jody Daniels worked in a Wilmington shipyard building blockade runners for the Confederacy until Union troops captured the city. Returning to his home, Jody received Union permission to haul food and other materials from Union-held New Bern to Confederate-held Washington in exchange for returning cotton needed by Union troops. To get this permission, he swore an allegiance and signed an oath to the Union. On the return trip, Confederate troops on the banks of the Pamlico River opened fire, severely wounding Jody, who died a week later, in January 1865, of blood poisoning. In later years, Josephus Daniels's foes maintained that his father was a Union sympathizer. As Josephus's biographer Lee Craig notes, Jody Daniels held anti-secessionist and antislavery sentiments, but he did not give material aid or service to the Union army.[1]

The war widow Mary Daniels, who was from a slave-owning family, moved with her three children, Josephus, Frank, and Charles, in 1865 to the cotton town of Wilson to live with her sister. Wilson had about 1,000 residents—40 percent of them Black—and was located fifty miles east of Raleigh in one of the most rural and conservative parts of the state. Daniels grew up in modest circumstances, raised by his mother, who ran the local post office—a Republican political patronage job—from the front part of her house on Tarboro Street.

Because there were no public schools, Daniels attended Wilson Collegiate Institute, a first-rate private school that not only emphasized the classics but also glorified Confederate heroes such as Stonewall Jackson. One of his fellow students was Charles Brantley Aycock, a lifelong friend whom he later helped become governor.[2]

His upbringing nourished his belief in white supremacy, the Jeffersonian sanctity of the small farmer, the Democratic Party, and the Methodist Church, which was the center of the Daniels family's social life. He was a lifelong abstainer from alcohol and tobacco and made a point of plainly dressing.

There were few better places to soak up politics than his mother's post office, which was a gathering place where men traded stories and collected their mail and newspapers.

By 1880, the eighteen-year-old Daniels left school to become editor of the *Wilson Advance*, a paper whose office he had been hanging around since he was ten years old. He purchased the paper for $2,000 ($62,000 in 2024 dollars) by securing a loan using his mother's house as collateral. Showing entrepreneurial talent, Daniels started the *Kinston Free Press* and purchased part ownership in the *Rocky Mount Reporter* within a few years. By age twenty-two, Daniels was president of the North Carolina Press Association.

While Daniels did not attend college, in 1885 he enrolled at the University of North Carolina law school and passed the bar exam. But instead of hanging out a shingle, Daniels fulfilled a long-held dream of owning a newspaper in the state capital when he purchased the *State Chronicle*. Although now largely forgotten, the *State Chronicle* provided Daniels with a dry run for his later ownership of the *News and Observer*.

The *Chronicle* was started in 1883 as a voice for reform by Walter Hines Page. It is striking that Raleigh produced two newspapermen who rose to national prominence in that era. Daniels and Page started as friends but became bitter rivals. Page grew up in Cary, now a Raleigh suburb, which his family had founded as a railroad town. Page, the more intellectual of the two young men, came from a more prosperous family and was college-educated. After a stint working for a New York newspaper, Page returned to Raleigh to start the *Chronicle*, financed by his family, as a progressive alternative to the more conservative *News and Observer*.

Page found it difficult to make a second daily newspaper profitable in a town of 10,000 residents—the size of the North Carolina town of Mount Airy today, model for the fictional Mayberry. Deciding to return to New York, he offered to sell the paper to Daniels. But Daniels initially lacked the money, and the paper was sold to a third party. However, Daniels got a second chance to own the paper—this time practically for free.

Daniels's financial backer was Julian Shakespeare Carr. The Durham industrialist and Confederate war veteran was one of the richest men in the South, having made a fortune selling Bull Durham tobacco before branching out into banking, textile mills, transportation, and electricity. The town of Carrboro is named after him. Carr became notorious in the twenty-first century when a racist speech he gave at the dedication of the "Silent Sam" Confederate memorial at the University of North Carolina in 1913 received wide circulation.

After the death of the previous *Chronicle* owner, Daniels asked Carr what he intended to do with the paper. The industrialist's holdings were so vast that he forgot that he owned the newspaper, kept no accounting of the money he invested, and was surprised to learn he had spent several thousand dollars on the paper. After Daniels assured Carr he could make the *Chronicle* profitable, Carr gifted the paper to Daniels, telling him, "If you succeed, you can pay me what you think it is worth." Daniels later paid him $1,000.[3]

During the seven years he owned the *Chronicle*, Daniels converted the newspaper into a daily with the largest circulation in North Carolina. His paper was known for its progressive politics, and Daniels himself was known for his ability to win the lucrative state printing contract and for his sponsorship of what was arguably the most influential newspaper columnist in North Carolina history.

Daniels hired Page—the former editor/owner—to write columns from his new home in New York, where he lambasted North Carolina's leadership of Confederate veterans, discounted fears of Black domination, and worried about a "priest-ridden society." His most famous columns were the so-called mummy papers, written in 1886, where he compared the state's leadership to long-dead Egyptians, calling North Carolina "the laughingstock among the states." While Daniels did not explicitly endorse those views, he readily gave them a platform because they created controversy and sold newspapers.[4]

A rising star, Page became editor of the *Atlantic Monthly*, the nation's most distinguished literary periodical in 1896; three years later he cofounded the book publishing giant Doubleday, Page & Co.; and in 1913 he became US ambassador to Great Britain.

In many ways, Daniels became heir to Page's ideas. Daniels pushed for improving the state's backward system of public education, supported increased educational opportunities for women, railed against corporate monopolies, and most of all crusaded against liquor in every way he could.

Daniels was developing a political philosophy. It was a blend of racism and Lost Cause mythology learned in a nineteenth-century southern cotton town. It included the grievances of the hardscrabble farmers who visited his mother's post office. There was a generous dab of small-town Methodism and its abhorrence of alcohol. It also reflected the views of a new generation of serious young southern thinkers—men such as Page, Aycock, state chief justice Walter Clark, and Leonidas Polk, head of the Farmers' Alliance. They were members of the Watauga Club, a social group formed in 1884 that pushed for better roads, schools, more modern agricultural techniques, and industrialization and helped start what would become North Carolina State University in Raleigh. The group still exists today.

Daniels was aligning himself with the younger reform faction of the Democratic Party but still maintained ties with the older Bourbon faction that included the old Confederate colonels, the railroads, and the industrialists such as Furnifold Simmons and Jule Carr.

One unintended legacy of Daniels's editorship of the *Chronicle* was that Durham, rather than Raleigh, became the home of Trinity College, later Duke University. The two cities were neighbors but had different histories: Durham was more industrial, while the state capital was more white-collar. Raleigh edged out Durham in 1890 for the location of a Baptist-affiliated women's college, now called Meredith College. The *Chronicle* crowed that Raleigh was "better suited to a college for the education of young women." That characterization offended Durham leaders, and its tobacco millionaires made a renewed effort, putting up substantial amounts of money and offering free land, to convince Trinity College—situated in Randolph County—to relocate to Durham. The Trinity trustees had previously announced that their new campus would be in Raleigh.[5]

Political patronage was a key to Daniels's early success at the *State Chronicle*. In 1887, Daniels convinced the legislature to name the *Chronicle* as the state printer—a contract worth about $4,000 per year ($139,000 in 2024 dollars), which he held until 1895. The patronage plum from the Democratic legislature helped keep Daniels's *Chronicle* financially afloat, bringing in more money than from circulation or advertising. In landing and keeping the state contract, Daniels displayed his political adeptness, working the boardinghouses where the lawmakers lived. In exchange for the contract, the state printer was the mouthpiece for the Democratic Party. But even with the state contract, the *Chronicle*'s finances were wobbly, the result of two daily newspapers trying to earn a profit in a small town.6

In 1892, Daniels sold his daily newspaper to North Carolina's governor, who wanted a campaign mouthpiece. Daniels then started a weekly called the *Carolinian* to provide him with a platform in the 1892 elections. While the weekly was not profitable, his strenuous advocacy for the Democratic ticket helped him land a Washington, DC, job in the administration of Democrat Grover Cleveland.

At age thirty-one, Daniels became chief clerk to Interior secretary Hoke Smith, a North Carolina native who became an Atlanta newspaperman, a white supremacist Georgia governor, and a US senator. In the job, which today might be called chief of staff, he handled federal pensions and political patronage. In his role as political hatchet man, Daniels later boasted that he "cut off so many Republican heads that even [Hoke] Smith asked me, 'in Heaven's name, to stop.'" Daniels sent much of his salary home to subsidize the struggling *Carolinian*, for which he continued to write.7

Moving to Washington with him in 1893 was his wife of five years, the former Adelaide Worth Bagley; their baby daughter, Addie; and a Black nurse. Adelaide, known as Addie, came from a socially prominent Raleigh family that had fallen on difficult times. She was the granddaughter of Governor Jonathan Worth, the daughter of a former Confederate officer, and a *Mayflower* descendant. They married May 2, 1888, at Raleigh's Presbyterian Church, but a minister employed a Methodist rite as a nod to Daniels's religious beliefs. Addie was nineteen and Josephus twenty-five.

The marriage was a step up for Daniels, the poor boy from Wilson. The *News and Observer* said the wedding involved "the crème de la crème of Raleigh society." Shown the clipping a half century later, Daniels wrote to son Jonathan, "Your mother may have belonged to that set—but not me.... You and I may get in on our wives' tickets, but in conviction and in radicalism we belong to the proletariat."8

The couple moved into Addie's mother's antebellum house at 125 E. South Street, a block from where Raleigh's Memorial Auditorium would later be built. The rambling two-story Greek Revival house was constructed in 1855 at a time when it was an upscale neighborhood. When the governor's mansion moved to Blount Street, most of Raleigh's finer families followed. It was a sketchy enough neighborhood that in 1908, their four-year old son, Frank, shocked a visiting family member by pointing out the local "whore house."

The Daniels family meals were prepared by "Aunt Zilphia," a former enslaved person who had been owned by Governor Worth and who stayed with the family after emancipation. Today, the house, which is a national historic property known as the Rogers-Bagley-Daniels-Peques House, is an office owned by Shaw University, a historically Black college. Daniels lived in his mother-in-law's house for the next twenty-five years, not owning a home until he returned from Washington in 1921 at age fifty-eight after serving as secretary of the navy.

During their two years in Washington, Daniels, his wife, and their first baby lived on the third floor in a DC boardinghouse. Most clerks lived in boardinghouses, eating at a common table with other boarders. To escape the summer city heat of 1893, Addie took their baby back to Raleigh, where the eighteen-month-old little girl died of an unknown ailment, possibly dysentery. They lost a second daughter in 1911, shortly after her birth.

Daniels was a natural networker, dining with senators and attending White House soirees. He turned down a federal post in the Oklahoma territory that potentially could have led to a Senate seat. But Daniels said his heart was in North Carolina journalism, and in January 1895, Daniels resigned from the Cleveland administration to return to Raleigh.

Buying the *News and Observer*

Like many newspapers of that era, the *News and Observer* had a complex lineage, having been created by mergers in an age when newspapers were financially weak and folded with astonishing regularity. Even today, the paper has difficulty keeping its founding story straight. For decades, the paper counted 1865 as its founding date—engraving it on the outside wall of its longtime McDowell Street headquarters and holding a centennial celebration in 1965. By 2015, the paper was erroneously publishing on its masthead that it was founded in 1894, the year Daniels purchased the paper.

The *News and Observer* is the descendant of two newspapers. The *Observer* was founded in 1876 by Peter M. Hale and William L. Saunders. It merged with the *Raleigh Sentinel*, founded in 1865, appearing as the *News and Observer* for the first time on September 12, 1880.

Samuel Ashe, the *News and Observer* owner, was a lawyer and conservative Democratic politician who ran the paper for fifteen years. The paper has been described as an "almost entirely unimaginative and unenterprising" Democratic organ and was soon struggling economically after it lost its state printing contract to Daniels and the *State Chronicle* in 1887, declaring bankruptcy during the 1894 recession.[9]

During a business trip to Chapel Hill in June 1894, Daniels met with Julian Carr, who told him that the *News and Observer* was nearing collapse and asked whether he was interested in editing the paper. If so, Carr said, he would front him the money.

Daniels purchased the *News and Observer* at a bankruptcy sale under a shroud of secrecy. Daniels feared that if powerful railroad executives learned that he was the buyer, they might swoop in and acquire the paper to keep it out of the hands of one of their leading critics.

The first news accounts of the purchase at the Wake County Courthouse on July 17, 1894, misleadingly announcing that J. N. Holding, a local lawyer, bought the paper. Holding was acting as an agent for Carr, who in turn was Daniels's financial angel. The transaction was so secret that even Holding did not know the identity of the buyer.

Daniels bought the paper with $10,000 in cash ($368,000 in 2024 dollars), plus $2,000 for legal fees and to cover an old debt. Of that money, $9,000 was a loan from Carr to Daniels. In addition, Daniels received credit for between $2,000 and $3,500—Daniels's account is confusing—as a form of equity in his weekly, the *Carolinian*, which was merged with the *News and Observer*. In return, Carr owned 5 percent of the paper, while Daniels owned 62.5 percent, with the other 32.5 percent owned by new shareholders.[10]

Having made his fortune, Carr helped Daniels buy the paper to pave the way for the latter's own entry into public life. It never worked out. He ran for the Senate in 1900, nearly ran for governor in 1896, and sought the navy secretary's job in 1912. Daniels's critics liked to taunt the Raleigh editor by asserting that Daniels "has taught himself to sneeze when Col. Carr takes snuff."[11]

So began 101 years of ownership of the *News and Observer* by the Daniels family—four generations of family ownership that stretched from horse-and-buggy days to the age of the Internet. Daniels was determined to publish a modern paper dependent on subscriptions and advertising—not on political patronage.

He sought to improve the physical plant, marketing, and news operations and to purchase the first three linotype machines in North Carolina. On July 30, 1894, he wrote a letter from the Interior Department to 100 leading North Carolina Democrats offering them one share of stock at $100 per share and a complimentary subscription to the paper. Daniels promised to promote the Democratic Party. More than 70 Democrats responded, including two future US senators and two future governors.[12]

The letter became part of the paper's lore, frequently mentioned in company histories. But Daniels biographer Lee Craig helped untangle the complicated deal. In describing Daniels's purchase, the paper has often minimized Carr's importance; it was better for a populist-leaning paper to be financed by grassroots Democrats than by a Durham tobacco and textile baron. By 1905, Daniels had repaid Carr's no-interest loan, and by 1926 he had bought out all his shareholders.[13]

Although the first issue of the paper in the Daniels era was August 12, 1894, Daniels did not quit his Washington job and return to Raleigh until January 1895. The paper was housed in a circa 1860s building located at 411–413 Fayetteville Street, a block north of what became Raleigh's Memorial Auditorium and across the street from what became the Sir Walter Hotel.

The venture was not a sure thing. Raleigh may have been the state capital, but it was a somnolent southern burg of 13,643 in 1900—just a third of the population of such modest-sized southern towns as Augusta, Georgia, and Wheeling, West Virginia. It was difficult for the paper to expand into the small towns and the cotton and tobacco farms that dotted Eastern North Carolina before rural free delivery was extended in 1902. (Prior to postal delivery, rural residents picked up the mail at post offices, which were often located at great distances.)

Still, Raleigh, the state capital, seemed like a city with possibilities. Raleigh's future as an academic center was coming together with new colleges, such as the future NC State University and Meredith College, joining Shaw University, St. Augustine's College, St. Mary's College, and Peace College. The city was beginning to industrialize with three new cotton mills. Telephone service and electricity were available. There would soon be fourteen miles of electric streetcar lines that would enable the development of new suburbs such as Boylan Heights, Cameron Park, and eventually Hayes Barton.

Daniels changed the name from the *News-Observer-Chronicle* to the *News and Observer*. He removed advertising from the front page and gave the paper a cleaner design and a new slogan: "First of All—the News." The paper soon doubled in size from four pages to eight pages and boasted of having the largest readership in the state. But it was a financial struggle at first, with Daniels borrowing money in 1894, 1895, and 1896.

Daniels wanted to rename the paper the *North Carolinian*, but his associates advised against dropping a brand name that had been around for three decades. Daniels said he might have renamed it anyway if business had been better and he felt he could take the risk.

In a larger sense, however, Daniels had superb timing because of the explosive growth of the newspaper industry—the newest communications technology of the era. The number of daily US newspapers grew from 574 in 1870 to 1,650 by 1899 and to 2,600 by 1909. The circulation of daily newspapers escalated over the same period from 2.8 million to 24.2 million. More people were literate, many could now afford the luxury of a daily newspaper, the advent of larger retail stores meant more advertising, and rural free delivery was just around the corner.[14]

CHAPTER THREE

War to the Knife

Daniels presided over a raucous era of newspapering in Raleigh, a southern cousin to the rough-and-tumble period of Chicago journalism made famous by the celebrated play *Front Page*. This was an age marked by highly personal journalism, with news stories routinely including insults and jibes and where the threat of fisticuffs and even gunplay were never far away.

As he was establishing himself in Raleigh, Daniels's most important adversary was Alexander Andrews, vice president of the Southern Railway. Daniels called his relationship with Andrews and the railroads "a war to the knife."[1]

It is hard to imagine today the power of the railroads. Think Amazon or Facebook. Before the rise of John Rockefeller's oil trust and Andrew Carnegie's steel conglomerate, the railroads were the nation's corporate Goliaths. In the age before automobiles and trucks, almost nothing moved around the country except by railroad.

"A railroad could make an industry or ruin a community merely by juggling freight rates," wrote historian Samuel Eliot Morison. "And among the major industries, they were the most notorious in abusing that power." Morison and other historians argued that the railroads virtually owned many state legislatures. "Members of the state legislatures were their vassals to be coerced or bribed into voting 'right' if persuasion would not serve," Morison observed. In southern cities, the railroads often subsidized such newspapers as the *Atlanta Constitution*, the *Montgomery Advertiser*, and the *Jacksonville Times-Union* in what historian Sid Bedingfield called the "New South industrial railroad complex."[2]

New York financier J. Pierpont Morgan was the colossus who dominated the railroads, especially those in the South, starting in the 1890s. The financial titan directed the Southern Railway, the Atlantic Coast Line, and the Seaboard

Line, controlling 6,000 miles of track south of the Mason-Dixon Line and east of the Mississippi River.

Morgan's man in Raleigh was Andrews, a Confederate veteran, engineer, and railroad executive. His Second Empire mansion, with a dramatic central tower and mansard roof, was located catty-corner from the governor's mansion, where it still stands as the Heck-Andrews House. With his wide girth, Andrews looked like the model for editorial cartoons of Wall Street barons. There was a question of which house—the governor's mansion or Andrews's mansion—was home to the most powerful man in North Carolina.

Andrews kept his grip on Raleigh by issuing free railroad passes to legislators, judges, and those in the newspaper business while financially lubricating the state's Democratic machine. Andrews or his associates set up a bar in one of the rooms of the Yarborough House, Raleigh's main hotel, and hired "fancy women" to keep lawmakers pacified, according to Daniels.[3]

At the same time, Andrews sat atop Raleigh society, with his invitations for social events highly coveted by the wives of many Tar Heel politicians. He entertained lawmakers and state officials in his private railcar, which he often kept parked in Raleigh. Most governors were said to be in Andrews's pocket. Daniels called him the "political overseer of North Carolina."[4]

Daniels had been a critic of the railroads since his days in Wilson. He campaigned for the creation of a state railroad commission to regulate the industry. He demanded reduced passenger and freight rates. He called for a fairer tax assessment of railroads. And he sought the annulment of a ninety-nine-year lease of the state-owned North Carolina Railroad to Southern Railway made in 1895 that was very favorable to the railroads. His feud with the railroads was part of his larger push for antitrust laws and his opposition to the American Tobacco Company's cornering the market on cigarette production. At Daniels's urging, North Carolina in 1899 became the first state in the country to create a corporation commission to regulate business.

Daniels never went as far as the populists, who called for government ownership of the railroads. Nor did Daniels sympathize with socialists—or at least with the politics of class struggle as viewed by Marxist socialism. Daniels was a self-made capitalist who believed in free enterprise and private property. But he thought that monopolies and concentrations of economic power distorted the marketplace and fettered competition. He attacked tax policies he thought favored the wealthy.

The conservative Democratic legislature protected the railroads, believing a laissez-faire approach to business was the best way to promote industrialization. Taking on the railroads was not for the fainthearted. "I wanted to learn whether the railroads owned North Carolina or whether North Carolina could control the railroads," Daniels later recalled.[5]

Andrews and the railroads used a variety of tactics to muzzle Daniels. Andrews first tried to buy Daniels off when he was editor of the *State Chronicle*. In 1889, Andrews offered to buy the *News and Observer* and make Daniels the editor with a hefty salary if he promised not to attack the railroads. Daniels said would not "sell myself" to the railroads. "I hate 'em with as holy a hatred as is possible but I am going to be, if possible, as 'wise as serpent [sic] & as harmless as doves,'" Daniels wrote his mother in 1886.[6]

After Daniels purchased the *News and Observer*, the railroads financed three successive newspapers to pressure him in the 1890s and the first decade of the twentieth century—the *Daily Tribune*, which lasted until 1897, the *Raleigh Morning Post*, which folded in 1905, and the *Raleigh Evening Times*. The newspapers did not make money, but they cut into the *News and Observer*'s profits. Only the *Raleigh Evening Times* survived and was purchased by the *News and Observer* in 1955.

Newspapers and railroads depended on each other. Newspapers needed the railroads to deliver newsprint and ink, to distribute the published newspaper, and to provide passes to allow journalists to cover out-of-town stories. The railroads needed newspapers to advertise ticket prices and schedules.

Putting pressure on the *News and Observer*, Andrews withdrew the railroad's free passes for the paper's employees that had been issued in exchange for printing the railroad's timetable. According to Daniels, Southern Railway also changed its railroad schedule to make it harder for the paper to make out-of-town deliveries.[7]

Daniels also believed the railroads used the paper's advertisers as leverage. During a modest smallpox epidemic in Raleigh, the *News and Observer* reported the number of cases daily. A delegation of merchants, fearful the coverage was scaring away trade, threatened to pull their advertising, but Daniels argued that the paper had an obligation to print the news. Daniels said the effort was orchestrated by the railroad-backed *Morning Post*.[8]

Daniels was not easily intimidated. When the legislature declined to cancel the ninety-nine-year railroad contract in 1897, Daniels denounced "the late disgraceful mob of bribe-takers, self-seekers, and corruptionists called the Legislature." He labeled one pro-railroad legislator from Halifax County "the senator from the Atlantic Coast Line Railway." The next day the lawmaker accosted Daniels on the Senate floor, lunging at him, while other senators broke up the fight.[9]

His feud with the railroads once led to his incarceration. Daniels sharply criticized a federal judge for granting a receivership of the Atlantic and North Carolina Railways. The judge fined him $2,000, which Daniels refused to pay. He did not allow his supporters to pay his fine, either.

So Daniels was arrested. "Before I would retract a solitary sentence of that editorial, or abase myself, I would rot in a dark dungeon all my days," Daniels wrote in a column, which began, "In the Custody of the United States Marshal, Room 28, Yarborough House." Confinement in Raleigh's finest hotel was not exactly a dungeon, especially because he was permitted to visit his pregnant wife (carrying his youngest son, Frank Sr.) and the newspaper office. North Carolina's First Lady sent him flowers.[10]

He was unchastened when released after three days by another federal judge. He denounced federal district court judge T. R. Purnell, the Republican appointee who had jailed him, as an "ignorant pygmy, a tyrant, a clown . . . puffed, distorted, craven, truckling, a puppet king, laughable figure, a constant menace."[11]

Fighting Editor

Daniels could be as brutal in his attacks as any toxic social media posting today. One of his chief targets was US senator Marion Butler, a populist leader and newspaper editor. On one occasion, the paper stated, "Marion Butler is a Judas Iscariot, who betrayed his state for thirty pieces of silver and then did not have the decency to go out and hang himself."[12]

Daniels liked to tell the story of a Republican legislator whom he had been attacking—a preacher with a fondness for the bottle. The man showed up at the newspaper to ask Daniels to lay off him. He noted that he planned to preach a sermon the next day and asked whether he would write something positive about that. The next day an item appeared in the paper announcing the legislator would preach the next day—"if he's sober enough to get there."[13]

As he once wrote to his mother, "I am prone to denounce men whose views are different from mine, especially when I know them to be influenced by selfish considerations. The only way to defeat a wrong scheme is to kill the man. I mean kill him as far as his influence goes. To kill him in the eyes of the people. You must give reasons for it & of course that maddens the man, but it defeats a nefarious plan."[14]

Sometimes disputes ended in fisticuffs. When Daniels was still editor of the *State Chronicle*, he won the lucrative state printing contract, snatching it from the *News and Observer*. Samuel Ashe, the *News and Observer* editor at that time, called on Daniels to forgo the profits from the contract and donate it to the state's Confederate veterans fund. Daniels interpreted the remark as a slur against his father, who was killed by Confederate forces while on a Union-commandeered boat.

When the two men met on Fayetteville Street, they exchanged words, Ashe swung either a fist or cane at Daniels and missed, and the two men grappled and traded swings before it was broken up by a legislator who had been walking with Daniels. Later that day, Ashe issued a news release boasting that he had "cowhided"—or whipped—Daniels, further infuriating him.

The next day in the capitol a few minutes before the start of a legislative session, Daniels spotted Ashe and attacked him, with both men rolling around on the floor trading punches before lawmakers broke it up. Minutes later, the two men were sitting on opposite ends of the press table, taking notes on legislative action. The fight was the talk of the state. Raleigh's mayor fined Daniels five dollars and court costs as the aggressor and Ashe one dollar and court costs.[15]

In 1910, Daniels used his paper to help defeat the Democratic machine that controlled Raleigh. After Daniels stepped off a streetcar, W. B. Jones, who headed the machine, confronted Daniels, pummeling him to the ground, where the two men grappled with each other until bystanders broke up the fight. Daniels said he did not punch back because he feared that Jones had a pistol in his pocket.[16]

Dave Jones, a top executive with the paper near the end of the twentieth century, recalled hearing a story—maybe true, but most certainly exaggerated—of some elderly woman who said, "I can remember my daddy saying that they didn't think they'd had a good day unless they'd knocked Josephus down on Fayetteville Street."[17]

In hiring newsmen, Daniels valued a sharp right hook almost as much as the ability to write a strong lead. The paper often ridiculed opposition politicians, including Representative Atwell A. Campbell, a Republican member of the 1895 legislature from Cherokee. Tired of being the butt of stories—the paper nicknamed him "Old Hoola Boom"—a drunk Campbell strode into the newsroom one night looking for W. E. "Billy" Christian, the writer who was criticizing him in print, holding "a big bulldog pistol" in his hand. "Where is the son of a bitch that wrote that article about me?" he demanded. "I'm going to lick a skillet of piss out of him."

Christian was a Raleigh native and University of Virginia graduate who had married Confederate general Stonewall Jackson's daughter. He also could handle himself in a brawl. While staffers dove under their desks, Christian "picked up one of the heavy split-bottom chairs we used and hit the drunken old intruder squarely on the head. He fell like an ox senseless," recalled city editor John Jenkins. Fearing he had been killed, a staffer fetched a doctor. "Of all things, we didn't want a dead legislator. Such things are hard to explain," said Jenkins. The lawmaker suffered only a concussion and could remember little of the incident.

On another occasion, Christian wrote critical articles about a Republican leader named Richard Pearson, and Pearson, in turn, insulted Christian. Christian grabbed a pistol and headed for the Park Central Hotel, where the lawmaker was staying, feeling his honor was compromised. As Pearson went up the stairs, Christian fired a pistol at him, barely missing him. Christian was hustled out of town on a train before he could be arrested. He returned several days later, after the incident had blown over. According to his city editor, Pearson did not press charges and "the Democratic policemen were not keen to do anything to a reporter who was pouring hot shot by ink and lead into Republicans."[18]

Fred Merritt, the paper's managing editor, was nicknamed the "Fighting Editor." Not only did the former Wake County legislator wield "a nasty quill," recalled Daniels, but he could use his fists. "Within a few years, he repulsed a dozen attacks from people who had been criticized in the paper," Daniels wrote. "He was thin and wiry and the best scrapper on the staff. I recall several fist fights in which he got the best of very large men, who thought they could silence criticism by resorting to fist fighting. After he had downed a two-hundred pounder, nobody wished to tackle 'the little bantam writer.'"[19]

Such fisticuffs became less frequent but did not entirely disappear. In 1925, Jonathan Daniels, a reporter who was the publisher's son, was slugged by the superintendent of Central Prison because he didn't like his reporting. The two fell to the ground fighting, and when they stood up, the superintendent hit him again, with an armed guard standing nearby.[20]

In those early years, the *News and Observer* was also fighting to make a profit. The paper lost $7,000 in 1894–95 and did not make money until 1897, three years after Daniels purchased it. By 1904, the paper had erased its debt and Daniels was on his way to becoming a wealthy man.

Circulation grew from 1,800 subscribers in 1894 to 6,200 in 1898 to 14,451 in 1910. By 1914, the *News and Observer* boasted that it had double the circulation of any North Carolina newspaper, but that soon changed as the Piedmont industrialized with new textile mills and furniture factories fueling population growth. The *Charlotte Observer* became the state's largest newspaper and a leading ideological opponent, supporting conservative positions and politicians. The *Greensboro Daily News* and the *Winston-Salem Journal* also became major news competitors.[21]

The paper's growing balance sheets were fueled by national advertising, first by patent medicines such as Ely's Cream Balm for Catarrh, The Sunflower for nerves and blood disease, McElwee's Wine of Cardui for leucorrhea, and Mrs. Joe Person's Remedy for dyspepsia. One Daniels critic said the paper "publishes advertisements of the most nefarious kind of quack remedies, fakes—advertising that has long been tabooed by a decent press."[22]

By the 1910s and 1920s, Raleigh was developing into a regional retail center, and the paper began featuring ads by Capital City Telephone Company, Stoddard-Dayton Automobile, Crinkley's Cash Department Store, Jacob Kline, Goodman Lazarus, Boylan Pearce, Hunter-Rand, the Raleigh Department Store, and Hudson Belk.

With its increased advertising, the paper began to look more like a modern newspaper. It began running the first color comic pages in the state. Among the cartoons—some of which were racist—were *Mary and Her Little Lamb*, *Sambo and His Funny Noises*, and *Uncle George Washington Bings, the Village Storyteller*. By 1909, the paper was carrying Associated Press reports on Major League Baseball games while sending sportswriters to cover local college sports. The paper began a "Women and Society" section, which included ads about classical concerts, vaudeville, and occasional lectures.

The arrival of rural mail delivery allowed the newspaper to expand into the Eastern North Carolina countryside. In the early years, printed newspapers were rolled by pushcart from the printing plant down Martin Street to Union Station, where the papers were loaded onto cars for rural distribution.

James L. Wood, who lived outside Raeford, about ninety miles southeast of Raleigh, received his paper at the turn of the century via two or three railroad changes before it arrived at his farm in a horse-drawn buggy. Later he received his newspaper via rural mail by 10 a.m. on weekdays and by 8 a.m. on Sunday.

In 1911, *Collier's* magazine sponsored a contest offering forty-eight prizes of fifty dollars for the best essay about a newspaper in every state. The North Carolina winner was G. M. Cooper, a country doctor from Sampson County. "I read the daily 'News and Observer' of Raleigh, N.C. That paper is an institution. It is read by something like seventy-five thousand people, two fifths of whom hate it like the devil, but read it just the same. Why? Because they must. Its policies make and unmake Governors, Senators, judges, and the lights of lesser magnitude. Politically, it is mightier than all of the politicians and bosses in the State, for the simple reason that is backed by public opinion."[23]

The paper was nicknamed the "Nuisance and Disturber" by critics before Daniels bought it. It was tagged "The Old Reliable" by the paper's salesman named Wiley Rogers.[24]

The paper was known for its aggressive reporting on state politics and circulation-building stories of sensational crimes. Reporters and tipsters sat around smoking, drinking beer, and talking politics with the politicians at Denton's Bar in the Yarborough House, where many lawmakers stayed. Many of the legislative decisions were made in closed party caucuses, and Fred Merritt, the managing editor, sometimes hid under the benches in the gallery of the legislative chambers to eavesdrop. When the Fusionist lawmakers met at the Wake County Courthouse, reporters climbed a tree to listen. Daniels sometimes made a post-midnight visit to the Yarborough House to talk privately with lawmakers.

Daniels worked long hours and always kept his door open. Throughout his career, he wrote in nearly illegible script with a stub pencil that someone else had discarded, sharpened with a pearl-handled pocketknife. He never learned to type.

The sign on his office door read: "OFFICE HOURS BETWEEN 9 A.M. AND 12 O'CLOCK MIDNIGHT. CAN BE SEEN AT ALL OTHER HOURS BY ANYBODY CALLING TELEPHONE 90."

"He sat then between a table piled with newspapers and a wastepaper basket which was built of split oak sticks to hold nearly half a bale of loose cotton," remembered his son Jonathan. By nightfall, the basket was filled with clipped newspapers. "Generally, when we went in, he would be talking to visitors, and, as he talked, cutting paper figures and serpentines out of discarded newspapers, with the pair of pocket scissors which are still the only jewelry he wears except for his watch."[25]

One of his forums was an editorial column which he signed the "Rhamkatte Roaster" (1902–47). The column featured brief and sometimes humorous observations in the folksy, misspelled dialect of an ill-educated farmer. Daniels noted that some people interpreted his name as "Joe-See-For-Us."

Few newspapers in the country so reflected the character of its proprietor. Shortly after he died in 1948, Daniels's star columnist Nell Battle Lewis wrote that as "the last noted personal journalist in the country," Daniels imbued the paper "from first page to last with his own unique personality. In a rising tide of wishy-washiness, he stood for something."[26]

CHAPTER FOUR

Crusader

William Jennings Bryan was Josephus Daniels's first political hero—a populist firebrand from the Great Plains who reshaped the Democratic Party from its Jeffersonian laissez-faire roots into a voice for the underdog.

Daniels was at Bryan's side during three presidential elections, elevating the provincial newspaper editor into an important player in national politics. In turn, Daniels made the *News and Observer* a Bryanite newspaper, casting the paper's political philosophy for the next century. Even well into the twenty-first century, Daniels's Bryan-influenced direction to the paper—that it be a tocsin, an antiquated word meaning alarm bell, for justice for the underprivileged and an opponent of the comfortable—continued to be printed on top of the editorial page.

The two met while Daniels served in the Cleveland administration and Bryan was a young and upcoming congressman from Nebraska. Daniels was attracted to Bryan's rural populism, his broad-shouldered and commanding appearance, and his booming speaking voice that allowed him to be heard in large halls in the days before electronic amplification. Describing him as a "young David with his sling, who had come to slay the giants who oppressed the people," Daniels said he wished he was Nebraskan so he could vote for him.[1]

Born two years apart, the two political brothers were so close that Daniels was sometimes mistaken for Bryan on Washington street cars. "They trusted each other's judgment about fellow politicians, and their families were close," wrote historian Michael Kazin. "Bryan and Daniels even dressed alike; they often wore the same string ties, pleated linen shirts, and old-fashioned frock coats."[2]

If Bryan had been elected president, Daniels would have likely earned a high spot in his administration. Kansas newspaper columnist William Allen

White jokingly referred to Daniels as the secretary of war in the first Bryan administration.

Bryan's reputation has declined over time, with many people remembering him as an old fool for his attacks on evolution in the famous 1925 Scopes trial in Tennessee. But he was a transformative politician, helping move the Democrats from their more conservative moorings to a party concerned with the poor and working people, skeptical about great wealth, and more inclined toward government activism. "Woodrow Wilson would erect his New Freedom, Franklin Roosevelt his New Deal, and Harry Truman his Fair Deal on the foundation of alliances and policies Bryan had laid," wrote Kazin.[3]

Populism rose from the growing economic and political polarization of American society. The pre–income tax Gilded Age produced some of the nation's most enormous fortunes and grandest mansions, including the Biltmore House in Asheville erected by a Vanderbilt. But many desperate farmers were barely holding on to their land.

The turn of the century saw a rise of giant corporations or trusts. Between 1898 and 1904, three-quarters of the early twentieth-century trusts were created, including the United States Steel Corporation, Standard Oil, Consolidated Tobacco, Amalgamated Copper, International Mercantile Marine Company, and the American Smelting and Refining Company.[4]

The carriages of North Carolina politicians often lined up in front of the Daniels family's South Street home to get Addie's home-cooked meals mixed with talk of an agrarian revolt. Jonathan Daniels recalled,

> Like similar residences in other Southern and Western small towns, it was a house of revolution. Men from even smaller towns, embattled farmers from the five-cent cotton fields, intense young lawyers, earnest schoolteachers, some angry old men, gathered in that house as they did in so many others to speak something more than restlessness about the country and the corporations, corn and cotton prices, high tariffs, and economic heartbreak. . . . Daniels did not describe the trust as a mere corporate and financial device. It was to him and his readers a deliberate conspiracy to starve the farmers and put small manufacturers out of business.[5]

Bryan, Daniels, and other populists ardently supported increasing the silver supply. It is hard for modern readers to grasp how monetary policy was a dominant and passionate political issue: gold, free silver coinage, greenbacks, and bimetallism. Daniels repeatedly used the *News and Observer* to tout free silver, while more conservative papers, such as the *Charlotte Observer*, backed the gold standard. Indebted farmers from the South and the West felt they were facing ruin because of deflation, causing them to repay their loans at higher real interest rates than they anticipated. They supported silver as cheaper money that would be easier to repay.

Daniels and Bryan saw the world through the same lens. They favored a reduction in tariff rates that they thought were hurting farmers. They railed against the evils of liquor and imperialism. They called for the breaking up of economic monopolies of giant corporations. And they shared an abiding faith in the nineteenth-century social gospel that emphasized using Christ's words to address social and economic problems as much as for personal salvation. The South was Bryan's political stronghold. Like Daniels, Bryan was blind to racism. During presidential campaigns, "he said little about the cruel and unequal treatment of Black Americans, even when it was a vital matter for his audiences," wrote Kazin. "Speaking before Democrats in Louisiana and North Carolina who were busy disenfranchising Black voters, he avoided the issue entirely."[6]

Trying to assess Bryan's nineteenth-century politics through twenty-first-century eyes can be bewildering. As historian Lawrence Levine pointed out in 1965 about Bryan, there was a "misguided effort to characterize him at various stages of his career as either a progressive or a reactionary, without understanding that a liberal in one area may be a conservative in another, not only at the same time but also for the same reasons."[7]

The Democratic National Convention in 1896 held in Chicago's Coliseum was one of the most astounding in American history. After trailing in early voting, Bryan won on the fourth ballot, becoming at age thirty-six the youngest major party nominee for president in US history.

Daniels attended the Chicago convention as a reporter but emerged as the state's new Democratic National Committeeman. The youngest DNC member in the country at age thirty-four, Daniels held the post for the next twenty years.

Even before winning the party post, Daniels had proved himself a highly skilled politician. He secured the state printing contract—a lucrative patronage plum—in 1887. He installed his own man, Furnifold Simmons, as state party chairman in 1892. And Daniels wangled a high-level appointment in the Cleveland administration in 1893. He often outmaneuvered older, more powerful men.

Presidential Politics

Daniels was an influential advisor in five of the next six Democratic presidential campaigns—from 1896 to 1916.

There were several reasons for Daniels's political success. He owned the major state capital newspaper in an age before radio, television, and the Internet offered competing sources for information. He was shrewd, understood the instincts of the white commoner, and was an expert networker. Behind a benign, friendly countenance, he was a tough, ruthless political operator who was willing to exploit racial divisions. "His black string tie, homespun face and rustic courtliness were the perfect cover for a full grasp of the art of politics and the arts of politicians," wrote historian James McGregor Burns.[8]

(Today's notion that journalists should not be involved in politics would have drawn guffaws in that era. Samuel Ashe, the previous owner of the *News and Observer*, had been both a state legislator and a state Democratic chairman. Daniels's leading rival, Marion Butler, the editor of the *Caucasian*, served as US senator and national chairman of the Populist Party. Another Raleigh newspaper editor, William Holden, the *North Carolina Standard* editor, served as governor. Clyde Hoey, a Shelby newspaper publisher/lawyer, was elected governor and senator. The 1920 presidential race featured two Ohio newspaper publishers, Republican Warren G. Harding, a former US senator, and Democrat James M. Cox, a former two-term governor.)

The 1896 election was arguably the first modern presidential campaign. Republican William McKinley, the Ohio governor, campaigned from his porch, relying on an unprecedented flood of corporate money to get his message across. In contrast, Bryan barnstormed across the country giving fiery speeches—the first presidential candidate to conduct a whistle-stop campaign.

With most of the nation's newspapers supporting McKinley, the *News and Observer* resembled a Bryan campaign publication. Bryan's every speech was given prominent front-page coverage through the fall, while McKinley was virtually ignored. When Bryan stumped in North Carolina, the paper practically treated it like the Second Coming. The day he arrived in Raleigh, an artist's half-page rendering of Bryan appeared on the front page with Bryan-related stories covering the rest of the page. The tenor of the coverage of Bryan's visit to Raleigh was conveyed by the news headline "The New Star That Has Risen in the West."[9]

In Raleigh, Bryan addressed a rally in Nash Square under electric lights. While the famed orator was speaking, a "great bug with fangs entered his throat, and he was compelled to seek assistance of a surgeon to remove the clawing bug," Daniels recalled in his memoirs. "Consternation ensued until the varmint was removed, and Bryan was able to continue." The incident was not reported in the paper, apparently because it might have held Bryan up to ridicule.[10]

Daniels rode the Bryan train across North Carolina and continued with the Great Commoner on his whistle-stop tour into the mid-Atlantic and New England states. Bryan's populist politics were polarizing, with much of the country's establishment viewing him as a radical. At Yale University, Bryan was hooted and jeered by students because of his opposition to the tariff. In the factory towns of Connecticut and Massachusetts, Daniels saw signs warning of factory closings if Bryan won. The *Charlotte Observer* called Bryan a "radical" and "not a fit man for president." The *New York Sun* warned that Bryan was a "socialist or a communist."[11]

But buoyed by large crowds, Daniels returned to Raleigh convinced that Bryan would win. The paper offered running election tallies in front of the Fayetteville Street office by using a stereopticon, a type of projector popular for entertainment before moving pictures, and by an employee reading bulletins. McKinley won 51 percent of the vote, with Bryan getting 47 percent. For the rest of his life, Daniels believed Bryan had won and contended that the election was "stolen from him by padding registration, buying election officers and every method known to political chicanery."[12]

In his rematch four years later, Bryan performed worse, with McKinley winning 51.6 percent to Bryan's 45.5 percent. Daniels played a more minor role in Bryan's 1900 campaign because he was preoccupied with the third white supremacy campaign in North Carolina.[13]

In 1908, Bryan ran for the third and last time for president, and Daniels again saddled up. Daniels spent much of the fall election at Bryan's headquarters in Chicago, where he was communications director. Having Daniels as a key advisor "helped inoculate him against charges that he was soft on racial equality," noted Kazin, a Bryan biographer. Bryan needed to carry the South and the border states to win.[14]

Daniels again converted the paper into a campaign mouthpiece, running daily front-page stories asking people to donate money to Bryan's campaign. The paper forwarded the donations to Daniels at Bryan headquarters in Chicago. The paper raised more than $4,000 ($137,000 in 2024 dollars).

Republican William Howard Taft easily beat Bryan by a 51.5 to 43 percent margin. Daniels was not a graceful loser, warning darkly of "the secret machinations of men with power that reached millions, and the corruption of the venal."[15]

Crusader

The *News and Observer* offices on Martin Street,
headquarters of the paper from 1907 to 1956.
(Reprinted with permission of the News and Observer.)

Daniels could afford to engage in presidential and national politics because the *News and Observer* was prospering. The paper was still small—8 pages during the week and 16 pages on Sunday. But Daniels looked for ways to drive up circulation and bring in more advertising. In 1899, the paper published a special 227-page end-of-century edition, profiling many of the towns and counties across the state. The edition was said to be the largest newspaper edition ever published, exceeding a 168-page issue by a Melbourne, Australia, newspaper. The paper immodestly declared the edition "the most remarkable achievement in the history of journalism."[16]

The paper often gave away prizes for new subscribers, including automobiles, pianos, house lots, and diamonds in 1912 and 1914, Atwater Kent Model 37 Radios in the 1920s, and a trip to the World's Fair in Chicago in the 1930s.[17]

Not only was the paper growing, but so was the Daniels family. Josephus Jr. was born in 1894, Worth Bagley in 1899, Jonathan in 1902, and Frank Sr. in 1904.

The growing paper moved into a new headquarters on 114 W. Martin Street, between Salisbury and McDowell Streets in 1907. The new three-story building was red brick with marble and granite. The first floor housed the editorial and business offices. On the second floor was an office of the Associated Press and five Mergenthaler typesetting machines. Pneumatic tubes whisked the copy between floors, making a whooshing sound. Passing pedestrians could watch the presses turn out their 12,000 daily copies behind two large plate glass windows.

The building experienced a disastrous fire in May 1913. The *News and Observer* suffered $65,000 in damages ($2 million in 2024 dollars), although the paper was only insured for $28,000. To finance the repairs, the paper asked 1,000 people to purchase annual subscriptions and also borrowed money.

The blaze was the first of three fires that damaged the paper. The newspaper burned again in November 1915. A third fire occurred—in its third headquarters, on McDowell Street—in March 1980, causing $4 million in damage ($15 million in 2024 dollars).

Tar Heel Politics

Following the white supremacy campaigns, North Carolina, like the rest of the South, was a one-party state, despite Republican pockets in the mountains and foothills. Democrat factions replaced party competition, mirroring the ideological splits found elsewhere in the country.

The dominant faction was the conservative Democratic wing, closely tied to the state's textile mills, utilities, and railroads. Its leader was Furnifold Simmons, who built the state Democratic organization—courthouse by courthouse—in what became known as the Simmons Machine (1898–1930). Fueling the organization was a patronage network of federal, state, and local jobs, almost exclusively going to whites. It was bankrolled by big business, and the organization sometimes resorted to fraud to win elections. According to Jonathan Daniels, Simmons was as powerful as any Tammany Hall political boss in New York City, usually able to name who would be the next governor.

Josephus Daniels was a leader of the Democratic Party's smaller populist wing, whose support tended to come from beleaguered white small farmers in the eastern part of the state, urban reformers, and labor unions.

Daniels had a complicated relationship with Simmons, whom he twice helped become state Democratic chairman. Daniels liked to portray himself as an outsider, maverick, and reformer. As he wrote late in life, "Whenever any political machine seeks to dominate, the *News and Observer* opposed such control and urges smashing every machine, city, county, state and national." That may be how Daniels saw himself, but the record shows something quite different.[18]

Daniels had dual roles as editor of the leading Democratic paper and a top party official. One observer described Daniels as having had "a coolly correct" relationship with Simmons.[19]

The paper did not endorse candidates in Democratic primary races because of Daniels's delicate position as a DNC member and because he did not want to divide the party. Only in the twenty-first century did the paper abandon the policy. Daniels would not even print letters to the editor attacking any of the Democratic candidates. His neutrality enabled him to play the role of party power broker, helping negotiate compromises in party conventions.

Daniels and Simmons clashed from the beginning. Daniels wanted to send his friend and ally Charles Brantley Aycock to the US Senate, where he could influence state politics for a long time. But Simmons coveted the Senate seat for himself and urged Aycock to run for governor in 1900, where he could serve only one term under North Carolina's constitution. Simmons prevailed and was a senator for thirty years.

Like other early twentieth-century governors, Aycock was a veteran of the white supremacy campaigns. Daniels was particularly close to Aycock, an old schoolmate who was a law partner of Daniels's brother Frank. He stoutly supported Aycock's education program and helped enshrine him as North Carolina's so-called education governor. But Daniels did criticize Aycock occasionally, despite their closeness, taking him to task editorially for dispensing too many pardons.

Daniels avoided confrontations with Simmons when possible. Daniels stayed neutral in the 1900 Democratic Senate primary, won by Simmons over Daniels's financial backer Julian Carr.

Daniels used the *News and Observer* to push an agenda that called for a progressive income tax, antitrust legislation, abolition of child labor, and women's suffrage. He championed lower tariffs, free silver, railroad regulation, increased education funding, secret balloting, and direct election of US senators. He backed workers' compensation laws to help those injured on the job and opposed efforts by banks to raise interest rates.[20]

Most often, Daniels was on the losing end of the fight.

In 1904, Daniels opened a campaign against child labor, with a page-and-half-long article written by A. J. McKelway, a Presbyterian minister from Charlotte who was a leader of the National Labor Committee on Child Labor. An estimated 24 percent of the state's textile workers were children, and the industry opposed most efforts to deprive it of cheap labor. The article included eleven photographs during an era when photographs in the *News and Observer* were rare. It was among the paper's first forays into both investigative and in-depth reporting. Despite Daniels's best efforts, the 1905 legislature rejected a bill forbidding the hiring of girls under fourteen. The industry claimed that every textile mill in North Carolina would have to shut down because 75 percent of the spinners were fourteen years or younger. The following year, the legislature passed a watered-down bill written by the industry, and in 1913 the legislature forbade children under twelve from working in factories. By contrast, the *Charlotte Observer*, closely aligned with the textile industry, attacked McKelway as "malignant and indecent."[21]

The *News and Observer* ran dozens of editorials on the need to reduce and regulate child labor in the coming decades. That included failed campaigns in 1935 and 1937 to convince the legislature—against heavy business lobbying—to adopt the Franklin Roosevelt–backed Child Labor Amendment to the Constitution allowing the federal government to regulate child labor.

Daniels was often disappointed during the first decade of the twentieth century with the conservative-leaning Democratic legislature. He argued in 1911 that the "Gulf Stream of Progress" had bypassed the state because of the influence of powerful corporate interests. "There must be a war upon excessive conservatism in States like North Carolina, which sit still and see other States going forward along progressive lines," opined an editorial.[22] That same year, the *News and Observer* began serializing chapters of the autobiography of former Wisconsin governor Robert La Follette, one of the nation's leading progressive reformers.

With the election of President Woodrow Wilson in 1912, Daniels sought to build support for a like-minded progressive movement in North Carolina. After continued setbacks in a conservative legislature in 1913, Tar Heel liberals held a progressive convention in Raleigh in April 1914 that proposed a series of constitutional amendments. Those included direct election of senators, an initiative ballot, a six-month school year, free public textbooks, creation of a state utilities commission, and other measures. But the convention was poorly attended, and when the regular state Democratic convention met six weeks later, it repudiated most of the proposals. Cameron Morrison, a conservative leader and future governor, declared, "We don't have to go to Nebraska, Wisconsin, or New Jersey to learn our democracy." A disgusted Daniels left the convention early.[23]

But some of Daniels's fellow progressives sometimes felt that Daniels faltered in their cause, preferring political power to reform. Daniels's abrupt turnaround during the 1912 Senate race is an example. The *News and Observer* had been sharply critical of Simmons for being too cozy with business and for his Senate votes on such issues as lowering tariffs. The paper had initially backed a primary challenge by Aycock, the former governor, before he died of a sudden heart attack. Many expected Daniels to then back North Carolina chief justice Walter Clark, one of the South's leading progressives and a Daniels mentor. But at the Democratic National Convention held in Baltimore that summer, Simmons supported Daniels's bid to be reelected to the DNC, and the *News and Observer* backed off its criticism of the senator, in what some progressives saw as a sellout.[24]

Public Education

Daniels was more successful in pushing for public education improvements.

There was a lot to improve. While the national average for elementary and secondary education spending at the turn of the century was $21.14 per student, in North Carolina it was just $4.56. Illiteracy for both North Carolina whites and Blacks was among the nation's worst. Four-month school terms were typical, and most children were not even enrolled.

The education push, like much else, was tied to racial politics. The 1900 state constitutional amendment requiring a literacy test for voting included the so-called grandfather clause exempting anyone whose descendants had voted prior to 1867—a move designed to make sure whites could vote. But starting in 1908, the law required all voters to pass such a test, and Democrats had promised during the campaign to improve education to make sure that whites in the future would not be disenfranchised.

Starting further behind, North Carolina led what historian C. Vann Woodward called "the great educational awakening in the South." In 1913, the paper helped push through the legislature an expansion of the school year to six months—prior to that it had the nation's second-shortest school year. But it took years of editorials to help convince the legislature to extend it to eight months in 1933 and nine months in 1943.[25]

In editorial after editorial, the paper called for increasing school appropriations, hiring more teachers, building more schools, creating rural high schools, and making education compulsory. The paper backed local school bonds and supported an equalization fund to help poorer rural counties. Starting in 1939, the paper supported federal aid for education, and it championed adding the twelfth grade to high school in 1942. During the first four decades of the twentieth century, the *News and Observer* published a special annual education edition.

Despite decades of championing improvements by the paper, North Carolina's public schools remained among the worst-funded systems in the country—a reflection of North Carolina's comparative poverty, its stinginess, and its racial politics.

Like Aycock, Daniels argued that North Carolina had an equal obligation to educate its Black children. But the reality was gross inequality that worsened over time. Average spending on North Carolina's schools between 1904 and 1920 was $3,442 for white schools but only $500 for Black schools.[26]

There is little evidence that Daniels ever crusaded for closing the gap, and the paper did not acknowledge the racial difference in teacher pay until 1933. He also held the racist view that few African Americans could benefit from a liberal arts education, preferring they focus on industrial training. But Daniels praised Julius Rosenwald, a Chicago businessman, for providing money to help build more than 800 Rosenwald schools for Black children in North Carolina. Daniels introduced Rosenwald at a dedication of a new school in the Method community outside Raleigh and made him his houseguest in April 1928.[27]

Daniels also championed the University of North Carolina, starting in the 1890s, when leaders of the denominational colleges sought to starve UNC of funding and limit it to just graduate education. Daniels was a member of the UNC Board of Trustees from 1901 until his death in 1948, often serving on its executive committee. For nearly a half century, Daniels was involved in many of UNC's crucial fights and decisions.

He championed the creation of North Carolina State University (known as North Carolina College of Agriculture and Mechanic Arts until 1918 and as North Carolina State College of Agriculture and Engineering until 1962) and later Women's College of the University of North Carolina (now UNC Greensboro). He headed the committee that led to consolidation of the three main campuses in 1932 into the UNC system. He nominated two of UNC's most influential presidents—Edward Kidder Graham and Frank Porter Graham. When Edward Kidder Graham died in 1918, Daniels's name was floated as a possible replacement, although Daniels rejected the idea, saying he was not qualified for the post. Daniels was a major ally of Frank Graham, who became a target of conservatives for his social activism, his pro-labor stance, his effort to clean up college sports, and his moving the engineering school from UNC to NC State University.

With talk of a move to oust Graham as president in 1936, Daniels offered to resign as ambassador to Mexico to return to North Carolina to help Graham fight his foes. Wrote Frank Smethurst, the paper's managing editor in a column, "If Frank Graham can be chased out of the presidency of the University of North Carolina . . . we North Carolinians have been kidding ourselves all along about having a university."[28]

Daniels was a powerful ally in building and protecting UNC. He sided with the university on such issues as teaching evolution and in protecting a pro-integration faculty member and in making sure UNC remained financially afloat during World War II by steering a naval training center to campus.

His work led to buildings being named in his honor on both the UNC Chapel Hill and NC State University campuses, only to see his name stripped off in 2020 because of his role in the white supremacy campaigns.

Besides education, Daniels's hobby horse was the prohibition of liquor. A teetotaler who refused to accept any liquor advertising in his paper, Daniels led an effort, backed by the churches, to prohibit or limit the alcohol sales, culminating in the statewide prohibition in 1908—twelve years before national Prohibition went into effect.

In the run-up to the May 1908 statewide referendum, the paper published dozens of articles, editorial cartoons, and editorials pushing for prohibition and attacking opponents. "The question for YOU in this hour IS: 'Will I vote with the preacher, the teacher, the women, the most progressive men of all callings who are doing most to advance the State, or will I vote with the liquor dealers, the liquor makers, the men who get money out of the business and those others who from a mistaken view of liberty vote to continue in North Carolina an evil that debauches many clever men while they live and then send their souls unshrived before their maker?'" read an editorial.[29]

More than just an editorial cheerleader, Daniels helped politically organize the state for the prohibition campaign and privately urged Simmons to do the same.[30] Like so many issues, prohibition had a racial component. A lifelong teetotaler and an ardent Methodist, Daniels undoubtedly believed that society would be better without alcohol. But he also sometimes mentioned alcohol abuse by Blacks when pushing prohibition. "Southerners, both newspapers and individuals, held that Blacks who were fairly docile and industrious became drunk, a menace to life, property and the repose of the community," wrote political scientists Hanes Walton Jr. and James K. Taylor.[31]

Rather than ending alcohol consumption, prohibition fueled a boom in the production of illegal whiskey, helping make North Carolina the nation's moonshine capital and, as a by-product of bootlegging, creating NASCAR's auto racing industry.

It wasn't just booze that worried Daniels. Long a priggish Victorian, Daniels campaigned to close houses of prostitution in Raleigh, helped block a production of a French sex farce involving adultery from being performed in his city, and complained of the "vulgarity" of sideshows at the North Carolina State Fair, the racy magazines found in men's barbershops, and the playing of baseball on the Sabbath. He was shocked by statues of female nudes in Washington's Corcoran Gallery of Art and in the revealing dress of opera singers in Paris. He discouraged smoking and campaigned to make divorce more difficult. He made sure that religious revivals were heavily covered by the paper. "The newspaper ranks next to the pulpit and school as educational and moral power," Daniels wrote in an editorial headlined "Editors Are Like Preachers."[32]

As part of what Daniels saw as the paper's responsibility for moral uplift, it ran a series of religious-themed columns, almost exclusively Protestant-oriented. Even after his death, the paper published the syndicated column called Daily Bread, written by A. Purnell Bailey, a Methodist minister from Richmond, from 1951 until 1978. A few weeks before he died, Daniels clipped a story about church activities, advising his staff to keep up the good work and included this note: "Remember, the *News and Observer* is primarily a religious paper—except in campaign years."[33]

It was a rarity when Daniels was not on one crusade or another. "A paper must always be for something and against something," Daniels said near the end of his career. "The editorial page has to make folks mad and glad. A paper is dead if it isn't a crusader."[34]

Daniels's politics and crusades earned him many enemies. In 1902, a conservative Greensboro legislator predicted that one day the state capital would be moved to Greensboro, adding, "We are going to leave nothing to Raleigh but the penitentiary, the asylum and Josephus Daniels." To which the *News and Observer* responded with an editorial headlined "Three Institutions to Keep Republicans Straight."[35]

CHAPTER FIVE

Wilson

One evening in January 1909, a man whose strong jaw, long nose, and pince-nez would launch countless editorial cartoons appeared at the open door of Daniels's newspaper office. "May I invade your inner sanctum?" asked Woodrow Wilson, president of Princeton University.[1]

Daniels was not totally surprised as he looked up from reading the first edition of the next day's paper. He knew Wilson would be speaking the following day at the University of North Carolina's commemoration of the 100th anniversary of Robert E. Lee's birth.

For the next decade, Daniels became a Wilsonian Democrat, helping elect him president in 1912 and reelect him in 1916 and serving eight years as his navy secretary. As he moved into Wilson's orbit, Daniels was part of a transformation of the American Left—from populism to progressivism, the next stage in what historian Richard Hofstadter called the age of reform. Daniels was a player in the three major phases of the reform effort—the agrarian revolt and populism of the 1890s, the progressive movement of the first two decades of the twentieth century, and the New Deal liberalism of the 1930s and 1940s. He was an intimate of the three leaders of the movement, Bryan, Wilson, and Franklin D. Roosevelt.

Both populism and progressivism argued that the federal government had been complicit in the consolidation of power by large banks, railroads, and other corporations that had betrayed the nation's founding principles. The social Gospel energized both. But there were differences: populists wanted less government, progressives more; populists believed government was broken, progressives believed they could fix it.

The two men clicked from the start in part because both had small-town southern roots. Daniels had heard Wilson's father, a Presbyterian minister, preach in Wilmington—one of several ministerial postings in the South. Wilson had attended Davidson College in North Carolina. As Princeton's president, Wilson, a Virginia native, sent his daughter Nellie to St. Mary's College in Raleigh because she was beginning to "talk like a Yankee."[2]

Few people rose as fast in politics as Wilson, from university president to New Jersey governor to president in three years. He started as a conservative Democrat who fought the political bosses and was a foe of Bryanism, governmental regulation, and labor unions. But as he campaigned for president, Wilson began moving away from his conservatism, distancing himself from Wall Street and broadening his appeal among the party's large Bryan/populist wing.

Wilson was a fresh political face, but because he was new, factions within the Democratic Party were still wary of him. The leading Democratic presidential candidate was House Speaker James "Champ" Clark, an old political warhorse from Missouri who had the support of most of Bryan's followers and many state and local politicians. Also in the race was House majority leader Oscar W. Underwood of Alabama. In North Carolina, Simmons's political organization was for Underwood, underscoring the conservative/liberal split in the party. But Daniels and other progressives prevailed in winning the state Democratic convention for Wilson.

Bryan was still the most influential figure in the Democratic Party. While he was not a candidate in 1912, he could influence the party's choice. This put Daniels, a top Bryan political lieutenant, in a pivotal position.

Daniels was well-informed about Wilson's efforts because he had his own man embedded in the campaign. Tom Pence, the paper's Washington correspondent, had a short but remarkable career. Born in Raleigh in 1873, he began working as the paper's Washington correspondent in 1905.

More than just a reporter, Pence was a gregarious, witty, well-connected political operator on a first-name basis with senators, cabinet secretaries, and diplomats. With Daniels in charge of the publicity division for the Democratic National Committee between 1896 and 1912—a part-time position—he brought in Pence to handle the daily work. In 1908, Pence coordinated publicity for the Bryan campaign. In 1911, he became press secretary for Governor Wilson, and during the 1912 Wilson presidential campaign, he headed the staff of the Democratic National Committee.

After Wilson took office, Pence used his two-room apartment above a Chinese laundry on Fourteenth Street to gather several nights per week with the Washington press corps, doling out the administration's spin and tidbits.

By 1916, Pence was in failing health, suffering from Bright's disease and heart and liver problems. When he died that March a day short of his forty-third birthday, the president, the postmaster general, the attorney general, and three senators showed up at his apartment to pay their respects before his body was shipped to Raleigh for burial.

It was a matter of luck that Daniels helped save Wilson's candidacy.

Bryan was a guest at Daniels's South Street home in 1912 when a New York newspaper published a damaging letter Wilson had written to a railroad lawyer five years earlier in which he said that he hoped a way could be found "to knock Mr. Bryan once and for all into a cocked hat." The letter reflected Wilson's earlier conservativism. There was panic in the Wilson camp, which feared he would lose his nomination chances if he alienated Bryan and his followers.[3]

Daniels and Bryan were preparing to travel together to a Democratic fundraising dinner in Washington. Daniels soothed Bryan and asked him to withhold comment temporarily. When Daniels got to Washington, he and Pence met with Wilson and his campaign strategists. Daniels helped convince him to lavishly praise Bryan at the Democratic dinner, helping defuse the crisis.

When the Democratic convention opened in Baltimore, Clark led in the early balloting but did not have the two-thirds majority needed under party rules to clinch the nomination. Some Wilson backers urged the New Jersey governor to withdraw as the convention dragged on, but Daniels counseled patience. On the forty-fourth ballot, the deadlock broke after Underwood withdrew and Bryan switched his support to Wilson.

The country was in the most Republican-dominated era in American history. Only one Democrat, Grover Cleveland twice, had been elected president since the 1850s. But the Democrats' prospects were much improved in 1912 because the GOP was divided between incumbent president William Howard Taft and supporters of former president Teddy Roosevelt, who split off and formed the Bull Moose Party.

Daniels was now one of the Democrats' most seasoned operatives in presidential politics, and Wilson brought him into his inner circle for the fall campaign.

Following the convention, Daniels moved to the seaside town of Sea Girt, New Jersey—Wilson's summer home—where he was one of nine advisors who helped him organize a national campaign and craft a message. Fearful of Roosevelt outflanking him on the left, the team pushed for what Daniels called "a militantly progressive" campaign focusing on such issues as lower tariffs, antitrust, and support for labor.[4]

In the fall, Daniels moved to New York to set up a press office for the Wilson campaign in the Fifth Avenue Hotel. Daniels was responsible for campaign literature and news releases, meeting weekly with Wilson in Sea Girt.

Daniels understood that the age of stump speeches, torchlight parades, and Bryan-like spellbinders was ending. The new way to reach voters was through the mass media of newspapers, as literacy spread and newspaper circulation exploded.

Daniels turned the *News and Observer* into a campaign mouthpiece for Wilson. The paper ran front-page articles soliciting contributions for the Wilson campaign, raising $14,000 ($442,000 in 2024 dollars), and front-page editorial cartoons tying Republicans to the trusts. On the Sunday before the election, the paper ran seventeen pro-Wilson articles, including one titled "One Hundred Reasons Why Wilson Should Be Elected."[5] Anticipating the political advertising of the future, Daniels believed in the effectiveness of repetition, pounding away on the same subject, week after week and month after month—even if his readers got sick of it.

Aware of the continuing power of racial politics, Daniels denounced Roosevelt as soft on race, noting that Roosevelt had dined with a Black man in the White House, had appointed a Black official in South Carolina, and had closed a post office in Mississippi when whites objected to a Black postmaster. The South was solidly Democratic, Daniels wrote in an editorial, because of "the realization that the subjugation of the negro, politically, and the separation of the negro, socially, are paramount to all other considerations in the South short of the preservation of the Republic itself. And we shall recognize no emancipation, nor shall we proclaim any deliverer, which falls short of these essentials to the peace and welfare of our part of the country. This attitude of the people of the South is profounder than reason and deeper even than experience. It is the Anglo-Saxon instinct of self-preservation."[6]

With the Republican vote splintered, Wilson won 6.2 million votes, with Roosevelt earning 4.1 million votes and Taft 3.4 million. The *News and Observer* began the tradition of running a drawing of a crowing rooster—a symbol of the Democratic Party—on its front page. Southern Democratic papers had used the rooster at least since the 1870s, and some considered it a symbol of white supremacy. Daniels regarded the rooster as the Democrats' true symbol, even though political cartoonist Thomas Nast made the donkey the party emblem.[7]

As a favorite of the president-elect, Daniels could expect a position in the Wilson administration, and his friends mounted a lobbying effort on his behalf. Daniels initially thought he would be appointed Interior secretary, but word soon spread that he was in line for navy secretary.

That prompted Walter Hines Page—an old college classmate and early backer of Wilson—to hurry to the governor's office in Trenton, New Jersey, in an unsuccessful effort to derail the appointment. During the eighteen years since he left Raleigh, his friendship with Daniels had curdled because of Daniels's racist demagoguery and his championship of Bryanite agrarian radicalism. Page had befriended President Theodore Roosevelt and had defended John Spencer Bassett, the Trinity College (later Duke) historian. After listening to Page denigrate Daniels, Wilson said, "You do not seem to think that Daniels is Cabinet timber." Replied Page: "He is hardly a splinter."[8]

News of the impending appointment prompted ridicule. After a series of navy secretaries who were Yale- or Harvard-educated New Englanders, some viewed Daniels as an unqualified country bumpkin. Others, such as Teddy Roosevelt, thought it was ridiculous that pacifists such as Daniels and Bryan would land cabinet posts. "The President who entrusts the departments of State and the Navy to gentlemen like Messrs. Bryan and Daniels deliberately invites disaster in the event of serious complications with a formidable foreign opponent," Roosevelt wrote in the *New York Times*.[9]

Daniels initially played to type. Attending one of his first Washington soirees, he bowed to a distinguished-looking foreigner, welcoming him to the United States, only to learn that he was a waiter—an episode that made the Washington newspapers.[10]

Being called a rube did not bother Daniels, who retained a skepticism of big-city dwellers and viewed the Jeffersonian yeoman as the ideal American. Daniels also knew that the southern barons of Congress—with whom he closely worked—were subject to the same ridicule. Being underestimated, as many country boys were, could be an advantage.

Daniels was hardly out of place in a ten-member cabinet that had the most southerners since the Civil War. Wilson biographer A. Scott Berg called the cabinet "mostly a team of Rebels—lawyers from the South who had pursued other professions and never shed their Confederate biases." Wilson thought that segregation was a way to promote racial harmony.[11]

Bryan and Daniels traveled by Pullman car together to Washington, after Bryan stopped off in Raleigh to speak to 8,000 people attending the North

Carolina Peace Conference. When the two men arrived in the capital, they were so regarded as a political package that Bryan was asked about rumors that Daniels would be navy secretary—as if Daniels, standing next to him, could not respond on his own.

Giving each of his cabinet secretaries nicknames, Wilson began calling Daniels "Neptune"—the Roman god of the sea.

CHAPTER SIX

Cup of Joe

Once you saw Josephus Daniels, it was difficult to forget him. Physically, he was unremarkable—five feet eight and half inches tall, pudgy, baby-faced, and slow moving—and he had a pleasant, modest, soft-spoken, and self-deprecating manner, combined with an easy laugh. All of that belied his brass-knuckles style on the printed page, his strongly held views, his racism, and a certain self-righteousness.

He dressed like no one else. He favored a tailored black frock coat in winter, white linen and seersucker in the summer, with string bow ties, semi-pleated and stiff-bosomed white shirts with stiff collars, high-topped shoes, a broad-brimmed Quaker-style black felt hat, and a gold-handled cane. One journalist wrote that Daniels resembled a living daguerreotype who should be serving in the 1850s cabinet of President Franklin Pierce. His white socks, pinned to the ends of his long drawers, went out of fashion during the Civil War, the journalist wrote. The *Times* of London called him "one of the most picturesque personalities in American public life." It was expensive to dress Daniels because such out-of-fashion clothes had to be custom-made.[1]

From the beginning, Daniels had to fight the image that he was a political hack. Daniels's experience in naval matters was so slight that he cited his father's profession as a shipwright in listing his seaworthy credentials. Even home-state papers ridiculed Daniels. The *Winston-Salem Journal* sneered that his marine experiences were confined to Raleigh's tiny Crabtree Creek and the Neuse River in an article headlined "Will Daniels Get Seasick?"[2]

The longest-serving navy secretary in American history courted controversy in Washington just as he did in Raleigh. As the *Guardian*, a British newspaper, observed near the end of his tenure, "Probably no Cabinet officer

Josephus Daniels speaking on Flag Day 1914 with his three political heroes sitting behind him on the platform. On the far left is Secretary of State William Jennings Bryan, to his left is President Woodrow Wilson, and on the far right is Franklin Roosevelt, assistant secretary of the navy. (Courtesy of the Library of Congress.)

in any Administration since the Civil War has endured so merciless a castigation as that to which Mr. Daniels was subjected from the moment of his taking office."³

Secretary of the navy was a far more powerful post in 1913 than it is today; there was no defense secretary to report to, and President Wilson believed in a strong cabinet-led government, so Daniels had broad leeway in directing the navy.

In prewar Washington, the federal government was so small that the entire Navy Department fit on two floors of the old State, War, and Navy Building—now the Eisenhower Executive Office Building. But there was nothing small about the third-floor corner office that Daniels inherited. The office was a huge, opulent room with crystal chandeliers, a marble fireplace, a large globe, John Paul Jones's sword hanging from the wall, and a mahogany desk large enough for twelve people to sit around. Diplomats and generals described it as the grandest office in Washington. Opening the French doors onto his balcony, Daniels was the only public official who could look down on the president next door at the White House. It was a Walter Mitty–type upgrade from his Martin Street newspaper office.

There were other perks. At Daniels's disposal was the USS *Dolphin*, a 256-foot gunboat/dispatch ship crewed by 152 men, which he used to visit naval facilities and take Sunday cruises on the Potomac—although Daniels tried to convince Wilson that they should both sell their government-owned yachts.

He rented three homes during his eight years in Washington—Single Oak, near Rock Creek Park; 3000 Woodley Road; and 1851 Wyoming in the fashionable Kalorama neighborhood. In the age when government limos came in the form of carriages, Daniels's commute featured a Black coachman and footman, Jordan and Willis, both wearing silk hats, with horses Nip and Tuck clip-clopping down Connecticut Avenue.

Daniels's mode of transportation may seem like a scene out of a Gilbert and Sullivan operetta. But Daniels took over a navy that had been greatly expanded under Teddy Roosevelt as part of a naval arms race and that stood as the third-largest in the world behind Great Britain and Germany. The fleet consisted of 259 ships, including 39 battleships and heavy cruisers, manned by 63,000 officers, sailors, and marines, with an annual budget of $144 million—roughly 20 percent of the federal budget.[4]

Shortly after taking office, Daniels launched an inspection tour of naval bases and shipbuilding yards from coast to coast. As a result of the trip, Daniels laid the groundwork for the creation or expansion of naval facilities in Pensacola, Florida; Charleston, South Carolina; New Orleans; California's Mare Island; and San Diego. Daniels was also instrumental in locating a tank training camp in West Raleigh, now the state fairgrounds site, and a marine air base near Morehead City. He was less successful in getting a Federal Reserve bank located in Raleigh—losing to the much larger cities of Richmond and Atlanta.

In his effort to familiarize himself with naval operations, Daniels became the first federal official to fly. Two months after he took office in 1913, Daniels went on an eight-minute training flight over the Naval Academy with Lieutenant John Towers in a rudimentary open-cockpit, 75-horsepower airplane. It was so dangerous that Tower crashed the plane the following week, killing his passenger and putting himself in the hospital for weeks.

Despite the modern technology, the navy was a hidebound institution, where admirals who had trained on sailing ships still wore old-fashioned cockade hats, powerful navy departments operated like private fiefdoms, and a social elite dominated the officer corps—many of whom looked down on the deckhands.

Although a nautical novice, Daniels was determined to reshape the navy in four significant ways: by modernizing the bureaucracy, improving the plight of the average sailor, more closely scrutinizing naval contractors, and improving morals if not morale.

From the start, Daniels alienated the navy's old seadogs by blocking their plans to concentrate power in the hands of admirals, installing his loyalists in key positions, and disregarding some navy traditions. The admirals were suspicious of Daniels's involvement in the peace wing of the Democratic Party, and Daniels brought his own Jeffersonian/Bryanesque prejudices to the job. During his eight years as secretary, Daniels dealt with an often-hostile officer corps.

Despite a genial personality and an unprepossessing appearance, Daniels could be very tough-minded, frequently going toe to toe with the navy brass and usually winning.

The navy hierarchy was composed of eight quasi-independent bureaus headed by powerful, entrenched chiefs—usually admirals—who were barely responsible to the navy secretary and competed for appropriations. Daniels broke the power of the bureau chiefs—who served indefinitely—by limiting their terms to four years, after which the chiefs could go to sea or retire. The sea duty requirement became known as the "Single Oak" policy, named after Daniels's house. He required naval officers to perform sea duty before promotion and stipulated that those promotions be based on merit rather than seniority.

Daniels also tried to democratize the navy. With many enlisted men poor and uneducated, he required officers to offer general education classes at sea. Congress blocked his plan to open the Naval Academy to enlisted men, but he did crack down on hazing in Annapolis. He was further derided for his decision to replace the seagoing designations of "port" and "starboard" with the civilian terms of "left" and "right"—although he was following a recommendation made by the navy brass.

But no action drew so much attention as Daniels's order in June 1914 prohibiting "the use of or introduction for drinking purposes of alcoholic liquors on board any naval vessel, or within any navy yard or station." There was such an ingrained tradition of drinking among old salts that people still use navy slang to discuss drinking: "three sheets to the wind"; "binge"; "down the hatch." The army had already banned alcohol on bases; and while enlisted navy men could not drink—only officers could—medical authorities had recommended the complete ban.

When naval officers appealed the decision, Daniels suggested the men drink coffee, leading sailors to refer to their coffee as a "cup of Joe"—one of several theories on the origin of the term. Newspapers widely ridiculed the move by "Holy Joe." One editorial cartoon dubbed Daniels "Sir Josephus, Admiral of the USS Grape Juice Pinafore."[5]

During World War I, Daniels extended the prohibition to a five-mile radius around major naval and marine installations, drying up entire towns such as Vallejo, California. In Annapolis alone, the home of the Naval Academy, his order closed an estimated thirty-six saloons, hotels, and club bars.[6]

When Daniels threatened to close the bars near the Port Royal Navy Yard in South Carolina, Governor Cole Blease said Daniels "can stick his Yankee money in his ears" and called him "a very small man [who] is not of the mental caliber to fill the position to which he has been appointed."[7]

On July 1, 2014, the navy loosened its policy of liquor on ships.

Daniels also ordered the end of the distribution of condoms to sailors heading ashore. "The use of this packet," Daniels wrote, "I believe to be immoral; it savors of the panderer. . . . It is the equivalent to the government advising these boys that it is right and proper for them to indulge in an evil which perverts their morals." Daniels later backtracked when he saw the growing rates of venereal disease, but not before earning the nickname "Joe Syphilis Daniels."[8]

In 1917 Daniels banned all houses of prostitution around naval and marine bases, leading to marine patrols and contentious efforts to shut down red-light districts in such cities as Seattle, Birmingham, and Newport, Rhode Island.

But those were nothing compared to the battle of New Orleans when he shut down Storyville, the city's fabled red-light district. New Orleans's largest revenue producer, Storyville covered twenty-eight blocks and gave employment to 750 women and countless jazz musicians from 7 p.m. until dawn and was so organized that there was a blue book providing the names of the women and musicians in each house.

Daniels had reactivated the navy yard in New Orleans, establishing a naval training center there. In September 1917, Daniels wrote to the governor of Louisiana and the mayor of New Orleans, ordering them to shut down Storyville, which he said was causing more casualties than enemy bullets. "Close Storyville or the Navy will close it for you," Daniels wrote. Mayor Martin Behrman made two trips to Washington to try to change Daniels's mind. "You can make it illegal, but you can't make it unpopular," Behrman said. Under the threat of a shutdown of the shipyard, the city complied. As Storyville closed at midnight on Daniels' deadline, prostitutes hauled away their belongings in wheelbarrows as a Black jazz band played the hymn "Nearer My God to Thee."[9]

With the houses of prostitution closed, employment for jazz musicians dried up, and many of the early greats—such as Joe "King" Oliver, Louis Armstrong, and Jelly Roll Morton—headed north to Kansas City, the South

Side of Chicago, and eventually Harlem. There were numerous reasons for the jazz diaspora, although Jonathan Daniels later claimed that his dad was "the father of jazz in America"—which seems an exaggeration.[10]

Daniels's use of his dictatorial powers "meant the end of legalized vice in all Southern cities," wrote historians Francis Butler Simkins and Charles Pierce Roland. "With the passing of the Daniels era, police-protected houses of prostitution were revived in many cities. They were never so blatant, however, as before 1917."[11]

Instead of being preoccupied with sex and booze, Daniels thought the enlisted men should look for moral uplift. He increased the numbers of navy chaplains and required Sabbath services onboard ships.

Race

If Daniels was indirectly responsible for the diffusion of jazz, he had a more active role in promoting the epic movie *The Birth of a Nation*. The silent film was one of the most profitable ever made—and one of the most racist—with a storyline that glorified the Ku Klux Klan and demonized Black people.

Even in 1915 the film provoked a backlash, with the NAACP leading a boycott of the movie in northern cities, inciting race riots and causing the film to be banned in some places. Needing the approval of the National Board of Censorship, the backers sought to build public support by getting political endorsements.

The movie was based on a trio of best-selling novels by Thomas Dixon, a Cleveland County native and sometime Raleigh resident. His books and the movie helped spark a Klan revival in the 1920s and prompted the KKK to take up cross burning—a symbol borrowed from Dixon's books.

Daniels arranged for movie showings at Washington's central post office and the US Supreme Court. Dixon, an old college friend of President Wilson, organized a showing at the White House attended by the cabinet. Lee Craig, a Daniels biographer, argues that Daniels's assistance was crucial to the film board approving the movie.[12]

The film, wrote historian John Hope Franklin and Alfred A. Moss Jr., "did more than any single thing to nurture and promote the myth of Black domination and debauchery during Reconstruction."[13]

Washington was a southern city of 350,000, of which nearly one-third were Black, the largest African American population of any American city. While most Blacks lived in some of the nation's worst slums, the creation of the civil service had enabled hundreds of African Americans to move into the middle class by working for the federal government in such departments as the postal service and the US Treasury.

Although Wilson was elected promising racial fairness, he disappointed the several prominent Black leaders who endorsed his candidacy. Wilson supported cabinet members who segregated their departments, after complaints from white federal workers. Wilson said segregation would result in less "friction."

At a cabinet meeting just weeks after taking office, Postmaster General Albert Burleson of Texas suggested segregating all Black federal workers. Although Daniels did not initiate the move, he almost certainly was in accord. Not then nor afterward did any cabinet member speak out against the new Jim Crowism. The segregation that started in the federal workplace spread to Washington's streetcars and residential neighborhoods, parks, beaches, and golf courses. Fans of the Washington Senators baseball team were now seated by complexion at Griffith Stadium.[14]

After having progressed under previous Republican administrations, "an almost impenetrable pall of gloom" settled over the Black community during the Wilson years, Franklin and Moss wrote.[15] Daniels extended Jim Crow policies in the navy to include cafeterias, bathrooms, and offices, ending a fifty-year tradition of integration in the navy bureaus. Blacks were banned from the Marine Corps. Black sailors were restricted to mess duty—serving white sailors rather than fighting—"to avoid friction between the races," Daniels said.[16]

"No colored man, however able or ambitious, may look to being anything other than a servant in the Navy," Swan Kendrick, a Black college-educated Mississippian who worked as a clerk in the War Department, protested to Daniels on behalf of the NAACP. Critics said Daniels should follow the lead of the army, where 50,000 Black soldiers saw combat in World War I. "Equality of selection, training and service have been found to work well with the land forces of the country, and there is no reason why it should not do the same on the sea," opined the *New York Age*.[17]

Daniels swatted down as "inadvisable and impractical" a proposal by a NAACP official that one navy ship be manned by Black sailors, with a white commanding officer, to demonstrate Black seamanship. He reversed a plan to have officers and seamen eat together when it was pointed out that it would lead to integrated dining. He accommodated South Carolina senator Ben Tillman by agreeing that a proposed clothing factory at a Charleston naval base should hire only whites.[18]

Black servants were the natural order for Daniels. He expressed surprise when Eleanor Roosevelt, the wife of his deputy, brought four white servants with her from New York. She was shocked when Daniels suggested that she replace them with Black servants—more in keeping with the southern custom. "Whom else," Daniels asked, "could one kick?" Eleanor never forgot the "almost brutal feeling" of the remark. When her white staff left, Eleanor replaced them with four Black servants but expressed reservations about the reliability of "all the darkies" on her staff.[19]

Following the war there was a vicious white backlash against the 367,710 Black veterans—including 200,000 who served in France—and other African Americans who took jobs formerly held by whites in war-related industries. There were mob attacks on Black people in twenty-six cities including Washington, DC, in what was called the Red Summer, claiming hundreds of lives and injuring thousands. Besides the white attacks, what was notable was that African Americans for the first time fought back. Historians Franklin and Moss called 1919 "the greatest period of interracial strife the nation has ever witnessed."[20]

The DC riot began with a false rumor of a white wife of a Naval Aviation Corps employee being raped—apparently, she was jostled and her umbrella stolen by two Black men. White servicemen, including many sailors and marines, began randomly beating Blacks, pulling them off streetcars. In Washington, as in other cities, the white press inflamed tensions.[21]

The NAACP appealed to Daniels to arrest the rioting sailors and marines, but he declined to take any action. In his diary, Daniels accepted the rumors of Black assaults on white women as fact and seemed unconcerned about the white-on-Black violence until African Americans began shooting back. After three nights of bloody rioting, Daniels ordered in marine and naval troops to help the army restore order. He made sure his Black chauffeur got home safely.[22]

Jim Crow Liberal

Although Daniels was a racial bigot, he did not subscribe to many of the prejudices of the age. He was a critic of antisemitism, supported the women's suffrage movement, denounced colonialism, and declined to engage in xenophobic immigrant-bashing.

In an era when Jewish Americans were widely discriminated against in employment, admission to resort hotels, membership in country clubs, and college admissions, Daniels became the Jewish community's point man in the Wilson administration. Daniels—named after the ancient Jewish historian Josephus—was influenced by his admiration for the good works of a Jewish woman in his hometown of Wilson and by his close friendship with a Jewish student at the University of North Carolina.

At the request of the Jewish Relief Committee in 1915, Daniels arranged to have two coal ships heading toward Turkish waters to make room for 900 tons of food and medicine for several thousand Jewish refugees stranded in Egypt during World War I. The navy continued to assist Middle Eastern Jews throughout the war. Speaking at a Zionist rally in Carnegie Hall in September 1918, Daniels was given a rousing five-minute ovation for helping Jewish refugees in Palestine.[23]

During the lead-up to World War II, when he was ambassador to Mexico, Daniels lobbied the Mexican government not to deport sixty Jewish refugees fleeing Nazi persecution. In 1940, Daniels was a member of the Council against Intolerance, a New York–based group led by a left-wing Jewish author who warned about the rise of the Nazis in Germany and fascism in the United States. Daniels remained a Zionist all his life. His last public appearance, wearing a yarmulke just days before his death in 1948, was at the House of Jacob Synagogue in Raleigh at a service marking the partition of Palestine. After his death, the Raleigh chapter of Hadassah, a Jewish service organization, donated money to plant 100 trees in Palestine in his honor.[24]

Daniels came to the rescue of Wilson's Supreme Court nomination of Louis D. Brandeis, one of the nation's leading progressive thinkers. Daniels helped swing two key Democratic members of the Senate Judiciary Committee in 1916, providing Brandeis with a 10–8 margin to help confirm him as the first Jewish Supreme Court justice in a bitter fight marked by antisemitism.[25]

The *News and Observer* in 1933, then under the direction of his Daniels's son Jonathan, backed UNC president Frank Porter Graham's ending of the quota for Jewish medical school students—a move that prompted the resignation of the school's dean. "There is no place for any Aryan doctrines now so familiar in Germany," the paper stated. "Any discrimination between Jews and Gentiles in [the school's] student body would be a repudiation of its ideals."[26]

After World War I, the nation was gripped by a wave of xenophobia, which resulted in Congress passing the first immigration quotas in 1921 and 1924 to restrict the entrance of Jews, Italians, and eastern Europeans who would, in the words of critics, bring "diseases of ignorance" to America.[27]

In North Carolina, Furnifold Simmons was a leading advocate for limiting immigration, attempting to keep what he called "the scum" of eastern and southern Europe from American shores. Daniels declined to join the anti-immigration backlash. Although worried about cheap foreign labor, Daniels told guests at a Democratic dinner in Washington in 1920 that "we must not shut doors to the men and women of other countries who have a mind to come to our shores by love of our institutions and a desire to share the blessings of liberty. The Democratic Party was born in hostility to laws denying a haven to the oppressed of other nations."[28]

Daniels had long been a champion of women's rights, a movement strongly linked with the Prohibition campaign. The two movements shared many of the same leaders, and both Prohibition and women's suffrage were enshrined in the Constitution in 1920. During debates over admitting women to the all-male Duke University and to Cambridge University in 1897, Daniels wrote that the young men at those schools "are destined to learn that there is no sex in brains."[29]

When women marched on Washington in 1913 to demand the right to vote, the *News and Observer* asked, "Have not the women of this country a perfect right to consider the questions that effect [sic] government? Are our mothers and sisters and daughters unsexed because they desire to vote?" In an address to the Women's Civic League in San Francisco in 1915, Daniels proposed that women be given the vote and men disenfranchised, and after ten years experts should study which gender governed better.[30]

He vigorously supported ratification of the women's suffrage amendment, which Simmons and his political organization opposed because they feared it would allow Black women to vote. In August 1920 Daniels returned to Raleigh, where he unsuccessfully lobbied the legislature for the amendment's passage.

Daniels's wife, Addie, cochaired the American delegation—along with suffragette leader Carrie Chapman Catt—at an international women's suffrage conference in Geneva, Switzerland, in June 1920. Daniels had thousands of copies of his wife's speech mailed across the country at the navy's expense, drawing press criticism for abusing his mailing privilege. Addie campaigned across North Carolina, urging lawmakers to back the amendment. When it failed in North Carolina but passed nationally, Addie went on the hustings again, urging women to register to vote. Daniels pioneered the hiring of women in both the navy and the Marine Corps and on the *News and Observer* staff.[31]

Daniels came into office as an ardent anti-imperialist who, like his friend William Jennings Bryan, was a critic of continued US involvement in the Philippines, captured during the Spanish-American War. Daniels disliked gunboat or dollar diplomacy, in which the navy provided muscle for American corporations operating in Latin America. But Daniels's anti-imperialism was tested during his tenure as navy secretary. The navy and the marines were instruments of American foreign policy, which put Daniels in the middle of several foreign crises.

Mexico was a foreign policy flashpoint, as a revolution, coup, assassination, and civil war unsettled the US southern border. To block military strongman Victoriano Huerta from receiving a shipment of German weapons, President Wilson ordered the navy fleet to Veracruz in 1914. Mexican authorities arrested two members of an American supply party that came ashore before releasing them with regrets. Admiral Henry T. Mayo demanded a twenty-one-gun salute from the Mexican forces for the two arrested Americans. Before the fracas was over, 126 Mexicans were killed in an event that severely damaged US-Mexican relations and would later backfire on Daniels.

Although the Democrats ran as anti-imperialists, once in office they dispatched gunboats into the Caribbean even more frequently than the "big stick" Republicans. It was true the region was beset by civil war, assassinations, bankruptcy, and mismanagement. But the Wilson administration also displayed a missionary zeal to spread democracy to the Caribbean—whether the populations there wanted it or not.

The American forces intervened to prop up a government in Haiti (staying nineteen years), to bring in the sugar crops in Cuba (remaining five years), to force the Dominican Republic to repay US loans (staying eight years), and to protect US citizens in Nicaragua (staying eleven years). Haiti was a particularly grim chapter of American involvement in the Caribbean. The US installed a puppet government, rewriting its constitution, implementing Jim Crow segregation, giving America power over its finances, impressing citizens into road gangs, and, with the marines, killing an estimated 3,000 Haitian rebels. The US occupation drew complaints from Black leaders and some Republicans, resulting in a nonconclusive congressional investigation. Daniels also sent a commission to Haiti in October 1920, which also drew no conclusions. "The Haitian occupation was unprecedented in both its duration and the extreme racism that characterized American behavior in the black republic," wrote historian Brenda Gayle Plummer.[32]

One of Daniels's many paradoxes is that he was a lifelong anti-imperialist and yet often dispatched the marines to act as police in other countries—although he was executing orders rather than enacting his own policy. In his memoirs, Daniels wrote that he was "not wholly in sympathy" with the use of the navy and marines in the Caribbean but had no choice.[33]

As Daniels's biographer Lee Craig notes, the navy secretary—who had jurisdiction over both sailors and marines—was by 1917 effectively running

Nicaragua, Haiti, the Dominican Republic, and Cuba. One cabinet colleague greeted him, "Hail, the King of Haiti"—which Daniels did not find amusing. "As the end of the Great War approached, the empire Daniels oversaw was larger than those of the German Kaiser, Russia's czar or the Ottoman sultan," Craig wrote.[34]

While Daniels played a supporting role in foreign policy flare-ups, he was center stage in dealing with defense contractors. Daniels brought a suspicion of business monopoly and collusion to the navy job, the branch being a major purchaser of steel, oil, cigarettes, uniforms, and other supplies.

Daniels had been in office a couple of months when he tossed out the identical bids of American steel manufacturers Bethlehem, Carnegie, and Midvale for construction of the battleship *Arizona*, later sunk at Pearl Harbor. When they returned the next day with identical bids, Daniels sent his assistant Franklin D. Roosevelt to New York City to meet with the British steel consortium leader. The American steel companies matched the British bid, cutting 10 percent off their earlier price.

Not satisfied with driving down prices, Daniels convinced Congress in 1914 to build an armor-making plant, locating it in Charleston, West Virginia. Construction began in 1917, despite objections from Republicans and steel manufacturers, who took out advocacy ads in the *News and Observer* in opposition.

Just as he did in Raleigh, Daniels put in long hours at his navy post, holding two daily press conferences, one each for the morning and afternoon newspapers. Despite his accessibility, Daniels was the subject of numerous hostile stories, particularly from the Republican press, which argued that his social experiments were affecting naval readiness. He was pummeled by such headlines as "Daniels in Open Disfavor with Men under Him" in the *New York Tribune* and "The Dangerous Pacifism of Josephus Daniels" in the *Pittsburgh Press*.[35]

By the end of his first year, Daniels was the best-known member of the Wilson cabinet, aside from Bryan. He had managed to alienate much of the naval establishment with his penchant for shaking up entrenched policies, and he was distrusted because he was a disciple of Bryan, one of the nation's leading pacifists.

The *News and Observer*

During his eight years in Washington, Daniels's name continued to appear on the masthead as the paper's president—and he was no figurehead. With his fortune tied to the newspaper, he influenced editorial policy, making sure it continued to be a Wilsonian paper, and pushed for road, health, and education improvements. He oversaw hirings, settled staff disputes, and returned to handle crises such as the fires in 1913 and 1915.

He divided the day-to-day management among four trusted, longtime colleagues: Edward E. Britton and later Robert W. Haywood as editors; Lee Alford, the printer; and Henry Bagley, his brother-in-law, running the business side. Daniels forced out Bagley because of his womanizing but helped him land a newspaper job in Fort Worth. He eventually hired Britton to be his private secretary in Washington. Family members would chastise Daniels for micromanaging the newspaper while serving in the cabinet.

The newspaper continued to grow and prosper during his absence with a circulation topping 20,000 by 1917, making Daniels a rich man. A sports page was added in 1913, comics in 1916, and suburban home delivery in 1917. The first separate comics section—four pages on Sunday—began in February 1920 with such strips as *Tom Sawyer and Huck Finn*, *Mutt and Jeff*, and *Bringing Up Father*. The paper soon added such classics as *Little Orphan Annie* and *Moon Mullins*. By 1929, the paper's daily circulation topped 40,000.

But the paper lacked the crusading fire that marked the years when Daniels was in Raleigh. Near the end of Daniels's navy tenure, Haywood begged him to return. "The paper has suffered by reason of the absence of a vigorous, fearless editorial policy," Haywood wrote.[36]

He also continued to be heavily involved in the University of North Carolina, serving on the trustees' executive committee and helping choose new presidents.

On a trip home in 1919, Daniels addressed a joint session of the North Carolina General Assembly, advocating a palette of progressive ideas, including women's suffrage, a strengthened primary law, a state income tax, a six-month school law, and the creation of a consolidated UNC system.

War Drums

When World War I began in July 1914, many Americans believed that the New World had no business jumping into an Old World conflict of obscure origins. News that Europe was becoming a slaughterhouse did nothing to tamp down antiwar sentiment in the United States. Alfred Bryan's "I Didn't Raise My Boy to Be a Soldier" sold 700,000 copies of sheet music.

The Wilson administration was under pressure from two opposing camps—the peace/isolationist wing of the Democratic Party, and a group, led by former Republican president Teddy Roosevelt, who wanted a significant naval buildup in preparation for a possible war. The Wilson administration initially took a go-slow approach to rearmament.

The navy's General Board, an influential group created in 1900, recommended that the Wilson administration build four battleships every year. Because of budget constraints, only two dreadnoughts had been constructed during the first two years of Wilson's presidency. Daniels argued that the United States had a sufficiently large peacetime navy and was skeptical of getting into a naval arms race. "The only use for the Navy is the same use which you have for a policeman," Daniels said in a speech at a North State dinner in Washington, a few months after taking office. "The Navy should not be made strong as a menace to other nations." Bryan, who spoke at the same dinner, noted how far the peace movement had come. "Daniels, how lonesome we used to be," Bryan said. "How gratifying it is, at last, to be able to walk down the main streets without fear of molestation."[37]

Both Daniels and Wilson also worried that an outbreak of war would jeopardize the great rush of reform legislation. The Wilsonian reforms included a progressive federal income tax, creation of the Federal Trade Commission and the Federal Reserve system, antitrust legislation, the establishment of the eight-hour workday, abolishing child labor, and the first federal aid to farmers.

Teddy Roosevelt was Daniels's most high-profile critic. Their differences started in the Cleveland administration, where TR, a member of the Civil Service Commission, decried Daniels's patronage decisions. Their divide deepened as the *News and Observer* criticized his presidency.

Their mutual hostility was on display during a rare presidential visit to Raleigh in 1905, when TR pointedly excluded Daniels from a lunch at the state fairgrounds—the only politically prominent person left off the list, which miffed Daniels. If anyone missed the symbolism, TR had Trinity College historian John Spencer Bassett—a famous Daniels target—at his side on his train trip across North Carolina. In a speech at what is now Duke University, the president gave a ringing endorsement of academic freedom. Although the *News and Observer* gave front-page coverage to TR's visit, it did not mention Bassett or the president's call for academic freedom.[38]

Now that Daniels was in public office and TR was a private citizen, turnabout was fair play. Daniels provided his critics with ammunition when newspapers reported that the gunnery scores of the Atlantic fleet were abysmal and that the crews of the *Texas* and the *New York*, the largest and most powerful battleships, had never fired a gun.[39]

Daniels ordered naval officers to honor the country's policy of neutrality by refraining from publicly commenting on the European hostilities. Soon word spread—falsely—that Daniels had ordered sailors and marines not to sing the British wartime anthem "It's a Long Way to Tipperary." (Daniels had backed the commandant of the Newport naval station who had banned the song.) Hearing the gossip, Wilson exploded, pounding his fists at a luncheon. "Daniels is surrounded by a network of conspiracy and of lies," Wilson declared. "His enemies are determined to ruin him. I can't be sure who they are yet, but when I do get them—God help them."[40]

Relationship with Wilson

Despite the barrage of criticism, Daniels had the support of the one person who mattered—the president. More than sharing a worldview, the two men forged a deep personal bond. "There was nothing calculated about the North Carolinian's devotion and loyalty; he simply loved the president and supported him without question," wrote historian Arthur Link, Wilson's chief biographer. "Wilson returned Daniels' love and trust with an affection equally warm . . . and the more Daniels' critics raged, the stronger Wilson's affections grew."[41]

The Danielses were frequent guests at the White House. The families' ties were such that Addie took one of Wilson's daughters, Eleanor, shopping and hosted a pre-wedding brunch in her home for another Wilson daughter, Jessie. After the First Lady died in 1914, the Danielses sent the president a cake for Christmas. Both Josephus and Addie wept when they received the president's reply: "It is fine to have a colleague that one can absolutely trust; how much finer to have one whom one can love!"[42]

Daniels was careful not to test the friendship. After Wilson's first wife died, the president fell in love with Edith Bolling Galt, a widow whom he asked to marry him. Key supporters feared that Wilson could lose the women's vote (women in some western states could vote) during his 1916 reelection campaign if he too hastily remarried. A cabinet delegation recruited Daniels to convince the president to delay the wedding. But Daniels recoiled from the "dangerous high and exalted mission of Minister Plenipotentiary and Envoy Extraordinary to the Court of Cupid . . . in the performance of which my official head might suffer decapitation."[43]

Franklin Roosevelt

If Daniels rarely challenged the president, Franklin Roosevelt was far from Daniels's yes man.

Daniels and his chief deputy made an odd couple. The handsome, aristocratic FDR frequented the exclusive clubs clad in expensive English-tailored suits, polished leather shoes purchased from London, and a starched high collar, wearing a bowler in winter or a straw hat in summer. Daniels—short, dumpy, and allergic to exercise—called the pre-polio FDR, who was six feet two, athletic, and well spoken, "as handsome a figure of an attractive young man as I had ever seen."[44]

Daniels was old enough to be FDR's father; the Raleigh editor was fifty-one and FDR thirty-one. Daniels was a small-town southern editor who learned his politics chatting up the cotton and tobacco farmers of Eastern North Carolina; FDR was a member of the Hudson Valley aristocracy, had attended Groton and Harvard, and was comfortable in yachting and high society circles. FDR had already crossed the Atlantic twenty times, while Daniels had never even been to Canada.

But for nearly eight years, they formed a team, working in adjoining offices. At the end of many working days, the two men gathered in Daniels's office with FDR trading gossip from the social clubs for Daniels's proffered tidbits from the congressional cloakrooms. Daniels was the only boss FDR ever had. Even as president, FDR addressed Daniels as "Chief," and Daniels always called Roosevelt "Franklin."

However, the Daniels-FDR relationship was often a difficult one, as a young and arrogant FDR bristled working under the reins of a seemingly unsophisticated older man and a social inferior.

They first met during the 1912 Democratic National Convention, where Daniels saw him as "the Democratic Roosevelt" with White House potential. But it was not until the inauguration that Daniels offered FDR, then a New York state legislator, the post of assistant secretary. Considered a shrewd judge of talent, Daniels was drawn to one of the most famous names in politics, FDR's progressive anti-Tammany views, and his charisma. Washington insiders cautioned him that FDR was so strong-willed and ambitious that he would try to run the department. Daniels replied, "A chief who fears that an assistant will outrank him is not fit to be chief."[45]

If FDR was grateful for the appointment, he did not show it. FDR privately described Daniels as "a hillbilly," sometimes mimicking his boss before his

Josephus Daniels (*right*) and his assistant, FDR, during World War I on the portico of navy headquarters, gazing down at the White House. (Courtesy of the Library of Congress.)

friends at the Metropolitan Club. As gossip about FDR's frequent patronizing remarks made the rounds on the DC social circuit, Interior secretary Franklin Lane warned Roosevelt that he should either be respectful or resign. After that, FDR toned down his sarcasm, and he was usually deferential in Daniels's presence. FDR looked for ways to please his boss, whether by attending a prayer meeting at Daniels's home or speaking at what is now North Carolina State University in Raleigh, declaring himself "a hayseed."[46]

Daniels understood that his golden boy deputy was the future of his beloved Democratic Party. There is a photograph of the two men on the balcony of the Executive Office Building looking down on the White House. Later, Daniels, whose smile is subdued in the photo, asked FDR why he was grinning. FDR said he always tried to look good in photographs. But Daniels said, "I will tell you. We are both looking down on the White House, and you are saying to yourself, being a New Yorker, 'Someday I will be living in that house'—while I, being from the South, know I must be satisfied with no such ambition."[47]

From the beginning, the two men approached the Navy Department from distinctly different perspectives. Influenced by the pacificism of Wilson and Bryan, Daniels was reluctant to engage in a naval arms race. Shaping FDR's views was his distant cousin Teddy Roosevelt, whom he idealized, who believed that an enlarged navy was critical if the United States were to take its place as a world power. It was remarkable that Daniels and FDR worked closely together for eight years, given their sharp differences over rearmament, the wisdom of entering the war, naval strategy, and even their pace of doing business—FDR a blur of activity and Daniels slow and deliberate.

FDR, however, could be a disloyal and scheming aide, feeding information to Daniels's Republican foes in Congress, intriguing with interventionists, undercutting Daniels's position in speeches, and spinning the story that he was doing most of the work. The *Wall Street Journal*, among other papers, called for FDR to replace Daniels.[48]

When World War I broke out in July 1914, FDR received a wire to return to Washington from his vacation home at Campobello off the Maine coast. FDR was dismayed by the lack of urgency he found when he returned. In an August 1, 1914, letter to his wife, Eleanor, who remained in Maine, he wrote, "Mr. D [Daniels] totally fails to grasp the situation." The next day he added, "These dear people like W. J. B. [Bryan] and J. D. [Daniels] have as much conception of what a war means as Elliot [their four-year old son] has of higher mathematics." On August 5 he wrote, "I am running the real work, although Josephus is here! He is bewildered by it all, very sweet, but very sad."[49]

When Bryan resigned as secretary of state in June 1915 because he believed the administration was abandoning its neutrality, FDR wrote to Eleanor that he was delighted with Bryan's resignation but was "disgusted clear through" that Daniels had not joined him.[50]

The Navy Department was more engaged than FDR portrayed, and FDR was not as focused on national defense as his letters to Eleanor might imply. FDR frequently had his eye on political office while serving as assistant secretary. He unsuccessfully sought a Senate seat from New York in 1914, he seriously considered running for New York governor in 1918, and he became the Democratic nominee for vice president in 1920.

Not only was FDR ambitious, but he chafed at playing second fiddle to Daniels. As one of FDR's biographers, Jean Edward Smith, wrote, Roosevelt "was still a pale second to Secretary Daniels and relegated to department housekeeping rather than grand strategy, and high politics to which he aspired."[51]

Relations between the two men were further strained by FDR's affair with Lucy Mercer, whom Eleanor had hired as her social secretary, a pretty twenty-two-year-old from an aristocratic background whose family had fallen on hard times. When Eleanor became suspicious, she fired Mercer. Five days later, in June 1917, she was hired as a navy yeoman and assigned to FDR's staff. When Daniels got wind of the Washington gossip, he dismissed her "by special order of the Secretary of the Navy," never providing any explanation. Daniels discreetly never acknowledged the FDR-Mercer affair in public or in his diary—a scandal that could have ruined FDR's political career.[52]

The affair became public after FDR's and Mercer's deaths when Jonathan Daniels wrote briefly about it in his book *The End of Innocence* in 1954 and provided more details in his 1966 book, *The Time between the Wars*. Jonathan, a Washington insider and aide to FDR, said his father never mentioned the Lucy Mercer affair to him. "He was a man who carefully could not see what he did not wish to see," Jonathan later remarked.[53]

FDR came to appreciate that behind Daniels's folksy persona was a keen political operative who was in his milieu in the Dixie-fied Washington, DC—where southern politicians dominated the Wilson cabinet and Congress. FDR later acknowledged that Daniels had provided him with a graduate-level course in Washington and southern politics—one that served him well when he became president.

Daniels's Capitol Hill connections were deep. Several were political comrades from the white supremacy campaigns. His best friend in Washington was Senator Benjamin "Pitchfork" Tillman of South Carolina, who led his white supremacist Red Shirts into North Carolina and who chaired the Senate Naval Affairs Committee. Furnifold Simmons was chairman of the Senate Finance Committee. Lee Overman was chairman of the Senate Rules Committee. Claude Kitchen was House majority leader and chairman of the House Ways and Means Committee, E. W. Pou was chairman of the House Rules Committee, and E. Yates was chairman of the House Judiciary Committee. All but Tillman were from North Carolina. As a result, Daniels successfully got his budget requests approved by Congress except for a large shipbuilding project he submitted after the armistice in 1918.[54]

After the United States entered the war, Daniels and FDR worked together more harmoniously. But even near the end of their eight-year partnership, there were blowups. In a Brooklyn speech in February 1920, FDR said the US Navy had been unprepared at the outbreak of the war, and to get the navy ready for action, Daniels had "committed enough illegal actions to put him in jail for 999 years." FDR's charges were either false or widely exaggerated.[55]

Both Daniels and Wilson were furious with FDR, and Daniels contemplated firing his assistant. But Daniels decided it was a bad time to fire such a high-profile official, with Wilson recovering from a stroke and three cabinet members having recently quit. Once again, Daniels had arguably saved FDR's career. "He was young then and made some mistakes," Daniels gently recalled their relationship years later in his memoirs. "Upon reflection, although I was older, I made mistakes too."[56]

By the summer of 1920, they had sufficiently patched up their relations that when FDR accepted the nomination for vice president in San Francisco, he asked Daniels to deliver a speech to the convention. (Nominees typically did not give convention speeches in that era.) Daniels traveled to Hyde Park to witness FDR's formal acceptance speech and campaigned for him across the Midwest.

Reelection Campaign

Wilson faced a difficult reelection in 1916, with many suggesting his victory four years earlier was a fluke caused by Teddy Roosevelt bolting the Republicans to form the Bull Moose Party. The GOP was once again united, this time behind former US Supreme Court justice Charles Evan Hughes. It was the Democrats who were feuding as Wilson's shift toward war preparedness had antagonized many progressive and rural voters.

Daniels was an inviting GOP campaign target, having angered rearmament advocates, drinkers, the steel industry, and customers of New Orleans bordellos to name just a few. In the Republican press, Daniels was portrayed as a narrow-minded pacifist, more interested in social experiments than rearmament.

Republicans erected billboards across the country reading, "A VOTE FOR WILSON IS A VOTE FOR DANIELS." The *Fort Wayne Daily News* complained that Daniels was playing into the hands of the enemy by his delays in building new battleships. "Yet his fault has not been treason; it is gross incompetence," read an editorial in the Indiana newspaper. "He is as stupid as he is vain and as biased as he is ignorant. His unfitness for the post he holds is notorious from one end of the country to the other." Hughes, the Republican presidential candidate, said Daniels was "a man of amiable qualities but unfit" and mocked his efforts to provide a seagoing classroom, saying that "we must pay less attention to punctuation and more to [gunnery] targets."[57]

Viewing Daniels as a political liability, Colonel Edward House, a top Wilson advisor—who had opposed both Daniels's hiring in the first place and the new First Lady, the former Edith Bolling Galt—discussed ways of convincing the president to dump Daniels. But Wilson would not hear of it.[58]

Daniels had plenty of defenders as well. An editorial in Tennessee's *Bristol Herald Courier* observed, "These newspapers cannot forget that Daniels is from the South; that he has driven liquor from American battleships and naval stations; that he has put a damper on snobbery in the Navy; and that he has tried to protect the government against hold-ups by manufacturers of armor plate and war materials and supplies."[59]

His most crucial defender was his boss. After meeting with a retired admiral, Wilson asked him to pass along a message to the Army and Navy Clubs, where many top naval officers socialized. "I wish you would inform those Naval officers who spend their time criticizing the Navy that I am behind Daniels 100 percent and nothing they can say can injure him."[60]

The Democratic National Committee assigned George Creel the task of performing a "rehabilitation" of Daniels's reputation. Creel, a Missouri-born newspaperman and a liberal, is regarded as one of the pioneering public relations experts. Creel said it was no small task because Daniels had been portrayed as "unfit, misfit, liar, incompetent, demagogue, and buffoon" after four years of press attacks. Creel wrote in his memoirs, "Not in our time was an official ever made the target for more savage and sustained assault." Creel believed that most of the allegations against Daniels were unfair, and he wrote an article defending Daniels that ran in dozens of newspapers across the country.[61]

(Although Daniels was often viciously attacked as navy secretary, I could find no criticism of his racism except in the Black press—an indication of the country's deep-seated racial prejudice.)

Daniels rarely defended himself, writing later, "I made it a rule from the first never to reply to critics, but to content myself with clear statements of policy. There were no serious criticisms until I denied lush profiteering to the armor-plate, smoke-less powder and other trusts which had been robbing Uncle Sam; until I thwarted the well-oiled lobby determined to exploit the Navy oil reserves; until I put an end to drinking on Navy ships and shore stations; introduced a measure (too small) of democracy and promotions by merit ... and refused to abdicate and let officers enamored by Prussianism run the Navy."[62]

Daniels resigned from the DNC, a post he had held for twenty years and where he was the ranking member, to campaign for Wilson's reelection, mainly in the Midwest. In October, the campaign asked him to go to New York City and raise money from two American titans—industrialist Henry Ford and inventor Thomas Edison. The men had requested Daniels because of their close relationship with him and their navy work.

Ford agreed to spend $200,000 for newspaper ads promoting Wilson ($5.6 million in 2024 dollars). But what was most memorable about the lunch at New York's Biltmore Hotel was the kicking contest between Edison and Ford, as the two old friends boasted of their physical prowess. Edison pointed to a chandelier with numerous globes and said, "Henry, I'll bet you anything you want to bet that I can kick that globe off the chandelier." At which point, Edison launched an over-the-head kick that shattered the globe to pieces. Ford tried and failed, and Edison spent the rest of the lunch gloating.[63]

The inventor and the navy secretary developed a friendship, with Daniels dining at Edison's home in West Orange, New Jersey, in June 1916, after which the inventor previewed a new project—the talking movie. However, the words and the actions were not quite synchronized. Edison later invited Daniels in 1918 to join him on a two-week camping trip through the Shenandoah Valley and the Great Smoky Mountains along with Henry Ford and fellow industrialist Harvey Firestone and naturalist John Burroughs.[64]

Daniels returned to Raleigh on Election Day, where early news reports had Hughes winning the White House. At midnight he took a Pullman car to DC, arriving in the morning, where he learned that late returns from California had made Wilson the first sitting Democratic president reelected since Andrew Jackson in 1832.

"Next to President Wilson himself," stated the *Atlanta Constitution*, "the election last week, vindicated Josephus Daniels, secretary of the navy, to a greater degree than it did any other one official."[65]

War

The American road to war began with the shocking German torpedoing of the British liner *Lusitania* on May 7, 1915, killing 1,198, including 128 Americans. The sinking dramatically shifted the Wilson administration policy away from pacificism to preparedness.

Wilson sent a note of protest to Germany. Bryan, who had been seeking a peaceful end to the war, resigned his post on June 8 because of the president's actions. Daniels had applauded Bryan's peace initiatives to end the war and owned one of the plow-shaped paperweights that Bryan had ordered made from old guns. But Bryan's resignation blindsided him. "I don't think in view of our long friendship you ought to have taken this course without talking to me about it," Daniels told him.[66]

The following month Wilson asked his army and navy secretaries to analyze the United States' security needs and make recommendations. Daniels proposed building 176 ships over three years at the cost of $600 million ($18 billion in 2024 dollars)—the largest peacetime construction program in American history. The plan would give the United States a two-ocean navy comparable to Great Britain's and Germany's.

Wilson's rearmament efforts divided the Democratic Party. A caucus of between thirty and fifty Democratic House members, led by House majority leader Claude Kitchen of North Carolina, opposed rearmament. After Congress approved the naval expansion plan, Kitchen remarked, "The United States today becomes the most militaristic naval nation on earth."[67]

Daniels's decision to stay in the Wilson administration showed his pragmatism—or a desire to hold power. Time and again Daniels cast his principles aside, whether joining the conservative Cleveland administration or allying himself with conservatives in the white supremacy campaign of 1898, engaging in gunboat diplomacy, or remaining with the Wilson administration on its path to war in Europe. As historian Michael Kazin noted, "Daniels's unbending faith could be remarkably supple when time altered the nature of both his friends and his enemies."[68]

Even as the navy prepared for war, Daniels hoped conflict could be avoided and said as much to Wilson. But the tipping point came in January 1917, when Germany declared unrestricted submarine war, gambling that they could force Great Britain out of the war before Americans could mobilize.

On March 20, 1917, Wilson gathered his cabinet members and individually polled them on whether the United States should declare war, leaving Daniels for last. According to one account, Daniels "spoke with a voice, which was low and trembled with emotion. His eyes were suffused with tears."[69]

"Having tried patience, there is no course open to us except to protect our rights on the seas," Daniels said. "It was the supreme moment of my life," Daniels wrote in his diary. "I had hoped & prayed this cup would pass." He described it as his "Gethsemane," which according to the Gospels was the garden at the foot of the Mount of Olives in Jerusalem where Jesus agonized over his fate.[70]

A generation later, as Hitler's troops poured over the Polish border, beginning World War II, Daniels wrote his son Jonathan that if he could do it over again, he would have voted against American entry into the First World War.[71]

Daniels's skepticism was not without merit. Few people today could articulate reasons for the industrialized mass slaughter of World War I that included heavy artillery, machine guns, poison gas, tanks, and airplanes. The war killed 9 million soldiers and 6 million civilians. It contributed to the Bolshevik Revolution in Russia, the rise of Nazi Germany, the Holocaust, and the splintering of the Middle East.

The United States had an unprepared force of just 300,000 men, which the German General Staff ranked "somewhere between Belgium and Portugal." The war required massive mobilization, with all American men between eighteen and forty-five required to register for the draft. Nearly 5 million served during the war.[72]

Although World War I was largely a land conflict, the navy had three important roles: transporting 2 million soldiers to Europe, containing the U-boat threat, and blockading Germany. The navy swelled from 65,000 members to 520,022 by the end of the war and from 300 vessels to 2,000.

Daniels was a member of a high-level war cabinet that met on Wednesdays in the president's study. Daniels worked to minimize profiteering, protected the navy's petroleum reserves from raids by oil companies, and negotiated a labor agreement with union leader Samuel Gompers to guarantee labor peace in the navy yards.

While few argued that Daniels was a gifted naval strategic thinker, he helped oversee a successful sea war. In several important ways, FDR was more of the innovator.

The significant innovations were the convoy system to protect cross-Atlantic shipping and the laying of anti-submarine minefields in the North Sea to bottle up the German U-boats. The British had rejected both ideas: they thought convoys made ships more vulnerable because they could travel only as fast as the slowest vessel, and they thought seeding ocean mines impractical. But because of the convoy system, the Americans did not lose a single troopship.

Daniels was initially skeptical of the mining operation because he feared violating international law and was doubtful it would work, but both Wilson and FDR championed the issue. About 70,000 mines were sewn across the

North Sea, but it impossible to determine their effectiveness because the war was nearing its end. Daniels was to call it "the most daring and original naval conception" of the war and not doing it earlier "the greatest naval error of the war."[73]

As he began to understand the importance of submarine warfare in 1916, Daniels refocused construction away from the major battleships and toward building 250 destroyers and sub chasers. But Daniels had to be pushed in that direction by FDR, after initially siding with the navy brass who did not want money diverted from building the more glamorous battleships.[74]

Inviting new thinking into naval affairs and submarine warfare, Daniels reached out to inventor Thomas Edison and made him the volunteer head of the newly established Naval Consulting Board to encourage suggestions from inventors.

Edison created a navy lab near Washington on the Potomac, which exists today as the US Naval Research Laboratory, to work on weapons, torpedo boats, submarines, and dynamos. Edison almost immediately found major problems: the United States was not plotting where Allied ships had been sunk. After two months of study by the staff, they determined that the British were using the same shipping lanes, making their ships particularly vulnerable.

Censorship

Daniels was the only newspaperman in Wilson's cabinet during a period of unprecedented government censorship.

At the urging of George Creel, Daniels proposed the creation of a Committee on Public Information to handle wartime propaganda censorship and to serve as a centralized clearinghouse for war-related news. The president appointed a three-member committee including Daniels to oversee the committee, with Creel as its chairman. The committee met only once, giving Creel wide latitude.

The navy censored thousands of journalists' dispatches, mainly from the war zone. Most censored stories involved articles about troop movements, anti-U-boat strategies, war preparation, and US defense installations. But they also included stories that could result in public dissatisfaction with the war, such as those concerning potential labor strikes, assassination threats against the president, war rumors, and photographs of dead American soldiers. In an age before there was a strong tradition of watchdog reporting, there was a widespread acceptance among newspapers of the censorship.

More controversial was the Espionage Act of 1917, which made it a crime to interfere with military operations, and the Sedition Act of 1918, which forbade Americans from using "disloyal, profane, scurrilous or obscene language" about the US government. Albert Burleson, the postmaster, carried out the most blatant abuses. He vigorously applied the new laws to suppress the distribution through the mail of seventy-five newspapers—mainly socialist or German-language newspapers.

Daniels was a moderate on the issue, agreeing with restraints on military information but worrying that Burleson was pushing censorship too far. "We cannot go after all the DF's (Damned Fools) we know," Daniels wrote in his diary. "We have better things to do." Daniels successfully argued in the cabinet against proposals to ban German-language newspapers and to allow newspapers to print the names of men killed or wounded.[75]

Regarded as the most repressive era in American history, the World War I years helped give rise to the creation of the American Civil Liberties Union in 1920. The Justice Department charged more than 2,000 citizens with sedition and convicted more than half of them. The censorship came at a time of widespread fear of sabotage. In 1918, forty-five US merchant ships were sunk by German U-boats off the American coast. German saboteurs committed 200 acts of sabotage against the United States.

Daniels sought to distinguish between the necessary censorship of wartime secrets and the public relations effort to build war support by the Committee on Public Information and the repressive measures of the US Post Office and the US Justice Department, which, he said, "carried a real danger." He later wrote, "Never at any time or in any degree was the Committee a machinery of concealment or repression."[76]

Daniels was skeptical of the so-called Red Scare, in which Attorney General Mitchell Palmer arrested 3,000 people with leftist sympathies in December 1919 and January 1920, deporting 556. Daniels wrote in his memoirs that "Palmer was seeing red behind every bush and every demand for an increase in wages."[77]

Back home, the *News and Observer* cautioned against paranoia, although it supported the arrest and deportation of such radicals as Emma Goldman. "It is seen that some of the alarm as to the movement toward Bolshevism and anarchy was merely a case of nerves," the Raleigh paper opined. The paper remained a staunch critic of anti-communist witch hunts, whether denouncing the House Un-American Activities Committee in the 1940s or the red-baiting of Senator Joe McCarthy in the 1950s. The Raleigh paper criticized McCarthy at every turn, arguing that he had "disgraced" the Senate and the nation.[78]

In a 1953 speech that garnered national headlines, Jonathan Daniels suggested that McCarthy's red-baiting was worse than the Ku Klux Klan. "If I had to take a choice between spoiled fish," Jonathan told a New York City audience, "I think I would prefer the KKK in bedsheets to the self-righteousness for profit, patriotism for politics and proscription for publicity which we see every day in the loud open in this land."[79]

Life in Washington

The Danielses were part of the Washington social whirl, frequently dining at the White House or entertaining Chief Justice Edward D. White or British and French diplomats.

The Danielses hosted the first post-reelection cabinet dinner on February 5, 1917, at their Wyoming Street house with Addie sitting between the president and Henry Ford. Dinners at their home began with a prayer by Daniels, and guests were served nothing stronger than Apollinaris water and red and white grape juice.

Daniels had ties to many of the most celebrated people in early twentieth-century American life. He recruited Thomas Edison to help battle German U-boats. He persuaded industrialist Henry Ford to run for the US Senate from Michigan in 1918—a race he lost. Admiral George Dewey, the hero of the Spanish-American War, was a friend and advisor. Captaining Daniels's yacht was William D. Leahy, who would serve as chief of naval operations during World War II. Future Arctic explorer Richard Byrd was a Daniels protégé. Famed revivalist Billy Sunday conducted a service at the Daniels home. Daniels coaxed John Philip Sousa out of retirement. It was over lunch that Daniels suggested that the band leader compose a march for an artillery unit—and the result was "The Army Goes Rolling Along," which became the army anthem.[80]

Daniels moved around the country, usually giving at least one war bond speech per week. At times, the war became personal. The navy secretary was stung by what he called "a vicious dirty article" in the *Greensboro News* in April 1917 that noted that none of his four sons was in the military. Several days later, his eldest son, Josephus Jr., a frail young man with poor eyesight working at the paper, enlisted in the marines, eventually serving in France as a first lieutenant. His two youngest sons, Jonathan, fifteen, and Frank, thirteen, were not of age, although Jonathan showed up at the office of army secretary Newton Baker, begging to be allowed to enlist. Worth, his second-oldest son, entered the Naval Academy with his father's help but dropped out when the war ended.[81]

News of the Armistice signing came over naval wires at 2:45 a.m., November 11, 1918. The navy had suffered 431 killed and 819 wounded, while marine casualties were 2,461 dead and 9,520 wounded.

Daniels had a good war; he was transformed from a widely ridiculed figure to a respected war leader. "American history records few instances of more nearly universal and complete reversal of public opinion regarding a man than is afforded in this instance of Secretary of the Navy Josephus Daniels," opined the *Atlanta Constitution* in 1918.[82]

On March 23, 1919, Daniels embarked on the USS *Leviathan*—a German passenger liner confiscated in New York—to help represent the United States in the peace negotiations in Versailles. After a nineteen-gun salute, he left with Addie, three admirals, and his Black servant Robert Gaines for a nearly two-month assignment.

Staying at the posh Ritz hotel in Paris, Daniels began what he called the Sea Battle of Paris, a dispute over the size of the world's postwar navies. The British wanted to maintain their naval supremacy and backed a plan with a fixed ratio of ships for each nation. The US House had just passed a three-year program of construction that would have made the American Navy the largest. The Americans thought the British were primarily concerned about maintaining their colonial empire. President Wilson left it to Daniels to work out a compromise.

The British launched a charm offensive targeting Daniels, including breakfast in Paris with British prime minister Lloyd George and a red-carpet trip to England. He and Addie had lunch with King George V and Queen Mary at Windsor Castle. (They had plovers' eggs, soup, chicken, cold tongue, and ham with salad and hot egg pudding.) King George reportedly offered to knight Daniels, but he turned down the opportunity to be addressed as Sir Josephus—a move that won him praise in the American press. The next day, a dinner was thrown for him at the House of Commons, attended by ninety-eight members and such luminaries as writer Rudyard Kipling and with speeches by Field Marshal Douglas Haig, the commander of British forces, and Lord George Curzon, secretary of state and former viceroy of India. After dinner, he met with Winston Churchill, then secretary of war, over cigars and brandy—for Churchill, that is, not the abstemious Daniels. The two men disagreed, with Churchill vowing that Britain would maintain naval superiority no matter the costs.[83]

In introducing Daniels to British readers, the *Times* of London described him as the American equivalent of the First Lord of the Admiralty and suggested the war had made Daniels's reputation. "Daniels, like most Southern Democratic politicians, was tainted with Bryanism, which, among other concomitants, included a pronounced tinge of pacifism." (No mention of racism.) But, the London paper said, "Mr. Daniels was putting the United States Navy's house in order on effective lines. The outbreak of war in 1917 found the United States Navy, as the country's first line of defence in a high state of readiness, limited only by its actual dimension. Within a very short period of time, as is now known, it developed a powerful offensive against the U-boat campaign and a strong defence for convoys."[84]

The negotiations led to an impasse with no naval arms agreement in the Treaty of Versailles. Afterward, Daniels was bitter that Republican president Warren G. Harding scrapped three battleships under construction, handing the British an ultimate victory—a turnaround from the years when Republicans were criticizing Daniels's pacifism.

Daniels toured the royal courts of Europe almost as a warlord. He lunched with King Albert in Brussels, met King Victor Emmanuel in Rome and Queen Marie of Romania, and dined with French prime minister Georges Clemenceau.

Daniels also toured the battlefields of France, particularly interested in Château-Thierry and Belleau Wood, where the US Marines had stopped a German advance. Addie took home shells from every battlefield, which she later used as bases for table lamps. At the German drill ground near Vallendar, overlooking the Rhine River, Daniels, Addie, and military brass stood as 25,000 marines of the Second Division passed in review.

Despite the cheers he heard in Europe, Daniels's last months in office were both anticlimactic and disappointing, with a stroke-felled Wilson unable to get his League of Nations agreement ratified by the Senate.

Republicans, who won back control of Congress in 1918, launched three months of election-year hearings into Daniels's performance as navy secretary. Their star witness was Rear Admiral William Sims, who had headed US naval operations in Great Britain and was among the most admired men in the navy.

He charged that Daniels's failure to send the full force of destroyers and anti-submarine craft to Europe immediately after the US entry had prolonged the war by four months, leading to the loss of 2.5 million tons of Allied shipping and costing an additional 500,000 lives. Daniels, who had feuded with Sims over the awarding of medals, called the charges an election-year "smear" and said Sims's anglophilism and his vantage point in London had prevented him from seeing the full picture. Daniels gave 1,400 pages of testimony. FDR deeply angered Daniels when, in a New York speech, he sided with Sims.[85]

With the Republican press baying for Daniels's head, the navy secretary once again proved himself a canny political fighter in the hearings that lasted from March 9 to May 28, 1919. He portrayed Sims as a petty egoist infatuated with the British hierarchy and more interested in awarding medals to deskbound officers than to seamen who had seen action. Parading friendly admirals to testify on his behalf, Daniels made sure that their statements were circulated to the sixty Washington news bureaus in time to make the afternoon dailies—and before the navy brass was cross-examined.[86]

The GOP majority concluded that Daniels's navy was not well prepared for the war either materially or strategically; a Democratic minority report concluded the opposite. Daniels had survived.

In a second GOP-led investigation, this one in 1920, both Daniels and FDR were rebuked by a Senate committee for conducting a sting operation into gay sexual activity involving sailors at a Newport, Rhode Island, training center. The probe had resulted in seventeen sailors being charged with sodomy. The Senate committee objected to navy investigators going undercover to entrap the young men, including allowing oral sex to be performed on them. Daniels had left orders with the Newport commandant to "clean up the place" before leaving for Europe, and FDR subsequently became involved. Both Daniels and FDR denied any knowledge of the tactics used.

Although a Wilson loyalist, Daniels blocked one final effort by Wilson—debilitated by a major stroke—to seek a third term at the 1920 Democratic National Convention in San Francisco. Daniels convened members of Wilson's cabinet on a battleship where the navy secretary was staying in San Francisco to shoot down the idea. The move angered Wilson but did not cause a permanent rift.[87]

Eight years as navy secretary had transformed Daniels from a provincial newspaper editor to a widely recognized national figure whose every utterance was quoted in newspapers across the country. A polarizing man, Daniels received mixed reviews from navy experts and historians.

"Courtly and modest, Daniels had an amiability that concealed an iron will and a remarkably wide-ranging intelligence," wrote Jean Edward Smith, a biographer of four presidents. "He was a tireless worker, a shrewd judge of people, and a longtime rebel against established authority. He suspected that what every admiral told him was wrong, and as one observer noted, nine times out of ten he was correct."[88]

But the *Washington Post* wrote in 1920 that the navy had been the victim of "nearly eight years of manipulation and mismanagement by a politician of the poor sort. How many American boys were sacrificed to the stupidity, procrastination, and blunders of the Navy Department under Josephus Daniels?"[89]

CHAPTER SEVEN

Between the Wars

The fifty-eight-year-old Daniels returned to Raleigh on March 21, 1921, as a celebrated figure. On his first day, he met with Governor Cameron Morrison, addressed a joint legislative session, and was feted with a reception attended by more than 5,000 people at City Auditorium. The next day he was back at his newspaper office.

Daniels had other opportunities. He turned down an offer from publisher Adolph Ochs to work for the *New York Times* but agreed to write articles about his navy years in the *Saturday Evening Post* and a thirty-part series for the National Newspaper Service.

Daniels had never owned his own home, mainly living at his mother-in-law's house on South Street. But at Addie's urging, they purchased land on a hill in the newly developing Hayes Barton neighborhood off Glenwood Avenue. Daniels bought eleven lots, initially envisioning a grand, rambling edifice that would include wings for his four sons—an idea that Addie rejected. As it was, Daniels gave land to his sons, resulting in three of his offspring living on the same block—forming almost a family compound.

Wakestone, as Daniels called his new house, took two years to build, with the family moving in late 1922. A naval architect had designed the house while Daniels was still navy secretary—an arrangement that would spark a congressional investigation today. Daniels liked to quip that the house was built with stones thrown at the *News and Observer* and paid for with hot air.

To finance the house that reputedly cost $100,000 ($1.8 million in 2024 dollars), Daniels hit the Chautauqua speaking circuit. He earned $250 per night telling war stories in such places as the Convention Hall in Muskogee, Oklahoma, and the Mankato Opera House in Minnesota, sometimes going on the road for six weeks at a time, speaking five nights per week. During the 1920s, Daniels made $25,000 per year (more than $420,000 in 2024 dollars)—$15,000 from the newspaper and the rest from speaking.[1]

From Wakestone, Daniels could take on all his enemies with booty from the Great War—a mounted five-inch naval gun from the *Kronprinz Wilhelm*, a passenger liner the German navy converted for use as a cruiser that was later seized by the United States and used as a troop transport called the *Von Steuben*. Daniels's successor as navy secretary gave him the gun in 1923 in recognition of his World War I service. Daniels claimed that because government property could not be removed, the navy designated Wakestone's front lawn as the nation's smallest naval base—a story that is probably a tall tale. The Freemasons owned the house from 1940 until 2021, when real estate developers managed to remove Wakestone as one of Raleigh's three National Historic Landmarks to tear it down and build new houses on the property.[2]

Daniels also turned to book writing, publishing *Our Navy at War* in 1922 and *The Life of Woodrow Wilson, 1856–1924* in 1924—two largely forgettable works.

Daniels turned down offers to buy the paper, including a $1 million bid from newspaper magnate William Randolph Hearst. As he told one newspaper broker, "Just suppose the newspaper was sold—what would we do? Where would be our forum? Where any lever? Where any life?"[3]

During his twelve years in the political wilderness under three Republican presidents—Warren Harding, Calvin Coolidge, and Herbert Hoover—Daniels was intrigued by the chance to return to public life. He flirted with running for elective office at least three times—the 1924 presidential race, the 1932 governor's race, and the 1942 US Senate race.

William Jennings Bryan floated the idea of a Daniels presidential run during a speech in Raleigh in 1923, hoping the party would nominate someone from the progressive wing to challenge Coolidge. Daniels-for-President Clubs popped up as far away as Compton, California, but were mainly in North Carolina.

Although a long shot, a Daniels candidacy was not out of the question. There were no strong Democratic front runners in 1924. Daniels had been at the center of national Democratic politics for more than a quarter of a century as a Democratic National Committeeman and campaign strategist and had worked in top jobs in two Democratic administrations.

Since leaving the Wilson cabinet, Daniels had maintained a high public profile and was the subject of hundreds of newspaper articles. He also gave dozens of speeches—probably hundreds—across the country, particularly in the Midwest, whether as part of the Chautauqua speaking circuit or in raising money for Methodist colleges or speaking at Democratic Party functions or religious gatherings. He acted very much like a presidential candidate at many stops: touring local farms and factories, meeting with local political leaders, and talking to local civic clubs. "He entered the limelight when he entered the Cabinet 11 years ago and he has never gotten out of it," the *Charlotte Observer* noted in 1924.[4]

Enhancing his reputation was the Teapot Dome scandal—the worst national political scandal until Watergate. The Republican Harding administration leased navy petroleum reserves in Wyoming and California to private interests at low rates without competitive bidding. Interior secretary Albert Fall went to prison for accepting a bribe, and Edwin Denby, Daniels's successor as navy secretary, was forced to resign for his role. Daniels had fiercely opposed oil industry efforts to grab the oil reserves when he was secretary.

Daniels never publicly said he was interested in the White House, but neither did he quash the effort. After 103 ballots over nine days, the 1924 Democratic National Convention chose John W. Davis, a corporate lawyer from West Virginia, as its presidential nominee.

Always the good party man, Daniels loyally campaigned across the Midwest for Davis, the conservative, rejecting overtures from the camp of the Progressive Party's presidential candidate, Robert La Follette, a Wisconsin senator, to be his vice presidential running mate.

In 1925, Daniels split with Bryan, his longtime political mentor. The friendship ended over the teaching of Darwin's theory of evolution—a controversy that swept across the South in the 1920s. In Bible Belt North Carolina, the anti-evolution movement had political legs. In 1924, Governor Morrison banned two biology textbooks from the public schools that taught evolution. A year later, religious fundamentalists lobbied the legislature to prohibit the teaching of evolution in public-supported institutions. The *Charlotte Observer* was a leading anti-evolution voice in the state. Seeking to enlist Daniels in the anti-evolution fight, Bryan met for hours in Daniels's office in Wakestone before a grim and silent Bryan stalked out.[5]

Although he was a devout Methodist, Daniels also had close ties to the University of North Carolina and had come to value academic freedom. "The issue is: Shall teachers in State-supported institutions of learning be forbidden to state to their classes the conclusions they have reached?" Daniels asked in an editorial titled "Liberty to Think." The anti-evolution bill was defeated.[6]

Bryan died later in 1925 after arguing against evolution in the famous Scopes trial in Tennessee. Although their last meeting ended on a discordant note, Daniels became one of Bryan's flame-keepers, raising money to erect a statue and hosting an annual Bryan dinner in Washington, DC.

In 1928, Daniels led the North Carolina delegation to the Democratic National Convention in Houston, where he supported Senator Cordell Hull of Tennessee, only to see New York governor Al Smith nominated for president. Daniels backed a dry plank at the convention, prompting poison-pen columnist H. L. Mencken, who liked his liquor, to ridicule the Raleigh publisher. "The new North Carolina is about everything that Josephus is not," Mencken wrote. "It is, in many respects, the most advanced of the Southern states; he is one of the hollowest and dumbest of Southern politicians."[7]

Ever the loyal Democrat, Daniels held his nose and backed Smith while his star columnist, Nell Battle Lewis, campaigned across the state for Smith. Smith's Catholicism, Tammany connections, and wet politics made him political poison in North Carolina. Senator Furnifold Simmons, the party chairman, bolted and helped carry the state for Republican Herbert Hoover. Simmons's political apostasy cost him his Senate seat in 1930, losing in the Democratic primary to Josiah Bailey. Although the *News and Observer* did not endorse in the primary, Daniels cited Simmons's long history of working in the Democratic trenches and voted for him.[8]

Progressivism for Whites Only

While Daniels never ran for political office, he used his bully pulpit to help shape political debate in North Carolina. Attempting to both industrialize and modernize what was still a poor rural state in the 1920s, North Carolina made a leap forward, plowing money into the University of North Carolina to make it one of the South's leading colleges and going deeply into debt to build one of the South's largest road networks. The effort paid off, with North Carolina becoming the most industrialized state in the South by the 1930s.

But it was, as historian C. Vann Woodward put it, "progressivism for whites only." Historians still debate whether any era that left out African Americans should be considered progressive at all. And Daniels reflected this.[9]

The Simmons machine still controlled North Carolina politics when Daniels returned from Washington in 1921. The candidate backed by the organization, Cameron Morrison (1921–25), had just taken office as governor in what was likely a stolen election.

Daniels became a frequent Morrison critic, even though they agreed on several important issues such as improving roads and building the University of North Carolina into one of the nation's top state-supported schools.

Daniels slammed Morrison for giving a $13 million tax break ($222 million in 2024 dollars) to Durham tobacco giant Liggett Myers Company in 1921. Daniels called on the governor to return from his summer vacation and reverse the action. Morrison replied that he would not do "the bidding of this imperial boss and would-be dictator to all officials in North Carolina." The governor said Daniels's "idea of justice to [corporations] is to kill them wherever he finds them." Daniels replied, "I am no more ambitious to be an imperial boss than he covets the royal trappings of the Duke of Durham."[10]

Morrison's ambitious program was financed through borrowing, so by the end of the 1920s, only New York had a larger per capita bonded indebtedness than North Carolina. Daniels accused Morrison of engaging in a "hysterical spending spree" and unconstitutional deficit spending. After leaving office, Morrison challenged Daniels to a debate—which the Raleigh publisher ignored.[11]

Daniels lambasted the governor when he appointed A. D. Watts, the Simmons machine's chief operative, as the state's first revenue secretary, questioning his character. Seventeen months later, Raleigh police arrested Watts on morals charges after finding a Black prostitute hiding under his bed in his apartment. Democratic lawmakers visited Daniels at Wakestone and tried unsuccessfully to have him kill the story. Watts resigned in shame.[12]

While Daniels feuded with Morrison, he had a better relationship with the string of corporate lawyers who served as governor in the 1920s and 1930s, largely backing the reform efforts of Angus McLean (1925–29), O. Max Gardner (1929–33), and J. C. B. Ehringhaus (1933–37).

But Daniels was always wary. He complained that the three "preach Jeffersonian democracy but they compromise with it when it runs counter to the interests of big business. Most of them represented big business in their law practice and naturally seek to make oil and water mix."[13]

Daniels was closest to Gardner, helping jump-start his political career when Daniels appointed him to organize Young Democrat Clubs across the state. But Daniels criticized Gardner's handling of the 1929 Gastonia textile strike and his inability to help tobacco and cotton farmers during the Depression. Daniels was disappointed when Gardner moved to Washington to become a super-lobbyist after his governorship.[14]

His son Jonathan, who became editor in 1933, continued the *News and Observer*'s tradition as a liberal burr, castigating Ehringhaus for failing to create a mini–New Deal in Raleigh and for not supporting the creation of a minimum wage.[15] Ehringhaus described the paper as "congenitally critical."[16]

Jonathan dismissed the next governor, Clyde Hoey (1937–41), as a Bible-thumping phony whose Sunday school lectures at Edenton Street Methodist Church were broadcast on radio but who also had a reputation as a womanizer. Jonathan judged him as "the perfect flowering of that American phenomenon, the show window Christian politician. He packs them in at Edenton Street, but he'll drive no money lenders out of any temple—indeed he'll quietly and piously help them to get in."[17]

The move to organize North Carolina's textile mills in the 1920s and 1930s widened the Democratic Party's ideological split.

Labor Wars

In 1920, Nell Battle Lewis was riding her horse past the *News and Observer* office when she impulsively dismounted, entered the building, and asked for a writing job. The editors seemed startled to see a young woman wearing riding breeches and boots. As she left, managing editor Frank Smethurst asked, "Does she always wear 'em?"[18]

Within a decade, Lewis became one of the South's leading crusading journalists, drawing praise from some of the biggest names in the newspaper business as a clarion voice for the downtrodden.

Lewis grew up in a prominent Raleigh family—her father was a well-known physician, and her brothers were businessmen. She broadened her horizons while attending Smith College, an elite women's school in Massachusetts, and serving in France with the YMCA during World War I.

She became the first woman to cover a North Carolina legislative session, writing about the defeat of the constitutional amendment to give women the right to vote. After the 1920 suffrage vote, Lewis was relegated to the pink ghetto of the women's section, where as "sassiety editress," as she called it, she chronicled teas, weddings, and which prominent citizens were staying at the city's four major hotels.

She made her reputation on her weekly column, called Incidentally, which began September 7, 1921, with a portrait of Raleigh's Nash Square, a description filled with racially loaded observations.[19] She soon made her column—also published in the women's section—into a hard-hitting platform where she crusaded for better child welfare programs, secret ballots, an eight-hour workday for children, construction of a separate women's prison, and creation of a reformatory school for Black girls. She also championed local cultural institutions such as PlayMakers Repertory in Chapel Hill.

"From the platform of one of the South's most influential presses and via prestigious national magazines and journals," wrote her biographer Alexander Leidholdt, "she gleefully deconstructed Ladydom and skewered the racial, religious, and political intolerance that the Ku Klux Klan, biblical literalists, and patriotic societies promulgated and which formed the bedrock of southern culture. She alternately mocked and scorned her state's powerful and exploitative conservative business establishment. In her newspaper column she also relentlessly punctured boosters, Babbitts, social snobs, and eulogists of moonlight and magnolias."[20]

Lewis was also an activist, earning a law degree from Columbia University, unsuccessfully running for the state legislature in 1926, and campaigning across the state in 1928 for presidential candidate Al Smith.

She made her reputation in North Carolina's labor wars of the 1920s. The textile industry in the late 1800s had moved from New England to the industry-starved South, where employers paid their workers less than half of what their northern counterparts had. When the industry experienced hard times in the 1920s, the mills cut costs, reduced pay, and required workers to increase their productivity. Efforts to organize in the South had always been a herculean task, because as W. J. Cash, a celebrated chronicler of the region, noted, the idea of collective action was associated with "Yankeeism, communism, atheism, alienism, and most of all race mixing."[21]

In 1929 the communist-controlled National Textile Workers Union tried to organize the massive Loray Mills in Gastonia, west of Charlotte. With the textile industry struggling, the Rhode Island owners cut the workforce from 3,500 to 2,200, implemented two 10 percent pay cuts, and required longer hours.[22]

When the workers walked off the job, Governor Gardner ordered in the National Guard at the request of local officials. There was nearly a solid wall of anti-union sentiment in the Carolina textile belt among newspapers, which joined with manufacturers, community leaders, and even clergy to break the labor movement. A front-page editorial cartoon attacking the union in the *Gastonia Daily Gazette* was captioned "A Viper That Must Be Smashed." The exceptions were the *News and Observer* and the *Greensboro Daily News*, which became a literate, thoughtful, progressive paper under the direction of Earle Godbey, Gerald W. Johnson, and Lenoir Chambers.[23]

In the mainstream press, Lewis was one of the few journalists who attempted to defuse the crisis, defend the strikers, and look at the root causes.

Lewis criticized the governor for inflaming the situation by using National Guardsmen as strikebreakers, and she labeled the anti-union *Charlotte Observer* "The Manufacturers' Pride and Joy."[24]

The situation deteriorated when heavily armed vigilantes burned down the union headquarters as the National Guard stood by. When the troops later withdrew, the sheriff's office deputized fifty men, armed with billy clubs, bayoneted rifles, and pistols, who attacked the strikers when they attempted a court-prohibited march.

Daniels mobilized the power of the state capital paper on the labor unrest and the vigilantism, dispatching his ace reporter, R. E. "Fleet" Williams, to Gastonia for five weeks of even-handed reporting and sending his star columnist to give her impressions.

"Barbarous Gaston" was the headline of one Lewis column. "As surprising and humiliating as it may be, it seems that we have a county in North Carolina which is in a condition of virtual barbarity—Gaston of course. . . . Members of the mob are allowed to do whatever violence they please, and it is impossible to apprehend or punish them. Unarmed citizens, including women, are attacked by official ruffians with bayonets and blackjacks. Persons are slammed into jail on the flimsiest pretext. Under the pretense of keeping it, the peace is continually broken, and the county insolently thumbs its nose at the law."[25]

The paper's editorial page was no less barbed. Daniels believed in industrialization but was skeptical of some of the New South philosophy, believing that mill owners—while bringing jobs—could also exploit their workers, particularly women and children. "Gov. Gardner can do no less than to demand the removal of the Sheriff of Gaston County, the removal of the thugs parading around as deputy sheriffs and if the civil authority of Gaston cannot restrain themselves from violence, declare martial law until such time as lawful civil police power can be set up," Daniels declared. While Gaston authorities warned of a Russian-style revolution, Daniels wrote, "they now have a creature infinitely worse than a whole cotton mill of communists, thuggery under the guise of law, doing the bidding of a corporation chartered in Rhode Island."[26]

When a Gastonia magistrate ordered strikers to leave company-owned housing, the deputies enthusiastically dragged their belongings out of the mill houses. The move prompted Lewis to write a fake advertisement:

BRING YOUR MILL TO NORTH CAROLINA
The State with All the Advantages

> LONG HOURS—LOW WAGES—PURE, NATIVE BORN,
> WELL BROKEN, ANGLO-SAXON LABOR
> MINIMUM LEGISLATIVE INTERFERENCE
> Night Work for Women. Eleven Hour Day for Children
> COMPANY-OWNED VILLAGES
> Where, if the workers get heady, you can turn
> them out of house and home.[27]

The *Gastonia Daily Gazette* sneered at the "short-haired, woman-lawyer-journalist from Raleigh" and condemned "the Mencken and Nell Battle types." David Clark, the editor of the *Textile Bulletin*, railed against the *News and Observer*'s "radical editors."[28]

The violence led to tragedy. Ella Mae Wiggins, a twenty-nine-year-old spinner, balladeer, and mother of five, was killed by a shotgun blast while riding in the back of a truck, becoming a national martyr to the national labor movement and the subject of books and novels. In June 1929, police chief Frank Alderholt and four deputies were shot trying to enter the union headquarters, with Alderholt killed.

Lewis and Daniels decried the shooting but demanded a fair trial, while the *Gastonia Daily Gazette* called for the electric chair for the "bunch of Russian anarchists." Lewis set up a defense fund for the sixteen workers who were indicted—with six convicted—for Alderholt's death, while the murderers of Ella Mae Wiggins were acquitted.

According to Australian historian John A. Salmond, the *News and Observer* provided the most balanced news coverage and most sensible editorials of the Gastonia strike. "Lewis' passionate angry columns in support of the strikers' rights were to earn her great calumny in some North Carolina circles," Salmond wrote in a book about the strike, "but they stand out today as reflecting a courageous, balanced engagement with the wider issues of class and economic hegemony that lay at the strike's core."[29]

Fred Beal, the lead organizer, fled to the Soviet Union to avoid prosecution but became disillusioned with communism and returned to the United States in 1938 to surrender. To ensure his safety, Beal asked three of the state's most prominent liberals—Jonathan Daniels, playwright Paul Green, and UNC president Frank Porter Graham—to accompany him when he turned himself in to authorities. Jonathan visited Beal in prison, where he served seven years, and lobbied to get his sentence reduced.[30]

The paper's pro-labor sympathies often left the mill owners fuming. In 1930, Cone Mills in Greensboro threatened to fire and evict any workers caught subscribing to or reading the Raleigh newspaper. "I wouldn't allow that trash to be thrown in my door," said T. O. Ward, a plant supervisor.[31]

While supporting the right to organize and strike, the *News and Observer* counseled against walkouts—urging mediation instead—saying strikes hurt the public, the workers, and the textile companies. "Nobody ever wins in a strike," the paper opined.[32]

The textile walkout in 1934 was the largest strike in American labor history, involving 400,000 workers walking off the job across the country, including tens of thousands at North Carolina plants. The paper criticized Governor Ehringhaus for ordering twenty-three companies of the National Guard to fourteen communities—the largest peacetime mobilization of troops in state history. "Now, North Carolinians under arms are sent against North Carolinians," the paper reported. "The soldiers of the State may use their force to break the strike of the State's workers. The State's troops may kill the State's people."[33]

But sending in the troops was extremely popular in a heavily anti-union state, and many criticized the paper's opposition. "I feel very strongly that there is concerted effort in the state and the South to break down labor in this strike and that then the liberties of the people are really jeopardized," Jonathan wrote his father, who was serving as ambassador to Mexico. "I know, however, that the majority of the propertied people in the state are of the opinion that the *N&O* is pretty radical."[34]

Jonathan was disconcerted when the Socialist Party attacked the governor but praised the *News and Observer*—which he judged helped the governor but didn't do much for the paper. But still Jonathan conferred by telephone with Norman Thomas, the socialist leader, when he visited the state—a fact that Jonathan kept out of print.

"The thing that worries me is this: I don't want to hurt the *News and Observer* if my views are too radical," Jonathan wrote his father. "If this were my paper alone, I wouldn't be worried. In modern slang: I can take it. But I don't want to go so far to the left that it will hurt you and the other boys."[35]

He need not have worried. The old man suggested he was ready to return to North Carolina from his post in Mexico to join the fight against the mill owners, whom he described as "powerful as any feudal lords." As he wrote to President Franklin Roosevelt in 1933,

> Not once, but a half dozen times in North Carolina, I have seen the just right of textile workers denied because a governor used the State troops on the side of the mills and against the employees. The troops

might as well have been under the direction of the mill owners.... The usual result of the mobilization of troops around mills is to give more power to the barons of industry in their resolve not to treat with their employees except upon their own terms.... When I reflect upon the refusal of owners, and the hard conditions in many mill communities, the cry Thomas Carlyle heard out of the French revolution rings in my ears. "How have ye treated us? How have ye taught us, fed us, and led us while we toiled for you?"[36]

The paper's prolabor stance contrasted with other major North Carolina newspapers. The *Charlotte Observer* was consistently anti-union, opposed efforts to regulate child or women's labor, and broke its own printers' strike and union in 1905. The *Winston-Salem Journal* helped bust a strike at R. J. Reynolds Tobacco Company in 1947 with headline accusations that the union was communist-ridden.[37]

But the *News and Observer*'s prolabor position was a strand of its populism DNA that often led it to champion the underdog. Virginius Dabney, a prominent Richmond editor, found the paper's stance remarkable. Dabney wrote that the Raleigh paper "is probably the most fearless paper in the South in its attitude toward economic and industrial questions. The textile and tobacco interests, the two most powerful groups in North Carolina, are treated as cavalierly by Mr. Daniels as if they controlled no advertising."[38]

Although Nell Battle Lewis was a leading voice for workers' rights, her star was eclipsed after the 1920s. She continued off and on as the paper's preeminent columnist until she died in 1956. She fought illness, including probably mental illness, according to her biographer. She became dependent on her conservative family; renounced many of her earlier liberal views, saying she had been "a radical dupe"; and became a political reactionary and a leading voice for segregation.[39] Even as her conservatism starkly contrasted with the paper's liberalism, the Danielses kept her on the payroll as a sop to conservative readers.

Marking the twenty-first anniversary of her column in 1942, Josephus took note of her political conversion in a letter she published in her column. "I loved you when you were so radical that I could not go all the way with you," he wrote. "I loved you when you were a real liberal and a militant progressive. I love you still, despite your lapse into conservatism where I cannot follow you. Come back to the liberalism that I still believe [is] in your heart, even if you sometimes stray from the fountain of equality and real democracy."[40]

Although unsparing of his enemies, Daniels was often tolerant of people who strayed from his advice, whether Lewis or FDR or, as we shall see later, his son Jonathan.

Lewis was the brightest of the paper's stars but not the only one. Few were more colorful than Ben Dixon MacNeill, a writer and photographer with a flair, packing his Speed Graphic camera in his classic Duesenberg as he chased juicy murders across the state. From 1920 until 1937, he was known for his purple prose and his not-always-accurate reporting.

A more sober newsman was Robert E. "Fleet" Williams, who joined the paper as sports editor in 1920 and became city editor, Washington correspondent, and associate editor, helping track Tar Heel politics for more than forty years before he retired in 1960. Holding everything together was Frank Smethurst, a Raleigh native who joined the paper in 1914. His talents allowed him to rise from reporter to become a widely admired managing editor in 1926—a post he held until his death in 1941 at age forty-nine.

Another stalwart was Neil Hester, who was the telegrapher in the days before wire or teletype machines. Skilled in Morse code and Phillips Code, he turned out 12,000 national and international news words per day or night. The equipment consisted of a telegraph key, sounder and relay, and the famous "blind" Remington typewriter with key bars made of hardwood. It was called blind because the incoming national and international news was written on the underside of the plate and what he wrote was invisible to the typist.

In pre-radio days, people gathered at the *News and Observer* building to get the results of big sports events, especially boxing matches. During the classic Jack Dempsey–Gene Tunney fight in 1927, 5,000 people assembled. Hester stood at the window with a pitcher of water, a bottle of "throat gargle," and a megaphone as he gave a blow-by-blow description. The World Series was played for ten years or more on a mechanical diamond erected on a platform in front of the paper, with the game updated as the Morse code operator received new information.[41]

The 1920s were a time of booming newspaper growth. Newspaper circulation in the state increased from 612,000 in 1901 to over 2 million by 1926. By now there were three leading newspapers in the state by size—the *Charlotte Observer*, the *News and Observer*, and the *Greensboro Daily News*. By 1924, the *News and Observer*'s average circulation had grown to 30,419. The paper was typically twelve pages during the week, and it could grow to forty pages on Sunday.[42]

While the paper could be fearless and its coverage of labor strife exemplary for its day, it was not by today's standards a high-quality newspaper.

Its coverage was often shallow, rarely exploring events in any depth, with as many as thirteen stories packed on the front page. But it was taking shape as a modern newspaper, with a sports section, a book page, a comics section, and a page devoted to women's interests.

The Depression

With the collapse of Wall Street in 1929, the paper faced a grim new economic reality, with both subscribers and advertisers slashing their spending. Nationally, newspaper advertising fell 40 percent between 1929 and 1933, and the *News and Observer* was little different—falling from fifteen pages on July 1, 1929, to ten pages on the same date in 1933.

The signs of economic hardship were everywhere. Forlorn merchants stood in doorways looking for missing customers. The unemployed hung around public squares, formerly well-to-do residents were seen in worn-out clothes and worn-down shoes, men's hair hung over their ears, self-rolled cigarettes replaced cigars, and vintage cars ruled the roads. In the countryside, farms that families had owned for generations were being auctioned at bankruptcy sales, while automobiles were being stripped and pulled by mules or horses—Hoovercarts, they were called.

By January 1932, the picture for the paper was bleak. Daniels had lost his bank savings with the collapse of the Commercial National Bank in Raleigh. The paper was losing money, salaries were being slashed, and Daniels was recovering from a serious car crash he suffered while being driven to a speaking engagement in Atlanta.

Daniels turned to an old Wilson administration colleague, Wall Street financier Bernard Baruch, for financial help. Baruch was a singular figure in American politics—a Jewish New Yorker with deep roots in South Carolina, where his father had been a Confederate medical doctor and Klansman. He had served as Wilson's mobilization czar during World War I. FDR sometimes vacationed at his South Carolina estate, and when Winston Churchill, out of office, visited New York, Baruch picked up the tab for his hotel, cigars, and brandy. It was Baruch who coined the term "Cold War." He was known to the public as the elder statesman who sat on the park bench in Lafayette Square dispensing advice.

He had not initially been impressed with Daniels, suggesting to Wilson that Daniels—then embroiled in a fight with the steel companies over the price of armor plate—be replaced by one of Baruch's Wall Street friends. But Daniels became a Baruch ally within the administration.[43]

Between the Wars

Baruch loaned Daniels $25,000 ($578,000 in 2024 dollars) to help him save the paper, a sum that Daniels paid back over several years from personal savings and from the paper's recovery. "Your kindness at that time was more valuable to me than you can know," Daniels wrote his benefactor. Baruch also gave money to other publishers and publications in distress, including his friend Condé Nast to save *Vogue* and *Vanity Fair* magazines, *Our World* magazine, and M. Lincoln Schuster to begin his publishing house, Simon and Schuster.[44]

The loan came with strings. In November 1934, the *News and Observer* challenged a proposal by a national firm to construct a $400,000 sewage disposal plant in Raleigh. Not only did the paper question the company's new technology, but it suggested that local officials were in an unseemly hurry to approve the deal—wording that suggested a hint of corruption to some.

Baruch sent a letter to Jonathan Daniels on behalf of the businessman involved, Simon Guggenheim, vouching for his friend and writing, "I believe in him just as implicitly as I would your father." A Guggenheim representative met with Jonathan, and during the meeting, Baruch followed up with a telephone call to Jonathan to underscore his point. "I know that I need not tell you that any friend of yours may always be sure of having the friendship of any member of the Daniels family and my friendship in particular," Jonathan wrote.[45]

The tone of the paper's editorials changed dramatically, with the paper hailing "the distinguished name" of the Guggenheims, vouching for their integrity, and writing that the sewage issue should be resolved by science and not politics.[46]

With the Depression causing widespread hardships for both taxpayers and local governments, the paper backed Governor O. Max Gardner in his sweeping reorganization in which the state took control of the schools, roads, and prisons while consolidating the UNC college campuses into one system. The state takeover extended the school year from six months to eight months but also resulted in a multi-year fight over how to finance the system.

Daniels and his son Jonathan spearheaded a crusade through the 1930s against passing a sales tax to finance the schools, noting that the tax fell disproportionately on the poor. Writing dozens of editorials, giving speeches, and even printing a clip-out petition in his newspaper for readers to send to lawmakers, Daniels wanted the schools to be financed by taxes on utilities and on luxuries such as cigarettes, soft drinks, and movie tickets. When business interests blocked alternative taxes, Daniels was in full roar. "The Power Companies and the Tobacco Companies have gotten all they want in the House revenue bill," he wrote in 1931. "It smells of cigarettes, tastes of coca cola, has the music of moving picture jazz and in its very sentences you can hear the roar of the water pouring over the dams of the power companies."[47]

With the close of the 1931 session of the legislature, Daniels began receiving hundreds of letters urging him to run for governor. Many of the letters were from small property owners facing foreclosure or educators experiencing drastic budget cuts. One delegation from Pitt County presented a petition signed by 300 people asking him to declare his candidacy. He had forsworn running for political office in his younger days, but now he was wavering. Family and friends counseled him not to, saying it could hurt the paper's influence.

The question became moot after he was seriously injured in a car accident in Atlanta on January 13, 1932, that left him with a badly lacerated scalp and an arm broken in several places. After being sideswiped by another vehicle, his car was forced down an embankment and into a tree. Daniels was a passenger, never having learned to drive. "You are one North Carolinian," said Governor Gardner, "perhaps the only one, who can say that when the governorship was practically in his grasp, he declined the crown."[48]

The sales tax was a driving issue in the 1936 Democratic primary for governor between conservative Clyde Hoey, the machine-backed candidate, and Ralph McDonald, an ardent sales tax foe and a liberal college professor from Winston-Salem. While the paper maintained its traditional neutrality in the primaries, Jonathan privately encouraged McDonald to run and voted for him. There was speculation that Jonathan would be named Democratic National Committeeman if McDonald was elected.[49]

CHAPTER EIGHT

Mexico

When Josephus Daniels's train crossed the Rio Grande into Mexico in 1933, he had the security usually accorded a visiting head of state. Six army officers and a railroad car of soldiers joined him at Nuevo Laredo, a dozen police detectives boarded at San Luis Potosi, and a squadron of airplanes monitored the train's progress from above. The train was still delayed several hours after it was discovered that a section of rail was torn up—an incident of suspected sabotage. Arriving in Mexico City, 360 policemen greeted Daniels. The police cordoned off half a dozen blocks to make sure he safely arrived at the embassy.[1]

President Roosevelt's appointment of Daniels as his man in Mexico had reopened old wounds in US-Mexican relations. Nineteen years earlier, Daniels, as navy secretary, had ordered the marines into Veracruz, resulting in the deaths of 126 Mexicans.

Both Daniels and FDR claimed to have forgotten about Veracruz, but the Mexicans had not. When FDR announced his choice, riots erupted. Protesters stoned the US embassy and handed out anti-American and anti-Daniels leaflets, with Mexican officials sending twenty rioters to a penal colony. So sensitive was the appointment that the Mexican government censored three major Mexico City dailies, barring them from editorializing about the new ambassador.[2]

Both the Left and the Right jeered Daniels's appointment. The Mexican Communist Party plastered Mexico City with posters calling Daniels a "murderer," while the American chamber of commerce in Mexico protested the appointment of the left-leaning Daniels.

From such an unpromising beginning, Daniels became the longest-serving US ambassador to Mexico in history. He won friends as the chief proponent of FDR's new Good Neighbor Policy—a reset from the old "dollar diplomacy" that had favored American corporate interests.

It was more than just friendship that earned Daniels his post. The *News and Observer* was a militantly Democratic paper in an era when most newspapers leaned Republican. In 1940, three-quarters of daily newspapers supported Republican Wendell Willkie over FDR.[3]

During the twelve years of Republican presidents, Daniels maintained his friendship with FDR. Shortly after FDR contracted the crippling disease of polio in 1921, Daniels visited him at his Upper East Side home, and FDR sought to display his vigor. "He hauled off and gave me a blow that caused me nearly to lose my balance," Daniels recalled. "He said, 'You thought you were coming to see an invalid, but I can knock you out in any bout.'"[4]

Their "Dear Chief" and "Dear Franklin" letters were so extensive that they were the subject of a 1952 scholarly book.

In 1932 Daniels stumped for FDR across the country, from North Carolina to California. The seventy-year-old Daniels was such an exhaustive campaigner that Norman Thomas, the Socialist Party presidential candidate, quipped to a Brooklyn audience, "I have never yet been able to find a real Roosevelt rooter except perhaps Josephus Daniels who says he raised him."[5]

Daniels lobbied for his old navy post, but FDR was not about to cede control to his aging former "chief," with whom he had often feuded during the Wilson years. Daniels talked himself out of an FDR proposal that he chair a shipping board to oversee transportation policy by arguing that the board was inefficient and should be merged into the Commerce Department. Roosevelt agreed. Daniels's second choice was the Mexican post, and FDR appointed him even though he had previously promised the ambassadorship to a Texas supporter.

Daniels was one of several unorthodox ambassadorial choices made by Roosevelt. FDR distrusted the 700-member Foreign Service, viewing officers as predisposed toward political conservatism and prone to prejudices of their wealthy WASP backgrounds: anti-immigrant, anti-Black, and antisemitic. "Roosevelt's principal ambassadorial appointments reflected measured contempt for the striped pants set," wrote FDR biographer Jean Edward Smith.[6]

After a three-week cram course in Washington, DC, Josephus and Addie left Raleigh on April 11, 1933, on a train trip to Mexico City—the State Department vetoed his initial plan to take a boat to Veracruz, fearing it would reopen old wounds. Daniels left behind his staff of eighty-seven at the paper, with his sons in charge.

Members of the left-wing Mexican opposition to Daniels confounded both friends and foes back home. As David Clark, editor of the conservative *Southern Textile Bulletin*, wrote, "We are wondering who misinformed them, for certainly, no good communist would wish to throw rocks at Mr. Daniels."[7]

The cultural divide between the two countries in 1933 was far greater than it is today, after the mass Latino migration changed the face of the United States. Crossing the border provided a stark contrast in wealth, food, culture, and language.

Mexico City, a sprawling city of more than 1 million people, was a hotbed of left-wing sentiment in the 1930s. The leading artistic lights were the husband-wife painting team of Diego Rivera and Frida Kahlo, both communists. In January 1937, Mexico granted asylum to Leon Trotsky, a leading Bolshevik whom a Stalinist henchman would assassinate in August 1940 in the capital. The Mexican government provided arms to Republican Spain and accepted 15,000–20,000 Republican exiles after losing to the Francisco Franco–led right-wing forces in 1940. (Daniels met with the Spanish Republicans but avoided meeting Trotsky to avoid providing ammunition to FDR critics.)

Before the revolution in 1910, Mexico was a semifeudal society. Most of the country's arable land was carved up in sprawling haciendas. Three percent of the population owned the land, and the landless peasants—most with Indigenous backgrounds—worked for low wages. American interest in Mexico exploded in 1910 after oil was struck near Tampico on the Gulf Coast. By 1921, Mexico was the world's second-largest oil producer.

Daniels's mission was to implement FDR's Good Neighbor Policy, which the president unveiled in his inaugural address. It was a broad statement subject to much interpretation. Still, it outlined a desire by the United States to treat Latin American countries respectfully as equals as opposed to commercial vassals, in which American companies set the policy and the US government provided the political muscle.

The policy was a good ideological fit for Daniels, despite his Caribbean experience as navy secretary. He had served as vice president of the Anti-Imperialist League, advocating independence for the Philippines. As editor he had opposed gunboat diplomacy, had backed land reform in Mexico, and was generally distrustful of big business. (In supporting Mahatma Gandhi's drive for Indian independence from the British raj, Daniels opined in 1930, "The white Man has made poetic talk about his burden, about his duty to the black and the brown and yellow. His gesture has always been two-handed. He may carry the Bible in one, but there's sure to be economic, political, and social oppression in the other. There are virtually no exceptions.")[8]

There was dread and apprehension about Daniels's arrival at the American Club, a gathering place for American expats in Mexico City, which was overwhelmingly anti–New Deal. The new envoy immediately began a charm offensive, seeking to win over skeptical Mexican leaders. Adopting a vigorous schedule that belied his seventy-one years, Daniels moved around the country, getting to know ordinary Mexicans. Despite his segregationist beliefs, Daniels mixed easily with Latinos, including many Mexicans who had Indigenous backgrounds.

Daniels's baptism by fire involved the anticlericalism of the Mexican government. Since the Spanish conquest, the Catholic Church had been a powerful and conservative force in Mexico, owning half of the land and holding the mortgages on much of the property. The church also oversaw education, but before the 1910 revolution, only 2.9 million of the country's 15.1 million people were literate. The country's 1917 constitution permitted state legislatures to limit church activity, believing it to be a reactionary force.

A pious Methodist, Daniels arrived in Mexico as an active churchman. He had taught Sunday school at Edenton Street Methodist Church in Raleigh for a quarter of a century, and his idea of a vacation was a church retreat at Lake Junaluska in the North Carolina mountains. Daniels tried to show support for religion by regularly attending Union Evangelical Church in Mexico City, speaking out for religious liberty, and lobbying behind the scenes to get Mexican officials to loosen restrictions on churches.[9]

But when Daniels gave a speech on July 26, 1934, to a seminar in Mexico City, all of that was lost. In his talk, Daniels voiced support for Mexico's efforts to push for universal education and said, "No people can be both free and ignorant." That sounds unexceptional today, but in the context of the Mexican government's efforts to secularize education, it was unwise and indiscreet.[10] His timing could not have been worse. That year, the Mexican congress was debating a constitutional amendment abolishing religious education.

Daniels's remarks created a firestorm in American Catholic circles, where religious publications and politicians with Catholic constituencies called for his ouster. The State Department received 10,000 communications dealing with Mexico and religion, with two-thirds calling for his firing. "How can you expect to save your soul, Mr. Daniels, when you aid and abet the godless gangsters of Mexico?" one North Carolina priest wrote to Daniels. There were resolutions in Congress calling for an investigation of religious conditions in Mexico and recalling Daniels.[11]

Daniels sought to clarify his remarks, noting he only meant to support universal education. FDR waved off calls for his firing and protected him from congressional attacks. Realizing he had become a political liability in Catholic strongholds, Daniels offered to resign during FDR's 1936 reelection campaign and weighed his options. He considered running in the Democratic primary for the Senate in 1936 against anti–New Deal incumbent senator Josiah Bailey of Raleigh. "North Carolina should be represented in the Senate by a progressive Democrat imbued with the principles of the great liberals of our party," he wrote to a friend. "It irks me to think of the possibility of the re-election of Senator Bailey who incarnates more of the Hamiltonian and Jefferson ideas."[12]

The White House was noncommittal about supporting his Senate bid. Daniels invited former governor O. Max Gardner, the head of the state Democratic organization, to Mexico City, but he too was noncommittal. His friends warned him that Bailey would be difficult to defeat, and his family urged Daniels to focus on his memoirs rather than a Senate campaign. Daniels also asked FDR if he could take over for ailing navy secretary Claude Swanson, but Roosevelt ignored the suggestion—and Swanson lived three more years.

Daniels attended the 1936 Democratic National Convention in Philadelphia. He backed liberal agriculture secretary Henry Wallace to be FDR's new vice presidential running mate, lunching with his old friend on the day he was nominated. Democratic officials asked Daniels not to campaign for FDR but to return to Mexico City, where he was less likely to stir the resentment of American Catholics.[13]

Daniels and Cárdenas

Daniels served during the terms of three Mexican presidents. His most important relationship was with Lázaro Cárdenas (1934–40), who is widely viewed as the most important Mexican political leader of the twentieth century and one of the most influential in Latin America.

The 1910 revolution had lost momentum when Cárdenas, a thirty-nine-year-old general and provincial governor, was elected president. Cárdenas, a populist and an agrarian reformer, revived the revolution by redistributing more land to the peasants, revitalizing the trade union movement, and nationalizing the US- and British-owned oil industry.

Daniels was an admirer of Cárdenas, viewing him as the Mexican version of Roosevelt and his New Deal and believing he was a Mexican patriot leading his country "out of feudalism into democracy."[14]

Cárdenas's program guaranteed trouble with the Wall Street bankers who in the 1920s had loaned hundreds of millions to the Mexican government, which had been unable to repay the loans during the Depression. An even larger crisis occurred when the Mexican government began taking the land in the Yaqui Valley, south of Arizona. Daniels saw justice in breaking up the large haciendas.

When the Mexican government expropriated foreign-owned oil fields in 1938, the oil companies' reaction was swift and decisive: they boycotted Mexican oil, made it difficult for Mexico to ship the oil, refused to sell new equipment for the Mexican oil fields, and launched a publicity campaign to dissuade American tourists from visiting Mexico as a dangerous land filled with bandits.

The Roosevelt administration was divided. Secretary of State Cordell Hull wanted the US government to side with the British and American oil companies. Although opposed to the seizures, Daniels and FDR wanted both to protect the Good Neighbor Policy and to ensure access to Mexican oil and political loyalty with World War II looming. The seizure of the oil fields was broadly supported in Mexico. Any effort to reverse the move, Daniels believed, would result in a revolution and the possible assassination of Cárdenas.[15]

Writing FDR during the oil industry dispute, Daniels exposed his distrust of the oil companies. "Mexico can never prosper on low wages, and we must be in sympathy with every just demand," Daniels wrote. "I need not tell you that as a rule the oil men will be satisfied with nothing less than the United States government attempt to direct the Mexican policy for their financial benefit. They are as much against fair wages here as economic royalists at home are against progressive legislation. They would have an ambassador who would be a messenger boy for their companies, and a government at Washington, whose policy is guided by Dollar Diplomacy."[16]

Daniels was no messenger boy for the oil companies. At times he was not even a messenger for the State Department. After the confiscation of the oil fields, the State Department issued a stiff diplomatic protest, followed by recalling the US ambassador home. Astonishingly, Daniels softened the rebuke on his own, telling Mexican officials that they should not view the American note as officially presented but merely as an unofficial expression of US views. More provocatively, he declined to follow instructions to return home. After several days, he received a belated authorization to remain in Mexico.

Daniels got away with his freelance diplomacy because he was a senior figure in the Democratic Party and had a better relationship with FDR than did Hull. If the president disagreed with the actions, Daniels would likely have been sacked.

Daniels's insubordination left Hull fuming. "Well, we are having lots of trouble in Mexico, and you know the President and Daniels have given the Mexicans the impression that they can go right ahead and flaunt everything in our face," Hull wrote a colleague. "Daniels is down there taking sides with the Mexican government, and I have to deal with these Communists down there and have to carry out international law."[17]

As a result of the oil industry boycott, Mexico experienced an acute economic slump. But Mexico never backed down. Just days after Daniels returned to Raleigh, negotiators between the oil companies and Mexico agreed to a financial settlement. The oil companies accepted compensation far below what they said the fields were worth.

Embassy Life

Daniels's long hours and constant touring surprised the embassy staff, who were expecting a more sedate schedule from an older ambassador—he was seventy when he arrived and seventy-nine when he retired.

The embassy was a walled compound with the official residence in one building and the chancery in another, with a beautiful garden in between. Daniels and Addie lived in huge rooms with seventeen-foot French windows, including a drawing room, a dining room, two small studies, and five bedrooms and baths.

At first, the thin air of Mexico City gave the Danielses some discomfort, but they grew used to it, along with mild weather and the view of two white-capped volcanos. They adopted local cuisines such as tortillas, frijoles, and enchiladas—exotic foods for many Americans in the 1930s. On occasion, Daniels dressed up in charro attire, while Addie wore a china poblana outfit. But Daniels avoided bullfights on moral grounds, and he never learned to speak Spanish, although he widely read Spanish history.

They hosted frequent alcohol-free lunches, teas, and dinners, with food served on silver plates by uniformed waiters. The guests included family and officials from North Carolina, Mexican leaders, politicians, diplomats, movie stars, journalists, and archeologists.

While in Mexico, Daniels began work on what would become a five-volume autobiography.

Addie, a large woman, increasingly found it difficult to host social events because of her severe arthritis, diabetes, hypertension, and a congestive heart condition that eventually forced her to use a wheelchair. After an examination in 1941, their son Worth, a medical doctor, advised the couple to return to

Raleigh, hoping it would improve her health—which they did in November 1941.

Like everything else, Daniels's Mexican legacy was the subject of divided opinion. David Cronon, a historian who authored a book about Daniels's Mexican sojourn, wrote that the ambassador "recognized that the days of forceful diplomacy, economic pressure, and old-style dollar imperialism were numbered. The United States could get much further with its smaller neighbors, he believed, by means of tact, discretion, patience and understanding. He rejected the Big Brother approach for the friendship-between-equals approach of the Good Neighbor Policy."[18]

Conservatives felt he was too soft toward the Mexican government. The *New York Journal of Commerce* complained that since Daniels had taken up his post, "American petroleum properties have been seized without compensation to their owners, and a policy of discouraging the collaboration of American capital and enterprise in Mexico's economic development has been pursued consistently."[19]

But others, such as Nobel Prize–winning novelist John Steinbeck, said he had a renewed pride in democracy after visiting Daniels in Mexico. "That is a great and humble man," Steinbeck wrote to poet Archibald MacLeish. "I don't much like the diplomatic class. But this man knows more about the Mexican people than his predecessors did, the common people. My admiration and affection for him are very great."[20]

CHAPTER NINE

Jonathan

When Daniels left for Mexico in April 1933, he turned the *News and Observer*'s management over to three of his four sons—although he never completely relinquished control. He closely read the paper, made frequent suggestions, and was consulted on important decisions.

Jonathan handled news and editorials; Frank Sr. managed the business side. Joe Jr., less talented than his brothers, held various business positions on the staff without much responsibility. Only Worth went his own way, becoming a physician in Washington, DC.

It was assumed that Jonathan would become editor; he was intellectually gifted and a graceful writer. Though a slightly rebellious son, he had a strong interest in journalism.

Born in Raleigh in 1902, Jona, as his family and friends called him, had advantages that were denied his father—an upper-class upbringing, a first-rate education, and an exposure at a young age to a wider, more sophisticated world. Like many such sons, Jonathan struggled to get out from beneath his father's shadow and put his stamp on the world.

Jonathan spent his formative teenage years in Washington, DC, where he attended St. Albans School, one of the nation's top prep schools whose graduates include some of the nation's political elite: Acheson, Bush, Gore, Kennedy, Lodge, Rockefeller, and Roosevelt.

His world included official trips with his father on the navy secretary's yacht, where he enjoyed diving off the side to swim. Answering the doorbell, he might find President Wilson, William Jennings Bryan, or leading authors, actors, journalists, and diplomats of the day. He watched Wilson's war message to Congress in the House chambers as a guest of the House majority leader. He rode to New York with Wall Street tycoon Bernard Baruch in his private railcar, ate dinner at the Ritz, and stayed at Baruch's Long Island estate.

In 1918, he enrolled at the University of North Carolina at age sixteen, having skipped two grades. He was a member of the Lost Generation, the Jazz Age group whom novelist F. Scott Fitzgerald described as having "grown up to find all Gods dead, all wars fought, all faiths in man shaken." Jonathan read such trendy magazines as *Vanity Fair* and the *Smart Set* and dreamed of becoming a famous novelist. He was such a free thinker that Governor Cameron Morrison complained that "the Daniels boy is over there destroying the faith of all the boys in Chapel Hill."[1]

His crowd included Thomas Wolfe, who later became North Carolina's best-known novelist, and Paul Green, a Pulitzer Prize–winning playwright. Jonathan and Wolfe were both editors of the *Daily Tar Heel*, the student newspaper, and they both acted at the newly created PlayMakers theater company. Jonathan appeared with Wolfe in two of Wolfe's plays.

A UNC classmate remembered when Jonathan approached some of his literary friends with a copy of Fitzgerald's first novel, *This Side of Paradise*. "He passed it around and when it came to Tom Wolfe, his hands trembled as he thumbed through it. And Jonathan said, 'Well boys if Scott Fitzgerald can do it, so can we.' Everybody then scrambled back to their rooms and started writing."[2]

Although not intimates, Jonathan and Wolfe were close enough to drain a bottle of whiskey together, and they stayed in touch after college. On one memorable occasion in 1937, Jonathan witnessed a famous literary blowup between Wolfe and his book editor, Max Perkins, a legendary figure at Scribner's publishing house who also edited Ernest Hemingway and Fitzgerald.

In Jonathan's telling, his brother-in-law Noble Cathcart, publisher of the *Saturday Review of Literature*, had hosted a dinner for Wolfe. Afterward the group reconvened at a speakeasy called Cherio's, where Perkins joined the party. Wolfe was already angry with Scribner's for not supporting him in a libel suit. After consuming large quantities of alcohol, Wolfe angrily accused Perkins of taking too much credit for rewriting Wolfe's manuscript and physically accosted him, pinning Perkins to a staircase post in the speakeasy. "He was threatening to pummel him there," Jonathan said. Jonathan said he and Cathcart pulled Wolfe off Perkins.[3]

But other accounts do not portray Jonathan as the peacemaker, describing him as needling an inebriated Wolfe before he blew up at Perkins—with physical blows narrowly avoided—an account that Jonathan dismissed as fiction. When Wolfe died in 1938 at age thirty-seven, Jonathan was one of his pallbearers.[4]

Jonathan's youthful rebellion against his straitlaced, Bible-believing father involved drinking plenty of bootleg whiskey—North Carolina began prohibition in 1909, ahead of most of the nation. He smoked, chased women, became an avowed atheist in his youth, and even experimented with smoking dope after some students stole cannabis indica from the medical school.[5]

Nicknamed "Dice Daniels" for his proficiency with craps, Jonathan swore off the game after he cleaned out several New York City friends, including poet Ogden Nash. Decades later, opponents still taunted him by calling him Dice Daniels. "We had a lot of radicalism in my generation," Jonathan recalled years later.[6]

Despite sewing his wild oats, Jonathan graduated in 1921 at age nineteen. He stayed an extra year to serve as editor of the *Daily Tar Heel* while earning a master's degree in Western literature, passing his oral exam on his second try. One summer, he interned as a police reporter at the *Louisville Times*, a paper owned by his mother's cousin Robert Bingham.

At a senior year dance in Chapel Hill, he met Elizabeth Bridgers, better known as Bab. She was on break from Smith College, a women's college in Massachusetts, and was a member of a prominent North Carolina family: her father had been president of the Atlantic Coast Line Railroad, and her sister was a nationally known playwright. Jonathan and Bab immediately hit it off, sitting up all night talking.

He joined her in New York after Bab dropped out of Smith to study art. Jonathan enrolled at Columbia University law school—a move encouraged by his father. Although he flunked every course, Jonathan had a grand time. Living in a brownstone walk-up, he attended Broadway shows most evenings with Bab, bounced checks on his father's bank account, flirted with socialism, and joined his father one evening in 1921 to dine with Franklin and Eleanor Roosevelt.

Jonathan was always drawn to New York City, frequently returning for meetings with publishers or for speeches, traveling in literary circles, and joining the prestigious Century Club. His idea of a good time, he once said, was "a few highballs with the boys on Broadway and then a good stage show."[7]

Back in Chapel Hill in the summer of 1923, he took a twelve-week review course—studying sixteen hours per day—and easily passed the bar exam, although, like his father, he never practiced law.

That fall, Jonathan and Bab married, and he began his career at the *News and Observer*. His father put him in his own editor-in-training program, rotating him in different jobs to learn the business—bill collecting, sportswriting, covering trials, and working the police beat.

The twenty-three-year-old Jonathan became the paper's Washington correspondent. In 1926, the couple had their first child, Adelaide Ann, before returning to Raleigh the next year so that Jonathan could help his father work on his multivolume autobiography and launch his own career as a novelist.

The couple was expecting their second child in December 1929; Bab underwent induced labor at Raleigh's Rex Hospital. When doctors performed a cesarean procedure, they found the uterus had ruptured at the place of the old incision from her first cesarean. The newborn died, and Bab's breathing became increasingly labored. The thirty-year-old Bab briefly improved with morphine, but soon she became so weak that she could not breathe independently. The scene was heartbreaking. With mechanical respirators not developed until midcentury, Jonathan and his brothers took turns performing artificial respiration to keep her alive. To relieve them, American Telephone Company employees trained in CPR volunteered. Bab was fully conscious, instructing the men when they were doing it right or wrong.[8]

Jonathan probably never fully recovered from her death, even keeping a photo of her at his own deathbed. He changed their daughter's name to Elizabeth, presumably to honor her mother.

Clash of Angels

Shortly after Bab died, Jonathan finished his novel, *Clash of Angels*, an allegorical fantasy concerning Jehovah and Lucifer. It was a philosophical novel that drew from Christianity, Islam, Judaism, and Zoroastrianism. His father tried to stop it, believing it to be sacrilegious. He asked Jonathan to join him on an evening carriage ride, requesting that his son postpone publishing the novel. Josephus argued that one should treat people's Christian beliefs with respect, and he worried "that in your early writings you might use your talent of satire unwisely."[9]

After its publication in March 1930, his father pronounced that "it was full of action and fire" and that his parents were proud of him. Daniels was willing to overlook the transgressions of his protégés—whether FDR or his son. The Freethinkers Society of America made the novel its book of the month selection, and political foes later used the book to attack Jonathan.

The book received decent reviews. The *Des Moines Register* described it as "a brilliant satire," and the *Atlanta Constitution* deemed it a "superb piece of craftsmanship." The novel earned Jonathan a Guggenheim Fellowship, allowing him to live a year and half in Paris (after all the famous writers of the 1920s had left), Switzerland, and Florence while he worked on his second novel—a satire on the Old South that never found a publisher.[10]

Returning to New York, Jonathan joined *Fortune*, a new business magazine started by famed publisher Henry Luce, where he made good money, drank too much, became lifelong friends with colleague and poet Archibald MacLeish, and found a second wife. In January 1932, he met Lucy Cathcart, the sister of his friend Noble Cathcart, editor of the *Saturday Review*. Both were unhappy—Jonathan was the grieving widower, and Lucy had dropped out of college and was estranged from her father. They found solace in each other in a marriage lasting forty-six years, producing three daughters.

Lucy was the daughter of a New York chemist credited with inventing Wesson Oil. She was educated in Germany but was proud of her maternal roots in such Old South citadels as Charleston, South Carolina, and Montgomery, Alabama. They were married in New York City on April 30, 1932. Most descriptions portray her as an attractive but cold and haughty woman. She thought Raleigh was provincial and the Daniels family nouveau riche. She was a sharp-tongued gossip who treated workers disdainfully. Jonathan liked to say there were two kinds of women from South Carolina—those who never owned a pair of shoes and those who treat you as if you never owned a pair of shoes. Lucy belonged in the latter category.[11]

Jonathan, Lucy, and six-year-old Elizabeth returned to Raleigh in 1932, despite misgivings about working "under a very dominant father." Both his father and brother Frank Sr. had pleaded with him to come home. In a "Dear Partner" letter, Josephus wrote, "It looks like it is about time to hang out the shingle, 'Jonathan Worth Daniels and Father.' From your early boyhood, I have looked forward to the time we would work in double harness on the *News and Observer*."[12]

When Daniels headed to Mexico, his logical replacement was Frank Smethurst, the paper's well-regarded managing editor. But Jonathan got the job after giving his father an ultimatum—"I'm going to be editor, or I'm going back to New York." Even though his father had doubts whether his thirty-one-year-old son was ready, Jonathan got the job.[13]

With financial help from his father, he built a home at 1540 Caswell Street, adjacent to Wakestone. It was a large and distinctive ivy-draped redbrick Charlestonian, with a circular staircase, high-ceilinged rooms, and elaborate moldings and whose privacy was protected by a high wall. (In 2022 the house was sold for $2 million.) In the words of historian Lee Craig, he made the home "a hub for Raleigh's fashionable set." But it was a fashionable set with an intellectual, bohemian flavor: a procession of writers, Jews, and New York editors who set it apart from most upper-crust Raleigh homes. Eleanor Roosevelt visited Raleigh so often that she was almost like another grandmother to the children. "Jonathan could seem like a character straight out of a F. Scott Fitzgerald novel—and that's the way he wanted it," wrote Craig. Still, Jonathan was a big fish in a small pond. Raleigh had fewer people than Lynchburg, Virginia, in 1930.[14]

Measuring five feet eight inches and weighing 170 pounds, the bespectacled Daniels was a wisecracker and a raconteur who could hold court for four hours, as he once did in playwright Paul Green's kitchen.

His refuge was his library, which was off limits to his four daughters and the servants. He often used a short pencil and notepad to write like his father, when working at home, with Lucy transcribing for him. He read and wrote prodigiously but had no other hobbies.

"Both of my parents drank too much," recalled their daughter Lucy. "But Father extolled the virtues of 'living dangerously' by smoking, drinking, and never shying away from the risks, while Mommy demanded order, cleanliness, and obedience beyond the capacity of most children."[15]

According to daughter Lucy, Jonathan had a temper and could be both verbally and physically abusive, sometimes using a belt on his daughters with such force that it left bruises and welts.[16]

Like many well-to-do southern whites, Jonathan depended on Black help to keep the household running. The nurse, Annie, served almost as a surrogate mother for the children, occasionally allowing the girls to climb into bed with her at night. Annie's mother, Octavia, was the family cook. In many ways, Lucy recalled, the Black help provided the love that her parents found difficult to express.[17]

Although father and son shared a similar liberal political philosophy, they differed on two significant issues—Prohibition and race.

Josephus thought alcohol was one of mankind's curses, while Jonathan thought bourbon was one of life's consolations. To accommodate their different views, Josephus sent his dinner guests over to either Jonathan's or Frank Sr.'s house for pre-dinner cocktails at five o'clock. Even so, the drinking ceased when his father walked over for a visit. Jonathan's daughter Lucy recalled that an unannounced visit by the old man caused a panic as she helped her parents scramble to hide their glasses behind books on a shelf. "Woe is me!" Jonathan exclaimed. "I can't even have a drink in peace!"[18]

The disagreement came to a head in 1933 during a statewide referendum on whether North Carolina should end Prohibition. His father scolded him for the paper's neutrality on the issue, but Jonathan said outlawing liquor was against his principles. Jonathan's solution was to visit his father in Mexico, leaving another person to write the Prohibition editorials. So strong was Josephus's influence that the paper declined to accept liquor advertising until the 1970s, long after Josephus had died.[19]

Race

It is hardly surprising that father and son held different views on race. Josephus was born during the Civil War, was raised during Reconstruction, and formed many of his ideas while living in the Black Belt of Eastern North Carolina with a recently liberated population of enslaved people. Jonathan was born at the dawn of the twentieth century, was raised partly in Washington, DC, was better educated, and had traveled abroad. "I was always very much to the left of my father on the racial situation," Jonathan recalled.[20]

While diverging from his father on race, Jonathan was also marinated in the caste system—a profoundly segregated world of Black maids, janitors, yardmen, cooks, and nannies. Traveling east through the farm country, he saw Black tenant farmers working behind mules in the fields and living in flimsy unpainted cabins hardly bigger than tiny tobacco barns.

As an editor/owner, Jonathan had more freedom to push for change than many other southern editors who were hired guns. But Jonathan moved slowly on race. His father was looking over his shoulder from Mexico, and the entire South was locked in such a segregationist straitjacket that no major white southern institution—ranging from governments to newspapers to colleges—dared call for the end of Jim Crow. Jonathan was both a creature of and a critic of the strict segregation system he was born into.

He gradually transformed the paper from a strident voice for white supremacy to one of the South's leading newspapers pushing for racial change. Jonathan's evolution on race was of such note that it was the subject of a 1982 scholarly book. "From the 1930s to the 1960s," wrote historian Charles Eagles, "his opinions gradually changed from an insistence on equal treatment of the races within the prevailing system of segregation to an endorsement of desegregation. His path was not straight or direct."[21]

Jonathan set a different tone early in his editorship. He expressed sympathy for the Scottsboro Boys, nine Alabama teenagers wrongly accused of raping two white girls. He described their 1933 conviction as "outrageous" and "shocking." He denounced lynching, drew attention to Black poverty, and worried about the unfair treatment that African Americans received in the courts.[22]

"I hope I am not making your newspaper too much the colored boy's friend," Jonathan wrote to his father in Mexico in 1933. Responding later, his father replied, "You have sometimes felt that I was too strong in my opposition to the recognition of the Negro in politics in our State. But I lived through the days of when they all had the ballot and I observed that 90 percent of them could be used to their own hurt and to the hurt of the better class of people."[23]

Jonathan argued that racial distinction was appropriate but not racial discrimination. But as Eagles observed, he failed to note that separation and distinction might necessarily involve inequality and discrimination.

North Carolina's justice system was lily-white, from the judges to the juries to the cops on the beat. In 1930 there were two Black police officers or deputy sheriffs in all of North Carolina; a decade later there were three. Without the vote, Black people were at the mercy of an all-white system. Newspapers were one of the few entities that could bring public pressure on injustices.[24]

W. E. B. Du Bois, a leading Black political intellectual/activist, had warned at the beginning of the century that the disenfranchisement of Black voters would have a profound effect on the system of justice. "Daily the Negro is coming more and more to look upon law and justice, not as protecting safeguards, but as sources of humiliation and oppression. The laws are made by men who have little interest in him; they were executed by men who have absolutely no motive for treating the Black people with courtesy or consideration; and finally, the accused lawbreaker is tried, not by his peers, but too often by men who would rather punish ten innocent Negroes than let one guilty one escape."[25]

Jonathan attacked the idea that crime was racial. Crime, he wrote, was rooted in poverty and a lack of education and opportunity. He called for the fair and equal administration of the law for all races—although he did not initially support the inclusion of Black jurors.

In 1936, Daniels charged that Greenville policemen used excessive force in employing blackjacks on two disorderly Black women at a dance at a tobacco warehouse, causing a riot. He wrote that the "use of blackjacks on women's heads or bodies is calculated to produce a riot anywhere in the world." He criticized a Greensboro judge in 1933 for exonerating a white policeman who claimed self-defense in shooting a Black man when the evidence showed the Black man had been shot in the back of the head.[26]

In 1935 he denounced the acquittal of Mecklenburg County jail officials who had held two Black inmates chained in a freezing cell, causing their feet to turn gangrenous, requiring amputation. "Whitewash for Brutality" was the headline of one editorial.[27]

Nell Battle Lewis, one of the paper's columnists, was even more pointed; addressing her "nominally Christian brethren," she called the abuse and the acquittal "shameful, disgraceful and sickening." In a sarcastic tone, Lewis wrote, "What the result of this trial actually says to them—and to an admiring world is 'Just a couple o' n———s—so we should worry?'"[28]

Lewis was well plugged into prison abuses. Besides her newspaper work, she did publicity for the State Board of Charities and Public Welfare, a state agency whose official duties included inspecting penal institutions and making recommendations for their improvement. She was outraged when a county coroner found no blame in the deaths of eleven Black convicts killed in a 1931 fire while trapped in an iron cage that was part of a mobile wooden stockade—part of Duplin County's road system. "We burned those eleven Negroes to death because in our selfish hearts we didn't give a damn what became of them, because we were cruelly content to leave them to whatever fate might befall," she wrote in a blistering column.[29]

In 1937, Jonathan challenged the death of a Black suspect shot by a Wake County deputy sheriff. "This case stinks to high heaven," he wrote. When the deputy denied shooting the Black man, Jonathan sarcastically suggested that the man had shot himself in the back while trying to escape. The deputy was later charged but acquitted.[30]

When Black activist Pauli Murray applied for admission to the UNC law school in 1938, Jonathan told a Chapel Hill audience, "I don't see how anybody can object to taking a graduate course with a Negro." But the paper took no editorial stand, virtually ignoring the issue.[31]

The *News and Observer*'s failure to support Murray's admission underscored the limits of Daniels's incremental approach to Black civil rights. In the 1930s he opposed Blacks serving on juries and opposed increased widespread Black voting rights, arguing that most were poor and uneducated and were subject to manipulation by unscrupulous politicians.[32]

Although he opposed capital punishment, Jonathan was one of the few southern liberals in 1935 to oppose a federal anti-lynching law, arguing that stopping extralegal killings was the responsibility of state and local officials. More than a dozen southern newspapers supported the federal anti-lynching law.[33]

Rarely were lynch mobs brought to justice. Such was the case involving Govan "Sweat" Ward, a twenty-five-year-old mentally ill Black man from rural Franklin County who decapitated a white farmer with an ax in 1935. The lynch mob—unmasked and in broad daylight—seized Ward from the custody of the local sheriff, driving him off before hanging him from a scrub oak with a cotton plow line. The sheriff claimed he could not identify the lynchers and failed to note any license plate numbers. The State Highway Patrol and the National Guard arrived too late except to witness the crowd of hundreds of men, women, and children who had gathered to observe the spectacle. No one was prosecuted.[34]

Jonathan was disgusted. "The blood lust that broke in Govan Ward's cracked brain yesterday morning spread to every man who joined in the carnival of killing made over his body," he wrote in an editorial. "It spread to a lesser degree to all those who came moved in morbid participation to view the swinging corpse of a crazy man and the marks that an equally crazy mob had left upon his dangling body."[35]

Jonathan favored more economic opportunities for Black people, arguing that cheap Black labor retarded southern progress, and opposed discriminatory wage policies. He called it "petty and cruel" when the Wake County commissioners cut the wages of Black janitors to raise the pay for white elevator operators (who were replacing the traditional Black operators). He also joined Black voices in complaining about efforts of some employers to exempt specific jobs, such as farmworkers and maids, that were dominated by Black labor from New Deal minimum wage codes. "The buying power of the Negro is as important to Southern prosperity as the buying power of the white," he wrote. He also called for the repeal of poll taxes levied by many southern states.[36]

Responding to reports of Black poverty in Durham in 1936, he wrote, "Conditions among lower-class Negroes in North Carolina and other Southern States constitute the deepest, the most dangerous poverty in the United States."[37]

He also encouraged better education opportunities for African Americans. Jonathan served on an advisory commission under Governor Ehringhaus that found in 1935 that many Black schools were ill-equipped, in poor repair, and inadequately heated and lighted and had insufficient staff.

Offended by inequality, Jonathan was angered when he noticed that a northbound train leaving Raleigh had steel cars for whites and an old wooden car for Black people. "When Negroes—as they do—pay the same price for transportation, they are entitled to the same safeguards and comforts for which white men get for the same price," he wrote in 1941.[38]

But Jonathan's efforts on behalf of Black residents were suffused with paternalism. When the Sir Walter Hotel, Raleigh's main lodging, moved in

1934 to end the employment of Black workers, Daniels objected, arguing there was a "preference for Negro servants in the South which it believes is shared by most Southerners." He added, "There is a relationship between the Negro servant and the white man, a courteous relationship, a graceful relationship that does not exist between white men and white men servants in other sections of America."[39]

Jonathan corresponded with James Shepard, the founder and president of what is now North Carolina Central University in Durham, the nation's first state-supported liberal arts college for Black students. Shepard frequently sought Jonathan's support in getting state funding from the legislature and asked for suggestions on planned speeches. But it was not a relationship between equal leaders of two important Tar Heel institutions. Shepard frequently played the role of a humble supplicant offering extravagant praise for Jonathan—a common practice for African Americans during the Jim Crow period.

Another correspondent was Walter White, the New York–based director of the NAACP, at a time when many southern whites saw that group as subversive. Although largely forgotten today, he was the leading civil rights figure of the 1930s and 1940s. A sophisticated, light-skinned man whose blond hair and blue eyes allowed him to pass for white, White risked his life by slipping into small southern towns in the wake of lynchings to determine the facts—sometimes barely escaping with his life. He then lobbied Congress to adopt anti-lynching legislation.

White saw Jonathan as a southerner who sympathized with the plight of southern Black people and tried unsuccessfully to convince him to back federal anti-lynching legislation. Jonathan argued that the states should combat lynching, not the federal government. Although Jonathan was worried about racial discrimination, he seemed equally concerned about a white backlash. "The whole question of the Negro in politics disturbs me, and while I do not regard myself as Simon Legree, I do suppose I share some white conservatism," he wrote White in 1936, referencing the antagonist in *Uncle Tom's Cabin*. Jonathan acknowledged that Black people were the subject of discrimination. But he said, "Unfortunately, however, the Negro group—and this is no reflection on the Negro; rather on the white man—is by and large in the South ignorant and poor and subject to improper pressures by one group or another." He continued, "If there is any problem in which I think the best course is one of making haste slowly it is the Negro question." Jonathan's views were shared among many white southern moderates/liberals of the era, including UNC president Frank Graham; UNC sociologist Howard W.

Odum; William T. Couch, director of the UNC Press; and Florida congressman Claude Pepper.[40]

Despite a lengthy correspondence, Jonathan was taken aback when White suggested in 1941 that they dispense with the "Mister" and address each other by their first names. "I guess that is race progress or sump'n," Jonathan wrote to a white friend. The "Misters" continued, and White eventually soured on Jonathan.[41]

John R. Larkins, who for several decades was the highest-ranking Black official in state government, said he admired Jonathan. But he noted a curiosity—Daniels would offer Black people only two fingers in a handshake.[42]

The paper provided "exceptionally extensive coverage" of routine Black life for a white southern paper, according to Eagles. During six weeks in 1936 examined by Eagles, the paper reported on the Black contributions to the Red Cross in Wendell, on improvements reported by the state's extension agent for Black farmers, on a concert by the Orange County Colored Teachers Glee Club, on the picketing of a Durham grocery by Black protesters, and on a meeting organizing support for a school bond issue. Although the paper did not regularly run obituaries of Black deceased, it did publish stories about the death of prominent Blacks. It also carried Black church news, but not in the regular Raleigh Churches Today column.[43]

But there were gaps in the news coverage on sensitive subjects. When Thomas R. Hocutt, a Black student, tried unsuccessfully to enroll in UNC's pharmacy school in March 1933, the *News and Observer* carried wire stories published on the inside of the paper but took no editorial position.[44]

Jonathan and the paper supported Black colleges, particularly Shaw University, as Jonathan had grown up across the street from the campus. He also supported better funding for the state's five historically Black public campuses—the most in the South. But he opposed a 1935 proposal by the NAACP to create law, medical, and pharmacy schools for Blacks, arguing that the state's priority was improving the funding for the existing campuses.[45]

The paper capitalized "Negro," which was unusual for a southern newspaper. Still, it used the term "Negress" to refer to a Black woman until at least 1943 and omitted the courtesy titles "Mr." and "Mrs." when referring to African Americans. Sexual assault was called "rape" when a Black person was charged but "criminal assault" if a white suspect was involved.[46]

In 1936 Foster P. Payne, dean of Shaw University, praised Jonathan for producing a paper that is "liberal in both its news and editorial policy" but complained of practices denigrating African Americans. He noted that the term "darkeys" appeared in an Under the Dome political column. He asked why parents of white babies were identified with the honorifics "Mr." and "Mrs." but not those of Black babies. "Is there any legitimate reason why there should be this discrimination?" Payne asked. "Are not all of these parents citizens of our state and nation? Are not all worthy of titles of respect?"[47]

Jonathan was troubled by the paper's policy on courtesy titles, noting that a white woman convicted of prostitution received the courtesy title of "Miss," while a notice of a lecture by a Black female home extension agent received none. When Jonathan later quizzed his father on the subject, the ambassador urged his son to "edge up" to the question. For example, Josephus allowed that the paper could refer to the wife of the president of Shaw University as "Missus." "It's better to do this without a definite policy at this time," he wrote in 1938.[48]

Although Jonathan seemed more attuned to racial injustice than most whites, he was still reluctant to challenge the racial code of segregation. At times, Jonathan regressed back to the racist positions of his father.

Following his father into the quagmire of race and academia, Jonathan in 1936 rebuked UNC English professor Eston Everett Ericson for attending a rally and then having dinner with James W. Ford, the Communist Party's Black vice presidential candidate. He objected to the two men dining together at a Black-owned hotel, saying, "The best way to preserve racial integrity is to keep the races wholly apart in their social relationships."[49]

UNC president Frank Porter Graham withstood pressure to fire Ericson, noting that the two men had had dinner before when they were students at Johns Hopkins University. Jonathan's liberal friends accused him of having gone "haywire." William T. Couch, director of the UNC Press, said Jonathan surely knew that both races informally dined together at southern universities and religious gatherings, despite the segregation laws. Couch sarcastically asked if he planned to establish "an inquisition" into interracial dining practices on college campuses.

Jonathan replied by saying he supported segregation but hated discrimination. "I believe I have shown that I am anxious to improve the conditions of the Negro in every particular," Jonathan wrote. "But I honestly believe . . . that the color line should be sternly drawn. I set this down in order that if it be considered treason to liberalism, my confession may be entered."[50]

In 1935, Jonathan expressed alarm when Black voters in Raleigh registered to vote to defeat a proposed city manager form of government for Raleigh—a measure the newspaper supported. Jonathan argued that poorly informed Black voters had been led by white politicians to defeat a good government proposal. "Daniels' main objections to Negro voting seemed to be that most blacks were poor and uneducated and therefore subject to manipulation by unscrupulous politicians," wrote Eagles. "As long as blacks, and perhaps even some whites, remain weak and illiterate, the paternalistic Daniels favored barring them from voting and permitting the superior whites to make society's decisions."[51] But as W. E. B. Du Bois wrote at the beginning of the century, "The power of the ballot we need in sheer defense—else what shall save us from a second slavery?"[52]

Jonathan declined to attend the landmark Southern Conference on Human Welfare, organized in Birmingham in 1938, to address the South's problems. When the conference called for the end of Jim Crow, Jonathan—almost always the racial gradualist—called it "a tragic mistake." He wrote, "It is not difficult to understand the impatience of those who watched the long suffering of the Negro in exploitation and injustice. But if progress is to be safe and sure, it must also be slow."[53]

Jonathan's views had begun to evolve in the late 1930s, accepting Blacks as voters, election officials, and trial jurors. By 1940 he argued that as a matter of "law and justice" registrars had to enroll qualified Black voting applicants. By 1941, he applauded the Wake County Board of Elections for placing Black election officials in charge of two predominantly Black precincts in Raleigh.[54]

Jonathan is often regarded as among the southern liberals or moderates of the 1930s and 1940 by such white writers as Gunnar Myrdal, John Gunther, Wilbur J. Cash, Morton Sosna, and George B. Tindall. But he was a gradualist, whose views incrementally changed from the 1930s until the 1960s.[55]

Southern Voice

During the Depression years of the 1930s, Jonathan emerged as one of the South's best-known editors—one who seemed more interested in the paper's editorial voice than in day-to-day news operations.

He was widely regarded as one of the South's leading liberals. "You are performing a highly useful service in prodding the sleeping South with keen and penetrating barbs," wrote Lucy Rudolph Mason, a leading southern union organizer. "It has to be waked up from within, not from without, and with sympathy rather than with anger."[56]

Like his father, Jonathan wanted his editorials to be hard-hitting and timely, abhorring editorial boards that sat around carefully weighing the pros and cons of an issue like some academic coffee klatch. Some of his best editorials, he once ruminated, came when "I said when my feet first hit the floor in the morning, 'I'll get that SOB today.'"[57]

"He was a short-fused editor who tried to attack the sin and not the sinner, but who so often ended up battering both," wrote colleague Herb O'Keefe. "He could be so deft in slicing up a man as a skilled surgeon with a scalpel. He could also be as blunt as a pile driver in pounding a straying Tar Heel right into the ground."[58]

Like other family members, he valued transparency. When he got a speeding ticket in Johnston County, he insisted that his paper write about it.[59]

Although Jonathan often traveled in elite circles, he did not believe in armchair journalism. His craft, not profession, Jonathan argued, had to be learned "from policemen, politicians, saints and sinners, arsonists, agitators, crusaders, and ham actors. Basically, ours is the skill of the public scold, the peeping Tom, the night watchman and the keepers of the Doomsday book."[60]

Jonathan was a terrible typist, whose fingers hit the keys harder and harder as his rage grew. He could destroy a typewriter ribbon in a few minutes, and he was known to beat a key out of his typewriter. Associates could guess how good an editorial was going to be by looking causally at the paper on which it was written to see how many holes he had punched in it with his angry typing.[61]

"Jonathan Daniels was a powerhouse of a man in personality and performance," recalled Clifton Daniel (no relation), who worked for him for four years in the 1930s and later became managing editor of the *New York Times* and President Harry Truman's son-in-law. "Jonathan held strong opinions and he strongly expressed them. The power of his voice was exceeded only by the explosiveness of his life. He immensely enjoyed being Jonathan Daniels and doing what Jonathan Daniels did."[62]

Pecking away on his typewriter in his library—the doors bolted to keep his daughters and servants at bay—Jonathan produced twenty-one books, mostly histories and biographies. He also wrote a weekly column on domestic issues called A Native at Large, which ran for twenty months in the 1940s in *The Nation*, a leading liberal magazine published in New York. While much of the magazine's essays focused on World War II, Jonathan concentrated on domestic issues such as lynching, the Okies, and filling stations, more as an observer than a crusader. The prolific editor also regularly contributed articles for other national magazines and wrote short stories and poems. He quit the column when he went to work in the Roosevelt administration. "During the 20 months of his association with *The Nation*, he has truly been a Native At Large, reporting the hopes and fears, the angers, and the issues [with] which the average American community is preoccupied," wrote *The Nation*.[63]

His best-known book, *A Southerner Discovers the South*, was prompted by a New York editor suggesting that he write about the new Tennessee Valley Authority project to produce energy for the region. The project intrigued Jonathan, who told his father that another book might "pull [him] out of the rut of non-accomplishment" and compensate for his failure to find a publisher for his second novel.[64]

To gather material, Daniels spent six weeks in 1937 traveling 3,000 miles, visiting Knoxville, Scottsboro, Little Rock, Natchez, New Orleans, Tuskegee, Atlanta, Tampa, and Charleston.

"Such a South I found," Jonathan wrote.

> I talked with governors and professors, with male and female patriots, with labor leaders and industrialists, educators and uplifters, engineers and chemists, and foresters and physicians. . . . But I also talked to hitch hikers and tenant farmers, to filling station operators, hillbillies, and Delta planters, to poets, and bartenders, to Syrians in Vicksburg and Cajuns in Louisiana, to a lovely, starry-eyed, aristocratic young woman in love with a liquor salesman, to a drunkard who lives and buys his liquor on the quarters which tourists give him for seeing the big house which his ancestors built, and everywhere to Negroes.[65]

Southern historian George Tindall called the best-seller "the most informative panorama of the South in those years."[66]

But there were also criticisms. In some instances, he used composite characters and wrote that he began the trip in Virginia when he actually started in Raleigh. He rarely interviewed Black people, believing they would not talk freely to a white stranger. Some of the racial descriptions make a modern reader blanch. Some conservative southerners accused him of fouling his own nest. But the book was perfectly timed, released on the same day the Roosevelt administration issued a report declaring the South the country's number one economic problem.

It was such a landmark study that nearly eighty years later, it was the subject of a scholarly book. "His account of his travels in *A Southerner Discovers the South*," wrote historian Jennifer Ritterhouse, "helped many readers see the region and its race and class issues more clearly and honestly than such 'extreme legends of the right and the left' as *Gone with the Wind* and *Tobacco Road*. Daniels achieved his primary goal of depicting a more complex and realistic South, whether or not he persuaded contemporary readers to support the New Deal–inspired initiatives that were trying to bring progress to his native land."[67]

A frustrated novelist, Jonathan had found his métier in longer-form nonfiction writing. Seeking to capitalize on his success, Jonathan immediately followed up with two more books—*A Southerner Discovers New England* in 1940 and *Tar Heels: A Portrait of North Carolina* in 1941.

His best-selling southern book gave him a national profile, and he was soon accepting speaking engagements at the most important universities, as well as corresponding with such famous public figures as Felix Frankfurter, Lyndon Johnson, Dean Rusk, Dean Acheson, Sumner Welles, Harry Truman, Adlai Stevenson, Eleanor Roosevelt, Gore Vidal, Sherwood Anderson, Thomas Wolfe, Archibald MacLeish, Arthur Schlesinger Jr., and Alistair Cooke.

His book on the South cemented Jonathan's place as one of the four most respected southern editors of the 1930s and 1940s, a group that also included Virginius Dabney of Richmond, Ralph McGill of Atlanta—both good friends of Jonathan—and Hodding Carter of Greenville, Mississippi. "They approached the prime of their lives and the pinnacle of their profession with a prolific and continuing output of daily columns, national magazine articles, speeches, and radio commentaries," wrote John Egerton, an astute observer of the midcentury South. "Whenever the quartet of editors wrote or spoke about the South, their words were as closely followed and as carefully listened to as those of any public figures of the time."[68]

CHAPTER TEN

Washington and Josephus's Last Days

With Addie's health failing, Josephus felt compelled to return home from Mexico in November 1941.

At age seventy-nine, Daniels resumed his twelve-hour days, editing the *News and Observer* and finishing his five-volume autobiography. Daniels had long believed that the secret of longevity was to stay active and engaged. His return meant that Jonathan was no longer the top news executive at the newspaper.

During Jonathan's first tenure as editor, 1933–42, the *News and Observer* was a full-throated backer of the New Deal—not surprising, since the proprietor was part of the Roosevelt administration. But when a New Deal critic asked Josephus whether he supported the president's program, he replied in the negative—it was too conservative, he said.

The paper supported FDR's controversial 1937 court-packing plan to enlarge a conservative US Supreme Court that had struck down some of the president's programs. "Tories hate this plan not because Roosevelt seizes power to lead but because they may lose the power to delay and destroy," the paper stated after the ambassador sent a telegram from Mexico urging editorial backing for the plan. Privately, Jonathan had his misgivings, writing to his father that he worried Republicans might reconfigure the court when they returned to power.[1]

"I am not afraid of any left dictatorship in this country," Jonathan wrote his father.

> The propertied classes are screaming terribly loud now, but the real danger in this country lies in a form of government close to fascism.

As a matter of fact, we practically had fascism under the Republican administrations which preceded Roosevelt's. My own judgement is that this country is due for a new period of get-rich-quick conservatism and that the overwhelming probability is that FDR will be succeeded by a conservative Democrat or a Republican. I'm very much afraid that he may make the powers of the executive so strong that they will be dangerous in the hands of such a man.[2]

Sharing his father's isolationist tendencies, Jonathan fretted that US entry into World War II would jeopardize FDR's New Deal and lead to anti-German hysteria. He worried about FDR's requests for increased military spending, saying, "All the Roosevelts love to run up San Juan Hill." He corresponded with aviator Charles Lindbergh, a leading isolationist, praising him for acting "almost alone as a great American patriot." A plunge into war "would divert American resources and American brains from this great American cause" (the economic recovery), Jonathan wrote.[3]

The ambassador encouraged Jonathan to provide prominent coverage of such isolationists as Lindbergh and industrialist Henry Ford. The elder Daniels was in a difficult position as a stalwart FDR supporter and an opponent of war. He suggested he might quit his post in Mexico and return to Raleigh to stand against "the folly" of another war.[4]

Just days before the outbreak of World War II, Josephus wrote to FDR urging him to hold a worldwide fireside chat calling on people to pray and petition their governments for peace. With German troops poised to invade Poland, the ambassador wrote his son: "What we have feared has burst upon us. We did everything we could, even if not in the best way, to urge the crazy Europeans not to commit suicide."[5]

A group of Jonathan's liberal friends, including UNC president Frank Porter Graham, novelist Paul Green, and William T. Couch, the head of UNC Press, urged Jonathan to support FDR's Lend-Lease program to send destroyers to England in 1940. "We believe that the destruction by Germany of the English way of living will leave the world poorer, will establish for generations a way of living in which the highest values of western civilization will be ruthlessly suppressed, in which brute force and war will be glorified, race prejudice and national hatreds cultivated, the ideal of paganism substituted for those of Christianity, and free men made slaves."[6]

Jonathan's isolationist views evolved as public support for the war grew and as the Wehrmacht marched across Europe. By March 1941, the paper was hailing congressional passage of the Lend-Lease Act and Jonathan was privately writing that while he still had reservations, "America has made its decision and . . . in our democracy I am bound by it."[7]

Despite his liberalism and his youthful flirtation with socialism, Jonathan was politically cautious. He rejected multiple requests that he join or sign petitions for liberal/left-wing groups or causes during the 1930s and 1940s. He cited a need for independence, but he was also wary of what conservative critics labeled communist-front organizations.

When he later applied for White House security clearance, he was questioned by unnamed security officials about his membership in the American Society for Peace and Intellectual Freedom and the American Committee for Non-Participation in Japanese Aggression. Jonathan said he had never heard of the former, and the latter included Secretary of War Henry Stimson. During a security interview, Jonathan declined an invitation to recant or further explain the paper's opposition to the red-hunting House Un-American Activities Committee. It didn't hurt that he had good relations with FBI director J. Edgar Hoover, an occasional lunch partner, who told Jonathan that the FBI had not been involved "in any foolish questioning" of him. Jonathan's FBI file described him as "definitely patriotic and loyal to the U.S."[8]

A restless spirit at age thirty-eight, Jonathan had been a novelist, newspaper editor, national columnist, and best-selling nonfiction writer. Now he wanted to follow his father into government service. Josephus suggested pursuing an ambassadorship in South America, but Jonathan wanted to be in Washington, proposing something along the lines of assistant secretary of the navy.

"It sounds coldly ambitious to write it down," Jonathan wrote his father, "but I want a place which would be a definite step up in the world for me. I consider the editorship of the *News and Observer* a very big job. Also, I think that in addition to it I have made some name for myself as a student of the contemporary American scene. . . . Maybe I'm merely ambitious," Jonathan continued. "If so, it is particularly your fault. I don't think much of a son who doesn't accept his father as a standard for competition. I'm racing with your career, and it is a hard race. I'm not ashamed to ask you to help me to keep up with you."[9]

With his father back at the paper, Jonathan was free to offer his services in wartime Washington. Two of his brothers joined the service—Joe Jr. once again donned his marine uniform, and Worth joined the Army Medical Corps. Frank Sr. stayed home to keep the paper operating.

Josephus lobbied FDR to hire his son, even boasting that he had dinner with FDR a few days after Pearl Harbor, although months later he acknowledged to his son that the president had been too busy to see him. Without his father's help, Jonathan likely could have landed in the Roosevelt administration. Only one in seven newspapers supported FDR's reelection in 1936. Jonathan was one of a small group of pro–New Deal editors who met at the 1936 Democratic National Convention to coordinate how to help FDR stay in the White House.[10]

"The more I see of American newspapers, the more I am convinced that they represent in nine cases out of ten, the personal slant . . . of the fellow who owns the paper," FDR wrote to Josephus in 1940. "Thank God you and the boys prove, though it is an exceptional case, ownership can still retain the old ideals of editorship."[11]

Josephus had been complaining about conservative press bias since his days with the William Jennings Bryan campaign. "When the Fathers demanded the freedom of the press, they did it not to enrich publishers but that they might be the tocsin of the people, uncontrolled by such power," Daniels wrote to a fellow diplomat in 1936. "Such papers as the *Chicago Tribune*, the *New York Herald-Tribune*, and *New York Times* and many others have ceased to be sentinels on the watchtower for the rights of people and have become protectors of wealth and privilege."[12]

Washington

Jonathan left Raleigh on February 22, 1942, to succeed First Lady Eleanor Roosevelt as director of the Civilian Mobilization Division of the Office of Civilian Defense. Jonathan and his family arrived in a city readying for war, with tens of thousands of new workers crowding into Washington and new federal buildings sprouting up everywhere. His office was in a plush converted apartment building facing Dupont Circle.

Jonathan and his wife and four daughters moved to 3404 Garfield Street in Washington, a square, three-story yellow stucco house near St. Albans School. There were hardships like rationing, but there were compensations as well, with the girls playing charades in the White House with FDR's grandchildren. Writer/poet Carl Sandburg, visiting Jonathan, read bedtime stories to the Daniels girls.[13]

For seven months, Jonathan worked at the Office of Civilian Defense, which supervised state and local defense councils and helped oversee volunteer efforts to salvage war material and conserve consumer goods. But Daniels was frustrated working for James M. Landis, a former Harvard Law School dean, who was disappointed that the agency had turned into a bureaucratic backwater. Adding to Jonathan's frustration, Landis had blocked a State Department assignment that would have sent Jonathan on a mission to India.

With Jonathan considering leaving Washington by summer, his father lobbied FDR to find a better post for him. Jonathan turned down an offer to serve on the Civil Aeronautics Board before being reassigned to the White House as a temporary troubleshooter for FDR.

His first assignment was carrying out what FDR called a "dirty job" of developing a list of wealthy young men who had landed cushy military postings in Washington, far from any combat dangers. FDR had been troubled during World War I by aristocratic young officers who had enjoyed what he called "the Saloon, the Salon, and the Salome" of DC. With the help of Hoover, Jonathan submitted a list of thirty-two men with such last names as Duke, Du Pont, Firestone, and Vanderbilt—including information about playboys bedding Hollywood actresses—to the president, who quietly ordered many of them transferred out of Washington.[14]

Jonathan almost followed his father into the Foreign Service. In March 1943, FDR nominated Jonathan to be US ambassador to New Zealand, but the nomination was blocked by Senator Josiah Bailey, a conservative North Carolina Democrat and longtime enemy of the Daniels family. Bailey was the principal architect of the Conservative Manifesto in 1937, which challenged many of FDR's New Deal programs and would become a blueprint for the ideological right. To bait Bailey, the *News and Observer* repeatedly reran the text of his speech, seconding FDR's nomination in 1936. The dispute was almost a family feud because the senator's wife, Edith Bailey, was distantly related to Addie Daniels, calling her "Aunt Addie."

The Daniels-Bailey feud can be traced back to at least 1901, when the *News and Observer* declared Bailey's paper, the *Biblical Recorder*, an organ of "corporation rule, imperialism, trusts and everything else that the National Republican Party stands for." As editor, Bailey had described the *News and Observer* as "a paper red-handed with personal and political persecution, reeking with the smell of personal ambition to rule."[15]

After FDR's reelection in 1936, there was a victory dinner in Raleigh. Bailey invited as speaker conservative Democratic senator Millard Tydings of Maryland, who criticized FDR's court-packing plan and other New Deal programs. Jonathan was so incensed that he helped organize a "Correct-the-Record" dinner a few weeks later in Raleigh, featuring Interior secretary Harold Ickes, an ardent New Dealer.

The Daniels-Bailey feud was a Raleigh legend. One story, perhaps true, was that Daniels made sure the *News and Observer* was delivered daily to the senator's home on Blount Street even though he was not a subscriber—presumably for instructional purposes. When Bailey was home, so went the story, he tossed the newspaper off his porch. Josephus had seriously considered challenging Bailey in the 1936 Democratic primary.

In a meeting with Bailey, the senator told Jonathan he was blocking his Senate confirmation because he was offended by his writings, including his description of Bailey as a person who "struts even when he sits down." Jonathan recalled Bailey saying that he was "personally obnoxious to him."[16]

In one account, Bailey said, "Young man. Would you vote for my confirmation if I were appointed to some job?" "Yes," replied Jonathan. "If it were someplace far off." To which Bailey shot back, "New Zealand isn't far enough off." The *News and Observer* ignored this juicy political feud involving its former editor and hometown senator until running an item several months later in Drew Pearson's nationally syndicated column.[17]

As a consolation, FDR named Jonathan one of six White House assistants, a position that did not require Senate confirmation. Jonathan worked out of the basement of what is now called the Eisenhower Executive Office Building—the same building where his father labored as navy secretary. He saw the president twice per week, usually after a news conference, along with other aides. His responsibilities included overseas aviation, the Department of Agriculture, the Rural Electrification Administration, wartime baseball, newsprint rationing, the Tennessee Valley Authority, selective service, and racial issues.

Jonathan was a liaison between FDR and an exceedingly ambitious young Texas congressman named Lyndon Baines Johnson, setting up meetings with the president and writing speeches for LBJ's reelection campaign in 1942. His most important role may have been helping Johnson, a lieutenant commander in the Naval Reserve, obtain some wartime experience in the Pacific to further his political career. When Johnson was in the White House, Jonathan kept an autographed photo of LBJ in his naval uniform on his newspaper office wall.[18]

He was also FDR's point man on civil aviation at a time when all new international flights were subject to presidential approval. Such industry giants as Pan American heavily lobbied Jonathan. One lobbyist sent Jonathan a coffin-size box of choice cuts of meat as a Christmas present during wartime meat rationing. Jonathan said he nailed the box up and returned it.

As a White House aide, Jonathan was in the middle of New Deal Washington—whether enjoying cocktails in House Speaker Sam Rayburn's bachelor apartment, lunch with heavyweight fighter Gene Tunney at the Mayflower Hotel, or movie nights at the White House.

Presidential Advisor on Race

Jonathan's most challenging task was advising FDR on race relations. African Americans supported FDR, with many leaving the party of Lincoln to vote for him. Complaining to friends that he didn't have enough to do in his White House post, Jonathan convinced FDR to allow him to oversee race relations beginning in the summer of 1943. "I know too well that at best this Negro question is one of the hottest, most difficult problems in the world," he wrote to FDR. "I can testify to that because I am one of those people who are suspect as radical on this question in the South and am regarded as still too conservative with regard to it by many Negroes in the North."[19] That Jonathan could be considered a radical on race relations—at least in his own view—only underscores how the South was locked in an ideological straitjacket on segregation.

Racial tensions were exacerbated by the war, as African Americans left the farm to work in defense industries and northern Black soldiers bristled at Jim Crow laws in towns near southern bases. In 1943 alone, there were 242 "racial battles" in forty-seven cities, according to Fisk University sociologist Charles S. Johnson. Race riots occurred in big cities such as Detroit and Harlem and also in smaller southern towns such as Durham, where fire destroyed four large warehouses, several private homes, a stable, a car company, and a restaurant. African Americans, who were being asked to defeat foreign dictators, wanted greater liberties and opportunities at home—an expectation represented by the so-called Double V campaign. Under the leadership of civil rights leader Ella Baker, NAACP chapters doubled in North Carolina, and membership grew to 10,000.[20]

"Here in America, we can claim that we have a democracy until we are blue in the face, we can sing our national anthem until we become hoarse," wrote Louis Austin, editor of the Durham-based *Carolina Times*. "But unless we realize the sanctity of human personality and the brotherhood of all mankind, we are going to have to pay a high price in human lives to win the war and in the end lose the peace." Austin's outspokenness made him the target of both an FBI and an IRS investigation.[21]

North Carolina governor Melville Broughton complained of a "violent and radical Negro press" writing "incendiary articles" that were menacing race relations. The new Black assertiveness generated alarm and fear of a Black rebellion in the white community, with rumors of maids forming "Eleanor Clubs" to conduct strikes or of guns purchased by African Americans through the Sears and Roebuck catalog.[22]

While not an outspoken segregationist, Jonathan's brother Frank Sr. believed in the racial status quo. In the summer of 1942, Frank Sr. wrote an alarmist letter to Jonathan accusing him of being in "with all the pinkeys and liberals tied up with the advancement of the Negro race." He said the average white working man disliked African Americans more than he did Japanese or Germans. If Blacks "keep insisting for more privileges," Frank Sr. wrote, "a worse condition is going to exist in North Carolina before very long than [in] the period from 1895 to 1902 because white people just aren't going to stand for it." If Blacks continued to push for equality, "the white people are going to rise up in arms and eliminate them from the national picture." He added that the Black push for rights "is going to mean that all of [the Black people] that can read and write are going to be eliminated in the Hitler style."[23]

Jonathan responded by trying to tamp down the talk. He penned an editorial for the *News and Observer* debunking the racial rumors, saying investigators found them baseless and that spreading such rumors hurt national unity and played into Hitler's hands. His brother was unimpressed. Frank Sr. wrote Jonathan that Eleanor Roosevelt was not welcome in the state because of her racial views and that she "ought to be kept at home and made to shut her mouth about the race question."[24]

Frank Sr. also unsuccessfully lobbied Jonathan in 1944 to keep open a tent camp recreation area in Raleigh's predominantly Black Chavis Heights neighborhood for off-duty African American troops to help keep them segregated.[25]

Shaken by his brother's letters, Jonathan wrote Lester B. Granger, head of the National Urban League, a New York–based civil rights group, saying that he had never been so disturbed by white-Black relations. While acknowledging that the Black push for equal rights "is logically strong," he warned that continued racial conflicts could lead to a fascist victory by the Nazis, or a fascist movement in the United States. Either way, Jonathan warned, the rise of fascism would hurt both Black aspirations and suppress liberalism.[26]

Writing to his friend Howard W. Odum, the noted UNC sociologist, on the same theme, Jonathan said, "I am more disturbed about race relations in the United States than I have ever been before. We seem to be almost back to the extreme abolitionists and the extreme slaveholders in the lines of discussion. Between them, people like ourselves seem to me to be left in a sort of awareness and futility together."[27]

Faced with ending the Great Depression and then winning the war, FDR attempted to avoid racially loaded issues for fear of alienating influential southern congressional leaders. By 1940, FDR was beginning to lose some Black support.

For a year and half, Jonathan's job was to monitor race issues and to keep a lid on unrest. He assembled a network of sources across the country on racial matters, tapping into eighteen federal agencies and examining newspapers serving Black communities. Jonathan had a Black deputy, and he developed ties with African Americans. He complained to his father that the Roosevelt administration was in "a tough spot," caught between southern white racists such as Mississippi senator Theodore Bilbo and the "extreme radical leadership of the colored people."[28]

One of the many flashpoints occurred in Hanford, Washington, where the atomic bomb was being developed as part of the Manhattan Project. Latino workers objected to being housed in the same dormitory as Black workers, but whites did not want to share accommodations with either group. Jonathan's solution was the construction of a third dormitory—with separate sleeping facilities for whites, Blacks, and Latinos—a similar situation to North Carolina's Robeson County, where there were separate school systems for whites, Blacks, and Native Americans.[29]

In 1944, Jonathan played a role in racially integrating the White House press conference, giving credentials to Harry McAlpin, a Black journalist, despite opposition from the White House Press Association. He lobbied the administration for more Black farm extension agents. He interceded on behalf of a Jewish airman—a former labor organizer—who was thrown into the brig when he complained of Black soldiers being mistreated at a Nebraska army base.[30]

But more often, Jonathan served as a brake on racial progress. He opposed creating a separate facility at FDR's Warm Springs facility for Black sufferers of infantile paralysis, leaving the center for whites only. He helped shoot down the idea of FDR adding a Black staff assistant. He suggested the attorney general postpone prosecution of the state of Alabama for blocking Black voting in Democratic primaries. He urged caution in opposing discriminatory practices of Washington's Capital Transit Company.[31]

He successfully recommended to FDR that the nation's first governmental agency devoted to racial inequality—the Fair Employment Practices Commission (FEPC), which FDR created as part of a deal to get civil rights leaders to drop a planned march on Washington in 1941—be declawed by moving it from semi-independent status and placing it under the control of a White House aide hostile to civil rights. The FEPC "was strangled in the house of its putative friends," Lawrence C. Cramer, the FEPC's executive secretary, wrote to Jonathan decades later. Jonathan would later say that his most important role was "to protect the war effort from tensions" rather than to "advance the Black people."[32]

Jonathan was almost certainly doing the bidding of FDR, who saw the push for civil rights as both a distraction from the war effort and as a threat to his New Deal coalition, which included white southerners. Although he may have been the liberal driving force of the twentieth century, FDR's views on race were stuck in an earlier age. Jonathan recalled FDR ridiculing Eleanor, mimicking her voice, saying, "Franklin, something has got to be done. The Negroes are not getting a fair deal." Civil rights attorney Thurgood Marshall, a future Supreme Court justice, accidentally overheard FDR in a phone conversation threatening to fire his attorney general if he scheduled any more phone calls with "Eleanor's n———s."[33]

White House Press Secretary

In January 1945, Jonathan was promoted to acting White House press secretary, replacing Stephen T. Early, who left for a private sector job. Jonathan was sworn in on March 29. The new job meant a government car and chauffeur for the first time—no small thing with wartime gas rationing. Jonathan wrote a friend that it was "a change of status almost like moving from the bleachers to the boxes."[34]

Jonathan became press secretary to a dying man who had only weeks to live. Close contact with FDR, including a morning meeting in the president's bedroom, with the chief executive wearing cigarette-burned pajamas and a loose bed cape, left him shocked at his rapid decline.

When FDR attended the Yalta Conference with Joseph Stalin and Winston Churchill in February 1945, he was so sick that Jonathan found some of the photographs "appalling." He chose the least unflattering photos for distribution to hide the president's dramatic decline from heart congestion. Jonathan misled the public, saying, "I have never seen the president looking so well. He is in grand shape." When a *Washington Post* reporter began raising questions about FDR's health, Jonathan visited him at his home to accuse him of falling for "French propaganda," assuring him FDR was fine.[35]

At one point, Anna Boettiger, FDR's daughter who lived in the White House and often acted as a hostess for her father, sought Jonathan's help in forming a protective ring around the president, screening visitors. Recalling the disabilities of the stroke-stricken Woodrow Wilson, Jonathan thought such an arrangement would be disastrous, providing too much power to the unelected, and nothing came of it.[36]

Jonathan Daniels (*in profile at left*) as President Truman's press secretary, briefing reporters on May 7, 1945, on the pending end of World War II. (Courtesy of Harris & Ewing, Harry S. Truman Library and Museum.)

The charade could not continue. Roosevelt died at his retreat at Warm Springs, Georgia, on April 12, 1945, of a cerebral hemorrhage. Early announced FDR's death, shouldering Jonathan aside, much to his irritation.

Jonathan was one of several aides in the Oval Office when Vice President Harry Truman sat behind the president's desk for the first time, having cleared the Resolute Desk of FDR's belongings but leaving everything else in the Oval office untouched. Feeling crushed and resentful, Jonathan said that Truman seemed "almost sacrilegiously small. . . . It seemed still Roosevelt's desk and Roosevelt's room. It seemed to me, indeed, almost Roosevelt's sun which came in the wide south windows and touched Truman's thick glasses."[37] Jonathan first judged Truman "tragically inadequate" for the job but soon changed his mind.[38]

Josephus was with best-selling writer John Gunther in Raleigh when he learned of FDR's death, retiring to bed all day sobbing at the news. Both Josephus and Jonathan rode the FDR funeral train from Raleigh to Hyde Park and then rode back to Washington with Truman as tens of thousands of mourning Americans lined the tracks.

Washington and Josephus's Last Days

Jonathan had the shortest tenure of any presidential press secretary to that point. Truman asked Jonathan to stay on for more than a month until his new press secretary, newsman Charles G. Ross, a high school classmate of Truman's, could take over on May 20. He offered Jonathan the job of director of the Rural Electrification Administration, which he declined.

The idea of returning to the paper under his father seems to have given him pause, and he sought a larger platform for his talents. For several months, Jonathan worked with Norman Cousins, the editor-in-chief of the *Saturday Review of Literature*, to start a general interest magazine, which would be a liberal alternative to such popular publications as the *Saturday Evening Post* and *Collier's*. Although the project had the tentative backing of Chicago retail magnate Marshall Field Jr., it never got off the ground. Jonathan also resumed writing, contributing articles to national magazines and completing his book, *Frontier on the Potomac*, and he did considerable public speaking.

Never afraid of controversy, Jonathan traveled to Richmond, where he criticized Virginia's poll tax, calling Virginia "both the cradle and the graveyard of democracy." That brought a retort from Virginia governor William M. Tuck, a lieutenant in the conservative machine of Senator Harry Byrd that controlled state politics, calling Jonathan "a disappointed and frustrated North Carolina politician who apparently is not taken too seriously even in his home state." Tuck said he did not know what qualified Jonathan to speak "unless it be that recently he secured a position as editor of his father's own newspaper."[39]

In February 1947, almost two years after he left the White House, the *News and Observer* announced that Jonathan was returning as executive editor overseeing the news operation, while his father, as president, remained in charge of the editorial page.

Not that Jonathan was happy being number two on the paper. His daughter Lucy said her father often seemed angry and discouraged. "It's terrible to have to live your life in another man's shadow," she remembers him grumbling. "We sometimes overheard him complaining to Mommy about problems with Grandfather's editorials or [brother] Frank's 'stupidity.' Mostly when we were with him, he was drinking bourbon peacefully or raging at or ridiculing someone—either one of us or a guest."[40]

World War II had changed the newspaper. Because of a newspaper print shortage, the paper was smaller. And with the male reporters off to war, the paper was mainly staffed by women. During the 1930s, the *News and Observer* newsroom had been a predominantly male bastion, with women, such as Nell Battle Lewis, working in a pink ghetto called the society page.

The paper hired five young women just out of college during the war; most had no experience or journalism training. Herb O'Keefe, an editor before being drafted in December 1942, conducted an after-hours journalism school for them, carefully going over carbon copies of their stories to point out mistakes or improvements. The women had successful careers—Marjorie Hunter became a mainstay in the Washington bureau of the *New York Times*, Jane Hall became the paper's first art critic, Margaret "Bette" Elliot started a newspaper and became a TV personality, and Frances Newsome became an executive with the state nurses' association.

Among the reporters who went off to war was sports editor Sam R. McDonald, twenty-two, who was killed in 1942 when his army bomber crashed. Reporter Jim Rankin served as a navy torpedo bomber pilot in the Pacific, rising to become a lieutenant commander. He survived World War II and Korea unscathed only to be wounded in the chest and shoulder—although not seriously—while covering a violent labor strike at a textile mill in Wake Forest for the *News and Observer* in 1951.

After Jonathan criticized the wartime paper—it was only eight pages one day—Frank Sr. replied, "I do not think local coverage by the *News and Observer* is a bit good, but then I do not know what we can do with only three girls and one man left."[41]

The wartime *News and Observer* could be shrill at times. It scolded North Carolinians who refused to cooperate with a blackout test in an editorial titled "Public Enemies."[42] But the paper did not engage in the hysteria whipped up by the *Charlotte Observer*, which claimed there were 2,000 subversives operating in the Charlotte area, including a spy ring in Salisbury. An FBI investigation found the charges groundless.[43]

Daniels's paper remained liberal on most issues. Josephus decried talk about the "Yellow Peril" as it applied to the Japanese, opposed excessive war censorship and war profiteering, and was angered by General George Patton's slapping of two shell-shocked soldiers. Josephus criticized British imperialist aims to restore European monarchies, argued for an independent India, and attacked proposals to require UNC faculty to take loyalty oaths.

With so many sons and fathers serving overseas, there was intense interest in war news. The 1940s saw the paper's most significant circulation gains, rising from 61,961 in 1940 to 112,034 in 1950. During the war, the paper frequently ran photos of "Tar Heels in the War Zone" and stories about those who were killed in action or had earned medals for their bravery. After the war, as the GIs returned home to start families, there was a surge in newspaper readership in the pre-television age.[44]

Josephus's Last Days

Josephus spent his last six years working in harness, surrounded by mementos of his career. On the walls of his newspaper office were the roosters that had once been the symbol of the Democratic Party—four of them on framed front pages proclaiming FDR's elections. In his study at Wakestone, there was a large Mexican flag given him by President Manuel Ávila Camacho when Daniels left Mexico "so you will always be under the Mexican flag."[45] Lining the walls were fifty original editorial cartoons featuring Daniels—collected by Addie—and thousands of books.

Spurgeon Fields, his Black chauffeur and valet, eased Josephus's routine, helping him dress and undress, giving him an alcohol rub twice a day, and helping him get in and out of the bathtub. Fields grew up on a farm near Oxford, holding several jobs before beginning work for Josephus in the late 1930s. After Josephus died, Fields became the chauffeur for his son Frank Daniels Sr. when he suffered macular degeneration. Fields died in 1994 at age eighty-seven.

On days when his chauffeur was unavailable, the non-driving Josephus rode a bus to the office and once even hitched a ride on a garbage truck.

After putting in a couple of hours at the office, Josephus would return home to work on his books. Josephus wrote a five-part autobiography—a stunning 3,004 pages that dwarfed even the longest presidential autobiographies. He quipped that his books should be bulky enough to be used as deadly weapons.

In the postwar era, Josephus's liberalism did not flag. He fought the passage in 1947 of North Carolina's right-to-work law, saying he had operated the *News and Observer* as a union shop for more than fifty years. He said working people were entitled "to just compensation, a voice in working conditions and wages, and collective bargaining."[46]

Underscoring the complexity of race and politics, Josephus, a UNC trustee since 1901, blocked an effort by a fellow trustee to oust sociologist Guy B. Johnson for publicly advocating racial integration in 1947. He also opposed efforts to cut the university's ties to the Chicago-based Rosenwald Fund because it was pro-integration. Josephus had not changed his segregationist views. But just like his stance on the teaching of evolution in the 1920s, Josephus often stood with UNC, even though it meant going against his personal beliefs.[47]

In defending segregation, Josephus argued that Black schools should be equal to white ones. When 400 Black students struck in Lumberton to protest the poor quality of their school in 1946, Daniels said school officials had a "sacred" obligation to provide equal facilities and urged state and local action to remedy the situation.[48]

While Josephus grew more liberal about some things, according to Jonathan he "was more fiercely rigid about the racial question." He was offended by Harry Truman's landmark President's Committee on Civil Rights in 1947, which recommended a more active role by the federal government in ensuring equal treatment of African Americans.[49]

Josephus still had plenty of political juice. He cut a deal to get the legislature to add the twelfth grade of high school in 1943 in exchange for him agreeing not to push for a statewide referendum outlawing alcohol. He used his clout with FDR to help land the World War II US Navy Pre-Flight School in Chapel Hill—a move that helped keep the campus open during the war years. Earlier, Josephus used his influence with FDR to change the Blue Ridge Parkway from its original proposed route through Tennessee to one through North Carolina. He played a role in creating Camp Lejeune Marine Corps Base on the coast, reminding FDR of how much he enjoyed pheasant hunting in the area when he was assistant navy secretary. The camp was named after General John A. Lejeune, who was Daniels's marine commander in Europe in World War I.[50]

Addie continued to deteriorate, suffering from congestive heart failure and arthritis. She died December 19, 1943, at age seventy-four, insisting on attending a speech by Vice President Henry Wallace in Chapel Hill the day before. Not only had Addie raised a family of four boys, but she had been outspoken on behalf of women's rights. She had entertained elegantly—although abstemiously—in Washington and Mexico City. As the granddaughter of a governor, she was not intimidated by presidents, statesmen, and industrialists. She was friends with Eleanor Roosevelt and a trustee at Peace College and Rex Hospital, becoming the first woman chair of the latter. She was also an important voice in opposing the proposed expansion of the state capitol in 1903 with large wings on the north and south, which the *News and Observer* described as "vandalism."[51]

Her funeral service was at First Presbyterian Church. In 1944, the Liberty ship the USS *Addie Bagley Daniels* was launched in Savannah, Georgia.

Josephus's devotion to left-wing politics remained undimmed. He introduced California congresswoman Helen Gahagan Douglas to a Raleigh audience; several years later, Republican Richard Nixon would attack her as the "Pink Lady" in winning his Senate seat. Daniels's old friend former vice president Henry Wallace had become so politically radioactive that the University of California at Berkley had denied him permission to speak. But when

Wallace brought his Crusade for Peace to Raleigh in 1947, Josephus not only shared a stage with him in racially integrated Memorial Auditorium—along with actress Ava Gardner—but made him his houseguest. He greeted him with an editorial titled "Man of the Courage of His Convictions." Wallace, in turn, singled out Josephus as one of the four leading progressives in the South. (Josephus pinched the bottom of a student standing on her tiptoes at the rally, according to Junius Scales, a young communist leader. If true, it was uncharacteristic of Daniels.)[52]

In his final months, Daniels made what turned out to be a goodbye tour. In June 1947 he gave a speech saluting FDR in Warm Springs, Georgia, Roosevelt's southern White House. In November, he was in New York City for a Woodrow Wilson Foundation dinner, sitting on the rostrum between Mrs. Woodrow Wilson and Eleanor Roosevelt. While in New York, he made a side trip to Hyde Park, where he spent the day with Eleanor Roosevelt, touring the grounds of FDR's home and reminiscing about their thirty-five years of friendship. On December 18 he visited Truman in the White House. Earlier, Truman had designated him "a special advisor" so that Josephus could say he worked in every Democratic administration during his life.

He died less than a month later. He had worked Friday, January 2, 1948, at the paper and attended church Sunday morning, but by that afternoon he had come down with a cold, which turned into bronchitis and then pneumonia. By the end of the week, he could not get out of bed, and by the following week he had drifted into a coma. As he battled for twelve days, the family received telephone calls from Truman, Mexican president Miguel Alemán, Eleanor Roosevelt, Bernard Baruch, and others seeking news. Newspapers across the country ran stories updating readers on his condition.

He died January 15, 1948, at Wakestone surrounded by family. He was eighty-five, having been born during the roar of cannons of the Civil War and having lived through two World Wars, a Depression, and the dawn of the atomic age.

Flags were lowered to half-mast on US naval vessels and installations worldwide. Hundreds who could not fit into Edenton Street Methodist Church braved the cold rain to wait outside. The navy sent a flower arrangement in the shape of an anchor, and North Carolina newspaper editors sent flowers in the shape of the number 30, the traditional symbol used in newspapers to end stories. There was a navy bluejacket and a marine to act as an honor guard and another sailor to play taps at Oakwood Cemetery. Among those attending the service were Eleanor Roosevelt and Edith Wilson, the widows of the last two presidents for whom he had served.

Eight Black men who had worked for Daniels or for the newspaper carried his body.

It is one of the ironies of the segregated South that while there was gross inequality, affluent white southerners such as Daniels lived cheek-by-jowl with Black people all their lives. In Daniels's case, he lived much of his life in a Black neighborhood, ate food prepared by Black cooks, was dressed and driven by Black servants, and was buried by Black body bearers.

By the time of his death, Daniels's role in the white supremacy campaigns had, if not been forgotten, receded into the background. None of the countless obituaries or editorials following his death mentioned his role in implementing and maintaining Jim Crow. The United States was still a racially segregated country—it was the law in the South and the custom in the North. Fifty years after Daniels's role in the white supremacy campaigns, almost every aspect of life across the country was segregated—including most colleges, the military, most neighborhoods, churches, and professional sports.

So Daniels's racism was unremarkable in 1948 America and therefore was not remarked upon. As judged by his contemporaries, Josephus Daniels was a great man—an underappreciated navy secretary, a peace-seeking envoy to Mexico, and a feisty southern liberal newspaper editor.

"A distinguished statesman," declared the *New York Times*. "Josephus Daniels was the greatest individual influence for the good of North Carolina the state has ever known," asserted the *High Point Enterprise*. "The greatest living Southerner," stated the *Atlanta Constitution*. Only the *Washington Post* struck a more skeptical note. "Josephus Daniels' generally fruitful and happy life was not without an element of tragedy. The tragedy was that he belonged psychologically to an agrarian America that no longer exists."[53]

Each generation views public figures through its own lens. By 2020, in the wake of public outrage over the slaying of Black citizens by white police officers and the rise of the Black Lives Matter movement, there was a renewed effort to dismantle statues connected to the Confederacy or of political leaders who advocated white supremacy. In June 2020, the Daniels family removed the Josephus statue from a public park across from what had been the *News and Observer* offices, and the Wake County Board of Education voted to rename Daniels Middle School. Campus buildings at North Carolina State and UNC were also renamed.

In an interesting historical footnote, Josephus's mansion was torn down in 2021 after it was stripped of its historical status. But the home of his Black chauffeur and servant, known as the Graves-Field House, was in 2024 the headquarters for Preservation NC, a nonprofit devoted to preserving old homes and other buildings.

He left an estate valued at $344,130 ($4.5 million in 2024 dollars), dividing it equally among his four sons. He had previously given half ownership of the paper to his sons in the 1920s, taking advantage of a Republican congressional measure repealing the gift tax. His sons donated his library, including 4,000 books and other items, to the UNC library. He left $500 (more than $6,525 in 2024 dollars) to his "friend and chauffeur" Spurgeon Fields and $100 each ($1,305 in 2024 dollars) to his gardener and maid.[54]

In his will, he noted that he had twice turned down lucrative offers to sell the paper and hoped that his descendants would do the same. He said he had never viewed the *News and Observer* "as property but [as] having an unpurchasable soul."[55]

In his last testament, he wrote, "I advise and enjoin those who direct the paper in the tomorrows never to advocate any cause for personal profit or preferment. I wish it always to be 'the tocsin' and devote itself to the policies of equality and justice to the underprivileged. If the paper should at any time be the voice of self-interest or become the spokesman of privilege or selfishness, it would be untrue to its history." This injunction appeared in some version on the *News and Observer* masthead until June 2019.[56]

"And now," announced the *High Point Enterprise*, "the 'Old Man'—North Carolina's finest citizen and most courageous editor and publisher— is dead. To his four sons—especially those now connected to the paper—falls the task of running the semi-public institution which the *News and Observer* has become."[57]

CHAPTER ELEVEN

Triumph and Despair

During the two years following his father's death, Jonathan Daniels plunged into two of the most famous political campaigns of midcentury America—one a stunning triumph and the other leaving him in despair.

Hardly anyone thought Harry Truman, the accidental president, would be elected to a four-year term in 1948. The Democratic Party was under assault from both the political Left and the Right—from Henry Wallace and his leftist, anti–Cold War Progressive Party, and from Strom Thurmond and his segregationist Dixiecrat Party. Most political analysts had conceded the race to New York governor Thomas Dewey, the Republican candidate, and the polls bolstered their judgment. The GOP was riding political momentum, having won control of Congress in the 1946 midterm elections.

No one had to explain the Democratic Party's plight to Jonathan, with segregationist sentiment strong in North Carolina and Wallace an old family friend. His eldest daughter, Elizabeth, worked in Wallace's campaign. Violence greeted Wallace during a campaign swing through North Carolina in August and September—he was pummeled with rotten fruit and prevented from speaking. The crude treatment drew criticism from Truman and North Carolina governor Gregg Cherry (1945–49). But Jonathan had little sympathy for his former Roosevelt administration colleague, scolding him in an editorial headlined "Like a Communist Bullet." "Henry Wallace came into the South not wishing to understand it but to irritate it. He has left the South not wishing to understand it but to use his unfortunate experiences in it as propaganda in the north and in the world."[1]

As Thurmond stumped across the state, Jonathan denounced "bush-league secessionists" who would deprive the South of "effective participation in the making of national decisions on the questions of race." But Jonathan avoided directly discussing segregation.[2]

The Dixiecrat threat grew out of Truman's appointment of the Committee on Civil Rights. The committee identified Jim Crow as a national problem and proposed a federal effort to ensure the rights of Black people. Outrage across the South greeted Truman's civil rights proposals, with most North Carolina politicians writing off Truman's chances of carrying the state and expressing fear that he would pull down the entire Democratic ticket. The *Charlotte Observer* denounced the civil rights program and left little doubt that it favored Dewey for president.

Jonathan was a lonely voice in North Carolina defending Truman as "a friend of the South" while offering a more nuanced response to the civil rights recommendations than his father had six months earlier. Jonathan supported specific civil rights proposals such as a federal anti-lynching law—which he had previously opposed—while opposing poll taxes, which North Carolina had abolished in 1920 but which eight mostly southern states still had on the books.

Jonathan was trying to hold together the fraying New Deal coalition. "Shun like equally venomous snakes the reactionaries and the leftists who today are engaged in trying to tear apart the liberal Democratic Party which is the hope of the South and the world," Jonathan told a Young Democrats club at UNC Chapel Hill in March 1948. Jonathan said he did not agree with all of Truman's civil rights recommendations. "But all the traditions of the Democratic Party in North Carolina, however, are in line with the goals the president seeks in the elimination of lynching, the freedom of the franchise and greater economic opportunity for the Negroes of the state."[3]

Jonathan was caught in a vise between Black voices pushing for more change and the paper's largely white readership, some of whom felt the *News and Observer* was too sympathetic to Black interests.

After his Chapel Hill speech, Paul R. Jervey Sr., editor of the *Carolinian*, a Black-owned newspaper in Raleigh, hailed Daniels as a "voice in the wilderness." Jervey wrote, "It might be said that Mr. Daniels' statement could have been much more vigorous in approval of civil rights legislation, but it is certainly true that in his speech before the students he had said more than any other prominent North Carolinian has said for the record."[4]

One white reader, C. C. Stone of Bailey, wrote a letter suggesting that Jonathan, Eleanor Roosevelt, Henry Wallace, Frank Graham, and Truman "ought to be deported to central Africa and turned loose on the banks of the Belgian Congo River where they would meet their social equals." Stone said the paper should change its name to "The Afro American Journal for the Advancement of N——s and Social Equality."[5]

S. Burke, a reader from Currie, complained about the paper's stance on race. "It is a far cry from the days when Josephus Daniels was one of the champions of white Supremacy to the puling thing the N&O has become now on its editorial page. Do you actually want it so your mother, wife or daughter cannot sit on a bus, in a theater, a café or any other public space without having a Negro sit by her? If so, you should move up North where the fondest dreams are to make of the proud people of the South a mongrel race of half-breeds—mulattos."[6]

Southern scholar John Egerton saw in Jonathan a conflicted man. "Jonathan Daniels was not entirely liberated from the old Southern habits of segregation when he went home to Raleigh in 1945," Egerton wrote. "But he was comfortable with diversity, and he certainly knew that momentous changes were bearing down urgently upon the South. He must have known, too, that when the crunch finally came, the only real choice open to him would be to leave the segs and take a lonely stand on the other side."[7]

By the fall, most political observers thought Truman was a dead man walking, with all signs pointing to a Dewey victory. The president embarked on something that had not been tried since William Jennings Bryan—an extensive whistle-stop tour that earned a place in American political lore.

One of the people the president wanted at his side was Jonathan, a Democratic wordsmith with a penchant for partisan rhetoric who helped Truman "give 'em hell."

Jonathan boarded the Ferdinand Magellan on September 17 in Baltimore—a private railroad car sheathed with bulletproof glass and armor plate for protection, preceded by a pilot engine to detonate any planted bombs. The seventeen-car train traveled 21,928 miles.

Before "the boys on the bus," there were "the boys on the train," which was equipped with two bars and a dining car. As part of the president's campaign brain trust, Jonathan wrote speeches for Truman and worked politicians who joined the train to have their backs slapped, knock down a few bourbons, smoke some stogies, and exchange jokes.[8]

After the first stage of the trip, Jonathan wanted to return to Raleigh, but Truman insisted he stay for the duration. The president wrote Jonathan's wife, Lucy: "I am very apologetic because I am taking your husband away from home, but he is making a tremendous contribution to the welfare of the country by going with me."[9]

The whistle-stop tour excluded the South, a traditional Democratic stronghold aflame over Truman's civil rights proposals. Jonathan was more optimistic about Truman's chances than North Carolina's Democratic establishment, which feared that the president was so toxic he might bring down the state Democratic ticket. Jonathan arranged for Truman to visit Raleigh on October 16 to open the state fair and to unveil the monument on the state capitol grounds to the three North Carolina natives who had become president. It was the first presidential visit to Raleigh since Republican Theodore Roosevelt spoke at the state fair in 1906. Truman drew huge crowds—75,000 at the fair and 25,000 along the motorcade route.

Despite being an unpaid campaign consultant, Jonathan wrote "an appraisal" of Truman for the *News and Observer*, touting the president's Confederate heritage and rural Baptist roots and arguing that he never called for ending segregation. Jonathan presumably found it reassuring that Truman still sometimes referred to Black people as "n——s." When Jonathan was later researching a Truman biography, the president's sister, Mary Jane, told him, "Harry is no more for n——r equality than any of us."[10]

Jonathan's dual role as editor and campaign advisor troubled conservatives, such as syndicated columnist Westbrook Pegler, who asked him years later, "How can you square your position as an editor with your partisanship and participation in the Truman regime?" Jonathan responded by noting how his father had once helped Pegler but did not address his question.[11]

Back in Raleigh in time for Election Day, Jonathan told his managing editor to ready the crowing red rooster—a Democratic Party symbol the paper printed during party victories.

Jonathan went to bed with the race too close to call. At 4 a.m., Truman woke him up with a call from Kansas City. "Well, Jonathan, we're in," the president said. Jonathan was on an early morning flight to Washington the next day when Dewey conceded. The *News and Observer* held off on the crowing Democratic rooster, running it two days after the election.[12]

Truman had pulled off one of the biggest upsets in American political history. He easily carried North Carolina, winning 58 percent of the vote, his second-highest vote margin of any state. Jonathan had been right about Truman's prospects in the state, and nearly every Democratic official in the state had been wrong. Party leaders had underestimated Truman's plainspoken, feisty, common-man appeal.

Just as his father had helped put Wilson in the White House in 1912, Jonathan could claim some modest credit for Truman's historic upset.

Truman headed to Key West, Florida, for a two-week post-election vacation of swimming, sunning, poker playing, and whiskey drinking at a submarine base that had become known as the Harry Truman Little White House. He brought along his cronies, including Jonathan, whom he picked up in New Bern, where he attended a service at First Baptist Church, fulfilling a campaign promise.

After ten days, Jonathan left, bringing home an offer to be the next US Navy secretary. Jonathan accepted on the spot, intrigued by the idea of holding the same post as his father. But there soon were difficulties. His wife, Lucy, did not want to move back to Washington. And the navy job had shrunk since his father's day, now reporting to Defense Secretary Louis Johnson, the leading Truman fundraiser, who opposed Jonathan's appointment. Jonathan eventually declined the offer.[13]

But Jonathan was now a White House insider, often dropping in to chat with the president and exchanging dozens of letters, which Truman always signed as "Harry." He obtained Truman's cooperation in writing an authorized biography, which became a bestseller in 1950, called *The Man of Independence*.

Jonathan toured war-torn Europe after Truman appointed him to the United Nations Sub-Commission on Prevention of Discrimination and Protection of Minorities. But Jonathan's segregationist views were sometimes a liability on the world stage. A Soviet diplomat charged that Jonathan was "more interested in protecting the right to discriminate against Negros than in preventing discrimination."[14]

Jonathan performed small favors for Truman. When there were disappointing advance sales for a Raleigh concert for his daughter, Margaret Truman, a striving concert pianist, Jonathan arranged for several local orphanages to receive tickets to pack the house.[15]

In February 1949, party officials elected Jonathan as the state's Democratic National Committeeman—representing North Carolina in national party circles—a post his father once held. Although some Democrats thought he was too liberal, Jonathan had the backing of newly elected governor W. Kerr Scott, a progressive maverick who had defeated the state's political machine.

Except for Charles Brantley Aycock and future governor Terry Sanford, no North Carolina political figure enjoyed such a close relationship with the *News and Observer*. When Scott ran for state agriculture commissioner in 1936, Josephus wrote to his son from Mexico, ordering preferential treatment. After Scott's election to the farm post, Josephus urged Jonathan to stop printing critical stories about Scott. "Kerr is not a great man, and he is not always wise, but he is such an improvement on his predecessor and such a great friend of ours, as was his father before him, that I should like us to treat him with every possible consideration," Josephus wrote in 1938.[16]

After serving as an independent voice and sometime critic within the Democratic Party for fifty years, the *News and Observer*, according to one detractor, was "working hand in glove with the governor of the state." Other critics went further. As conservative columnist Eula Nixon Greenwood put it, "It becomes more apparent every day that [Jonathan] Daniels is the boss of the Democratic Party in North Carolina."[17]

Dr. Frank

After US senator J. Melville Broughton died of a heart attack in March 1949, having served just two months in office, Scott asked Jonathan whom he should appoint to replace him.

When the governor shared some fifty names of possible Senate appointees, Jonathan noted the absence of the name of Frank Porter Graham, president of UNC. Scott relit his cigar and asked, "Well, do you suppose we can get him?" Jonathan replied he hoped so, and the governor dispatched him to Chapel Hill.[18] Graham initially rejected the idea, saying there were projects he wanted to wrap up at the consolidated university before his retirement. Jonathan wore him down over nine days by appealing to his sense of duty. Graham had answered his country's call before: he had joined the US Marines during World War I, had settled labor disputes for FDR during World War II, had served on Truman's Committee on Civil Rights, and was dispatched to Southeast Asia to negotiate the independence of Indonesia.

Graham was both a beloved avuncular figure and strongly disliked because of his social activism, especially for his push to reduce poverty and improve the plight of Black people and for his support of union-organizing efforts.

Josephus had closer ties to Graham than did his son. Josephus had tried to hire Graham for his navy staff and had written a letter helping Graham enlist in the marines after being rejected because of his short stature and poor eyesight. Graham had tutored one of the Daniels boys at a Raleigh public school, and Daniels had lobbied Graham to accept the UNC presidency in 1930 and had later offered to return from Mexico to fend off the "reactionaries [who] resent you making the University the dynamo of justice and liberalism and democracy."[19]

Appointing Graham to the Senate in 1949 was one thing, but getting voter approval in the subsequent election in 1950 was quite another because of Graham's liberalism. In a letter to Eleanor Roosevelt, Jonathan wrote that the "only possible way" his opponents "could defeat Frank would be in a horrible n——r-communist campaign."[20]

Graham's chief opponents in the Democratic Senate primary were Willis Smith, a prominent Raleigh lawyer, and former two-term senator Robert Reynolds from Asheville, a populist showman seeking a political comeback.

Jonathan should have remained neutral based on journalist ethics, his father's example of neutrality in primaries, and the sensitivity of his post as a DNC member. But having recruited his old friend into the race, Jonathan was not about to stay on the sidelines. He immersed himself in the contest, using the paper as a pro-Graham megaphone, ignoring negative stories about Graham, participating irregularly in strategy sessions, raising campaign money among Truman's network of supporters, and asking President Truman for help. He later described himself—along with the campaign manager—as a "principal sort of first lieutenant" in the campaign.[21]

Nor was Jonathan above questionable tactics. He asked the White House to dig up dirt on Reynolds's World War I record, but nothing was found harmful to Reynolds.[22]

Jonathan became a campaign issue. Rivals called Jonathan the "real behind the scenes campaign manager" and claimed he was Graham's "undisputed political boss." The *Durham Sun*, a pro-Smith paper, ran an editorial cartoon portraying Jonathan and Scott as puppeteers pulling Graham's strings. Reynolds called Jonathan the "self-appointed commissar of North Carolina politics."[23]

The 1950 Senate primary was one of the most vicious in North Carolina history. Smith supporters first portrayed Graham as sympathetic to communists and, when that did not work, pivoted to racial appeals—an issue on which he was vulnerable, having served as one of two southerners on Truman's Committee on Civil Rights. The Smith campaign further accused Graham of being a stalking horse for racial integration and fanned racial hysteria not seen in North Carolina since Josephus helped lead the white supremacy campaigns.

This time, the *News and Observer* was on the receiving end of racial animus. The reaction of some readers to the paper's endorsement of Graham was bitter. Someone at the Carolina Country Club spat in Frank Sr.'s face. Sam Ragan, the managing editor, received telephone threats and verbal harassment. Jonathan forbade his children to answer the phone because of obscene calls. On at least one occasion, stones were thrown at Jonathan's house. Even the newspaper office offered little sanctuary, with Nell Battle Lewis, now a conservative Smith backer, screaming at Jonathan, "I hope all your children have n———r babies."[24]

In a letter to Truman, Jonathan described Smith's bid as "a Dixiecrat campaign coated with sugar at the high level and operated with brass knuckles at the precinct level." Unlike the campaigns of noted southern racist politicians such as Senator Eugene Talmadge of Georgia and Governor Theodore Bilbo of Mississippi, Jonathan wrote, Smith's campaign was the "cold-blooded, advertising agency technique employed to arouse prejudices for the purpose of reactionary politics."[25]

A week before the primary, Jonathan wrote a signed editorial titled "Sound the Tocsin." He praised Graham and noted his father's devotion to him. "The attacks on Frank Graham have turned this primary from an election into an assault on decency, character, and service in North Carolina," Jonathan wrote. "It is time for the 'tocsin' of Democratic decency to ring across North Carolina."[26]

Graham led the May 27 primary with 48.9 percent, followed by Smith with 20.5 percent and Reynolds with 9.3 percent. Because Graham did not win a majority, Smith called for a runoff for June 24. Stepping up the race tactics, Smith won with 51.7 percent compared to 48.2 percent for Graham.

As the Smith supporters gathered in the ballroom of the Sir Walter Hotel in downtown Raleigh, they sang a popular campaign ditty: "We'll hang Dice Daniels from a sour apple tree, while we go marching on."[27]

A stunned Jonathan wrote the president, "I didn't believe what happened on Saturday could happen in North Carolina, but I have never seen the effectiveness of race fear and race hatred in a political campaign before. The nearest thing I ever saw to it was what happened in the Al Smith campaign in 1928." Of course, Jonathan was born after his father's white supremacy campaigns.[28]

The campaign left Jonathan in despair and increasingly in the political wilderness. A conservative backlash against civil rights led to a shift to the right both in North Carolina and nationally. Jonathan chose not to seek reelection to his DNC seat in 1952 rather than be swept out by resurgent party conservatives.

At the 1952 Democratic National Convention, Jonathan supported Senator Adlai Stevenson of Illinois, while most of the North Carolina delegation backed segregationist senator Richard Russell of Georgia. Daniels and Stevenson knew each other from the Roosevelt administration, and they sometimes met when Stevenson visited his sister in Southern Pines. Jonathan was discreetly approached about his availability for the vice presidential slot, although nothing came of it.[29]

He stumped for Stevenson across the country, from a ballroom in Oklahoma to a Polish Catholic Church in Pennsylvania. Among other subjects, Jonathan decried what he called "the crudest slanting" of news coverage seen in his thirty years in the business.[30]

He supported Stevenson again for president in 1956, but Stevenson kept Jonathan at arm's length for fear of alienating conservative southerners. Jonathan chastised him in 1955 for his comment that Stevenson didn't have any aggressive notions about civil rights. "This is a time for aggressive notions by those of us who are not willing that Ku Kluxers in pleated bosom robes run the party down here or anywhere else."[31]

The nation's press backed Republican Dwight Eisenhower by a four-to-one margin.[32]

Jonathan worked closely with Kerr Scott's 1954 Senate campaign, particularly in defanging the race issue that cost Graham the same seat four years earlier. When conservative Democratic senator Alton Lennon's campaign began distributing racist leaflets in the primary, the Scott campaign obtained copies and leaked them to the *News and Observer*, which obliged with three front-page stories a day before the primary with the blaring headline "Alton Lennon Forces Flood State with 'Phony' Race Issue Leaflets."[33]

Jonathan also raised money for Scott's Senate race. After Scott was elected, he reached out to his Senate friends, including Lyndon Johnson, to help Scott get desirable committee assignments. LBJ promised to help, writing Jonathan, "I shall do my dead level best for him . . . because I knew when you signed up with Johnson many years ago that you were very select in the company you keep."[34]

Jonathan was often the target of Republican darts. When Senator Barry Goldwater campaigned in Raleigh in 1953, he attacked Jonathan, saying he had "put many professional and businessmen on a [sacrificial] political altar. He has done this with his propaganda."[35]

Southern liberals were in retreat. Conservatives such as David Clark, editor of the *Southern Textile Bulletin*, complained that the *News and Observer* "would not hesitate to sell the South 'down the river' if it would benefit them either politically or financially."[36]

The defeat of Graham, the South's most visible liberal, marked the end of the era. For the rest of the 1950s, Jonathan and the paper fought a rear-guard action against a rising segregationist tide in the South.

CHAPTER TWELVE

Civil Rights and Integration

Two months before the Supreme Court's landmark *Brown v. Board of Education* decision in 1954, Jonathan Daniels delivered a nationally broadcast address on racial integration to the National Urban League meeting in New York's Waldorf Astoria Hotel. Providing a rosy assessment to the civil rights group, Jonathan predicted that if the Supreme Court ordered the schools integrated, the South would greet it with "the good sense and good will of the people of both races."[1]

But that hope was severely tested in the coming years as a powerful white backlash developed. Jonathan's New York speech underscored the impossibly fine line southern moderates were trying to walk as he praised efforts to upgrade Black schools yet said he viewed "with apprehension" the day the Supreme Court outlawed segregation.

The end of school segregation had long been anticipated in the national press, such as in a 1953 series in the *Minneapolis Tribune* by pioneering Black reporter Carl Rowan headlined "Jim Crow's Last Stand." As southern scholar John Egerton wrote, "For at least two years before the court's ruling on *Brown*, anyone who was paying the slightest attention to the daily news in the United States knew that a momentous decision was coming on the question of school segregation." Black activists and civil rights organizations had been filing court cases to challenge Jim Crow segregation for decades, with some piecemeal success. By 1951, for example, Black students were enrolled at UNC's medical, law, and graduate schools.[2]

The *News and Observer* delivered a muted reaction to the *Brown* decision, urging the South to respond with "composure and good sense." Opined

Jonathan, "The South has never needed wisdom more nor fury less than it does at this moment." The Raleigh paper's moderate response was in keeping with most major North Carolina dailies.[3]

Before the court's *Brown* decision, no major southern newspaper editorialized against Jim Crow segregation laws. After the decision, some southern moderate editors such as Virginius Dabney in Richmond and John Temple Graves in Alabama defended segregation. Others, such as Jonathan Daniels, Ralph McGill of Atlanta, Mark Etheridge of Louisville, and Hodding Carter of Mississippi, searched for a quickly evaporating middle ground.[4]

While never quite calling for school integration, Jonathan counseled obedience to the law and put the paper on the side of racial progress. He attacked segregationist candidates such as I. Beverly Lake Sr. and separatist groups like the Ku Klux Klan and the more respectable Patriots of North Carolina, doing so during an era when North Carolina had 112 Ku Klux Klan Klaverns—the largest number in the country, according to a 1965 congressional report.[5] He slammed southern politicians such as Arkansas governor Orvall Faubus for his efforts to block the integration of a Little Rock high school in 1957. He sharply criticized Virginia's policy of massive resistance—closing public schools rather than integrating—and dismissed the Southern Manifesto, which attacked the *Brown* decision and was signed by most southern congressmen, as stirring false hopes.

In June 1957, amid talk of massive resistance across the South, Jonathan urged the Raleigh school board to accept the application of Joseph Hiram Hold, a fourteen-year-old Black student, to the all-white Broughton High School. Even though Broughton was three miles closer to his home than a Black high school, his application was rejected. "From all reports, this boy by any standard of accomplishment meets every qualification of desirability as a pupil—except that he is colored," Daniels wrote.[6]

Jonathan became a leading regional voice, giving speeches across the South and arguing that it would be "the most tragic proposal ever" for southern states to shutter their schools rather than integrate and that such action would amount to "seceding from civilization." Newspapers across the country reprinted Jonathan's remarks.[7]

North Carolina's official response to school integration was the creation of the Pearsall Commission, first formed under Governor William Umstead (1953–54) and then, after his death, reorganized by Governor Luther Hodges (1954–61). In April 1956, the Pearsall Commission proposed a constitutional amendment allowing residents to abolish their public schools by a majority vote and empowering the state to provide tuition grants to parents to send their children to private schools. This was sold as a safety valve for communities worried about school integration. The measure passed, but no community ever abolished their public schools. But it was also, as historian Charles Eagles has noted, the height of mass resistance to school integration in North Carolina. Voters approved the plan by a four-to-one margin in September 1956, with the backing of such Democratic Party moderates as US senator Kerr Scott and future governor Terry Sanford. It was opposed by the NAACP. The *News and Observer* and the *Winston-Salem Journal* were the only two major papers in the state to oppose the plan.

Jonathan at first supported the work of the Pearsall Commission and accused the NAACP of "rocking the boat" with its demands for immediate integration. But Jonathan eventually turned against the plan, believing "it would turn back the clock in North Carolina so far as public education is concerned for a century."[8]

Trying to find the center when there was not much of a middle, Jonathan called for voluntary integration—a position that satisfied no one.

Jonathan's stance on the Pearsall Plan was not popular with many readers for whom segregation was still an article of faith. Many felt like Dan H. Jones of Farmville, who in 1956 wrote the paper, "*The News and Observer* obviously and stridently favors integration but has for two years consistently avoided saying so in so many words. Why?" Jonathan replied, "The *News and Observer* has not said it 'favors integration' for the simple reason that it does not favor it. It believes that separation of the races in the public schools can be maintained substantially within the law, without closing the schools. The *News and Observer* is, however, opposed to present proposals in attempted evasion or defiance of the law which would endanger public education."[9]

Jonathan ran editorial after editorial attacking the Pearsall Plan, urging voters to reject the constitutional amendment. During the month before the September 8 referendum, the paper nearly every day reprinted the governor's own words on the editorial page: "Just one year ago Governor Hodges said: 'Abolition of the public schools and their replacement to a most uncertain extent by private ones is a last-ditch and double-edged weapon. If that weapon is ever used in North Carolina, its results will be appalling in ignorance, poverty, and bitterness.'"[10]

Hodges privately protested that the Raleigh paper "has definitely decided to complain about almost everything I do." He later wrote that the *News and Observer* endorsed "integration but hasn't the courage to say so." Jonathan and Hodges, classmates at UNC, never got along, although his brother Frank Sr. maintained cordial relations with the governor.[11]

Backers of the Pearsall Plan feared the paper's attacks. When Hodges asked Pearsall Plan supporters what else could be done, Representative Wilson F. Yarborough of Fayetteville recommended they "cut the current off that operates the presses at the *Raleigh News and Observer* the week of the election." Representative Joseph C. Eagles of Wilson wrote, "Ban the *N&O* from eastern N.C."[12]

Two days after the referendum passed, Pearsall Plan supporters conducted a mock funeral on the capitol grounds. It featured a casket labeled "JD" and a sign proclaiming, "Mourning the Death on Sept. 8 of jo-nathan [sic] Daniels Racial Mix Master from Beaufort County sympathizers." Another poster read, "School Integration sired by *Raleigh News and Observer* / slain by Tom Pearsall / Rest in Pieces."[13]

Jonathan later recalled, "I guess I got worse beat on that than anything I undertook. But it was a devious device, and never once have they dared to use it," referring the Pearsall Plan. "And to propose that it was just a plan to gain time is a lot of crap. It was exactly the plan that was proposed by Virginia. But instead of being undisguised massive resistance, it was sort of a half-way disguised massive resistance."[14]

While Jonathan championed a middle path, his liberal-turned-conservative columnist, Nell Battle Lewis, took a segregationist hard line. She thought the Pearsall Plan did not go far enough in opposing integration, she supported the Southern Manifesto, and she championed staunch segregationist politicians such as I. Beverly Lake Sr., who would run for governor in 1960 and 1964. She declared the Supreme Court's *Brown* decision one of the two worst things that ever happened in the South—the other being the Civil War. Lewis also called for UNC to investigate whether the campus had become "a comfortable nest for Muscovite fledglings." She was viewed by some as the strongest segregationist voice in the state, and her columns were reprinted in the publication of the Patriots of North Carolina, a segregationist group. "I declare," wrote segregationist editor James J. Kilpatrick of Richmond, "I don't see how you keep your job there. If I were Jonathan Daniels, which heaven forfend, I think I would fire you before breakfast." Jonathan said he kept Lewis on because she added "an element of spice" to the newspaper. "It's a good thing for our readers to get opposing points of view," he wrote to a friend.[15]

Jonathan continued to speak throughout the 1950s against racial injustices. He criticized Greensboro hospitals for refusing to accept Black patients, backed federal housing legislation, urged the integration of the state's two medical societies, and admonished both a Craven County jury for acquitting a wealthy white farmer accused of murdering his Black tenant and a white Apex police chief for beating a Black man.[16]

Jonathan expressed shock and outrage at the 1955 acquittal of two white men for the savage murder of Emmett Till, a Black fourteen-year-old, for allegedly whistling at a white woman in Mississippi. "It would be harder to think of a sadder thing for the South—and the thousands of good, justice loving white people in it, in Mississippi and everywhere else," he wrote.[17]

He lashed out at "hoodlum white trash" who jeered at Dorothy Counts when she integrated a Charlotte white high school in 1957. "Dorothy Counts has shown herself a more dignified, better trained, even a 'better-bred girl' than those who spat upon her." That proved too much for one reader, Thomas Iverson of Beaufort, who called the editorial "the most disgusting piece of trash I have ever read."[18]

When sit-ins began in February 1960 in Greensboro and quickly spread to Raleigh and lunch counters across the South, Jonathan split hairs. He wrote that a restaurant owner could serve who he or she wanted but said it was wrong to take the money from Black customers at other store counters but refuse to provide lunch counter service. When the US Supreme Court ruled segregated lunch counters to be illegal, Jonathan accepted the integration of lunch counters.[19]

The paper gave prominent coverage to the sit-ins, putting the story on the front page nearly every day for a month. It carried wire stories for sit-ins in other cities and staff-written stories for Raleigh demonstrations. The *News and Observer* covered visits by the Reverend Martin Luther King Jr.—something not all southern newspapers did.

The paper was more cautious on its editorial page, rarely taking a stand—neither criticizing the protesters nor defending them. "It was a transition time," recalled Frank Daniels Jr., Josephus's grandson and a young executive on the paper. "We didn't want a revolution. We wanted evolution."[20]

In 1962, Jonathan joined thirteen other southern white liberals in writing essays for a widely publicized book called *We Dissent*. The introduction said of the group, "They do oppose—they most emphatically dissent from—the rabid segregationists and all their works: the White Citizens Councils, the Ku Klux Klan, the closers of public schools, the wielders of clubs at bus stations, the advocate of interposition and nullification and other legal absurdities invoked in the name of freedom and state's rights."[21]

As the demand increased to open restaurants, theaters, pools, and other accommodations, Jonathan supported the work of a biracial committee to end discrimination. "Raleigh was not Little Rock, Arkansas," Jonathan wrote.

"It was not Oxford, Mississippi. And it's not going to be Birmingham, Alabama. It could indeed, be the Southern city which, facing a serious problem in reason and goodwill, set a pattern which will serve as a model for 'human beings dealing with one another,' as Mayor [William G.] Enloe put it, in the American South."[22]

The paper's coverage of the sit-ins won praise from Foster P. Payne, dean of historically Black Shaw University, whose students were heavily involved in the demonstrations. "At a time like the present in Raleigh," Payne wrote, "when there may often be tenseness, irritation, hot-headedness and distortion, it is good to have you and your newspaper continue your dedication to and the practice of calmness, truth, fairness, good sense and good will." But other Black readers, such as Mrs. Mable Pearl Lilly of Raleigh, expressed disappointment that the *News and Observer* was not more supportive of civil rights protests. "Lately, I realize you feel that there is a set pace for us and we should want to stay in our place. . . . We don't want this bitter fight. However, whatever we have had we have had to fight all the way for it."[23]

The biracial committee that Jonathan supported resulted in seventy-six businesses agreeing to extend equal service to Blacks. Jonathan's brother Frank Sr. was involved in the effort in which a group of businessmen encouraged local businesses to integrate, his segregationist views having somewhat softened since the 1940s.[24]

The paper took a moderate tone toward the landmark Civil Rights Act of 1964, which banned discrimination in public places and in employment, and the Voting Rights Act of 1965, which outlawed literacy tests and other discriminatory voting practices. "Southern Congressmen who already are mapping plans for a filibuster against the President's legislative proposals should confront this matter not with bluster and bullheadedness but in the knowledge that the states have not lived up to their responsibilities in a problem which now racks and sorely tries the whole country," the paper opined. And in another editorial, the paper said, "Certainly the recognition grows that no brutal barriers should be permitted barring members of any American group because they are members of that group from essential public facilities."[25]

Still, during the critical months of the debates over the civil rights bills, the paper's support was tepid at best. The paper provided wire service coverage of the debate in Congress—often on the front page—but was largely silent on its editorial pages. Jonathan's caution on the civil rights bills echoed that of many southern moderates.

For the segregationist view, North Carolina residents could turn to Jesse Helms, a commentator on Raleigh's WRAL-TV, who called the 1964 civil rights bill the "single most dangerous piece of legislation ever introduced in Congress" and something "that the communists would very much like to see enacted."[26]

Jonathan's moderation on civil rights drew praise from national publications and rebukes from conservatives. Helms in a television editorial complained in 1962 that *Time* magazine portrayed the South as "a festering jungle of depraved white people and persecuted Negroes." Helms said, "*Time* magazine's heroes in the South are Harry Golden, Ralph McGill, Jonathan Daniels, and the Freedom Riders—plus, of course, Martin Luther King." Golden and McGill were southern journalists.[27]

Conservatives periodically sought to provide an alternative to the *News and Observer*'s liberalism. In 1979, a group of mainly conservative Raleigh construction executives and automobile dealers announced plans to start the *Raleigh Newsweekly*, but it never got off the ground.[28]

The most successful effort by conservatives was the creation in 1991 of the *Carolina Journal*. It was a project of the John Locke Foundation, a Raleigh-based think tank funded in large part by Raleigh retail executive and former state representative Art Pope. Such conservative groups were not segregationist but supported more libertarian economic solutions.

Raleigh, a city dominated by state government and a state university, was a tough environment to launch a competing newspaper in because it did not have corporate leaders with deep pockets. In 1937, Winston-Salem's tobacco, textile, and banking tycoons succeeded in buying out the two daily newspapers from Owen Moon, an ardent New Dealer whose politics offended the business establishment.

After Raleigh's stores and restaurants were integrated, Jonathan became less patient with demonstrations. He agreed with Democratic governor Terry Sanford (1961–65) that there should be less marching and more effort to find solutions. He opposed the historic 1963 March on Washington because he feared violence. But southern racial moderates like Jonathan were being marginalized. The timetable of change was being dictated by African American activists who were taking to the streets as part of their freedom movement.

Looking back on his life in 1972, Jonathan, who was a part-time historian, said he understood that his views on race—which had evolved over the years—might not seem very advanced to contemporary ears. "But I was far enough ahead then to be suspect as a 'n——r lover' by some whites and to have the appreciation of many of the most ardent Blacks."[29]

The Reverend Martin Luther King Jr., the civil rights leader, strongly criticized moderates like Jonathan in his 1963 "Letter from Birmingham Jail." He expressed disappointment in moderates who seemed more interested in preserving social order than in supporting social justice. "I have almost reached the regrettable conclusion that the Negro's greatest stumbling block is not the White Citizens' Councilor or the Ku Klux Klanner, but the white moderate who is more devoted to 'order' than to justice."[30]

"King's criticism fit Jonathan Daniels because he did insist that social order be maintained, did hope that reasonable compromises could be achieved to avoid demonstrations which often led to violence, and did consider gradual change more effective," wrote Charles Eagles.[31]

Sunset

Jonathan's *News and Observer* became less of a crusading force as the sixties wore on. Perhaps the aging Jonathan was losing some of his youthful fire. Or maybe it was because he was becoming an absentee editor. He built a house on Hilton Head Island in South Carolina in 1963 and began spending more time book writing on the island and paying less attention to the newspaper. Jonathan sold his Raleigh house in 1965, renting an apartment for when he was in town. Increasingly, the editorials were written by his son-in-law Tom Inman.

"Father, you have been letting the paper down," his daughter Lucy wrote in 1965. "This makes me very sad because I have been taught to regard the N&O as the most valuable thing we have." She advised him to either devote his energies to the paper or turn it over to someone else—most likely her husband, Tom Inman.[32]

The paper remained staunchly Democratic during the sixties. Jonathan supported his old New Deal colleague Lyndon Johnson's Great Society programs to enlarge the social safety network and Governor Terry Sanford's anti-poverty programs and efforts to expand job opportunities for Blacks. In 1963 there were rumors that LBJ would appoint Jonathan as ambassador to Mexico, but that was a trial balloon posted by his friend and syndicated columnist Drew Pearson.[33]

A note of skepticism about the Vietnam War began creeping into the paper's editorials in 1966, and by January 1968, the paper stated that "increasingly there is agreement that the US should never have committed a field army to Vietnam." That was before the Tet Offensive later that month, which shifted public opinion against the war.[34]

Jonathan held a low estimation of conservative Democrats, including the state's two senators—Sam Ervin Jr. and B. Everett Jordan—writing privately that "I can never remember an occasion in my lifetime when we had two such reactionary senators in Washington." His friend Frank Graham urged Jonathan to run for the Senate in 1960, which would provide a progressive ticket along with Terry Sanford's candidacy for governor.[35]

After the conservative state leadership of the fifties, Jonathan believed that North Carolina needed a jolt of liberal activism because "we are still poor, still ignorant, still losing our sons and daughters" to outstate migration. In Sanford—a brother-in-arms from the Kerr Scott and Frank Graham campaigns—Jonathan believed he had his man.[36]

The paper's coverage of the 1960 Democratic primary for governor between Sanford and segregationist I. Beverly Lake Sr. was so pro-Sanford that it won Jonathan private plaudits from Sanford's campaign manager, Bert Bennett, for his "courageous stand." To help Sanford win the election, Jonathan even sought to muzzle Frank Graham's pro-integration speeches, worrying that he would stir up racial antipathy during the primary.[37]

The Raleigh editor also helped Senator John F. Kennedy's presidential campaign, preparing remarks for him to deliver during a swing through North Carolina. Kennedy's victory in the state, a top Kennedy aide wrote to Jonathan, "is a strong testimony to the power of the *News and Observer*'s good sense."[38]

Jonathan was regarded as such a front-runner to become Kennedy's director of the US Information Agency that he was contacted by job applicants and Washington real estate agents. After Kennedy named TV journalist Edward R. Murrow to the post, he appointed Jonathan to the USIA's advisory commission—a position that Jonathan felt was useless. He was more successful in getting a new guided missile frigate named the USS *Josephus Daniels*, after Jonathan lobbied historian Arthur Schlesinger Jr., a special assistant to JFK and Vice President Lyndon Johnson. A large photograph of the ship, launched in 1963 to mark the 100th anniversary of Josephus's birth in 1962, was prominently displayed in the *News and Observer* headquarters for decades.[39]

Jonathan remained close to the Sanford administration, contributing to his inaugural speech and providing him with advice. He helped protect Sanford, quashing a story about a proposed shady land deal. The Sanford administration was going to sell some West Raleigh property to a real estate developer who was a major Sanford backer. Jonathan talked the administration out of it, saving Sanford from a potential scandal because of the appearance of rewarding a donor. "He loved Terry and would do anything for him, which wasn't the way to do it," said Roy Parker, the paper's chief political writer, referring to Jonathan helping Sanford avoid a scandal. Despite Jonathan's killing the land deal story, Parker said the reporters generally had a free hand to pursue stories objectively. Jonathan was mainly involved in editorial writing rather than in newsroom decisions.[40]

Jonathan's coziness with Sanford sometimes made life difficult for his reporters on the campaign trail. Covering a 1960 gubernatorial rally by Lake, the segregationist, in rural Robeson County, reporter Gene Roberts avoided a mob assault only because he was warned by a local newspaper editor. When Lake started verbally attacking Roberts, he was already halfway out the door. The local editor pulled him into his darkened storefront office, where they got on their hands and knees and peered through venetian blinds as six to eight men passed by with bricks in their hands, shouting, "Where did that goddamned reporter go?"

After filing his story, Roberts called the police for help to get out of town. "I had a little foreign car, a Morris Minor, and the local editor had basically impressed on the local police chief that it wouldn't be great for the town image to have a *News and Observer* reporter killed or beaten up on the streets of Lumberton. So, they put these two big police cruisers before and after my car and went with me all the way to the Fayetteville city limits and got me in another jurisdiction and left."[41]

That sort of favoritism toward certain candidates changed when Claude Sitton became editor—the first non-Daniels to hold the post. When Sanford ran for the US Senate in 1986, a *News and Observer* story made a point about his advanced age in his attempt to become a rookie senator. Sanford clipped the article and sent it to the paper, scribbling a note: "This is from my friends?" The clipping with the Sanford note was pinned on the paper's bulletin board that served the political staff as a point of pride.[42]

During the 1950s and 1960s, the paper had a team of political reporters who were arguably as good as those with any regional newspaper in the country. They included Jay Jenkins; Simmons Fentress, a future *Time* magazine columnist; and David Cooper, who went on to a distinguished career at the *Detroit Free Press* and the *Akron Beacon Journal*. They also included such *News and Observer* stalwarts as Roy Parker, Bob Brooks, and Woodrow Price.

Gene Roberts, the son of a Wayne County school principal, achieved the most fame, eventually covering the civil rights movement and serving as Saigon bureau chief of the *New York Times*. He became one of the most influential editors of the twentieth century, editing the *Philadelphia Inquirer* when it won seventeen Pulitzer Prizes in eighteen years, finishing his career as managing editor of the *New York Times*. He also wrote, with Hank Klibanoff, a Pulitzer Prize–winning history of covering the civil rights movement called *Race Beat*.

While in Raleigh, Roberts was a groundbreaking reporter. In 1961, Roberts wrote a powerful four-part series about the gross inequality of job opportunities between the races. He focused on an all-Black Pitt County high school and what had happened to the forty-student graduating class of 1959. Of those who stayed in North Carolina, not a single person had a job above day laborer or maid. The class valedictorian worked as a maid, as did nine of her classmates. Two or three of the males had gone north and landed jobs like baker and truck driver that were unavailable to Black graduates who stayed home. Roberts called every Black college in the state—North Carolina had eleven, the most in the nation—and not one had ever had a corporation send a job recruiter to campus, while 393 companies visited the historically white University of North Carolina at Chapel Hill in a recent year.[43] "A lot of pretty moderate newspapers would have had problems, I think, with that story, but Raleigh ran it," said Roberts.[44]

Roy Parker was from a family that owned several small newspapers in the state's rural northeastern corner. After cutting his teeth on the family papers, he joined the *News and Observer* in 1957. He served as the paper's Washington correspondent from 1963 to 1971, leaving the newspaper in 1972 to work on a gubernatorial campaign. He later was the founding editor of the *Fayetteville Times*.

"Tense and sardonic, Roy would stalk in late in the day and go into a manic two-fingered typing trance, turning out page after page of copy," remembers Gary Pearce, a former colleague. "He had more sources and more scoops than any [other] reporter in Raleigh."[45]

Like many state capital newspapers, politics was the *News and Observer*'s meat and potatoes. During certain periods in the 1960s, the paper published brief stories on every statewide bill introduced in the legislature. Its front-page political column, Under the Dome, was mandatory reading for anyone interested in Tar Heel politics.

Under the Dome was started on January 15, 1895, shortly after Daniels bought the newspaper. For decades it ran only during legislative sessions. It began appearing daily on September 3, 1934, calling itself Under the Dome: Capitol News and Comment, broadening to cover all of state government and politics.

For decades, some state officials checked Under the Dome the first thing in the morning to make sure they were not the subject of an unfavorable article. Many politicos also used the column to plant stories or trial balloons.

The 128-year run of Under the Dome makes it a candidate for the nation's longest-running political column.

"For anybody interested in state politics, that was like a Bible," said former Durham mayor Steve Schewel.[46]

One reason North Carolina politics was regarded as relatively clean was the paper's intensive and aggressive coverage of state government and politics. Unlike some other states, North Carolina has not been dominated by a single publication but has had strong newspapers in Raleigh, Charlotte, Greensboro, and Winston-Salem, all with statehouse bureaus working in a hypercompetitive environment for scoops so that no newspaper could sit on a story. Many of the state's major television and radio stations also had Raleigh bureaus.

Gene Roberts would later recall covering the civil rights moment in the South, big labor and the auto industry in Detroit, and the Vietnam War. "But when it came to sheer competitiveness, there was no contest, really. The state capitol beat in Raleigh was the hottest league I ever played in. This had a lot to do, I think, with how seriously newspapers took state government coverage."[47]

If politics and government were the paper's raison d'être, then tobacco was a close second. Tobacco was the major cash crop for Eastern North Carolina. Every topic about the leaf received extensive coverage, from price controls to the opening of tobacco auctions to discussions about the best chemicals and pesticides. Visiting journalists were sometimes puzzled by the number of tobacco stories, which often seemed arcane to an outsider. But such attention was little different from other newspapers' treatment of local industries—such as Detroit and automobiles or Texas and oil and gas.

Early in the twentieth century, the abstemious Josephus Daniels had been critical of smoking, associating it with the Duke American Tobacco trust, with one 1901 editorial headlined "Poison Mind, Body and Heart." But he supported farmers growing tobacco.[48]

Under Jonathan the paper became a cheerleader for tobacco. In 1960, Jonathan said a smoker in Eastern North Carolina was "doing his utter patriotic duty." A year earlier, the paper had opined, "It could indeed be argued that since Sir Walter Raleigh introduced tobacco to the world, no new discovery has given so much pleasure to man with less proven harm."[49]

But even Jonathan wondered whether he was whistling past a graveyard. "As a heavy cigarette smoker, I hope I am right in minimizing the dangers of tobacco," Jonathan, who smoked unfiltered Camels, wrote to a reader in 1964.[50]

The *News and Observer* was too small to be a great regional newspaper. Roberts noted that when he was hired, the staff was only about a third the size of the Norfolk-based *Virginian Pilot*, despite similar circulations. Raleigh was a government and university town and did not have the same advertising base as Norfolk, which had triple Raleigh's population. While focusing attention on government and political news, the paper had few reporters covering the community or such issues as health, medicine, colleges, or religion.[51]

A bare-bones staff produced the paper. In 1965 there were only forty editorial staffers—and only nine of those were women, who mostly wrote features about domestic life and cultural stories.[52]

With Jonathan disappearing in Hilton Head, Woodrow Price and Sam Ragan took on increasingly important roles with the paper, providing much of the direction of post–World War II coverage, with Jonathan mainly reigning over the opinion page.

A native of Elizabeth City, Price joined the *News and Observer* after wartime service in 1946. He was a government/political reporter but was probably best known for writing an outdoors column, In the Open, on hunting and fishing for twenty-eight years.

During Price's tenure as managing editor, 1957–72, the paper broke such stories as the weekly delivery of cases of liquor to room 215 of the Sir Walter Hotel, where most lawmakers lived when in session. The booze was distributed by the liquor industry in 1957 to slake the thirst of lawmakers—a story richly illustrated with surreptitious photographs by Lawrence Wofford.

The *News and Observer* had a cadre of talented photojournalists who helped tell the North Carolina story. Among the best of them were Robert Willett, Steve Murray, Scott Sharpe, Gary Allen, Corey Lowenstein, Mike Sargent, Greg Gibson, Burk Uzzle, Julia Wall, Ethan Hyman, Robert Miller, and Chuck Liddy. Many more could be included on the list.

Price exemplified the cozy relationship between the paper and Democratic leaders, accepting appointments from three governors. Sanford appointed Price, then managing editor, as chairman of the North Carolina Outer Banks Seashore Commission in 1962, to preserve the barrier islands from development. Price played a significant role, working with the federal government, in expanding the Cape Hatteras National Seashore and creating the Cape Lookout National Seashore. In 1969, Governor Bob Scott (1969–73) appointed him chairman of the State Ports Authority. Price became an issue in the 1972 governor's race when Republican gubernatorial candidate Jim Gardner said Price was unqualified for the post. Price countered that he was qualified and hadn't sought the position, and besides, "I have always been a friend of the Scott family, starting back in the early '40s." Governor Jim Hunt made Price a member of the State Wildlife Commission in 1976, shortly after he retired from paper.[53]

Such government experience gave Price important sources and an understanding of the workings of government. But it also raised questions about the paper's ability to aggressively report on Democratic administrations. Price had fishing and hunting buddies in nearly every state agency, which kept him very plugged in. If a story would reflect poorly on his friends, he passed along the tip to another reporter to do the story.[54] The paper had a long history of blurring such lines. Other newspapers often broke critical stories about *News and Observer* favorite Governor Kerr Scott.

Coziness between journalists and government officials was not the only practice that would today raise eyebrows among those concerned about press ethics. Freebies for underpaid reporters were a way of life well into the 1950s, with formal company procedures for requesting tickets twenty-four hours before a basketball or football game, rock concert, or dance.

Although politics and state government dominated the paper's coverage, it offered a broader menu of stories. The newspaper's first full-time general interest columnist was Charles Craven. From 1949 to 1980, Craven wrote his daily column, Byways of the News, often about the beer drinkers and pool room habitués of Rusty's Cafe with nicknames like Barrel Gut Hogan, The Count, and Little Man. One day in 1971, Governor Bob Scott picked up Craven and his pool hall cronies in the state limousine and took them to the mansion to play pool. A gruff former college football player from Asheville who saw action in France and Germany in World War II, Craven was once called "the Damon Runyon of Martin Street."[55]

Several specialty columnists became the longtime faces of the paper. Bugs Barringer, a Rocky Mount photographer, wrote a garden column, Bugs in the Garden, from 1951 until 1993. Bill Humphries wrote The Farm Observer column from 1953 until 1973.

During the 1970s, the paper's star general interest columnist was Jack Aulis, who wrote a folksy, often humorous column while traveling around Eastern North Carolina. He hunted and pecked his columns with one arm, having lost the other arm as a marine during the battle of Iwo Jima. His successor as the bard of the East was Dennis Rogers, a rail-thin, bearded chain-smoker known for tooling around on his Harley-Davidson with a gift for writing about the lives of ordinary people.

The paper's best-known sports columnist was Dick Herbert, who for twenty-nine years oversaw the rise of the Atlantic Coast Conference from his perch as the paper's sports editor before retiring in 1971. He served as president of both the US Football Writers Association and US Basketball Writers Association and was the first sportswriter honored by the Naismith Basketball Hall of Fame.

In 1965, the paper celebrated its 100th birthday with a special edition that was a record 332 pages. The paper had a circulation of 150,000. It hosted a dinner at Memorial Auditorium honoring all those who had been named "Tar Heel of the Week," the Sunday profile of interesting North Carolinians begun in January 1950. The paper enraged some readers in 1969 when it made Howard Fuller, a controversial Black activist, Tar Heel of the Week.

The paper was beginning to modernize. Its system of non-staff correspondents, paid by the story, was replaced by bureaus in Ahoskie, Greenville, Wilmington, Jacksonville, and Fayetteville. The women's page, then called Women's Society News, was revamped, and pictures and stories about new brides (uniformly white) were moved inside the features section in 1964 rather than appearing on the section's front page—years behind other newspapers.[56]

Culture

While Jonathan presided over the editorial page, running the newsroom was Sam Ragan, the son of a Granville County tobacco farmer who became an influential cultural figure in North Carolina. Ragan was a striking figure, a tall man with flowing white hair, a bow tie, a wide-brimmed fedora, and a chain-smoker's voice described as a whiskey baritone. He started work at the paper in 1941, served in military intelligence in the Pacific during World War II, and was named managing editor in 1948 and executive editor in 1957. Ragan made the newspaper a cultural force in the state, earning him the nickname "North Carolina's Literary Godfather."

The newspaper had long taken a strong interest in cultural affairs. Josephus saw the *News and Observer* as an educational tool, and the paper took its education mission seriously by publishing popular literary and historical material. In the first decade of the twentieth century, the paper regularly ran short stories in its Sunday edition, such as Arthur Conan Doyle's Sherlock Holmes detective tales, sometimes starting them on the front page. In 1910 the paper began running "one-page classics" in its Sunday edition, highly condensed versions of such classics as George Eliot's *Daniel Deronda*, Virgil's *Aeneid*, and Washington Irving's *Rip Van Winkle*.

The paper built its literary reputation during a five-year period, 1909–13, when Daniels published the *North Carolina Review* as a monthly sixteen-page literary and historical newspaper supplement. The *Review* explored such subjects as the Revolutionary War's Battle of Moore's Creek and the lives of O. Henry and Henrik Ibsen. The *Review*'s managing editor was R. D. W. Connor, the state archivist who later become the first Archivist of the United States. The *Review* ended after the *News and Observer*'s fire in 1913. It served as a model for later book review pages in the state. The *Review*'s range of articles was emulated by the *North Carolina Historical Review*, which was started in 1924 and is still being published by the state today.[57]

The book page first appeared in February 1922, four months after the *Greensboro Daily News* began the first book page in North Carolina. During its first year, the *News and Observer* offered a $10 prize for knowledge of American literature. It also gave $100 in 1923 for the best short story based in North Carolina, with lesser cash prizes for runners-up. The paper published the winning short stories.

The book page was one of the newspaper's strengths. Michael Skube won the Pulitzer Prize for Criticism for his book reviews in 1989, and J. Peder Zane won the Distinguished Writing Award from the American Society of News Editors in 1999. Both were book editors.

"To some degree," said Gene Roberts, "every paper I worked on felt compelled to give some attention to books, but there was a kind of feeling about that on the *News and Observer* that was just kind of a little bit more intense, and a little more that you had an obligation to worry about the writers out there, and that sort of thing."[58]

The paper encouraged poetry, publishing the column Today's N.C. Poem from 1923 until at least 1970. The poems, which ran on the editorial page, were usually about ten lines and dealt with natural beauty, religion, children, and love. The column provided an outlet for Tar Heel poets.

The emphasis on writing started at the top. Josephus wrote nine books, and Jonathan, a frustrated novelist, wrote twenty-one books, with one by Josephus and three by Jonathan winning major state awards.

While the paper's cultural coverage tilted heavily toward white authors, it did not ignore Black writers. A local reviewer called Richard Wright's 1940 classic novel, *Native Son*, "one of the most powerful novels of all time." Jonathan's rave review of *Native Son* for the *Saturday Review of Literature* described it as "authentic powerful writing about a young Negro driven by his cramped destiny to crime." He wrote of the book—banned in some places in the South—that "there are few pages in modern American literature which will compare."[59]

The paper publicized an upcoming talk of W. E. B. Du Bois, the editor of the Black paper *The Crisis*, at Shaw University in 1926 and defended the

1931 appearance of poet Langston Hughes at UNC against critics. It also publicized the local appearances of novelist Zora Neale Hurston in 1940 and ran a profile of J. Saunders Redding when he became the first Black author to win the Mayflower Cup, an award for the best book written in the state in 1943, for *No Day of Triumph*.[60]

The paper had Black reviewers as early as 1935, when Jonathan asked James E. Shepard, the president of what is now North Carolina Central University, to review *The Bottom Rail*, a book about life in the Deep South for Black Americans.[61]

Black author Charles W. Chesnutt's novel about the 1898 Wilmington massacre, *The Marrow of Tradition*, received a mixed review from Nell Battle Lewis in 1923—two decades after it was published. Still, she wrote, "There is a great deal of truth in it which the liberal-minded reader must admit." In her 1924 review of Walter F. White's novel about Black Americans, *The Fire in Flint*, Lewis found the book biased. "Yet it contains much bitter truth and many things to make us ashamed."[62]

Jonathan Daniels promised to have historian Helen G. Edmonds's 1951 book, *The Negro and Fusion Politics in North Carolina, 1894–1901*, laying out the lies of the white supremacy campaigns, reviewed, but there is no record that the paper ever did. Perhaps it sliced too close to the bone.

Nell Battle Lewis often wrote about literature and North Carolina authors when she wasn't commenting on political matters. That mantle was taken up by Sam Ragan in 1948 through his column Southern Accent, which continued until 1996, switching from the Raleigh paper to *The Pilot* of Southern Pines when he became editor. During the column's forty-eight-year run, Ragan championed southern literature and North Carolina writers. Celebrated North Carolina novelist Reynolds Price remembered as a high school student hardly sleeping Saturday night because he knew Ragan would mention his name in his Sunday morning column.[63]

Ragan, who wrote six books of poetry, was a cultural innovator who used his newspaper perch to champion the arts. While editor, he served as director of the North Carolina Arts Council, making hundreds of speeches around the state promoting literature. In the early sixties, he helped create the North Carolina School of the Arts in Winston-Salem, one of the nation's first state-supported residential conservatories. He helped birth the Friends of the College series in 1959, which over the next thirty-five years presented 226 concerts to 4 million people in Reynolds Coliseum at North Carolina State University. The subscription series was one of the nation's cultural bargains, bringing to the arena the New York Philharmonic conducted by

Leonard Bernstein, the New York City Ballet, Leontyne Price, Itzhak Perlman, and many other national treasures at a ticket price that schoolteachers and retirees could afford.[64]

Democratic governor Bob Scott named Ragan as the state's first secretary of cultural resources in 1972, and in 1982, Democratic governor Jim Hunt named him the state's poet laureate for life—both after he left the paper. Like the Danielses, Ragan had close ties with the Democratic Party, writing a friendly book about the Sanford administration in 1964 titled *The New Day*. Prior to Scott's election in 1968, Ragan organized a group of intellectuals to brainstorm ideas about how Scott should deal with social unrest.

By the time Peder Zane arrived in 1996 to take over the book page, he inherited one of the state's cultural institutions—one with a close relationship with a rich network of local novelists such as Lee Smith, Clyde Egerton, and Jill McCorkle who were willing to contribute. Acclaimed poet Fred Chappell wrote a poetry column. Important North Carolina books were certain to be reviewed, as well as many nationally significant works. Zane's column and the two pages of book reviews helped add intellectual heft to a paper that served serious readers, many of them connected to local universities or the new high-tech industries of the Research Triangle Park.[65]

The paper also played a role in the social life of the state. The Women's Society News Page listed not only the marriages but the balls, dances, and other social activities for middle-class and upper-middle-class Eastern North Carolina. At the insistence of the Daniels family, the paper continued to give prominent coverage to the Miss North Carolina contest and to the debutante balls, which the staff often bridled at covering.

Florence King, who wrote for the women's page in the mid-sixties, described life chronicling the debutantes, brides, and their mothers of what she called the "southern gynecocracy." Wedding announcements were sacrosanct. If an announcement was left out of the paper, there might even be a question of its legality in some minds.

"Because of such intense deep-seated emotions," King wrote, "the Southern Women's Department is forced into a nerve destroying sense of eternal vigilance. If one little thing goes wrong with a wedding write-up or photo, panic ensues. Above all, no matter how crowded our pages were with ads, we had to make sure that a wedding account appeared in the paper the next day. If it did not, we had to deal with a hysterical mother of the bride."[66] Those marriage announcements yellowed in family albums as reminders of one of the most important landmarks in a person's life. They could also awaken the dreams of young girls.

Frances Davenport of Williamston said that as she was growing up in rural Martin County, her family could not afford a *News and Observer* subscription. One Sunday, when she was eleven, a carrier left a newspaper in her yard, perhaps by mistake. "I devoured every word of it several times," she recalled years later. "I dreamed of being a beautiful bride one day, just like those in the *News and Observer* and vowed when I was older and richer, this would be my paper. And so, it was."[67]

CHAPTER THIRTEEN

Frank Sr. and Frank Jr.

By the time the *News and Observer* moved into its new building on McDowell Street in 1956, the newspaper had long been a Tar Heel institution.

The paper's 1907 building at 114 W. Martin Street had outlived its usefulness, and it was never that grand in the first place. "That building's whole inside was dark and dank," wrote Lucy Daniels, Jonathan's daughter.

> The bathrooms were literally tiny, foul-smelling closets whose doors had to be held shut. In winter it was cold, in summer hot and airless. The entire place was dirty and rundown and permeated with the flat, lethargic smell of paste and copy paper. Upstairs, where the reporters worked and the public seldom visited, was infinitely dirtier, with a black dust coating everything. One of the most puzzling contradictions of my early years was how this powerful institution, revered not only by the Daniels family but also by the Democratic Party, the State of North Carolina, and everybody anywhere who believed in freedom of speech and the rights of the oppressed, could be housed in such a dilapidated building.[1]

With postwar advertising on the rise, many newspapers built new offices in the 1950s. The new 40,000-square-foot building at 215 S. McDowell Street had air conditioning, an elevator, shining steel columns, and aluminum louvers that operated like venetian blinds. In a special edition printed to celebrate the new headquarters, the paper described the transition as "one from grime to glamour."[2]

But the "glamour" soon wore off, and by the twenty-first century, the building was looking shabby, with the air conditioning and the elevator frequently broken. After a visit to the paper, James Goodnight, a billionaire software entrepreneur from Cary, is said to have disdainfully remarked, "What a dump!"

During the 1970s, the paper enlarged its footprint, purchasing and then tearing down the Andrew Johnson Hotel on the corner of Martin and Salisbury Streets and the Park Central Hotel on the corner of Martin and McDowell Streets. Both hotels were decrepit, and by the 1970s one or the other had housed an adult bookstore and a gay bar, when such establishments were considered furtive and served as hangouts for prostitutes. The Park Central, a seven-story building erected circa 1893 with a distinctive turret, had once been fine enough to lodge President William Howard Taft. Historic preservationists protested its demolition to no avail because Frank Daniels Sr. saw it only as a rat- and roach-infested eyesore. The newspaper in 1994 built a 30,000-square-foot addition, a post-press building to store newsprint and provide office space.[3]

The McDowell Street building had three floors—one for each of the Daniels sons now running the business. The first floor belonged to Josephus Jr., who by all accounts was the least capable of the Daniels sons. He held such positions as business manager, advertising manager, and company president but had fewer responsibilities than those titles would imply.

The second floor housed most of the business functions, and that is where Frank Daniels Sr. and then his son Frank Jr. kept the paper financially afloat. The offices of the *Raleigh Times*, a competing afternoon paper, were also found on the second floor.

Jonathan ruled the third floor, where the news/editorial staff churned out the news and editorial copy. Frank Sr. and Jonathan tended to stay off of each other's floors. Many other papers had a strict line between the business and editorial sides, to keep financial considerations from influencing news judgment. But the division was particularly rigid at the *News and Observer*—perhaps in part to keep the peace in the family.

Frank Sr.

Frank Sr. lacked his brother Jonathan's flamboyance, national profile, and politics. What he had was a capacity to run a growing business, an even temperament, and enough self-confidence that he could defer to Jonathan's

News and Observer offices on McDowell Street,
the paper's home from 1956 to 2017.
(Reprinted with permission of the News and Observer.)

large ego—although Jonathan never published his own name in the paper's masthead.

Besides possessing business acumen, Frank Sr. was attuned to the local community, stopping daily at a local drugstore to share a morning coffee with the city's merchants, bankers, and real estate developers. Frank Sr. was a joiner, participating deeply in the civic, political, and professional life of the town—from hospital boards, the Chamber of Commerce, and the United Fund to state and national newspaper organizations. Frank Sr. served as chairman of the State Board of Public Welfare from 1948 to 1956. He was active in local politics, championing a city manager form of government for Raleigh after World War II and recruiting city council candidates.

He was close to moderately conservative Democratic governor Luther Hodges, accepting his appointments to the state tax commission and the Research Triangle Institute. "My brother is quieter than I am—I think a better North Carolinian," Jonathan wrote. "He stays at home and meets the payroll and helps run the hospital and the cemetery." It was Frank Sr. who guided the paper through the difficult Depression years. "If it had not been for my father, I don't know if the *News and Observer* would have made it," Frank Jr. said.[4]

Frank Sr. spent his entire career working on the paper's business side. After graduating from UNC in 1927, he began work in the press room, training in production, circulation, advertising, and the business departments.

He became treasurer in 1935, general manager in 1942, president in 1956, and publisher in 1966 before moving to the part-time position of chairman in 1970 after he was slowed by a heart attack.

A handsome six-foot-two, he married Ruth Aunspaugh, the attractive daughter of the co-owner of a Norfolk insurance agency, in November 1929 at Raleigh's First Presbyterian Church. They built a stately 6,631-square-foot Georgian-style house—with a tax value of $2 million in 2022—next to his father's house on Glenwood Avenue in 1931 and lived there the rest of their lives. There they raised two children, Frank Jr. and Patsy. Although Frank Sr. was a reader, his home did not have the intellectual atmosphere of his brother Jonathan's home. The talk was more likely about the Carolina-Duke game, Wrightsville Beach, or prominent Raleigh families. He played tennis when he was young but was not a golfer despite his membership in the prestigious Carolina Country Club.[5]

Frank Sr. almost certainly softened the anger at the paper from the conservative-leaning business community. Although Frank Sr. was more conservative than other family members, he remained what he called "a straight-line Democrat," raising money for Democratic candidates and rejecting invitations to attend GOP fundraising dinners for Richard Nixon and other Republicans.[6]

Although the paper's political viewpoint was liberal Democratic, the *News and Observer* was conservatively run—reflecting Frank Sr.'s experience in the Depression and his fear of debt. The paper had a modest profit margin of around 12 percent in the mid-fifties, as Frank Sr. preferred to reinvest in the company rather than further enrich the family. That profit margin crept up to around 24 percent by the time the family sold the paper in 1995—far below the 30 to 40 percent margins that some national chains demanded of their newspapers. Although part of the city's elite, Frank Sr. avoided ostentation and never owned a vacation home.[7]

"I think it is a legitimate point to say they were willing to live a more modest middle-class or upper-middle-class existence in the service of doing good journalism," said Ted Vaden, the paper's only ombudsman, who handled reader complaints. "They could have milked a lot more from the paper than they did and as did their fellow publishers around the country."[8]

In many ways, the paper was old-fashioned. Into the 1970s, Frank Sr. personally handed out bonuses and prizes such as cameras or wristwatches at the Christmas party, dressed as Santa Claus—a tableau that many found patronizing. When Ferrel Guillory, the paper's new political reporter, was assigned to rove the state to interview voters in the run-up to the 1972 elections, he asked whether he could rent a car; his family had only one car, and his pregnant wife was due to deliver shortly. He was told that the paper didn't pay for rentals, but Frank Jr. gave him the keys to his Buick.[9]

"The paper was run a little bit like a country store when I got there," recalled Claude Sitton, who was hired as editor in 1968. Payroll statements were written in longhand on a legal pad, and a newsman who had been fired three times was still coming to work because nobody had told him not to. When Fred Crisp Jr. arrived in 1969 as retail advertising manager, he was shocked to find that his advertising salesmen had to share telephones and that the department lacked graphics and art specialists deemed essential to sell advertising.[10]

Frank Sr. was a principled man. After a raid of a lake cabin owned by his editor, Claude Sitton, turned up a stash of marijuana, Sitton inquired of the publisher about whether the paper should run a story. Sitton had rented the cabin to a young couple, who had brought in the dope. Frank Sr. said to publish: "Live by the sword, die by the sword." Later, when Frank Sr. was pulled over for a minor traffic offense, he gave what Sitton said was his first-ever order: "Put this in the paper."[11]

The paper was reluctant to invest in new kinds of media, reflecting its Victorian-era patriarch. Josephus advised his son Frank Sr. in 1939 not to participate in a radio deal. "I strongly believe that in the long run we should stick to the *News and Observer*, give it all our thought, initiative and attention," he wrote from Mexico. "Put all your eggs in one basket and watch the basket is a good rule."[12]

The paper briefly experimented with branching out to television and radio—a growing industry that ended the newspaper's monopoly on news. By 1947, 44 percent of the American public got most of their news from radio, compared with 48 percent for newspapers.

In 1947, the *News and Observer* purchased a 5,000-watt radio station, called WNAO (later WKIX), which went on the air March 21, 1948. With little expertise in radio, the station suffered from a lack of professional management. It struggled to turn a profit against Raleigh's two established radio stations—WPTF, backed by deep-pocketed Durham Life Insurance Company, and WRAL, which created the Tobacco Radio Network and its Dixie FM network, connecting it to 370 stations across the South.

WNAO and WNAO-FM were purchased in December 1952 by Sir Walter Television and Broadcasting Company for $250,000 to begin the

Raleigh-Durham region's first television station, with the paper maintaining a share of ownership. But channel 28, initially located in a small building adjacent to the newspaper, used a poor-quality UHF signal that many televisions of that era could not receive. WNAO-TV aired for four years, from July 1953 until December 1957, before being put out of business by new stations—WTVD in Durham and WRAL in Raleigh—that received federal licensing for stronger VHF signals. Frank Jr. said in the end the paper got "very little out of it."[13]

Skeptical that radio or TV would be lucrative, Frank Sr. was not comfortable dabbling in a new media. The paper flirted with television in later years. The Daniels family expressed interest in buying an Alabama TV station in 1975, discussed a joint venture bid on television rights to air thirty-eight Atlantic Coast Conference basketball games in 1981, and talked about getting into cable television in 1984, but nothing panned out.[14]

"We never did buy TV; we should have," Frank Daniels Jr. said after his family sold the paper. "We should have bought radio. Should have gotten into cable. Should have, should have, should have."[15] When the paper broadened its interests in the 1970s, it mainly stayed within its expertise and comfort zone—running small southern newspapers.

In June 1955, the *News and Observer* purchased the *Raleigh Times* for about $500,000 ($5.7 million in 2024 dollars), which the family of John Park had owned since 1911. The afternoon newspaper was started in 1879 as the *Evening Visitor* and changed its name to the *Raleigh Times* in 1901.

The *Raleigh Times* was often a more politically conservative newspaper, and Josephus Daniels attacked it as a voice of the railroads. But the economics of sustaining two separate newspapers, especially in small cities, had become untenable. *News and Observer* executives had considered purchasing it as early as 1938. Raleigh was one of only two cities in the country with fewer than 100,000 people having two separately owned newspapers in 1955.

The Park family initially proposed a merger with the *News and Observer* with a joint operating agreement, but Jonathan and Frank Sr. saw no benefit of joint ownership. The *News and Observer* had a daily circulation of 125,008, while the *Raleigh Times*' circulation was just 15,310.

Frank Jr.

After purchasing the *Times*, Frank Sr. asked his son, a second lieutenant in the air force, to return from Japan to help with the family business.

Frank Jr. was born in 1931 and grew up in the family compound. During summers, he worked at the paper, starting as a copyboy, fetching the mail, and delivering proof pages. He attended public schools until his last two years, when at his father's insistence he transferred to Woodberry Forest, an all-male prep school in Virginia where many of North Carolina's wealthy families sent their sons. The headmaster lectured young Daniels: "Frank, you come from a very, very well-known family and you have a very nice smile, but if you don't start studying, neither one of them will do you a damn bit of good."[16]

Although he never graduated from high school, Frank Jr. had sufficient credits to get into the University of North Carolina. In Chapel Hill, Frank Jr. worked in the advertising department of the *Daily Tar Heel*, the student newspaper; served as president of the student honor council; spent a semester in law school; and trained in the Air Force Reserve Officer Training Corps, graduating as a commissioned officer in 1953. He had hoped to become a pilot but failed the physical. Frank Jr. trained in San Antonio and St. Louis before returning home to marry Julia Jones of New Bern.

The two had met in the ninth grade at Broughton High School, when she was a new student. "I remember she had on a plaid skirt and had nice tits," Frank Jr. said. They dated off and on through college. "She likes to say I was too sophomoric," Frank Jr. said, "and as I like to say, she didn't drink or screw."[17]

Julia Jones graduated from Converse College, where she was class president, in Spartanburg, South Carolina, and was teaching elementary school in Raleigh before her marriage. Like her husband, she became an important civic leader in countless organizations. There is a Daniels Auditorium in the North Carolina Museum of History, for which the Daniels family gave $150,000 toward its construction. The Julia Jones Daniels Center for Community Leadership is the Junior League's Raleigh headquarters.

They married at the Church of the Good Shepherd in Raleigh, but Frank Jr. was soon posted first in St. Louis and then Japan. Air force life in Japan was no hardship. The couple lived in an attractive house in the mountains, thirty minutes from the Itami Air Base. Frank Jr. enjoyed his work as a supply officer and the benefits of the Officers' Club enough that he thought about making it a career.

But on June 4, 1955, the couple's first anniversary, his father called and asked him to come home. Frank Jr. joined the paper in January 1956, going to work in the advertising department—the beginning of his publisher-in-training program.

The family always assumed Frank Jr. would become publisher. Joe Jr. had one adopted son, who was not interested in the business, and Jonathan had four daughters. Women were not considered for leadership positions at the paper in the era's patriarchy.

The transition from father to son began when Frank Sr. suffered two heart attacks, requiring extended bed rest. In 1971, Frank Jr. became the newspaper's publisher. Frank Sr. kept his office and secretary and came into the paper daily to manage short-term investments until he died in 1986. Frank Sr. was reluctant to cede authority, and Frank Jr. developed a process of doing things and asking for permission later.[18]

He also brought a more informal leadership style; even his most junior employees called him Frank, while everyone called his father Mr. Daniels. Frank Jr. learned the names of most of his employees. Like his father, he tended to be a micromanager rather than a delegator.

With a winning smile, a quick sense of humor, disarming candor, plenty of charm, and a powerful position, Frank Jr. was what the British called a "clubbable" man. He was friends with the movers and shakers, whether bird hunting in South Carolina or playing golf with Carolina basketball coach Dean Smith at Figure Eight Island, where both men owned homes.

"Frank Jr. was one of the fifteen people who owned and ran the state," said Rob Waters, a veteran editor on the paper. It was a role that Josephus or Jonathan could have also claimed.[19]

From Senator Terry Sanford to Governor Jim Hunt, Tar Heel politicians courted him by frequently soliciting his opinion—and often his campaign contributions—and he was not shy about giving either. Even as some publishers such as the *Washington Post*'s Katherine Graham stopped donating to candidates, Frank Jr. continued not only to make contributions but to hold fundraisers at his house—rejecting pleas from his reportorial staff that he end the practice.

"Frank loves politics," said Dick Jenrette, a Raleigh-born Wall Street tycoon and old college buddy. "Frank loves talking about politics and he's a pretty shrewd observer, but he prefers to play a little bit behind the scenes."[20]

His irreverent attitude was on display in 1996 when Charlie Sanders, a Democratic Senate candidate and Harvard-educated pharmaceutical executive, cardiologist, and a friend of the publisher, appeared before the paper's editorial board seeking an endorsement. Frank Jr. asked him what he thought of the paper's coverage of the Senate campaign. Sanders said he thought it was fair but objected to a profile (incidentally, written by me) that described him as "patrician."

"God damn, Charlie," Frank Jr. said with a smile, breaking the tension in the room. "You sure come across as patrician." Frank Jr. could be remarkably candid and was an inveterate cusser.

Frank Jr. also moved easily in national newspaper circles, forming friendships with industry giants such as Kay Graham, publisher of the *Washington Post*, and Arthur "Punch" Sulzberger, publisher of the *New York Times*. He was part of a close-knit, exclusive group that called itself "the gang" whose members hung out together at meetings of the American Newspaper Publishers Association. "The group partied together, competed on the golf course and tennis court together and played practical jokes on one another," wrote Susan Tifft and Alex Jones, authors of a history of the *New York Times*.[21]

Frank Jr. and Kay Graham had "sort of a flirtation," said Jenrette. "Kay Graham adored Frank. He knew just how to play her."[22]

"In the old days—I'd guess you call it pre-women [lib]—he'd walk into a room where everybody would be real serious, and he'd say to me, 'Hiya, Hot Lips,'" said Graham. "I loved it. I thought it was funny. He knew how to tease, how to have fun." Graham signed one short note to Frank Jr. "xx Hot Lips Senior."[23]

He was constantly traveling across the country—whether attending professional meetings or scouting out potential newspaper properties to buy. As head of the Associated Press and various industry trade groups, he traveled to Tokyo, Seoul, Zurich, and Berlin. He met six presidents, Pope John II, and Nelson Mandela.

Sulzberger traded on his friendship with Frank Jr. in helping his son get a starting job. Many publishers want their children to begin learning their trade on another newspaper. "Sit down, fasten your seat belt, put on your spectacles, light up a good cigar and read on," Sulzberger wrote to Frank Jr. in February 1974. "A young man named Arthur Ochs Sulzberger Jr. will, this spring, God willing, be graduated from Tufts University, and in the fall after a summer of loafing and other unmentionable things, wants to start in the newspaper business. Unfortunately, after I was born, the witty, urbane sophisticated mold was broken and thrown away, but Arthur, nevertheless, is really a pretty intelligent kid and if he weren't my son, I would hire him myself." He added, "Just be grateful that I am trying to peddle my son and not myself."[24]

Young Sulzberger moved to Raleigh in 1974 with his live-in girlfriend, Gail Gregg, who enrolled at UNC to earn a graduate degree. They rented a condo in West Raleigh, often tooling around town on his Kawasaki 900 motorcycle or his Porsche—an indication that he had means beyond his $150 per week salary at the *Raleigh Times*.

Sulzberger was a general assignment reporter, and he fit in with the twenty or so reporters who were also mainly young and single. He was "absolutely, totally green," said Mike Yopp, the managing editor. "We would not normally have hired someone like Arthur with zero experience. It was much like dealing with a college intern." Sulzberger would send his clippings to Seymour Topping, a top *New York Times* editor who was a mentor, griping that the editors made him write short sentences and short words. "It's annoying as hell," he wrote. He mailed one clipping to Topping with the comment, "Being a small-town paper, it was naturally rewritten by my over eager editor. The sad effect of having time to spare." Topping discreetly arranged to have his *Raleigh Times* editors send Sulzberger's raw copy to New York so he could compare it with the published version to help improve Sulzberger's writing.[25]

The unpretentious Sulzberger was popular with his *Raleigh Times* colleagues. Like other reporters, he was required to type obituary notices sent from funeral homes; he called himself "the friend of the dead." His immaturity, awkwardness, and boyish looks made it difficult to envision him having the gravitas to become the publisher of the world's most influential newspaper.

After work Sulzberger would drift over to the Players' Retreat, a beer-only bar near North Carolina State University that was a reporters' hangout. He enjoyed cookouts where there was plenty of Southern Comfort, dope, and dancing. "Arthur Jr.'s two and half years in North Carolina may have been the happiest in his life," wrote Tifft and Jones. "The paper made him feel that he was a member of the team, that he belonged, that he could just be himself."[26]

Sulzberger and Gregg married, and after graduating, she took a job as an intern with the Associated Press wire service before becoming editor of the *Western Wake Herald*, a weekly paper in the Raleigh suburbs. Sulzberger spent his last six months in Raleigh working in production and advertising. In 1976, his father arranged for him to get a reporting job in London with the AP, while Gail landed with UPI's London bureau.

Arthur Jr. was publisher of the *New York Times* from 1992 until 2017, during which time the paper won sixty-one Pulitzer Prizes.

Labor

The *News and Observer* was involved in protracted labor negotiations in the 1930s—so the story goes—when Frank Sr. suggested that the parties agree on an arbitrator. The union negotiator proposed Josephus Daniels, who was due home from Mexico for a visit. "Nothing doing," said Frank Sr. "The old man would give the plant away. We've got to make a living out of it. Pick another arbitrator."[27]

Josephus had been an honorary member of Raleigh Typographical Union No. 54 since 1904, the only publisher in the country to be so singled out. He was known to pay for the funerals of his employees from his own pocket. Not only did the paper tend to side with workers during the labor strife of the 1920s and 1930s, but he was a forceful advocate in other ways.

During a meeting of the Press Institute in Chapel Hill in 1932, there was a move to pass a resolution calling for North Carolina papers to support "open shops" in which employees didn't have to join the union. The anti-union resolution was blocked when Daniels's sons threatened a walkout by the *News and Observer*.[28]

In 1947, Josephus was the most prominent person to testify against an open shop bill in the legislature, which made North Carolina a right-to-work state. He said it was unconstitutional and unfair to working people because twenty-one other organizations in the state had licensing boards, which were in effect their own closed shops. The paper also editorially opposed congressional passage of the Taft-Hartley Act, earlier that year, which prohibited closed shops and otherwise restricted union activity.[29]

Even so, Josephus was also a businessman. "I don't want you to get saddled with too many high-priced men on the *News and Observer*," he wrote Jonathan in 1938.[30]

The tension of being a liberal business owner continued down the generations. As Frank Jr. later wrote his uncle Jonathan, "I shall endeavor to be the liberal publisher—liberal that is except when it interferes with profits."[31]

The Daniels family defeated an effort by the paper's reporters to form a guild in 1970 and instead offered generous raises and promoted anti-union reporters. After defeating the drive, management told reporters involved in the effort that they had no future with the paper.

The union guild supporters put out a newsletter called *The Tocsin*, noting that many of the nation's best newspapers had guilds. They argued that the *News and Observer* was not really "a career paper" and had lost some of its best reporters to better-paying newspapers. Wayne Hurder, a reporter involved in the organizing effort, said pay was the biggest issue. There was also unhappiness over a short-lived city editor and concern about Claude Sitton's role in directing both the news and the opinion page.

Management was dismissive. "It was a rather odd combination of folks—two or three young militants, two or three of our charity cases, and one of our very good reporters," Sitton wrote to Jonathan.[32]

The organizing drive petered out after three to four months, when management offered raises—increasing pay to $180 per week—to longtime staffers such as columnist Charlie Craven and police reporter Bob Lynch, who withdrew their support for the guild, according to Hurder. Gene Marlow, a talented reporter who would later become a Washington bureau chief for Media General Newspapers, was told he had no future with the paper.[33]

The paper's back shop had long been unionized. Since the 1800s, the composing room employees had been represented by the International Typographical Union. The company and union operated on a verbal agreement until the late 1930s, when the first written contract was executed.

The paper's employees eventually came to be represented by three unions. The International Typographical Union represented the composing room employees and the printers; the International Printing Pressmen and Assistants Union represented the pressmen, paper handlers, janitors, stockroom workers, and others; and a third local union represented engravers.

The climate changed in the late sixties when the newspaper moved to photocomposition, switching from hot type to cold type over eight years ending in May 1973. The $1.2 million conversion meant the loss of jobs for the keyboard operators who set type on the linotype machines; they were no longer needed because of the newer technology. The number of composing room employees—foremen, typographers, and technicians—were reduced from 101 to 57, and the number of proofreaders dropped from seventeen full-time and part-time employees to seven.[34]

Management had marathon negotiations with its mailroom employees that stretched over eleven years and 160 negotiating sessions, prompting the International Typographical Union to file a complaint with the National Labor Relations Board alleging that the newspaper was not negotiating in good faith. At one point around 1970, the paper's management drew up contingency plans for a threatened strike that never occurred.[35]

The paper eventually shed its unions. The International Printing Pressmen and Assistants Union voluntarily ceased to represent building maintenance employees in the late 1970s. The engravers voluntarily gave up their contract in 1979. The pressmen voted to decertify in 1981, and the composing room and mail room employees voted to decertify in 1983. By 1983, Frank Jr. boasted to the newspaper's board of directors that the paper was "union-free."[36]

Like many business executives, Frank Jr. was anti-union. After receiving a letter from an Atlanta attorney congratulating the newspaper for its investigation leading to the conviction and jail time for state AFL-CIO president Wilbur Hobby, Frank Jr. replied, "I am fearful that our stories are being so successful in exposing Hobby that we will get a competent union president."[37]

The paper faced a difficult situation of shedding skilled workers during modernization. But its stance certainly opened it to charges of hypocrisy, given its pro-union slant on its editorial page. "Grandfather Josephus was very supportive of labor and had labor unions," Frank Jr. later recalled. "Then I spent fifteen years getting rid of them."[38]

Jonathan's Passing

Jonathan, meanwhile, was fading from the scene, spending more of his time book writing in Hilton Head and less time in Raleigh. By the mid-sixties, Jonathan was a largely absentee editor, retiring as editorial director in 1968. After retiring, Jonathan was rarely seen in the newsroom.

Jonathan's retirement coincided with the breakup of the New Deal coalition that had permitted the Democrats to control the White House and the statehouse for decades. With the rise of the civil rights movement, the white South began voting mostly Republican in national politics.

Jonathan busied himself with the *Island Packet*, a twice-weekly newspaper he started, writing a weekly column called Sojourner Scrapbook, while churning out the last of his twenty-one books and hosting well-lubricated sundowners with his mostly rich Republican friends.

Jonathan was fading, drinking too much, smoking heavily, and depressed about his failing eyesight and age. Lucy went first in January 1979 at age seventy-four. They had been married forty-six years, with Lucy helping him with his books and columns, particularly spelling and grammar.

Alone for his last two years, depressed, legally blind, suffering from emphysema, and dependent on oxygen, the literary-minded Jonathan thought of himself as a modern version of Shakespeare's tragic figure King Lear and began calling his daughter Lucy "Cordelia." Not that Jonathan helped himself, refusing to move back to Raleigh to be near his family or give up his vices.

"This is damned hard, Lucy," Jonathan told his daughter. "Old age is the worst of God's pestilences."

"Father, are you afraid of dying?" his daughter asked. "Not entirely," he replied. "I have some longing . . . I expect to see Mother and Father again. Also, your mother and Babs."

"You do believe in heaven then?" she asked.

"More and more every day," he replied.

He had moved a photo of Babs, his first wife who had died tragically during childbirth, next to that of his second wife, Lucy. An atheist in his youth, Jonathan had returned to his father's faith in later life. "For psychologists, heaven is an illusion," he told his psychologist daughter. "But don't scorn an old man, Lucy."[39]

Jonathan died in November 1981 at age seventy-nine in Hilton Head, where he was buried—six years younger than his father had been and with less robust health in his last years, perhaps testimony to Josephus's abstemious lifestyle and Jonathan's bourbon and Camels–infused habits.

Jonathan was both a maverick and someone who enjoyed being in the back rooms. He pushed for racial change, but slowly. He was an advocate for the disadvantaged but lived in an elegant house and drove luxury cars. He could be harsh, or maybe just clear-eyed, in his judgments of even his closest allies: his father, he said, was a racist; Eleanor Roosevelt was a disagreeable nag; Frank Porter Graham was an egoist more concerned about his image than in winning elections.[40]

Jonathan Daniels was a larger-than-life figure, a polymath who got drunk with novelist Thomas Wolfe, shot craps with poet Ogden Nash, served as FDR's last press secretary, and played poker with Harry Truman. Along the way, he wrote twenty-one books and edited a progressive newspaper that circulated in one of the most conservative regions of the South.

Jonathan was one of a quartet of midcentury southern editors, wrote author John Egerton, who sought to be "a bridge between the Old South and the New, between the painful past and hopeful future."[41]

CHAPTER FOURTEEN

Claude Sitton, the Outsider

With Jonathan heading off to his Hilton Head sunset, the family searched for a successor.

The third generation of Danielses produced one promising newsman, Derick Daniels, the son of Worth Daniels, a Washington, DC, physician, and a grandson of Josephus. Jonathan recruited Derick after he graduated from UNC and later sought to convince him to become editor. But small-town life held no appeal for Derick. "I couldn't have been happy living in Raleigh, addressing the Kiwanis Club on Friday," he once said. "I wouldn't fit in. I love big cities."[1]

Derick was the Daniels family's glamour boy, a high-living executive famous for squiring attractive young women, for his drinking, and for daily smoking four packs of Benson & Hedges. He was editor of the *Detroit Free Press* when the paper won the Pulitzer Prize for its 1967 Detroit riot coverage. He later became a top executive with the Knight Ridder newspaper chain.

When Hugh Hefner hired him in 1976 to become president and chief executive officer of Playboy Enterprises, his cousin Frank Jr. quipped, "He was attracted by Playboy because it had the three things in the world he enjoyed most: drinking, gambling and women."[2]

Before heading to Playboy, Derick threw a notorious farewell party in Miami, renting a Coconut Grove home once used as the movie set for the pornographic classic *Deep Throat*. The male and female servers and bartenders wore only G-strings. His girlfriend, Mary-Jeanette (known as MJ) Taylor, wore a floor-length, hand-painted open coat with her breasts swinging free, nipples covered by star-shaped pasties. Derick wore a gold lamé jumpsuit.

Derick, forty-seven, and MJ, twenty-two, were married after that, the second of his three marriages.[3]

Frank Sr. was shocked at Derick's antics, but Jonathan saw him as "a figure for a neo–Scott Fitzgerald novel." Jonathan was inspired to write a bawdy poem to his nephew, which read in part: "Old ears can still recall your cries at bitten breasts and driven thighs, the moans you made, the breathless quiver, the kiss you gave back to the giver."[4]

Many of the third generation of Danielses were women, but they were not considered for executive positions in that era.

Among the potential candidates for the *News and Observer*'s editor was Tom Inman, Jonathan's son-in-law, who oversaw the editorial page and whom Jonathan championed to be his successor. Also in the group were syndicated *New York Times* columnist Tom Wicker; *New York Times* reporter Gene Roberts; and Sam Ragan, the longtime managing editor.

The family eliminated the candidates one by one. There were doubts that Inman would make a robust editor. Wicker had no interest in giving up his national perch to return to his native North Carolina. And it was felt that Ragan, the laconic poet, did not have the drive or crusading temperament of Josephus and Jonathan.

There is disagreement on why Roberts—widely viewed as one of his generation's best editors—was eliminated. Frank Jr. said he favored Roberts, but his father and Jonathan thought he was too inexperienced. Roberts believes Frank Jr. blocked his appointment because of his pro-union views. Nothing in the Danielses' papers sheds light on the decision. Roberts says the failure to get the *News and Observer* post was a blessing in disguise, enabling him to shine in Philadelphia and New York. Another possibility for the position was Don Shoemaker, a UNC graduate who had edited the Asheville paper and would later become the editor of the *Miami Herald*. But Jonathan said that while Shoemaker was very able, Raleigh was not ready to accept a Jewish editor of the paper.[5]

In 1968, Claude Sitton became the first and only nonfamily member to edit the paper during the Daniels era. Sitton, a Georgia native, was a reporting legend, having covered the civil rights movement in the South for the *New York Times*.

As Gene Roberts once noted, Sitton was "a bona fide son of the South," with a lineage that included Confederates, railroads, circuit-riding preachers, bluegrass, and gospel music.[6] He was taught how to plow a cotton field by an old tenant farmer named Gus. He learned from his mother to love the written word and despise racist demagogues such as Georgia governor

Eugene Talmadge. At Emory University in Atlanta, he became interested in news reporting and politics.

"That was the South crushed by its past," Sitton said in a speech, "the South of the one-horse farm, the poll tax and one-party politics, the South of Jim Crow and lynch law."7

Like many farm boys, Sitton wanted to see the world. He served a stint in World War II in the Atlantic with the merchant marine and then in the Pacific as a boatswain aboard an LST, a navy landing craft used in amphibious operations. Sitton said Japanese fire did not scare him as much as a typhoon with seventy-five-foot waves that broke the ship's steering cables.

After the war, Sitton worked as a wire service reporter in the South and later in New York. Living in Greenwich Village, he fell in with a beat crowd that included Allen Ginsberg, Jack Kerouac, and William Burroughs—although Sitton, with his straitlaced persona and close-cropped hair, seemed the antithesis of a beatnik. Wanting to work overseas, he joined the US Information Agency. He was assigned two years to the American embassy in Ghana, where he watched the British colony become the first Black African nation to earn its independence, which helped mold his views on race. He later worked in Tehran.

Back in the states, Sitton was working for the *New York Times* when the civil rights movement began in the South—one of the most powerful American stories of the twentieth century. Turner Catledge, the Mississippi-born editor, was looking for a native southerner who had the smarts, drive, and talent to tell the nation about the Black struggle at its most dangerous point.

The bland-appearing Sitton could have passed as an accountant—a man of average height with thinning hair and a stoic bearing. Only his firm chin, runner's body, and intense stare stood out.

"He was about to set into motion a level of reporting that would establish the national standard for two decades," wrote Gene Roberts and Hank Klibanoff, who chronicled the reporting on civil rights in their Pulitzer Prize–winning history called *The Race Beat*. "Nobody in the news business would have as much impact as he would—on the reporting of the civil rights movement, on the federal government's response, or on the movement itself. Sitton's byline would be atop the stories that landed on the desks of three presidents. His phone number would be carried protectively in the wallets of civil rights workers who saw him, and the power of his byline, as their best hope for survival."8

Covering a fast-evolving story, Sitton sometimes worked six weeks without a day off, missing major family events in his Atlanta home. One night he arrived at the airport at 11 p.m. and flew out the following morning at 3 a.m.

Sitton was in Oxford when efforts to integrate the University of Mississippi in 1962 erupted into a bloody riot—what Sitton called the last battle of the Civil War. He was in Birmingham when Bull Connor turned on the fire hoses and sicced the dogs on civil rights marchers. He was in Jackson when NAACP leader Medgar Evers was gunned down. He was in Montgomery when Governor George Wallace stood in the schoolhouse door. And he was in a lot of smaller places where he shined a journalistic light.

Covering a white South seething in anger, the *New York Times* man was often met with hostility—even with his Georgia accent.

One evening at Mount Olive Baptist Church in rural south Georgia, he was with a small group of voting rights activists when they heard car doors slam outside. With chilling novelistic detail, Sitton conveyed the terror as Terrell County sheriff T. Z. Matthews and his deputies confronted the group meeting in the sanctuary. Sitton recounted how one deputy smacked a heavy flashlight in his hand while another ran his hand over his cartridge belt. A list of the license plates of those attending was read out loud. "We want our colored people to go on living like they have for the last 100 years," the sheriff said.

When the sheriff asked Sitton to identify himself, Sitton shot back, "I'm an American, sheriff. Who are you?"[9] When Sitton returned to his rental station wagon, he found sand had been poured into the gas tank and air let out of his tires. Several weeks later, the church was burned to the ground.

"I thought, by God, that's the end of us," said Bill Shipp, an Atlanta reporter who was with Sitton. "He did not flinch and he didn't back down. He was a brave man. But he was more than just brave. He was a first-rate journalist. When Claude was around, we all gathered in his room to compare notes. He was the kind of unofficial squad leader of the reporters covering civil rights."[10] President John F. Kennedy and Attorney General Robert Kennedy read Sitton's story. Within hours a task force of Justice Department lawyers and FBI agents had descended on "Terrible Terrell," and within two weeks, a voting rights complaint was filed in a county where only 51 of the 8,209 Black residents were registered.

When the first alarm went out in the middle of the night about three missing civil rights leaders in Neshoba County, Mississippi—they were killed and buried by the Klan with the help of local sheriff's deputies—the calls went to the FBI, the US Justice Department, and Sitton. Parts of Mississippi were in a homicidal rage. The first reporters to arrive in Philadelphia, Mississippi, were Sitton and Karl Fleming of *Newsweek*. The sheriff told them they were traitors to "our precious Southern way of life" and ordered them to leave town—a notion seconded by a gang of white toughs who "promised violence against the lying, mongrelized Northern press."[11]

Back at their hotel, the manager threatened to evict Sitton. "Look, tell these folks that they can shoot me," Sitton said. "But I guarantee you that there will be five just like me to get off the plane at Jackson airport tomorrow, and they'll be right up here to cover the story." Shotgun-toting men arrived at the hotel inviting Sitton and Fleming to "take a ride with us out in the country." Instead, the two reporters packed their bags and left town, returning later when things had calmed down to report the story.[12]

Sitton recalled meeting Easy Steptoe in the small southern Mississippi town of Liberty. Steptoe, an elderly Black man, had been helping organize local voter registration. Steptoe could be forgiven for thinking that he was living on borrowed time because Black men from Liberty had already been killed, while others had been flogged or driven off their farms. Steptoe said he was glad to see Sitton and another white reporter. "I'm proud to see yawl, for as long as yawl's here, I know I got a few more minutes to live."[13]

To remain inconspicuous, Sitton and Fleming developed a reporter's notebook in which they halved a stenographer's pad, so it could be hidden away in a coat jacket—now the industry standard. He had shatterproof glass installed in his spectacles after a fellow reporter was thrown through a plate glass window. In southern restaurants he refused to sit with his back to the front door. He was the model of professional circumspection, never having more than two drinks and smoking only moderately. His frequent traveling companion, Karl Fleming, a North Carolina native, later wrote, "I imagined it felt almost like being behind enemy lines in some hostile and warring country. Who could you trust? Who could you turn to if you got in real trouble? Who would come to your aid if you were dragged out of your motel room in the middle of the night? Who would care if you were waylaid and killed in our car on a dark country road?" Southern-bred reporters such as Sitton and Fleming were particularly hated because they were regarded as traitors to the South.[14]

In 1964, Sitton was named the *New York Time*'s national editor, overseeing ten regional bureaus, fifty-two full-time reporters, and 225 part-time correspondents. But Sitton was soon entangled in office politics, caught between the New York editors and the leaders of a powerful Washington bureau.[15]

Looking to leave, Sitton considered several southern newspapers, including the *Louisville Courier-Journal* and *The State* of Columbia, South Carolina, before deciding on the *News and Observer*. Sitton was probably tipped to the

Raleigh opening by Wallace Carroll, editor/publisher of the *Winston-Salem Journal* and a former *New York Times* colleague.[16]

In hiring Sitton, the Daniels family understood it was getting a strong-willed individual who would continue the paper's crusading voice. "If Mr. Sitton's career has been inordinately distinguished, the tradition of the Raleigh newspaper is rich and colorful," opined the *Greensboro Daily News*. "It should be a happy match, for Mr. Sitton is cut from the same tough journalistic mold as the N&O's Josephus and Jonathan Daniels."[17]

For twenty-two years, Sitton set the tone for the paper in a dual role as the chief news executive and head of the editorial page. He improved the quality and professionalism of the paper. Sitton stressed investigative work, government watchdog reporting, and politics. He attempted to move the newspaper away from its close association with the Democratic Party, even as the paper continued to endorse mainly Democrats.

Shortly after taking office, Sitton told a business group that "popularity is not a legitimate goal of a newspaper," which suited both Sitton's vision of the newspaper and his personality—he was too intense and had too many sharp edges to be a glad-hander. There was a recoil from Sitton's strong views. "You must have hired Sitton from Russia," Willie York, a prominent Raleigh real estate developer, wrote Jonathan.[18]

Sitton seemed driven, even on his days off. He hiked the Appalachian Trail with his wife, Eva. His company car was a GT Mustang, the fastest American-made automobile. In quieter moments, he loved country and gospel music and played a passable guitar.

The newspaper had slipped in the late sixties with Jonathan often an absentee editor and because Ragan did not push his staff. Other newspapers were challenging the *News and Observer*, including the *Charlotte Observer*, which under the new Knight Ridder chain ownership—and gifted editor Pete McKnight—was plowing money into its operation, hiring away some of the Raleigh paper's star reporters, adopting a more progressive edge in its editorials, and racking up prizes. The *Winston-Salem Journal*, under Wallace Carroll, was also experiencing a golden era.[19]

Sitton was determined to inject rigor into the operation and to change the newsroom culture. "He sort of hit the place like a tornado," remembered Gary Pearce, a former reporter and editor at the paper. "He was a very strong, forceful guy, huge reputation as a newsman, and you suddenly had this feeling that the standards and expectations had been ratcheted up."[20]

Claude Sitton, the reporting legend whom the
Daniels family hired to run the paper.
(Reprinted with permission of the News and Observer.)

The paper, Sitton declared, was too provincial and too boring. He cited one day's newspaper that carried such headlines as "Columbus ABC Profits," "Morgan to Speak in Goldsboro," "Oxford Town Board Spurns Court Parking Order," and "Henderson Returns Water Pipes."[21]

The paper could afford to be more ambitious under Sitton because the Research Triangle Park, one of the nation's most prominent high-tech research and development centers, was about to turn the Raleigh–Durham–Chapel Hill region into a fast-growing Sunbelt dynamo. By 1970, Raleigh had grown to 122,000 residents.

The paper's business in the 1950s had been "lousy," with the cash flow—profits before taxes and debt obligations—about 12 percent, according to Frank Jr. Profits would rise dramatically in the 1960s and even more so in the 1970s, eventually reaching 25 percent under the Daniels family ownership. "We could have gone up to 40 [percent]," Frank Jr. said. "There were newspapers that went beyond 35 and 40 [percent]."[22]

The seventies brought a wave of prosperity with new shopping centers and residential subdivisions being erected on old farmland, and with it a sharp spike in advertising fueled by department stores such as Hudson Belk, K-Mart, Sears, Boylan Pearce, and J. C. Penney and supermarkets such as Colonial and Winn-Dixie.[23]

There was a churn at the newspaper's top, as Sitton assembled his team. Ragan purchased *The Pilot*, a small-town paper in the golfing resort of Southern Pines, where he continued to be a significant cultural figure in the state. Woodrow Price stepped down as managing editor but continued to write his wildlife column while running the business desk before retiring.

Sitton's majordomo of the newsroom was Robert L. Brooks, who was managing editor during most of Sitton's era, from 1972 to 1986. Brooks joined the newspaper in 1946 as a sportswriter after serving in the Marine Corps in the Pacific in World War II, entering as a private and discharged as a first lieutenant. He was a tough, demanding old-school journalist who outworked everyone in the newsroom. Brooks would start his day at 8:30 a.m. Colleagues could set their watch by when Brooks grabbed his fedora at five o'clock to go home for dinner with his family before returning for several more hours to put the paper to bed. When he left again, he took home the first edition of the paper and thoroughly proofread it, with copy editors sometimes getting post-midnight calls asking them to correct paragraph 24 of a story buried inside the paper. He required reporters to show him key documents that the stories were based on and to have multiple sources on controversial stories.

Brooks pushed his small staff to be aggressive and to "get it first but get it right." He chewed out reporters and editors who did not measure up, his face getting red, while also providing attaboy pats on the back to those who delivered. "He was the toughest son of a bitch I ever met," said Pearce, who was an editor under Brooks. "He scared the shit out of me; he really did. He did the same thing with reporters. Brooks's theory of management, I think, was pretty much formed when he was in the marines and never changed."[24]

His style worked less well with women or later generations of reporters. He once instructed a junior editor to push a reporter, Leslie Wayne, a talented woman reporter who later worked for the *New York Times*. He told the editor, "You've got to kick her in the balls."[25]

Because Sitton was such an iconic figure, many young journalists from across the South wanted to work for him. Some went on to successful careers with the *New York Times*, the *Philadelphia Inquirer*, *Newsweek* magazine, and the *Herald Tribune* in Paris and in academia. Among the most notable were Ferrel Guillory, who influenced a generation of political reporters at the *News and Observer* as well as headed the editorial page—pushing for a more rigorous analytic approach—before leaving for academia, and David Zucchino, who became one of his generation's best foreign correspondents with the *Philadelphia Inquirer, Los Angeles Times*, and *New York Times*, winning two Pulitzer

Bob Brooks, the managing editor who ran the
newsroom as if he were still in the marines.
(Reprinted with permission of the News and Observer.)

Prizes. Other young journalists became editors of the *St. Louis Post-Dispatch* and the *Greensboro News and Record*.

The most influential was Pat Stith, a folksy investigative reporter whose aw-shucks demeanor, tobacco chewing, buzz haircut, and cowboy boots caused many politicians and government officials to underestimate him—often to their great regret.

By the time he retired in 2008 after thirty-six years on the paper, Stith fooled no one; his voice on the telephone or his appearance at an office was enough to send shivers down the spines of the powerful across the state.

There had been little tradition of investigative reporting at the paper until Sitton hired Stith in 1972 from the *Charlotte News* and gave him the flexibility and time to engage in months-long investigations. Among those keenly feeling the changing nature of the Sitton regime was Democratic governor Bob Scott (1969–73).

Scott, a member of North Carolina's most famous political clan, had close ties to the paper. He remembered the days when Jonathan had advised his father, Governor W. Kerr Scott; his grandfather, nicknamed Farmer Bob Scott, was a friend of Josephus's. Bob Scott had appointed Woodrow Price, the paper's managing editor, chairman of the State Ports Authority. But Scott became angry about Stith's investigations of his administration, which he characterized as "character assassination." He had had several run-ins with Frank Jr., the paper's publisher, including one at a manufacturing plant dedication in Wake Forest. The governor told the audience that the paper should develop a product "that would cause the newspaper to self-destruct whenever the percentage of the half-truths they print gets above 50 percent that now seems to be the company policy." Scott wrote in his diary, "Later Frank told me he thought it was a clever statement. I replied, 'I meant every damned word of it.' He replied, 'I know you did.' He started to extend his hand for a handshake, but I gave him a look of disgust, turned away and walked off."[26]

Stith became one of the nation's best investigative reporters. He was recognized at first for his dogged digging and later for his innovative use of computer technology to accompany his shoe leather. His work drew the attention of Stanford University professor James T. Hamilton, who sought to quantify some 150 Stith investigations in his 2016 book, *Democracy's Detectives: The Economics of Investigative Journalism*.

He found that Stith's investigations resulted in the passage of thirty-one new laws and saved taxpayers millions of dollars. There was hardly any issue involving watchdog reporting that did not attract Stith. He examined psychiatric centers, highway and bridge repair, lax DUI prosecutions, campaign reporting violations, crooked use of odometers, misuse of credit insurance, and the shortcomings of the state's Dickensian unemployment compensation program.

He examined the abuses of overweight trucks, missed payments to nursing homes, the power of the billboard industry, and the lack of regulation of the safety of well water. State employees were fired or demoted because of his stories. His series on cigarette smuggling by organized crime had him checking under his hood before starting his car. The state AFL-CIO president went to prison after Stith discovered he was illegally using federal training money. Wake County Schools superintendent John Murphy resigned in 1981 after Stith reported that he had used school phones for private consulting work and had provided consulting contracts to those who had hired him for consulting work. In 1996, Stith was the lead reporter on a team that won a Pulitzer Prize for a five-part series on hog pollution in the state that resulted in a state moratorium on new pig farms.

"These laws affected multiple policy areas: public safety, environmental protection, criminal justice, civil rights and health care," Hamilton wrote. "The impacts were spread out across millions of North Carolinians, since the reforms affected people in multiple roles, for example, as workers, drivers, consumers and patients."[27]

Not only was Stith given time to conduct his investigations, but Sitton had his back. Late one Saturday night in early 1972, an IRS agent from Atlanta called Stith at home and said he wanted to meet with him. Although the IRS investigator did not say what he wanted, Stith knew—he had just written a story saying the IRS had recommended the prosecution of thirteen men associated with Democratic governor Bob Scott's 1968 campaign, and the agent wanted to know the source of the story.

Stith called the paper's city desk, and soon Sitton was on the phone, telling him not to meet with the agent. Instead, Sitton dressed and went to the paper, collecting a reporter and photographer, and surprised the IRS agent by showing up at his hotel room after 11 p.m. Sitton stepped back, the photographer snapped the agent's picture in his pajamas, and Sitton told him if he wanted to talk with one of his reporters he should do it properly—making an appointment at the paper. The agent met with Sitton but got no information.[28]

"Frank Jr. said one time, 'We needed an editor that had the killer instinct,'" recalled Dave Jones, the paper's top business executive. "And I said, 'Well, we don't have to worry about that because Claude kills them and then kicks the body.'"[29]

The *News and Observer* of the 1970s

The *News and the Observer* of the early 1970s, when I started at the paper, would have been recognizable to earlier generations of journalists. There were newsroom veterans who had begun working for the paper in the 1940s.

Stories were still banged out on typewriters, and the term "cut and paste" was not a computer function but the product of the scissors and paste pot that were on every reporter's desk for rewriting and rearranging paragraphs. Unpublishable stories were literally "spiked"—that is, impaled on a metal desktop spike. Reporters were required to use two pieces of carbon paper—one for the paper's files and one for the Associated Press, which ran a version of many of the paper's stories. Stories from Washington were sent by Western Union.

A crescendo of noise rose as the evening deadline approached, with the clatter of typewriters joining that of the teletype machines delivering news from wire services; curses expanded in frequency and volubility as the pressure grew. One short-fused editor was famous for regularly kicking a small trash can across the room. Another editor would have been rendered nearly mute if not for some variation of the word "fuck." Later in the evening the giant presses two floors below the newsroom would start to rumble.

Stories were still dictated over desktop telephones, the most advanced technology in the newsroom. The cries of "copy" could be heard as copy boys scrambled to take stories from editors and place them in pneumatic tubes that whisked them down to the composing room.

The smoke-filled newsroom was old-fashioned in other ways. There was an old-time police reporter who had a stogie permanently protruding from his lips and who was known to don diving gear to help in police searches. Stith kept a series of Styrofoam cups on his desk to act as spittoons for his stream of tobacco juice. The managing editor, Bob Brooks, was not the only person who still wore a fedora.

The newsroom comprised mainly white males, although that was changing. There were only a few Black reporters, and most women journalists worked for the Today's Woman section. Obituaries were taken over the telephone by inmates on work release from the women's prison in Raleigh. One of the inmates, a hardened platinum blonde, was carrying on during work breaks on the roof with one particularly libidinous male reporter—or at least that was what the reporter claimed.

In one significant change in 1973, the paper switched from the traditional hot metal typesetting machines, known as linotypes—an 1800s technology. Using letterpress printing, this method injected molten type metal into a mold, resulting in slugs that were used to press ink onto paper. The new technology used phototypesetting that was controlled by a computer keyboard.

Despite the modest pay and long, irregular hours, there was a romance to newspapers. Reporters got a front-row seat to history, learned the back story, often uncovered things that officialdom wanted to keep quiet, or simply raced to the big fire. In the age before the Internet or cable news, reporters got the hot news before anyone else. Some of the news came over machines connected to the wire services. The wires had alarm bells with the number of bells going off announcing the importance of an event.

When he came to the paper, "Sitton brought the soul of the *Times* with him," wrote journalist Barry Yeoman. "He retained his passion for liberal causes such as civil rights, but he also brought his old newspaper's just-the-facts approach to journalism. 'I'm an old newsman,' he says—and that's reflected in the paper he edits."[30]

His Sunday column offered a vigorous progressive voice that showed a sharp analytical mind and a graceful writing style. The column frequently pushed against the state's conservative inertia—from improving the state's underfunded public schools, to stricter environmental enforcement, to improving race relations, to supporting the university and opposing conservative politicians such as Jesse Helms.

On economic questions, Sitton put the paper on the side of the little guy. The paper often found itself at odds with the business community. He helped derail tort reform that would have profited insurance companies by limiting accident victims' rights in court. Sitton's father had been a conductor on the Southern Railway who during the Depression had been demoted to brakeman. When the elder Sitton broke his back on the job, Southern Railway tried to deny him benefits. Only after hiring a leading claims lawyer was the elder Sitton able to collect benefits, which he used to take up farming in north Georgia.[31]

"Silence in the face of injustice is not neutrality," said Sitton in a speech accepting an award from the local chapter of the American Civil Liberties Union. "It is, instead, cowardice."[32]

In 1983 Sitton was awarded the Pulitzer Prize for his commentary. On the day the Pulitzer was announced, Sitton was out on his daily four-mile jog at 6 a.m. when one of the paper's carriers pulled his car over and rolled down the window. "Congratulations Claude," said the carrier. "You just keep on writing that bull and I'll keep throwing it."[33]

The paper was the leader in the South in covering the brown lung disease that was harming textile workers, according to the *Columbia Journalism Review*—although the *Charlotte Observer* would later win a Pulitzer after having been chastised by the *Review*.[34]

"One of the great things about the *News and Observer* is that they were pretty damn fearless," said four-term Democratic governor Jim Hunt (1977–85, 1993–2001). "They had editors who would call it like they saw it, and they had a bunch of reporters who were not intimidated by anybody. They were pretty tough personally, wouldn't give in to you. They were pretty hard chargers, I think by and large, more than other papers."[35]

Among the paper's crusades was opposition to creating a second state-financed medical school at East Carolina University. Also opposing the project was the state university administration and much of the Piedmont establishment, which felt North Carolina could not afford to finance two public medical schools. But the school had strong backing in Eastern North Carolina, the most rural part of the state where there was a shortage of physicians. After seeing how the medical school served the east for twenty years, Frank Jr. later said the paper's opposition had been a mistake.[36]

Civil Rights

Sitton took command of the paper after the first wave of civil rights activism in North Carolina, marked by lunch counter sit-ins. But there was still plenty of activism, particularly in the eastern part of the state. The *News and Observer* took what Sitton called "a moderate to liberal approach" that was "in tune with the thinking of middle-class Blacks."[37]

Sitton, who ran the editorial page, had little toleration for disruptive tactics. The paper called the seizure of Duke University's registrar's office by Black student activists in 1969 "hoodlum behavior pretending to an intellectual or moral cause." The paper was also skeptical of many of their demands, such as the creation of an all-Black dormitory and a student-run Black studies program.[38]

When civil rights activist Golden Frinks led "jail-ins," disrupting Raleigh traffic, and sought to create a tent city, Sitton was unimpressed. He said that while the Reverend Martin Luther King Jr. broke the law in practicing civil disobedience, "the illegal activities in downtown Raleigh are of a different stripe": they "cheapen the idea of non-violent protest."[39]

The paper pushed for full racial integration of the public schools and chastised local officials in counties when they took steps to maintain segregation. When a federal official in 1969 temporarily upheld the Raleigh school system's voluntary "freedom of choice" plan, the *News and Observer* said the city's school board should use the time to "to develop its own plan for eliminating schools that are either mostly Black or mostly white. And that includes limited busing."[40]

Such views infuriated Jesse Helms, the conservative WRAL-TV commentator, who said the paper favored integration "at any cost." Helms said federal officials should be informed "that the *News and Observer* does not in this matter speak for the people of Raleigh and that it seldom does on any matter."[41]

The paper pushed for the merger of the Raleigh and Wake County school systems, a move aimed at fostering integration and successfully preventing a repeat of the pattern in many northern cities—a largely poor Black city surrounded by affluent white suburbs. Frank Daniels Jr. lobbied for the merger, donated to the merger campaign, and provided free advertising to the effort.[42]

Sitton made sure there was an unrelenting drumbeat of merger stories, even when there was little news to keep the issue on the front burner. "This was the Claude Sitton show," said Linda Williams, the paper's school board reporter in the mid-1970s. "He was going to make that merger happen. . . .

He decided that integrated schools were the right thing to do, which it was, and he saw the white flight happening and saw that Raleigh was going to end up with a mostly Black city school system, surrounded by whites."[43]

But Sitton was privately skeptical when it came to court-ordered busing. "The busing issue has created a problem for us editorially," he wrote to Jonathan in 1970. "I do not feel that we should support mass cross-town busing which could prove even more detrimental to the best interests of public-school students than segregation." If the Supreme Court ruled in favor of busing—which it did in the landmark Charlotte case of *Swann v. Charlotte-Mecklenburg Board of Education* in 1971—Sitton said the paper would have to reluctantly go along with it for reasons of law and order. Three years later, Sitton's views seemed to have evolved; he said that without busing, "we undoubtedly would see a shift back to the old pattern where the quality of public education depended on the quality of the neighborhood."[44]

Jonathan was also skeptical of busing, telling former governor Terry Sanford that antibusing protests were being driven by "a deep, self-righteous anger of the decent [white] lower middle class. Apparently, no liberal is supposed ever to express dissent against the stupidities of those who presume to be our leaders of the way to be one happy prejudice-less society. But race balance is not the whole business of education."[45]

The paper gave minimal attention to Southeast Raleigh, the majority-Black quadrant of the city, reporting its problems such as crime and poverty but not covering the culture or how people lived. "There was no coverage from the viewpoint of the Black community in Southeast Raleigh," said Williams, who is African American.[46]

Bob Brooks, who oversaw much of the paper's coverage, could be forward-thinking. He greenlighted Gene Roberts's groundbreaking racial discrimination series in the early 1960s. But he also had blind spots. Brooks dismissed the request of Connie Laibe, a Harvard-educated reporter, to chronicle Oxford's two orphanages—one for whites and one for Blacks—as a nonstory. She later wrote the Oxford story after joining the *New York Times*.[47]

One of the most potent racial controversies of the era involved the Wilmington Ten, a group of activists convicted of firebombing and conspiracy for their role in the racial disturbance in the Port City in February 1971. After the group—mainly high school students—were cumulatively given 282 years in prison, there was an international outcry.

Concerned that the Wilmington Ten case was besmirching North Carolina's reputation, Jonathan sought reassurances that the paper had thoroughly examined the situation. Sitton said the paper had conducted three investigations by young, pro–civil rights reporters and was unable to discover any evidence that the Ten had been railroaded. Still, the paper argued editorially for the commutation of the sentences—which Sitton declared were excessive.[48]

One of the most contentious investigations of the Sitton era was the failure of the federally funded Soul City development that began in the 1970s in Warren County. Soul City was one of sixteen projects subsidized by the federal New Communities program, created in 1968 to help private developers build racially and economically diverse new towns. But as the program lacked capital, good locations, and expertise, only one of the developments was financially successful—The Woodlands, located outside Houston, which had a deep-pocketed natural gas mogul behind the project. The plug was pulled on Soul City in 1980, and three years later the entire New Communities program was ended.

Of all the New Communities projects, none was riskier than Soul City. The other projects were located near major metropolitan areas. Soul City was situated in one of the poorest counties in America—an isolated rural, majority-Black county on the Virginia border. The county has fewer people living there today than it did in 1880.

Soul City was the brainchild of civil rights leader Floyd McKissick, who wanted to reverse the flow of Black migrants out of the South by building a city—while integrated—developed by African Americans and that would especially appeal to Black people.

The obstacles were numerous. McKissick had no experience as a real estate developer, the Soul City name made some industrial prospects leery, there were no deep financial pockets behind the project, and the rural location meant that everything had to be built from scratch—schools, water, sewer, industry, parks, housing, shopping centers, and so forth.

The project received $29 million from federal grants and loan guarantees ($165 million in 2024 dollars) awarded by the Nixon administration, after McKissick, a lifelong Democrat, switched his registration to Republican and campaigned vigorously for Nixon's 1972 reelection.

Stith's investigation resulted in a series in March 1975 that raised questions about the project. The stories noted the political connections, the interlocking directorships, the hiring of family members, and most importantly how little there was to show for taxpayers' money spent—"no industry there, no shops, no houses—no Soul City."[49]

Sitton was also troubled by the Soul City project from the beginning, viewing it as a move toward racial resegregation. As early as 1971, the project's supporters said the paper's skeptical coverage "smacks of functional 'racism.'" The North Carolina Association of Black Lawyers—a group that included McKissick and others involved in the project—asserted that the paper's coverage was "racially inspired."[50] That assertion was underscored in a book published in 2021 by Thomas Healy, a Seton Hall law professor, who worked as a reporter in the paper's Durham bureau during the 1990s.

Although Healy noted that Soul City was "a highly improbable venture" because of the barriers of trying to "build a city out of nothing," he advanced the thesis that the project was unfairly killed by an unlikely Right-Left coalition of Republican senator Jesse Helms and the *News and Observer*.

"What doomed Soul City was not just the size of its ambition but, at least in part, the color," Healy wrote. "Like nearly every other effort to improve the lives of Black people, it was subjected to a level of scrutiny, second-guessing, and outright hostility that other ambitious ventures rarely encounter."[51]

But it was Democrat Jimmy Carter's administration—including his housing secretary Patricia Harris, the first African American woman cabinet member—who pulled the plug on Soul City after concluding it could not succeed.

Sports

Perhaps even more controversial was the paper's investigation of North Carolina State University basketball coach Jim Valvano.

The Triangle is one of the nation's leading hotbeds for college sports, with college football having been important in the first half of the century and basketball a regional passion since the 1940s. Duke, Carolina, and North Carolina State have avid followings, and the fierce school rivalries dominate water cooler talk—and taunting—year-round.

The *News and Observer* has long served as a watchdog on college sports, raising questions about commercialization, professionalization, and cheating. In 1935, UNC president Frank Porter Graham, heading a national college group, proposed radical reforms that included a ban on recruiting, ending athletic scholarships, and no preferential treatment of athletes. Powerful alumni opposition killed the plan.

Supporting Graham's plan, Josephus wrote that commercialism in football was "a part of a dangerous commercialism which creeps into all good things, and . . . should be rigidly excluded."[52]

Sitton was a vocal skeptic of big-time college athletics. He graduated from Emory University, which does not participate in intercollegiate sports. Sitton criticized UNC's firing of football coach Dick Crum in 1987 because of his mediocre record, saying a university with intellectual pretentions shouldn't behave like a football factory. He called the firing "a business most grubby, one with little of the honesty and all of the greed that marks the professional game."[53]

Among those who agreed with Sitton was UNC president William C. Friday, one of the nation's most widely respected academic leaders. "He [Sitton] became very hard about sports, but it was an earned position because he realized how corrupt it was," said Friday. He said Sitton's views helped shape his own, leading him to become founding cochair of the Knight Commission on Intercollegiate Athletics in 1989 to consider reforms to college athletics.[54]

Valvano was an immensely popular coach with a quick wit and an engaging manner who led the Wolfpack basketball program to an improbable NCAA championship in 1983 and who would later be widely admired for his courageous battle with cancer that would take his life. His success on the basketball court led the Raleigh school to name him athletic director in 1986.

But there were soon questions about whether Valvano's drive for success had caused him to loosen too many institutional controls on the athletic program. In January 1989, the paper reported that Simon and Schuster was about to publish a book, called *Personal Fouls*, by Peter Golenbock, a national sportswriter and author. The book portrayed a program out of control: players illegally selling sneakers and tickets, drug use, admissions standards lowered for athletes, players' grades changed to keep them eligible. In one case, a star player was admitted with an SAT college board score of 470—a test taker gets 400 for just signing his or her name—who told a tutor he could not name the country located to the south of the United States. Sniffing a scandal, the *News and Observer* bore down hard on the controversy with a string of stories mainly written by John Day and Liz Clarke.

Irregularities were found by the UNC board of governors, which appointed a committee to investigate the allegations. The NCAA put the North Carolina State basketball program on probation, and both Valvano and Chancellor Bruce Poulton resigned. Poulton complained of "the malicious motives" behind the *News and Observer*'s coverage and editorials, saying they had "damaged my reputation."[55]

The stories created a backlash, with the paper receiving hundreds of letters and phone calls from irate fans, some threatening and obscene. During a football game between NC State and Georgia Tech, an airplane flew over Carter-Finley Stadium with the trailing message "Just Say 'No' to The N&O! Go Pack." The paper was still eliciting boos more than a decade later when an ad for the paper appeared on NC State arena's Jumbotron. "I have never observed such unabashed, biased reporting toward an individual or toward a quality institution as I have seen in your shameless attack on Jim Valvano's integrity and the name of our fine university," wrote one reader, Jim White of Cary.[56]

The paper's aggressive coverage of Valvano and Poulton led to internal divisions. Among those who thought the paper went too far were Frank Jr.; Dave Jones, the general manager; and sports columnist and former sports editor Joe Tiede. In retiring at age sixty-two after thirty-three years with the paper, Tiede expressed his disagreement "with editorial and news policy which I felt was far too strongly negative towards college athletics." But Sitton was always skeptical of sportswriters' willingness to critically examine sports, writing privately that they "consider themselves members of the sports establishment and defenders of the faith."[57]

Twenty years later, the *News and Observer* uncovered a scandal at UNC, where for fifteen years, fake classes were created mainly to keep athletes academically eligible. The scandal prompted authorities to place the school under sanctions and academic probation. Football coach Butch Davis was fired, athletic director Dick Baddour retired, and Chancellor Holden Thorp took a job at another school. The paper found some 200 lecture courses in the Department of African American Studies that never took place, dubious independent study courses, and improper help from tutors. Many of the students in the courses were football or basketball players.

Dan Kane, an investigative reporter, was dogged in his reporting, despite an angry response from some Carolina fans. "There have been violent threats, angry screeds, Twitter flame campaigns and an entire website predicated on the punitive hideousness of Dan Kane's existence," a *New York Times* reporter wrote. "Someone sent Kane an email wishing him a lingering death by bone cancer. Someone else tweeted him a photograph of a noose."[58]

Yet despite occasional investigations, the paper helped build the sports-crazy culture by emphasizing sports coverage as a circulation builder. The paper attracted many talented sportswriters including Dick Herbert, Caulton Tudor, Bruce Phillips, A. J. Carr, Gerald Martin, Barry Svrluga, and Luke DeCock.

Politics

Sitton attempted to make the paper more professional and less partisan, but for Republicans, it seemed like a barely discernible evolution. The paper did not endorse its first Republican candidate—a GOP judge candidate—until 1988.

The *News and Observer* was part of a small band of daily newspapers that supported liberal Democratic presidential candidate George McGovern in 1972 against incumbent Richard Nixon, a Republican, who garnered 93 percent of the newspaper endorsements nationally. In the same year, in a Democratic presidential primary in North Carolina that the paper dubbed "The Dixie Classic," former North Carolina governor Terry Sanford faced Alabama governor George Wallace. Sitton wrote dispatches from Alabama showing how poorly the state had fared under Wallace's leadership, but Wallace won easily anyway.

Jonathan admonished Sitton for not being supportive enough of Sanford in his 1972 presidential bid, urging him to more strenuously back him in 1976 when Sanford was preparing for a second White House run. "There are battles which the N&O was born for," Jonathan wrote. "This is one." But Sitton replied that he was more concerned about the *News and Observer* being perceived as too biased in favor of Sanford.[59]

Sitton disliked printing conservative opinions in his paper. He complained to a newspaper syndicate that one of their writers, Washington, DC, social columnist Betty Beale, had a pro–Richard Nixon bias. "We are not going to permit our columns to be used for right-wing Republican puffery week in and week out," Sitton wrote.[60] He also groused about printing letters to the editor that disagreed with the paper's opinion—which is the point of letters to the editor. The paper's progressive tradition extended back to the days of the horse and buggy, so it would have been a remarkable reversal if it had suddenly become an advocate of Ronald Reagan or Donald Trump.

"The Danielses have long memories," Frank Jr. told the Kinston Rotary Club in 1989. "The N&O's social function is to play an adversarial role in relations to government and other public institutions, to provide a voice, not only for you and me, but also for those in our communities who, because they are economically or educationally deprived, have no forum or influence with government or business."[61]

The *News and Observer* could not have been a progressive crusading newspaper without the blessing of Frank Jr. As Harold Evans, the celebrated editor of *The Times* of London who interned at the *News and Observer* in 1957, once noted, "Ultimately, all stands or falls on the judgment of the proprietor."[62]

Although many on the staff believed Frank Jr. was more conservative than Sitton—or Josephus or Jonathan, for that matter—that view was not borne out in his correspondence, where he repeatedly defended the paper's philosophy. When a subscriber complained about the bias on the editorial page, Frank Jr. wrote back, "The editorial page of the *News and Observer*, since my grandfather bought it in 1894, has always been partisan. It is our soap box. We work hard to be even-handed in our news coverage. We believe, for example, that the Republican Party and the majority of its candidates speak for those who are financially and educationally better off than others in our community. For that reason, among others, we espouse candidates of the Democratic Party."[63]

Frank Jr.'s instinct was to back up his reporters. When a major car dealer and advertiser visited the publisher to complain about a column by Dennis Rogers, which cast car dealers in an unflattering light, Frank Jr. asked the man if his customers carried a copy of the dealer's ad in the paper when they visited his lot. The man was at least partially mollified.[64]

After Sitton retired, Frank Jr. presided at editorial board meetings, most often agreeing with the positions of his staff. One exception was when he reversed the paper's stance and supported building a new sport arena on the western outskirts of town instead of downtown.[65]

One's view of the paper often depended on a reader's politics. Even when it criticized Democrats, the paper was often seen as a useful trip wire. "I never heard a cabinet secretary say, 'Governor, we got a massive fuck-up here,'" said Gary Pearce, a longtime advisor to Democratic governor Jim Hunt. "You'd only find it out when you read it."[66]

Governor Jim Martin, the state's only two-term Republican governor (1985–93), saw the paper as an adversary. In 1990 the newspaper ran a story—reported by me—about how Martin was using his state-paid research office to collect political information on his opponents. A relatively minor transgression, the incident blew up after Democratic attorney general Lacy Thornburg promised an investigation. Martin—at home sick with a severe throat and sinus infection, and according to some accounts taking powerful cough medicine—left his sickbed to hold a rambling, at times incoherent ninety-minute news conference in which he angrily dared Thornburg to take him away in handcuffs. The coverage of the news conference further inflamed him. On a Saturday morning, the governor—still ill—went to the *News and Observer* office and personally delivered a three-page "Dear Claude" letter to Sitton. He declared that he was finished with politics because "it's too brutal for me."

The governor wrote that he could not wait to respond until he got well because the paper "could be relied upon to print every leak, every mean joke, every vile accusation, every lie for that matter. After 'The Old Reliable' (as you call yourself) had worked me over for another week, there wouldn't have been enough left of my reputation worth defending. I knew from experience that your paper has been bitterly hostile to every Republican leader ever since 1896, when Governor Daniel Russell, the last Republican before [James] Holshouser, took the state printing contract away from you." (Actually, the state printing contract was taken away from Josephus Daniels—which he won as editor of the *Chronicle*—when the Democrats lost control of the legislature in 1895.)[67]

Sitton's dual role in charge of both news and opinion was an unusual arrangement. Most newspapers enforced a wall between the news and editorial departments.

Frank Jr. came to regret Sitton's twin roles but did not want to force the issue and risk losing his star editor. "I just didn't have the balls to step up to deal with him," Daniels later said. When Sitton retired in 1990, Frank Jr. separated the news and editorial functions.[68]

How much influence Sitton's editorial views had on news coverage was a matter of debate—even within the newsroom. When Sitton's editorial page was crusading on a subject, reporters often received a stream of memos, passed to the managing editor and then to the reporters to follow up on.

Ferrel Guillory, the head of the editorial page during much of the Sitton era, said Sitton's memos grew out of questions he had about news stories—issues that needed a follow-up—rather than out of an effort to shape the news.[69] But other staffers were troubled by the spin that Sitton required on his news pages. "He would have editorials he wanted to write, and he would send a reporter out to generate the story that he wanted to write the editorial about," said Ted Vaden, a former editor. "A lot of stories got assigned and done that were not real news." Midlevel editors often were told what kind of stories their reporters were expected to come back with, rather than told to pursue the facts with an open mind.[70]

Sitton later defended the lack of separation, saying most readers saw the paper "as an entity" rather than as separate departments. Overseeing news and editorials, Sitton argued, gave him information that helped both sections.[71]

In part, Sitton and Frank Jr. got along because the publisher gave his editor freedom to operate. But there were some underlying tensions. Sitton complained when he was left out of a meeting between the publisher and Wake County schools superintendent John Murphy, who was complaining about the paper's coverage. In his diary, Frank Jr. noted that Sitton was "jealous of his territory and his responsibilities. I'm worried that he is trying to cover too much and not let folks fuck up—comments to reporters, subeditors, perhaps too much influence. He thinks the same thing of me."[72]

Sitton threatened to quit in 1977 over a disagreement regarding whom to endorse in the nonpartisan Raleigh mayor's race. Frank Jr. wanted to endorse the incumbent, Jyles Coggins, a real estate developer and a conservative Democrat. Sitton backed challenger Isabella Cannon, a seventy-three-year-old liberal and retired librarian who ran as the little old lady in tennis shoes. When Sitton threatened to quit if the paper endorsed Coggins, Frank Jr. backed down. The paper endorsed Cannon, who became Raleigh's first female mayor, while Frank Jr. wrote a front-page letter endorsing Coggins.[73]

A year earlier, there had been another clash, when Frank Jr. wanted to continue the family tradition of running on the front page a red rooster—a symbol of the Democratic Party crowing—after Jimmy Carter was elected president. Frank Jr. kept a big lead plate with the red rooster on his wall. Sitton objected that printing a red rooster would reflect poorly on the paper's ability to project impartiality on its news pages. As a compromise, the rooster was run on the editorial page. After the 1976 election, the rooster was permanently retired—a trend made easier by the decline of the Democratic Party.[74]

Sitton was jealous of his turf. After losing his job at *Playboy*, Derick Daniels was hired by Frank Jr. as a part-time consultant for the non-Raleigh newspapers owned by the News and Observer Publishing Company. The move angered Sitton, who apparently saw Derick as a threat. Frank Daniels III, who succeeded Sitton as editor, later described his predecessor as "a control freak."[75]

Under Sitton the newspaper's strength was comprehensive news coverage and hard-hitting editorials. But it could be one-dimensional. The newspaper tended to be gray in its presentation, Sunday-sermon serious in its news columns, short on analysis, and lackluster in its sports, features, and business coverage. Although highly intelligent, Sitton was not a man of letters like Jonathan or Sam Ragan. When a colleague urged him to assign a reporter to interview Aaron Copland, the nation's most celebrated composer, who was in Raleigh in 1976 to guest-conduct the North Carolina Symphony, there was no story because Sitton had never heard of him.

Jonathan complained in 1977 that "dullness" marked the entire paper under his successor—from the book page to the Under the Dome political column to Passing Scene, the social column. "We desperately need some brightness," Jonathan wrote Frank Jr. "I think the paper's news coverage is excellent but where we should be showing personality we come off as a bore."[76]

When a third-grade teacher named Betty Debnam proposed a children's section, called the Mini-Page, in 1969, Sitton hated the idea. But Debnam won the support of Frank Jr., and the Mini-Page ran for thirty-seven years, syndicated in 500 newspapers. Debnam was later elected to the North Carolina Journalism Hall of Fame.[77]

"The world of the *News and Observer* revolved around a few blocks around buildings: city hall, the General Assembly, and the school board," recalled Linda Williams, a reporter and editor said. "It was government-heavy, process-heavy, coverage."[78]

Sitton was talented and courageous. But his leadership style did not encourage dissent from reporters and subeditors. Personally driven, he pushed to get the most of his undersized staff, which often meant long hours. The *News and Observer* was a tense, highly competitive, and often unhappy newsroom headed by a hard-driving boss famous for his temper. It was a sink-or-swim organization, not a nurturing or democratic one. Not every reporter flourished in such an environment. "Claude is an intimidating person," said Ted Vaden. "He had a grim visage. He could get very angry. He would push back hard if you argued with him or criticized the coverage."[79]

Sitton constantly pressed for enlarging the newsroom, but the paper still operated with a smaller staff than many similar papers. In 1975, the combined staff of the *News and Observer* and the *Raleigh Times* was 95 newsroom personnel compared with 156 for papers in Charlotte, 152 in Richmond, 131 in Norfolk, and 108 in Columbia, South Carolina. Those figures did not include photographers, library staff, or part-time employees. Sitton said he never had enough reporters.[80]

Race and Hiring

Like much of the newspaper industry, the paper was mainly staffed for decades by whites in professional positions, with Black people more likely to be working on the loading docks or as janitors.

White-owned newspapers began to slowly integrate after World War II, and by 1955, twenty-one Black reporters were working mainly for papers in the Northeast and Midwest. The first southern paper to integrate was the *St. Petersburg Times*, which hired its first Black reporter in 1951 and at the same time integrated its water fountain and restroom.

The *News and Observer*'s first Black reporter was Grover C. Bailey, hired in 1962. A Raleigh native then living in Brooklyn, Bailey walked into the newsroom on Christmas Day in 1961 while home visiting his family. Sam Ragan, the executive editor and a poet, asked what he was doing, and Bailey showed him poetry he had written. Ragan called six weeks later and offered Bailey a position, starting as a copy boy for six months before moving to write about entertainment. A shy, introverted man, Bailey worked for the paper for eighteen years, until 1980, when he became editor of the *Carolinian*, a Raleigh newspaper serving the Black community. The only Black reporter on the paper for years, Bailey said he always was treated fairly.[81]

In 1974, Sitton recruited Linda Williams, a Fayetteville native, army brat, and UNC journalism school graduate who later became a reporter and editor for the *Wall Street Journal*, *Los Angeles Times*, and other publications before returning in 1997 to Raleigh as a senior editor.

Covering local schools, Williams was often pigeonholed into covering stories involving Black people or Black institutions. She was, for example, assigned to interview Black singer Natalie Cole, even though she knew little about music. Finding such assignments confining, Williams left the paper in 1976. "I didn't have a bad experience with the *N&O*," Williams recalled. But "it was always clear that I was THE Black reporter."[82]

The paper was criticized for its lack of diversity. Ralph Campbell, a Black community leader in Raleigh, complained in 1979 about the lack of African Americans on the staff, to which Frank Jr. replied that it was a problem plaguing the entire industry.[83]

A white liberal activist picketed the paper in 1990, noting that only 5 percent of its journalists were Black people, according to a 1990 survey by the American Society of News Editors. Only the *Des Moines Register*—located in an overwhelmingly white state—had a worse record among sizable dailies. By comparison, 11.3 percent of the *Charlotte Observer*'s news staff was African American. "Sitton may have won a Pulitzer Prize for his reporting on civil rights struggles in the 1960s, but he would win no prize for the commitment he showed to Black people during his editorship of the N&O," Harrill Jones said in a letter to the paper. The paper responded by saying that 4.8 percent of its full-time news and editorial staff were minorities, compared with a national average of 7.8 percent, and that 30 percent of all its employees were minorities.[84]

Sitton later said there were several obstacles to hiring more minority staff, including the lack of a Black middle class in Raleigh and the difficulty of finding qualified Black journalists "who could handle the language of idiomatic English well enough to work on the *News and Observer*." He wrote to several journalism schools and organizations in the early 1970s telling them that he was "eager" to hire Black reporters. But there were three historically Black colleges in the Triangle, and other newspapers were better able to recruit Black journalists, suggesting that minority recruitment was not a high priority for Sitton.[85]

Minority recruitment improved markedly when editor Anders Gyllenhaal hired Will Sutton, a New Orleans native and the son of a college professor/president. He served as assistant and deputy managing editor from 1996 to 2005. As the former editor of the *Post-Tribune* in Gary, Indiana, and soon-to-be president of the National Association of Black Journalists, Sutton had broad national contacts.

"Too many papers like the *N&O* were doing good, aggressive civil rights coverage, but they themselves didn't have that diversity in their newsrooms," Sutton said. That, said Sutton, made it difficult for the paper to see the community from the Black perspective.[86]

Sutton helped with high-profile hires, including bringing Linda Williams back to the paper as a senior editor and Nikole Hannah-Jones, who covered the Durham school system for the paper from 2003 to 2006. In 2017 she was a recipient of the MacArthur "Genius Grant," and in 2020 as a *New York Times* writer she won the Pulitzer Prize for her 1619 Project, which examined the country's legacy of slavery and which prompted a national debate about American history. Another hire was Jemele Hill, who became a high-profile ESPN *SportsCenter* anchor who tangled with President Donald Trump on the issue of white supremacy and Black athletes kneeling during the playing of "The Star-Spangled Banner."

Other notable hires included Barry Saunders, a talented and popular writer whose column—ranging from sharp commentary to down-home humor—ran for twenty-four years before he was laid off in 2017 as part of cutbacks at the paper. Rochelle Riley, who reported for the *News and Observer* in 1980–81, was a columnist for the *Detroit Free Press* from 2000 until 2019, when she left to become director of arts and culture for the City of Detroit. She is the author of the 2018 book *The Burden: African Americans and the Enduring Impact of Slavery*. Kelly Starling Lyons, another former reporter who was Black, has written sixteen children's books, several of them award-winning. Bridgett A. Lacy, a former reporter, has written several food-related books.

During the 1990s, the paper hired its first Black executives and invited its first African American to join its board of directors.

In 2000, when the paper was part of the California-based McClatchy chain, Orage Quarles III, an African American, was named president and publisher of the paper, a post he held until he retired in 2018. He was named publisher of the year by the trade publication *Editor and Publisher* and was chairman of the Newspaper Association of America. In 2020, Sharif Durhams became the paper's first African American managing editor, staying only a year.

Regardless of race, the talent that flowed through the newsroom continued to improve starting in the 1980s, when the paper was staffed with journalists who later worked for such national papers as the *New York Times*, the *Washington Post*, and the *Wall Street Journal*. The paper's alumni included Ben Sherwood, who became president of Disney-ABC Television Group and head of ABC News; James Bennett, who became editor of the *Atlantic* magazine and editorial page editor of the *New York Times*; David Baron, who became a Harvard law professor, assistant attorney general in the Obama administration, and a judge on the First Circuit Court of Appeals; Erin Kelly, who became an MIT professor; and Lucy Daniels Inman, who became a North Carolina Court of Appeals judge. During the 1970s and 1980s, the paper had two reporters with law degrees.

Retrenchment

As the Sitton era neared an end in 1989, the paper underwent a period of introspection about its future.

A study by a newspaper task force, aided by a consultant, recommended the paper run local news more prominently and boost its cultural and entertainment coverage to compete with the growing free weekly tabloids. The paper was too gray and had stories that ran too long, which no one read. There was too much political/government news, and the paper was too Democratic with a readership that was becoming increasingly Republican. The paper moved the long-running Under the Dome political column off the front page, and the editorial and news functions were separated.[87]

As part of the rethinking, the paper refocused its attention on the fast-growing Triangle region. To free up money, the paper made two consequential moves—pulling back circulation from Eastern North Carolina and closing the *Raleigh Times*.

The *Times* was a lively afternoon paper with a circulation of about 30,000 that covered Raleigh more extensively than the *News and Observer* did. It had better-written features and sports pages. In 1973, A. C. Snow replaced the retiring Herb O'Keefe as editor. Snow's folksy column, Sno' Fooling, became an institution well into the next century for both papers. Sitton had overall responsibility for the *Raleigh Times*, with the paper's managing editor reporting directly to him. Though it was understood that the afternoon paper would have its own "somewhat more conservative" editorial voice, it was hardly conservative.[88]

Afternoon newspapers across the country were on life support as reader habits changed. In North Carolina, the *Greensboro Record* and the *Charlotte News* had been killed. The last edition of the *Raleigh Times* appeared November 30, 1989. Closing the *Times* saved the company $850,291 ($2.1 million in 2024 dollars). It also increased the *News and Observer* staff from 80 to 120 overnight, allowing it to beef up local, cultural, and business coverage.[89]

The paper saved another $331,723 by cutting circulation in thirteen counties in the rural eastern part of the state. When Sitton became editor, the paper's circulation extended from Chapel Hill east to the coast and from Virginia to the South Carolina border. No newspaper in the country had such a high percentage of subscribers outside its retail trading area. The paper calculated that it was losing $80 per year for every home delivery in Eastern North Carolina.

The paper withdrew from the east in stages, first cutting circulation in the Wilmington and Fayetteville areas. (The *News and Observer* tried to buy the *Wilmington Star-News* for more than $11 million—or $68.4 million in 2004 dollars—but lost out to the *New York Times* in 1974.) Other cutbacks in rural areas followed.

The paper's decision to withdraw was traumatic. Kay Horner noted the reception in rural Warren County when subscribers began receiving notices. "When I arrived in Warrenton Wednesday night for choir rehearsal, I found a choir on fire," wrote Horner. "Theirs was not a fire fueled by religious fervor, but rather fueled by a notice from the capital city's venerable *News and Observer*. Along with those of us from Littleton, Warrentonians had that day received their pink slips (and I do mean pink, the shocking variety) from the N&O. . . . The notice included not one word of explanation, not one word of regret, and not one word of thanks to the subscribers for their faithfulness lo these many years. It was, in short, a one-page, big-print exercise in arrogance."[90]

There were cries of anguish all over Eastern North Carolina. "I cut my teeth on the *New and Observer*," wrote Carol Y. Henry of Fountain. "My mother strongly believed that the Southern Baptist Church, the Democratic Party and the *News and Observer* were the epitome of all that was important."[91]

The town of Beulaville's board of commissioners passed a resolution protesting the decision, as did several chambers of commerce. Letters from disappointed subscribers underscored how ingrained the newspaper had become in people's lives.

J. W. Taylor of Weldon wrote that the announcement put a damper on his retirement, pointing out that he had been a faithful reader since 1947. "It probably doesn't matter that my first luxury upon arising in the morning is being, now that I can enjoy my retirement, to saunter out to pick up the N&O to enjoy with the first cup of coffee."[92]

June B. Long of Roanoke Rapids wrote, "I learned to read on my hands and knees on the living room floor bent over the funnies section. I can't understand why the *News and Observer* even is published except to bring the news of the state to eastern North Carolina. Our local newspaper is as next to nothing as a paper can be."[93]

Joseph H. Thigpen of Williamston wrote that the paper was essential to his digestion. "The paper and I usually go to the bathroom together. There I peruse the sports pages, letters to the editor, Tumbleweeds and Al Capp in the comic section, determine how much bias or slant there is in the news stories and enjoy Erma [Bombeck] and [Lewis] Grizzard. My digestive system needs your paper. Ex-lax is habit forming although more reliable than 'The Old Reliable.'"[94]

Sometimes the cries were political. "Will we abandoned to the wolves in [Jesse] Helms' clothing?" wrote Martha H. Holloman of Scotland Neck. "Do you care that this section of our state is rife with conservatism and, yes with reactionism, and after the 30th of this month may well become rifer?"[95]

CHAPTER FIFTEEN

The Neighbors' War

The feud between the *News and Observer* and Jesse Helms was not your typical neighborhood brawl.

Just as the Danielses had played a role in the rise of Democrats Woodrow Wilson, Franklin Roosevelt, and Harry Truman, Jesse Helms and his allies figured prominently in the ascent of the religious right and the election of Ronald Reagan. They may have been neighbors, but they viewed the world through different keyholes.

"It is a matter of common knowledge that this publishing family has been selling out the South at least two generations earlier," Helms, then an aide to Senator Alton Lennon, told a Raleigh civic club in 1953.[1]

To a startling degree, many of the participants in this political feud were neighbors living in greater Hayes Barton, an upscale West Raleigh neighborhood built in the 1920s not far from downtown. Helms lived across the street from Wakestone, Josephus's mansion, and the Daniels boys' houses were within spitting distance. Willis Smith, whom Helms helped elevate to the Senate and then served as his top Senate aide, lived a few blocks away. Just down Glenwood Avenue resided A. J. Fletcher, the TV station owner who played a crucial role in launching Helms's political career.

The history of Helms and the *News and Observer* traces to the 1930s, when Helms, the son of a Monroe police chief, was a student at Wake Forest College, then located in the nearby town of Wake Forest. Frank Smethurst, the paper's managing editor, spoke to Helms's journalism class, and afterward Helms approached him about a job. A few weeks later, Helms began work as an overnight proofreader, making the sixteen-mile commute by train. When he was offered a job as a sportswriter with the paper, he quit school and went to work.

It was where Helms discovered both his love of words and the love of his life. Dorothy Coble, a recent UNC graduate and the daughter of a Raleigh traveling shoe salesman, was editing the society page. Helms wooed her by leaving a cola and a small pack of peanuts on her desk. Their first date was an assignment—her coverage of a dance at NC State, which featured crooner Frank Sinatra. They were married October 31, 1942. By that time, he had switched jobs, working as first a reporter and then an editor for the *Raleigh Times*. After serving as a navy recruiter during the war, Helms returned to his old job as city editor of the *Raleigh Times* but soon decided electronic media was the future and began a series of radio jobs.

Jesse's in-laws, the Cobles, lived across the street from Wakestone, and on Sunday afternoons, Jesse and Dot would stroll across the street to visit with "Mr. Josephus," who sometimes gave Jesse a book from his large library. "The prestige of the paper," Helms once complained, "died with Josephus Daniels." But he also had reservations about the old man, noting that Josephus had decried Congress and the US Supreme Court as being insufficiently liberal for several generations. He described Jonathan as "bleary-eyed and haggard," but if "I ran a newspaper like Jonathan, I wouldn't sleep well either."[2]

The relationship between Helms and the paper was irreparably torn during the 1950 Senate Democratic primary. Jonathan helped engineer the appointment of liberal Frank Porter Graham to the Senate, and Helms, working as a radio reporter, aided his opponent, Willis Smith, a conservative who defeated Graham with a campaign of vicious race- and red-baiting. By 1953, Helms frequently denounced the "left-wing" press and warned that many people were wondering whether such slanted coverage by newspapers deserved constitutional free press protections.[3]

Through the 1950s, Helms and the *News and Observer* warily circled each other. Helms became a lobbyist for the state's bankers and accused the paper of sabotaging a rewrite of the state banking laws. When Helms was elected to the Raleigh City Council, he and the paper sparred over a 1958 visit by Martin Luther King Jr. to the city's Broughton High School. Helms warned of possible violence, which prompted the paper to accuse him of needlessly stirring up trouble. Helms threatened to sue the paper; Jonathan privately dismissed Helms as "a reactionary pipsqueak."[4]

A. J. Fletcher, a Raleigh attorney and owner of WRAL-TV, in 1960 recruited Helms to become one of the nation's first television editorialists. Helms finished every evening news broadcast with a four-and-a-half-minute editorial called *Viewpoint*.

Fletcher wanted a TV station that would be a conservative counterpoint to the Raleigh papers. "I am determined, to the extent possible, to convince our viewers that the so-called Welfare State is another name for Communism, but without the machine gun; that is, the implementation by force of the state's decrees," Fletcher wrote in a letter. "For fifty years no voice like this has been heard in this area, since the morning and afternoon newspapers, both owned by the same family, headed by Jonathan Daniels, former Assistant to President Truman, have been so far to the left that they barely escape being behind the Iron or Bamboo curtains."[5]

On his second *Viewpoint* segment, Helms concluded by saying, "There is substantial evidence to indicate that many North Carolinians are becoming increasingly distrustful of the major daily newspapers they read, and that respect for the integrity of the newspaper profession may be on the wane."[6]

Helms criticized the *News and Observer* at least seventy-six times during his twelve years on the air—one of his favorite targets, along with the civil rights movement, Martin Luther King Jr., social programs, and college protesters.

He said the Raleigh paper was unfair to segregationists, busing opponents, the John Birch Society, power companies, and the Speaker Ban Law, which barred communists from speaking on state-supported campuses. He criticized the paper for dropping *Little Orphan Annie*, a conservative-leaning cartoon, and for supporting Medicare, the federal health insurance for seniors.

He variously described the paper and its editor as "vicious," "pious," "left-wing propagandists," and the voice of "the far left" and accused them of engaging in "demagoguery," "ultra-liberal elitism," and "sophomoric journalism." He called the paper the "knee-jerk voice of liberalism" and the "errand boy for every left-wing cause" and referred to the paper as "character assassins" who engaged in "fabricated" reporting, McCarthyism, "slanderously, irresponsible journalism," and printing "poisonous libel." He decried the "cowardly tone" of editorials, their "astonishing ignorance," and their "screaming epithets."[7]

He particularly loathed Jonathan. That was evident in a 1968 editorial following the Orangeburg Massacre. Three students were killed and twenty-eight wounded by police while attempting to integrate an all-white bowling alley three blocks from the historically Black South Carolina State University campus. Most of those wounded were shot in the back. The federal government indicted nine police officers, who were later acquitted by a jury.

Visiting Orangeburg a few days after the tragedy, Jonathan wrote a measured column in which he blamed the city's leaders—white and Black—for failing to address long-festering wounds and grievances. "Dilatory complacency was the killer in Orangeburg last week and complacency, delay, talk without action make in America—and not alone in South Carolina—the meat on which the Rap Browns and the Stokely Carmichaels feed and thrive. All is quiet in Orangeburg, but the consciences of its best people should not be still and that last is true elsewhere where blood has not yet been spilled."[8]

Helms denounced the "tearful" piece, saying, "Mr. Daniels seizes upon the society-is-to-blame thesis" for the violence. Helms argued that the bowling alley owner was within his rights to bar Black customers, just as the *News and Observer* was within its rights to have an all-white reporting staff. (It had one Black writer.) "Mr. Daniels proceeds to paint a picture suggesting that America's only hope of avoiding violence is for every citizen in every community to surrender to the demands of agitators and the easily agitated," Helms said. "Jonathan Daniels may regard it as a 'bloody police reaction,' but to others it may seem more the serving of notice that mob violence will not be tolerated."[9]

Helms maintained he was the authentic voice of North Carolina and not Jonathan or the paper. He may have been right, since Helms served thirty years in the Senate, tying a state record.

In 1972, Helms took a leave of absence from his TV job to seek the Republican nomination for the US Senate. The paper opposed his candidacy and did not let up after he was elected, dubbing him "Senator No" because of his many votes in opposition to progressive programs and appointments—an epithet that Helms readily embraced.

Although many dismissed Helms as a one-term wonder and a right-wing crank who rode into office on President Richard Nixon's coattails, his critics badly underestimated him. Between the 1964 defeat of Barry Goldwater and the 1980 election of Ronald Reagan, Helms became one of the leading conservative voices in America. Stressing opposition to abortion, civil rights, and gay rights, Helms put together a national organization, helping elect senators in North Carolina and across the country and playing a critical role in Reagan's 1980 election. He rose to become chairman of the Senate Foreign Relations Committee and a *Time* magazine cover boy.

Claude Sitton and Helms—two small-town boys of the same generation from the segregated cotton South—fought each other for two decades. Helms thought he knew the minds of white southerners and was determined to be their champion. Sitton had stood up to some of the toughest redneck sheriffs in the South. If Bull Connor, George Wallace, and the Klan couldn't intimidate him, Helms certainly would not.

Sitton regularly hurled editorial thunderbolts at Helms, while the senator frequently used the paper as his whipping boy as he campaigned in the sweet-smelling tobacco warehouses and barbecue restaurants across Eastern

North Carolina. Helms took to joking on the stump that a mutual friend once asked Sitton if he would write something nice about Helms if he died. And Sitton supposedly replied, "Only if he does so soon."

In retrospect, Sitton said it was "a wasted cause" to criticize Helms, because it just made him more popular with his supporters. When Helms was at WRAL-TV, Jonathan had ignored Helms. But Sitton said the paper was obligated to pay attention to Helms when he became a senator.[10]

Helms was a juicy target for Dwane Powell, the paper's cartoonist from 1975 until 2019. He often drew Helms with huge glasses and googly eyes and in caveman regalia, complete with a club. Showing a sense of humor, Helms lined a wall of his Washington Senate office with Powell cartoons.

Powell was a guitar-strumming Arkansas country boy with an easy way and a folksy manner, which belied his instinct for the jugular. Tweaking the high and mighty for five decades, Powell became a Raleigh institution, winning several national awards. Four collections of his cartoons were published.

The Helms–*News and Observer* feud was intense because Raleigh was so small. Bob Brooks, the paper's managing editor who directed the paper's political coverage in the 1970s and 1980s, disliked Helms from the time they were in the same Sunday school class at First Baptist Church. Brooks found Helms self-righteous and dismissive of other people's views, even in Sunday school.

Attacking the news media has been a favored tactic of conservative politicians for decades—from Barry Goldwater to George Wallace to Donald Trump. Denigrating the press, particularly in rural settings, Helms watched as his supporters menacingly crowded around reporters before urging them to give them space—saying it was just their editors who were the problem. The *News and Observer*, Helms once declared, was "a suck egg mule," which is a southernism for someone who is an irritating, worthless liability.[11]

Relations between Helms and *News and Observer* reporters covering him were often fraught. For instance, I was denounced across the state by name in 1982 by Helms and his protégé Senator John East after I wrote a story about how Helms's combative style was hurting the federal tobacco program in Congress. I was also attacked in Helms's newsletter, which was reprinted in small papers across the state. I learned of the attack when my Washington, DC, cab driver—a white man from Oxford, North Carolina, who subscribed to his hometown paper—gave me an earful after learning the identity of his passenger.

At a rally attended by 600 people at a Goldsboro tobacco warehouse in 1990, Helms delivered a laundry list of reasons why the liberal news media was ruining America—finishing by pointing his finger at me and saying, "As represented by Rob Christensen, who is sitting right there." A writer for the *New Yorker*, who was in town, jerked in his seat, glanced around, and remarked, "That would be scary, if this crowd wasn't so damn old."

Relations between Helms and the paper were particularly acrimonious during the 1984 Senate race. Helms defeated popular Democratic governor Jim Hunt in what was called a battle for North Carolina's political soul.

During the 1984 Republican state convention held in Raleigh, Helms's strategists engineered the ouster of *News and Observer* reporters from the gathering. What set them off was a *New York Times* story—reprinted in the Raleigh paper—that reported that President Reagan had warned Helms against encouraging a plot by right-wing elements in El Salvador to assassinate the US ambassador there. Helms denied the story, and his allies denounced the Raleigh paper as "the Jim Hunt hit squad."

Dan Hoover and I, two of the paper's reporters, were evicted by cheering delegates, some of whom stood on their chairs, amid shouts of "Over there, over there" and "Throw the bastards out." As sergeants-of-arms led us out, Barry McCarty, the presiding officer, intoned, "The cancer has been surgically removed." Several days after the event, Helms telephoned me and said he had nothing to do with my ouster. But for several years in the early 1980s, Helms refused to talk to me after I wrote a lengthy article about how the senator was exploiting the state's racial divide for political gain.

Helms was hardly alone in despising the *News and Observer*. Take the 1984 Democratic primary for governor that included Lieutenant Governor Jimmy Green, a mossback later convicted of tax fraud. During one campaign swing, I accompanied Green, who stopped at a string of country stores, at each stop pointing me out to the good ol' boys as the *News and Observer* reporter who was causing him so much trouble back in Raleigh. After he made me sweat, we would jump in the same car and head toward the next stop, where the performance would be repeated. It was cheap entertainment for Green.

Among the conservatives who hated the paper was David Funderburk, a former US ambassador to Romania and a future congressman who accused Sitton of attacking "anyone to the right of Karl Marx." He wrote to Sitton, "Are you such an insecure and incompetent writer that you fear the intelligence of the reader to discern the truth after seeing two sides?"[12]

After Sitton underwent surgery correcting a minor heart malfunction in 1982, a Helms admirer feigned astonishment. "Surely you are mistaken," he exclaimed. "It couldn't have been Claude. He doesn't have a heart."[13]

While Republicans complained about the paper's coverage, they understood that the paper's liberalism had alienated many conservative voters and that attacking the paper was political gold. When Frank Jr. described Helms as "the prince of darkness," the Helms campaign quickly used the insult in fundraising letters.[14]

Democrats like Governor Jim Hunt saw a lot to like in the paper's coverage. "He [Helms] was a racist, and they said so when not many people would," Hunt said. "Most people were afraid of him. . . . In a society when the racist/segregationist position and influence was so powerful, the *News and Observer* was telling another story, reporting what I thought was the truth."[15]

Although the paper was not intimidated by Helms, its leadership seemed rattled by the attacks. Frank Jr. told the paper's board of directors that the Helms-Hunt race was difficult because the paper became part of the news rather than just reported it. "The alliance between the Moral Majority or conservative Christians and the political right wing is a potent one, and many of them use us as the focal point of their frustration that everybody doesn't agree with them," he said.

Frank Jr. further noted that a Helms-connected group, Fairness in Media, had launched a campaign to take over CBS News. "I shudder to think what they would do if we were a broadly held public company rather than a privately owned one," he said. He pointed out that at a recent Helms fundraiser, Republican senator John East received a standing ovation when he proposed an effort to take over the Raleigh paper.[16]

Helms lashed out at other newspapers he regarded as liberal, such as the *Charlotte Observer* under Pete McKnight and the *Greensboro Daily News* under Bill Snider. But it was more personal with his hometown newspaper, where he started his career and where he was neighbors with the Danielses.

The 1990 Senate campaign between Helms and former Charlotte mayor Harvey Gantt, an African American, was another brutal campaign. It featured a Helms TV ad of white hands tearing up a job application and a voice saying the applicant had lost employment because the job had to go to a Black applicant. The tactics were so bad that the Republican Bush administration successfully sued the state Republican Party for intimidating Black voters by sending cards into minority neighborhoods questioning whether they could vote.

Following the Helms-Gantt campaign, Accuracy in the Media (AIM), a conservative media group based in Washington, launched a campaign against the *News and Observer*, charging that the paper was heavily biased against Helms. AIM is a group that blames the media for losing the Vietnam War, described candidate Barack Obama as a socialist with dangerous left-wing connections, and is skeptical of global warming.

The AIM newsletter focused on two items that ran in the *News and Observer*. One was an editorial cartoon showing a Black man standing in his doorway observing two white men bearing burning crosses while a third says, "Hi, we're from the Helms campaign. Can we put a sign in your yard?" The newsletter also criticized an article I wrote that noted that at least fifteen Helms supporters had also contributed to the campaign of David Duke, a former Klansman running for the US Senate in Louisiana. The paper received several hundred postcards from around the country because of the AIM effort.[17]

Helms and Sitton warily circled each other. One day Sitton and several colleagues were having lunch at the cafeteria of the Hudson Belk department store in downtown Raleigh when Helms and his chief political strategist, Tom Ellis, came in. Spotting Sitton several yards away, Helms shouted, "How is your hammer hanging today?" Sitton, a bit of a bluenose, was still fuming when he got back into the office about Helms using such coarse language in front of ladies.[18]

In 1989, Helms tested Sitton's prudery. The paper had criticized the senator's efforts to bar the federally funded National Endowment for the Arts for financing "indecent" or sacrilegious art. Helms went after the art of Robert Mapplethorpe—a winning issue for Helms because it involved the hot-button issues of homosexuality and public subsidy of art. Helms said that Sitton should let the public see the homoerotic art and judge for themselves, shipping some samples to Sitton. "Oh my God," Sitton exclaimed when he was shown photos of Mapplethorpe's work that included such explicit photos as the painter with a bullwhip inserted in his anus. To fulfill his promise of making available the art, Sitton quietly had an envelope with the photos put at the paper's main reception desk but didn't publicize its availability, and apparently no readers came by to look at them. Helms won that battle.[19]

Like many newspapers, the *News and Observer* tiptoed around homosexuality during most of its history. One of the first references was an Associated Press story in 1967 about "sex deviates" in which the state mental health director lamented that only thirty homosexuals had been admitted to state mental hospitals for treatment of their affliction. During the AIDS epidemic, the newspaper decorously described gay sex as "an exchange of body fluids." In one sensational murder case in 1972, a lesbian relationship was euphemistically described as "their shared love of Morgan horses." Unlike civil rights, the paper was slow to editorially support the emerging gay rights movement in the 1980s. The paper named its first openly gay managing editor in 2020.[20]

Sex of any sort made the paper's editors skittish. The paper pulled the *Doonesbury* comic strip, drawn by Garry Trudeau, when it depicted an unmarried couple sleeping together—implied rather than shown. Brooks, the managing editor, wanted the cartoon dropped altogether, but instead, Sitton moved it from the comics section to the editorial page.[21]

When Sitton retired at the end of 1990 at age sixty-five, the mandatory age, Daniels gave him a horse named Jesse. Draped over the horse was a blanket that read, "You've ridden Jesse for 22 years. Now you can continue riding him." Sitton retired to Oxford, Georgia, not far from where he grew up. He helped establish a journalism program at Emory University. He was also a citizen activist, attending town council meetings as a watchdog, and was particularly outspoken on such issues as local airport expansion and privatization of municipal garbage collection. He died of congestive heart failure in 2015 at age eighty-nine.

When Frank Jr. retired in 1996, he received a letter from Helms written in Chinese. Translated, it read, "Congratulations and thanks a lot for your newspaper's help to my re-election to my fifth Senate term. If I didn't have your newspaper's opposing stand, I could have not been elected in 1972."[22]

CHAPTER SIXTEEN

Frank III, the Fourth and Last Generation

In searching for Claude Sitton's successor, the Danielses' first instinct was to dip into the same well. Frank Jr. courted Howell Raines, an Alabama native who was a rising star at the *New York Times*; he would win a Pulitzer Prize for his writing on his childhood remembrances before becoming the *Times*' executive editor in 2001. When Frank Jr. began recruiting him, he was working as the paper's London bureau chief. Raines flew from London to meet separately with Daniels and also with the leadership of the *St. Petersburg Times*, which was also recruiting him. In New York, Arthur Sulzberger Jr., the future publisher, urged him to remain with the *Times* if he wanted to be the paper's editor one day. He decided to stay with the *Times* after being offered the job as Washington bureau chief.[1]

That left the door open for Frank Daniels III, who had argued that none of the prospective candidates would sufficiently change the newspaper, which at the time was experiencing a recession. "We would not have challenged ourselves differently, in my mind, if we brought Howell on board," Frank III said. His father decided to give his thirty-four-year-old son a chance, even though Frank Jr. later acknowledged that "he really didn't have the background for it."[2]

The paper had been edited for nearly a century by three larger-than-life crusaders with national reputations—Josephus, Jonathan, and Sitton. Some family members were skeptical that Frank III could fill their shoes. "The problem with Frank III was that he never was really experienced," said Lucy Daniels, Jonathan's daughter. "I had seen my grandfather, father, and Claude Sitton." She added, "What did he know about running a newspaper?"[3]

The appointment was similarly met with staff skepticism because Frank III had scant newsroom experience. He had been groomed to take over from his father on the business side as publisher. Three decades later, Frank III ruefully said he never gained the full confidence of his staff, many of whom did not understand or appreciate how he was attempting to transform the paper.

It was not unusual for family members to work for the paper. Frank Jr. had hired eight other relations. However, he established rules to minimize nepotism, requiring relatives to get experience at other newspapers if they expected to advance to a supervisory position. He often had family members start at the bottom to learn the business—whether climbing into the dirty presses to empty out ink pockets, leaving the person covered in ink, or working the newspaper routes. When he sold the paper, his son was editor; a nephew, Bobby Woronoff, was chief financial officer; and another nephew, David Woronoff, was a sales executive with the family-owned magazine *Business North Carolina*, based in Charlotte.[4]

Frank III had long been the publisher-in-waiting. After attending Raleigh public schools, he followed his father's path, spending his final three years of high school at Woodberry Forest prep school in Virginia. An angry Frank Sr. had to be talked out of cutting off the family's donations to UNC after Frank III was rejected for admission to Chapel Hill, while Spurgeon Fields III, the son of the family's Black chauffeur, was accepted. Fields later became a Raleigh attorney, while Frank III graduated with an economics degree from Duke University.[5]

If his family's liberal views were unusual for an upper-crust clan in a conservative-leaning area, Frank III's philosophy was more in line with Raleigh's old families. He gravitated toward a libertarian's belief in limited government during his formative years. "I had a very liberal social view and very conservative political view," he said. "So, I ended up already pulling off a little bit different from the traditions of the *News and Observer*."[6]

To learn the family business, Frank III spent a year working for the *St. Joseph News-Press and Gazette* in Missouri as a reporter covering utilities and hospitals before moving on to the *Ledger-Star* in Norfolk, where he covered the city's waterfront. While in Norfolk, he married Teresa Davison, a credit analyst for a local bank who had grown up in Oklahoma, the daughter of a senior vice president for Phillips Petroleum Company. They had three children, Kimberly, Frank IV, and Joseph.[7]

In 1981, his father brought him back to Raleigh to continue learning the family business. He worked as a circulation sales manager, in classified and retail advertising, and then in the business office, preparing the paper's

Frank Daniels III, the last family editor of the *News and Observer*. (Reprinted with permission of the News and Observer.)

budget and doing financial analysis on potential acquisitions. He eventually became publisher of *Business North Carolina*, which was owned by the *News and Observer*.

Frank III did not have many fans among the paper's business executives, who saw him as a highly opinionated and entitled boss's son. They also viewed him as a spendthrift and erratic manager, whether deciding on his own to spend $80,000 to purchase a hot air balloon for promotional purposes, or missing a payroll at the business magazine, or unilaterally canceling an important newsprint contract. But Frank Jr. had felt stifled by a controlling father and was determined to give his son maximum independence.

In August 1990, the company announced that it would give the keys to the kingdom to Frank III, replacing Sitton on November 1. The change could hardly have been more dramatic: the two men had different worldviews and rarely talked, and Sitton had championed Raines to be his successor. "While I respected Claude," Frank III said, "I doubt Claude respected me."[8]

Among the assumptions that Frank III brought to the job was that the paper was out of touch with its more conservative readers. "The *News and Observer* was a very agenda-driven, perceived-to-be-very-biased newspaper," Frank III said a decade after he left the paper. "And in my frank opinion, it was a very biased newspaper. I mean, the newsroom wasn't biased because they deliberately went out to be biased. It was biased in their inputs."[9]

As an example, Frank III cited the lack of coverage of Russell Capps, a conservative activist and Jesse Helms wannabe who headed the Wake County Taxpayers Association. Capps's politics were on display in an unsuccessful 1990 run for the state House, when he described South African leader Nelson Mandela as "a terrorist, not a political prisoner," with strong communist ties.[10]

Under Frank III's leadership, the newspaper increased coverage of Capps. The number of articles mentioning Capps grew from four in 1990 (the last year of Sitton's tenure) to fifty-eight in the next three years, helping propel Capps to a seat in the state House in 1994. Among Capps's first initiatives was a bill to ban all hiring preferences based on race, sex, color, or ethnicity.[11]

Frank III was not reactionary, and his laudable goal was to broaden the newspaper's outlook and community connections. He later called Capps's victory "an unintended consequence, but accurately reflected the mood of Wake County." Regardless of intentions, Frank III helped advance the career of the sort of politician that several generations of his family had tried to keep out of public office.[12]

He was not the only family member frustrated with the paper. His mother, Julia, thought the paper was too negative and didn't provide coverage of issues she cared about. Julia, an active civic leader, was more conservative than her husband, although she was discreet about their differences. She became more politically active after the Daniels family sold the paper. In 2012, Julia was state co-chairwoman of Republican Mitt Romney's presidential campaign. In 2015, their home hosted a fundraiser for GOP presidential candidate Jeb Bush. "It was held in Julia's half of the house," Frank Jr. quipped.[13]

Frank Jr. avoided friction with his son regarding editorial policy by giving Frank III control of the newsroom, while the father presided over the editorial board, run by Steve Ford, a Yale-educated veteran journalist.

Marion Gregory, a veteran journalist, became the paper's first female managing editor, providing an experienced hand in running the newsroom. Gregory, the daughter of a longtime Danville, Virginia, editor, had started with the *Raleigh Times* in 1962 and had risen—after taking some time off to raise her family—to become the *News and Observer*'s features editor in 1984.

Newsroom skepticism about Frank III as a lightweight frat boy was reinforced by episodes such as one during a recruiting trip to a national Black journalist convention in Atlanta in 1994. After dinner one evening, Frank III ordered the taxi—accompanied by senior editors Anders Gyllenhaal and Judy Bolch—to go to the Cheetah, a famous upscale Atlanta strip club. Gyllenhaal fumed, while a bemused Bolch found the exotic scene educational. This was a far cry from his great-grandfather padlocking the fleshpots near naval stations but certainly in keeping with his cousin Derick Daniels's tastes.[14]

Despite such misadventures, Frank III markedly improved the paper during his five years as executive editor. He poured money into the newsroom, became a national pioneer in digital journalism, vastly expanded the business staff, and pushed coverage into Chapel Hill and Durham to help make the paper the leading journalistic voice of the Triangle.

In some ways, Frank III's lack of a journalism background proved to be an advantage, arguably providing iconoclastic leadership that bordered on the visionary in several instances. Frank III "was the disruption that the *N&O* needed to become a much better newspaper," said Melanie Sill, who later became editor of the *News and Observer* and the *Sacramento Bee*. "Frank was right about some key things. I don't know that the *N&O* would have been able to make the changes if Frank had not come in."[15]

As an owner/editor like Jonathan, Frank III invested more money into the news operation, nearly doubling its budget. The newsroom staff grew from 120 in 1989 to 198 in 1993. The largest increases were strategic. To accommodate the paper's focus on the Triangle, the paper enlarged the Durham and Chapel Hill bureaus, with 18 new reporters hired for Durham alone. As Raleigh became less of a government/college town, the business staff was expanded to 11 journalists. The news/editorial budget grew from $3.6 million in 1991 to $5.4 million in 1994.[16]

Financing the expansion was a booming Triangle economy that fattened the newspaper with advertisements. By 1990, Raleigh's population had grown to 212,092. In keeping with its tradition, the Daniels family continued to reinvest in the paper while remaining satisfied with more modest profit margins.

The paper was hiring not just more reporters but more seasoned journalists. For much of the paper's history, the *News and Observer* was where young reporters learned their trade before moving to better-paying jobs on larger metropolitan papers. Under Frank III, the paper hired reporters who had previously worked in wire service bureaus in Moscow and Eastern Europe and veteran editors from the *Los Angeles Times*. That trend would continue after he left, with the paper bringing on science writer Jon Franklin, who had won two Pulitzer Prizes for the *Baltimore Sun*.

A generation earlier, the paper was so tightfisted that reporter Gene Roberts was denied moving expenses from Virginia when he joined the staff. In contrast, Frank III sent reporters to London, Brazil, and Budapest to pursue stories.

Frank III sought to modernize the newsroom culture and to make it more collaborative. No longer would thunderbolts be issued from the corner editor's office. A professional staff of news researchers would provide reporters with more help and training. More decisions would be made by midlevel editors. The paper was given a brighter design.

The paper also featured more vivid writing, sometimes too vivid. Dan Neil, the paper's automobile columnist, wrote about cars with verve and imagination. In 1996 he authored an R-rated review of a Ford Expedition, describing a backseat tryst with his girlfriend, noting that "this was loving, consensual and—given the Expedition's dual airbags, side-impact beams and standard four-wheel anti-lock brakes—safe sex."[17] Neil's irreverence eventually got him fired from the Raleigh paper, but it carried him to the *Los Angeles Times*, where he won a Pulitzer Prize for his auto writing in 2004.

Frank III relied heavily on consultants—from a Boston firm that led staff brainstorming sessions, to a design consultant to modernize the paper's appearance, to urban expert Neil Pierce, who provided an outsider's look at the Triangle's future. He was also entrepreneurial, starting *The Insider*, a subscription-based electronic newsletter mainly targeting lobbyists, providing detailed information on state government that the paper once printed.

He preferred to leave the paper's daily operations to his staff, instead focusing on the big-picture initiatives. Frank III's most prominent and expensive project was his effort to move the paper into the Internet age. By 1995, Amazon.com, eBay, Craigslist, and Match.com had established their presence online, and Microsoft was launching Windows 95. But as cultural historian Joseph Campbell has noted, no industry in that era was as ill-prepared for the digital age—still using Victorian-era production and distribution methods—or more inclined to dismiss the disruptive potential of the Internet as newspapers.

The Raleigh paper transitioned from typewriters to desktop computers earlier than most newspapers. In 1994, the paper created Nando.net, one of the nation's first online service providers, and began publishing *NandoTimes*, an electronic newspaper.

Frank III's business background served him well in thinking differently about the future of business. He immersed himself in the new technology and was willing to consider new ideas—such as the time he floated the idea of buying the paper's readers fax machines so they could receive the newspaper with that technology.

Frank III hired outside Internet experts. But much of the digitalization work was done by investigative reporter Pat Stith and Lany McDonald, who

Celebrating their Pulitzer Prize in 1996 are (*left to right*) reporters Pat Stith and Joby Warrick and editor Melanie Sill. (Reprinted with permission of the News and Observer.)

modernized and expanded the old library with a modern research team, increasing staff from four to fourteen. That was a far cry from the days when the library was called the morgue and consisted mainly of banks of filing cabinets filled with newspaper clippings in thousands of small manila envelopes. The paper organized a national conference in 1993 on computer-assisted reporting that brought 500 journalists from across the country to Raleigh. The *New York Times* sent a team of executives to Raleigh to examine Raleigh's web operation.[18]

The investment in journalism paid off when in 1996 the paper was awarded the Pulitzer Prize for Public Service, the highest award in journalism. The series examined the power of the huge hog industry and particularly how it affected water quality in Eastern North Carolina. Titled "Boss Hog," it took seven months to report and write the five-part series by the investigative team of Pat Stith, Joby Warrick, and Melanie Sill.

Rob Waters, a veteran editor with the *Los Angeles Times* and the *Philadelphia Inquirer* who joined the paper in 1994, was struck by the quality of the reporting staff and the extensive and talented research, graphics, and photography departments. "It was an amazingly good midsized paper that was punching above its weight," he said.[19]

Despite the paper's success in the early 1990s, there were storm clouds on the horizon. Frank III told a journalism conference in 1993, "I don't think it is too far a stretch to say the newspaper industry is all timbered out, good mostly for holding the past together. The smart money on Wall Street that sucked the money out of the industry in the '80s thinks so. While newspapers still make a lot of money, it is pledged not to the future, but to the past." Two years later, the Daniels family would sell the paper.[20]

Selling the Paper

In the early seventies, Cleves Rich, the youngest daughter of Jonathan Daniels, began a restaurant in New York's Greenwich Village called the Front Porch that specialized in soup and gourmet sandwiches. At first, it was so successful that she and her business partner opened two additional New York eateries. But the restaurant business in Manhattan is highly competitive, and Rich was not an experienced restaurateur. Rich used her *News and Observer* stock as collateral, and when the dining establishments ran into trouble, she looked for more cash.

Like many of Josephus Daniels's grandchildren, particularly the women, Rich's links to the patriarchal Raleigh newspaper had weakened. The Daniels family may have been politically liberal, but it had a traditional view of gender roles. The boys were often groomed for management positions, but not the women. With the rise of the feminist movement, though, she wondered where the women executives were. "Father always told me when I was a screaming little girl that 'A voice ever sweet, gentle, and low is a wonderful thing in a woman,'" Cleves wrote the stockholders in 1972. "So, in a soft voice, I ask why there is no woman on the board of directors?"[21]

The issue confronting Frank Jr. was one that many family-owned companies increasingly faced with each generation: too many family members chasing too little money.

Josephus left the newspaper's stock to his four sons—three of them who ran the paper and a fourth who practiced medicine in Washington, DC. But now there was a third generation—Frank Jr.'s generation, nine children, and most did not work for the paper. They were now scattered in New York City,

Asheville, Miami, New Mexico, and elsewhere. They saw the paper more as an investment than a family legacy from which they derived little prestige. Dividends per share had risen from $25 in 1977 to $84 in 1988, and the paper was rapidly growing. Gross annual revenues increased from $21 million in 1976 to $75 million in 1985.[22]

As the paper's worth grew, it became apparent to many in the third generation that the sale of the newspaper would generate far more money than their modest dividend checks. The tensions promised to worsen in the fourth generation—Frank III's—which included twenty-four cousins.

Suitors had been knocking on the paper's doors for years, viewing Raleigh as a desirable, fast-growing Sunbelt market. Those included the Hearst chain, the Gannett newspaper chain, and Jack Kent Cooke, owner of the Washington Redskins. There were also some merger flirtations between the Raleigh paper and *The State* in Columbia and the *Charleston Post and Courier* that went nowhere.[23]

In 1988, Frank Jr. rejected a lucrative offer—from an unnamed company, but probably Gannett—for roughly $200 million. Because of the size of the offer, Frank Jr. felt obligated to reveal it to the family shareholders, which he later judged a mistake. This was the first time that some family members understood how much the company was worth. About six months later, four of his cousins—Derick Daniels and three of Jonathan's daughters, Lucy, Cleves, and Adelaide—proposed selling the company. The split was largely along family lines. Frank Jr.'s family, which was running the paper, opposed the sale, while Jonathan's daughters, who had little role in the paper's operations, wanted to sell. The failure to engage the Daniels women in running the paper was coming back to haunt the family.[24]

Several Daniels women actually had newspaper ties. Lucy Daniels, son of Jonathan, worked briefly as a reporter for the *Raleigh Times* and wrote a best-selling novel in 1956, *Caleb, My Son*, about a Black family in the South divided over integration. She eventually became a clinical psychologist. Her daughter, Lucy Inman, worked for the paper as a reporter in the 1980s before she became a lawyer and an appeals court judge.

"You couldn't be somebody as a girl," said the elder Lucy, the last surviving of Jonathan's daughters. "The only way to be somebody was to write. That is why I wrote seven books."[25]

Elizabeth Daniels Squire, another of Jonathan's daughters, worked as a reporter in Connecticut and a columnist in Beirut before moving to Asheville, where she authored at least eight mystery novels and wrote a palmistry column that appeared in the *News and Observer*. Another daughter, Adelaide Daniels

Key, also of Asheville, was heavily involved in gay rights and supporting children with special needs. Years after divorcing her husband, she became one of the first North Carolinians to marry her same-sex partner in 2007.[26]

Although Frank Jr. acknowledged that some of his female cousins were talented, he said "there was no way a woman was going to get a shot at the top slot."[27]

Anticipating the family ownership split, Frank Jr. acquired a string of smaller newspapers, mainly in North and South Carolina. In 1989, he sold five newspapers in South Carolina for $74.1 million to McClatchy, another family-owned newspaper company based in Sacramento, California. The *News and Observer* used the proceeds to help buy out the four cousins who wanted to cash out, keeping the business in the hands of the five cousins who did not want to sell—Frank Jr. and his sister, Patsy Woronoff; Worth Daniels Jr.; Edgar Daniels, son of Josephus Jr.; and Elizabeth Daniels, daughter of Jonathan.

The sale of the papers bought the Daniels family more time, but family-owned papers were a vanishing breed across the country. In North Carolina, chains had already snatched up most of the family-owned dailies: Knight Newspapers purchased the *Charlotte Observer* in 1955, Landmark Communications bought Greensboro's *News and Record* in 1965, and Media General acquired the *Winston-Salem Journal* in 1969.

The transaction helped forge a growing relationship between the *News and Observer* and McClatchy. In 1990, Erwin Potts, the president and chief executive officer of McClatchy and a North Carolina native, joined the Raleigh paper's board of directors.

In an audacious move in the spring of 1991, Frank Jr., his son, and the paper's attorney, Russell Robinson of Charlotte, traveled to San Francisco to interest James McClatchy, the McClatchy chain publisher, in a merger of the two companies. Frank Jr. hoped the Daniels family would have three seats on the McClatchy board and might in time become the dominant partner in the merger. Not surprisingly, the much larger California company rejected the offer.[28]

Because he was tech savvy, Frank III was the first family member to voice alarm that a radical restructuring of the newspaper industry was looming. He warned that the Internet would ravage the newspaper's classified advertising, which represented about 50 percent of the company's profit.[29]

Although his father thought the prediction was too pessimistic, Frank Jr. was worried about mounting costs. The paper had accumulated $126 million in debt to finance the family buyout and $40 million in debt to buy and install eighteen flexographic printing press units to replace its old letterpress printing presses in 1995. The company faced principal loan repayments of $2 million per year starting in 1996. It had rapidly expanded into Durham, and the paper's Internet project, Nando.net, was expensive. The *News and Observer* had moved from "being moderately in debt to being heavily in debt" at a time when the paper needed a new plant and money for other projects to stay competitive, according to Frank Jr.[30]

"There were a lot of projects," said Bobby Woronoff, the newspaper's treasurer and business manager. "You had to have a lot of things go right to pay it off."[31]

Frank III thought the debt was surmountable, but he was burned out. He believed he was constantly being second-guessed by the newsroom and his business colleagues, and he felt pressure from the family to produce more money. And he was increasingly skeptical of the future of newspapers.

To plan for the paper's future, Frank Jr. formed a five-member operating committee. It included his son and three top executives of the company—his nephew Bobby Woronoff; Fred Crisp, the general manager; and Dick Henderson, who was vice president for sales. The group met twice a year, usually at the Governor's Inn in the Research Triangle Park, to talk about acquisitions and the company's long-term plans. Not looking to sell the newspaper, Frank Jr. had worked out a succession plan for when he retired at age sixty-five in 1996: Crisp would become publisher and Henderson would become general manager.[32]

The news executives seemed clueless about the economic forces that were about to engulf them. Henderson wrote in 1993 that while the paper faced a "tough" business environment, the paper's competition would come from "TV, cable, shoppers, telephone systems, telephone directories, direct mail, radio, outdoor advertising, Yellow Pages, niche publications and other new entrants." There was no mention of the Internet—the powerful force about to overwhelm print media.[33]

At a meeting of the operating committee in 1995, Frank III said he was sufficiently worried about the newspaper industry's future that he wanted to sell his stock. He predicted the newspaper industry's business model would begin to feel the pain in 2003, collapsing between 2006 and 2008. (The newspaper began its first major layoffs in 2008.) Frank III attributed his insight to "pure dumb luck," but it was more likely the result of his interest in technological change and his background in business and because he was a bit of a newsroom outsider. Frank III saw the future more clearly than many experienced news executives around the country who had a vested interest in traditional newsrooms. In some ways, Erwin Potts later remarked, Frank III had been "almost prophetic."[34]

Frank Jr. said he never thought he would be the last generation of Danielses to own the paper. But now, his son and heir wanted out. Emotionally fraught, there were tearful discussions between father and son. But it turned out to be a financially smart move for the family.[35]

Learning of the decision to sell, Potts asked Frank Jr. if McClatchy could make a preemptive bid. After a newspaper consultant was brought in to assess the paper's value, lawyers from both sides negotiated the deal. The sale was announced simultaneously on May 17, 1995, in Raleigh and Sacramento.

McClatchy agreed to pay $372.6 million for the *News and Observer*—$250 million for the stock and an agreement to assume the paper's $120 million debt. The deal also included six weekly newspapers, *Business North Carolina* magazine, *The Insider* newsletter, and Nando.Net. The *New and Observer* had 1,285 full-time and part-time employees at the time, with a daily circulation of 153,000 and nearly 200,000 on Sunday.[36]

Standing on a desk in the middle of the newsroom, Frank III told his staff that 101 years of Daniels family ownership was ending. A few people cried.

The Daniels family got top dollar. McClatchy paid more than seventeen times the paper's net income. Analysts said the *News and Observer*'s operating margin of 20.3 percent was within industry standards, although Gannett ran a 28 percent margin.[37]

The Daniels family's timing was propitious, coming before the industry collapse. Amazon billionaire Jeff Bezos bought the much larger *Washington Post* for $250 million in 2013. The entire thirty-newspaper McClatchy chain was sold to a hedge fund for $312 million in 2020.

The Danielses: Post-*N&O*

After the sale, Frank Jr. eased into long-planned retirement. He kept his hand in newspapers with his ownership of *The Pilot*, the Southern Pines paper started by Sam Ragan. His nephew David Woronoff was publisher and was so successful that *The Pilot* was named the best community newspaper in the country. Frank Jr. continued his civic and political involvement, working out of an office on Fayetteville Street decorated with political cartoons of his grandfather Josephus. He died in 2022 at age ninety.

His son, Frank III, became a tech entrepreneur. He worked seven months as president of McClatchy Interactive, which was spun off from the paper.

Great fortunes were made in the tech world during this period, but it was still a risky business where timing was everything and where there were far more failures than success stories.

In 1997, Frank III invested heavily in a company he started called Total Sports LLC, to carry sports on the Internet—a new concept. His firm was acquired by Quokka Sports Inc., a San Francisco–based company, in exchange for Quokka's stock. But Quokka filed for bankruptcy in April 2001, and with it, Frank III lost his investment.[38]

Frank III later became president and CEO of Vital Source Technologies Inc., a Raleigh-based company that distributed content for schools. He subsequently moved to Nashville, where he got a new start and a new marriage. He was CEO/editor of Wakestone Press, a small nonfiction publisher, before becoming a metro columnist for four years for the *Nashville Tennessean*. He was later laid off as part of cutbacks by the Gannett newspaper chain. In 2018 he became president of FW Publishing, which publishes four Nashville-area magazines and newspapers.

CHAPTER SEVENTEEN

The Decline of Newspapers

Two years after the paper's sale, Frank Jr. ran into Jesse Helms in Washington, DC. "Frank. I'll be damned if the *News and Observer* isn't a helluva lot worse than even when you had it," Helms said.[1]

Most readers could not immediately tell the difference when they picked up the paper. The *News and Observer* and McClatchy were an ideological fit, with both papers having a progressive tradition and a culture of public service—one reason Frank Jr. sold the paper to McClatchy.

The Raleigh paper was making a transition that many family-owned newspapers had previously made—adjusting from local ownership to being part of a chain and now answering to corporate owners located on the other side of the continent. No longer could an irate reader call Frank Jr., the paper's publisher/owner, at home—his telephone number always listed—or grab him on the golf course of the Carolina Country Club.

During the first decade under McClatchy's ownership, the paper prospered, continuing to be profitable and producing good journalism while maintaining local independence. Fred Crisp, a longtime business executive with the paper, served as transition publisher from 1996 to 1999.

Completing the transition to McClatchy, Orage Quarles III became the paper's publisher in 2000. The Modesto native was a newsroom management veteran—twenty-four years with Gannett before McClatchy hired him to be the publisher of the *Herald* in Rock Hill and then of the *Modesto Bee*. He served as the Raleigh publisher for eighteen years until his retirement in 2018—working to protect the paper's diminishing budget, keeping the paper in its downtown location rather than moving to the suburbs, appointing the paper's first ombudsman, and expanding coverage of Southeast Raleigh's Black community. He also allowed reporters to operate independently without interference and continued the Daniels family legacy of readily opening the checkbook for lawsuits to force public agencies to abide by open records and open meetings laws. Speaking to a group of business and government leaders shortly after his arrival, Quarles, with a smile on his face, said, "The job of the paper under me will be to piss you off."[2]

A disciplined man famous for short, efficient meetings and for keeping in superb physical shape, Quarles seamlessly fit into Raleigh's predominantly white power structure, serving on numerous prestigious boards. He had an upbeat personality, priding himself on being forward-looking rather than focusing on past injustices. He liked to say he was a publisher who happened to be Black rather than a Black publisher. He said it helped that key figures in the community—the police chief, the sheriff, and the school superintendent—were also African Americans.[3]

During the McClatchy era, a new breed of editors led the paper who saw themselves as news managers rather than crusaders. None had the larger-than-life personality of those from the Daniels family era, nor was any involved in politics. These editors were Anders Gyllenhaal (1996–2002), Melanie Sill (2002–7), John Drescher (2007–18), Robyn Tomlin (2018–21), and Bill Church (2021–24).

Gyllenhaal grew up outside Philadelphia in the town of Bryn Athyn, founded in the late nineteenth century by the adherents of Swedenborgianism, a small Protestant sect based on the teachings of an eighteenth-century Swedish scientist and theologian. His only brother, Stephen, became a successful Hollywood director, and his nephew and niece, Jake and Maggie Gyllenhaal, became well-known actors. But there was nothing Hollywood about Anders.[4]

Anders helped raise his family when his father, a high-powered business consultant, battled alcoholism. Gyllenhaal brought a new management style to the paper—self-effacing, deliberate, and so quiet he was sometimes accused of mumbling. He preferred sweaters to power suits, and in his spare time he played the banjo in bluegrass groups and was an avid birdwatcher, writing a book about endangered species with his wife, Beverly Mills, a former *News and Observer* reporter, in retirement in Raleigh.

He had built his career with the *Miami Herald*. Starting as a reporter before moving into editing, he absorbed the managerial skills of the well-run Knight Ridder chain. In 1991, Gyllenhaal was hired as metro editor of the *News and Observer* by Frank III. He moved up to managing editor and then editor in 1996—the first McClatchy-appointed leader.

Anders Gyllenhaal, editor from 1996 to 2002, the first editor after the *News and Observer* was purchased by the California-based McClatchy chain. (Reprinted with permission of the News and Observer.)

The paper was on a steady arc of improvement until the industry collapsed. In 1999, the *News and Observer* was named the sixteenth-best newspaper in the country in a survey of 100 US editors conducted by the *Columbia Journalism Review*—even though it was the country's sixty-seventh-largest paper. Only the *St. Petersburg Times* and the *Dallas Morning News* were ranked higher in the South.[5]

It was called "an ambitious and aggressive newspaper that has actually been getting better in recent years" in a 2002 book, *The News about the News*, on the state of journalism. "The *News and Observer* stands out from most American newspapers because of its ambition and its execution," wrote the authors, Leonard Downie Jr. and Robert G. Kaiser, the *Washington Post*'s executive and associate editors. "It's easy to put out a daily newspaper that rarely or never does good, original reporting."

"A good paper has a culture of excellence," they wrote. "The people who work for it know the difference between thorough, resourceful, tough-minded journalism and pap. A weak paper doesn't challenge itself or its readers. . . . Raleigh, its region, and the state of North Carolina are all better communities because the *News and Observer* is their newspaper."[6]

The authors cited such stories as the Pulitzer-winning investigation into the state's hog industry and a four-part series in 1999 by education writer Tim

Simmons about how North Carolina's public schools were failing its Black children. Also cited was a 2000 story by Dan Kane about how the campus police chief at NC State University used $2.2 million of unspent salary and benefit money to buy fancy computers, a truck for himself, and an expensive office renovation. The chief was fired six days later, and his boss was reassigned.

During the 1980s, 1990s, and the first decade of the 2000s, the paper had a stable of talented journalists. They included future or past Pulitzer Prize–winning reporters such as Pat Stith (*News and Observer*), Michael Skube (*News and Observer*), Lisa Pollack (*Baltimore Sun*), Cornelia Grumann (*Chicago Tribune*), Nikole Hannah-Jones (*New York Times*), Dan Neil (*Los Angeles Times*), Joby Warrick (*Washington Post* and *News and Observer*), and Jon Franklin (*Baltimore Sun*). George Polk Award winners included Todd Richissin (*Baltimore Sun*), Sally Jacobs (*News and Observer*), Craig Whitlock (*Washington Post*), and Hannah-Jones. Some became successful authors.

In 2002, the paper's newsroom had 260 journalists, including 100 reporters assigned to different departments: metropolitan news (about 60), sports (12), features (12), and business (10). The paper also had sixteen photographers, six graphic artists, and a professional research staff of eight.[7]

Gyllenhaal was one of the rising stars of McClatchy, which was aggressively buying newspapers on its way to becoming the nation's second-largest newspaper chain. He became editor of the *Star Tribune* in Minneapolis in 2002, editor of the *Miami Herald* in 2006, and then vice president for news and Washington bureau chief for the McClatchy chain in 2010. The newspaper industry recognized his talents by naming him chairman of the Pulitzer Board and of the Poynter Institute in St. Petersburg, Florida.

In 2002, Melanie Sill, the managing editor, succeeded him as editor. The paper had slowly moved to include more women at every level, from street reporters to the executive suites. Marion Gregory had been named managing editor by Frank III in 1990. The paper hired women general interest columnists—Nicole Brodeur, Ruth Sheehan, and Mary Miller.

Sill grew up in Hawaii—one of five children of a skilled mechanic and a schoolteacher—who came to North Carolina to attend UNC journalism school, married a local boy, and stayed. She started working for the paper in 1981 as a features writer, working her way up to managing editor. Among other things, Sill oversaw the paper's "Boss Hog" series that won the 1996 Pulitzer Prize. Although tempered by a sense of humor and an easy laugh, she was tough and driven and expected a lot from her staff.

During her five and half years as executive editor, the paper covered destructive Hurricanes Fran and Floyd, the 9/11 terrorism attack, and the

Raleigh-based Carolina Hurricanes winning the Stanley Cup hockey championship in 2006.

The most difficult story during the Sill era was the Duke lacrosse case—when a Black stripper falsely accused several white Duke University athletes of raping her at an off-campus party where she had been hired as an exotic dancer. The 2006 incident created a national and international media frenzy because it was too juicy to ignore. The story "conformed too well to many preconceived notions of too many in the press: white over Black, rich over poor, athletes over non-athletes, men over women, educated over non-educated," wrote media critic Daniel Okrent.[8]

Durham County district attorney Mike Nifong—facing an election in a city with a politically strong Black community—fanned the flames, giving more than fifty interviews describing the athletes as "hooligans" and saying a rape had occurred. (Nifong later resigned and was disbarred.) The *New York Times* ran more than 100 stories on the case. There were many media voices quick to judge, such as CNN Headline News' Nancy Grace, who said, "I'm so glad they didn't miss a lacrosse game over a little thing like gang rape."[9]

The problem was that the story was wrong—the stripper had falsely accused the Duke lacrosse players.

The *News and Observer* played an important role—both good and bad—as the major print outlet in the region. The paper broke the story on March 24, 2006, with a front-page article that said, "All but one member of the Duke lacrosse team had reported to the Durham police crime lab" for DNA testing. "Police think at least three of the men could be responsible for the sexual assault, beating, robbery, and near-strangulation of one of two women who had an appointment to dance at the party March 13, according to a search warrant." The next day the paper ran what one media critic called a "one sided, sympathetic portrayal" of the woman, not naming her in keeping with its policy of protecting the identity of rape victims.[10]

There was angry pushback from the nascent blogosphere. The lacrosse case helped launch the public careers of two conservative Duke students—Richard Spencer, the eventual leader of the alt-right, and Stephen Miller, President Trump's leading immigrant strategist.[11]

The *News and Observer* soon began unraveling the stripper's account. Sill, who had questions about the narrative, put reporter Joseph Neff on the story, and he began documenting the weakness of the case and instances of prosecutorial misconduct. Neff, a Columbia Journalism School graduate who spoke a West African dialect from his days as a Peace Corps volunteer, was a seasoned, award-winning investigative journalist who lived in Durham. He had wide contacts in the local courthouse and the legal community and a record of exposing prosecutorial misconduct.

"I had a leg up because I'm from here, because I am sourced and because I cover these issues," Neff recalled. This was good old-fashioned shoe-leather, just-the-facts reporting, and as Neff put it, "I didn't give a shit about the narrative of race, class and gender."[12]

Neff wrote that the "accuser gave at least five different versions of the alleged assault to different police and medical interviewers and made shaky identifications of the suspects. To get warrants, police made statements that weren't supported by information in their files."[13]

Assessing the news media's coverage in their book *Until Proven Innocent*, writers Stuart Taylor Jr. and K. C. Johnson concluded that the *News and Observer* "distinguished itself after its lamentable first few articles." Taylor and Johnson, among the early skeptics of the rape narrative, wrote that "while the paper's left-leaning editorial board virtually ignored the case, reporters Joseph Neff and Benjamin Niolet produced by far the best news coverage of any newspaper in the country."[14]

Under Sill's and Quarles's leadership, the paper began in 2006 to address its role in the white supremacy campaign of 1898 and the Wilmington massacre and coup d'état. The project was prompted by the state-sponsored *1898 Wilmington Race Riot Report* published in May 2006. The paper hired historian Timothy B. Tyson to write a sixteen-page special section called "The Ghosts of 1898." This was an effort at racial reckoning conducted a decade before the Black Lives Matter movement.[15]

Sill left the paper in 2007 to become executive editor of the *Sacramento Bee*, McClatchy's flagship paper. After three and half years in Sacramento, she became executive editor and later vice president of Southern California Public Radio. Under her leadership, SCPR was rated the most listened to public radio station in the country.[16]

Both Gyllenhaal and Sill directed a talented staff. Nancy Barnes became editor of the *Minneapolis Tribune, Houston Chronicle*, and *Boston Globe* and headed National Public Radio's news operation. Steve Riley became editor of the *Houston Chronicle*. The paper served as a talent pipeline for the *Washington Post*, sending more than a dozen staffers to the paper.

John Drescher, who succeeded Sill, moved to an editing job at the *Washington Post* at the end of his tenure as editor of the *News and Observer* in 2018. Drescher came to Raleigh as a ten-year-old, after his father was transferred to Raleigh by IBM in 1971, where he worked as an engineer/executive. Reserved and quiet, Drescher started as a reporter for the paper in 1983. He left the paper

John Drescher, the editor from 2007 to 2018. (Reprinted with permission of the News and Observer.)

in 1986 to work as a reporter and then editor at several major newspapers in the Carolinas before returning in 2002 as managing editor. When Sill left for California, Quarles elevated him to executive editor.

Drescher had obtained what he said was his dream job—editing his hometown paper—but it was a compromised dream. He spent the subsequent decade managing decline. To better connect with his staff, he moved his office from the executive suites to the newsroom.

Just months after Drescher became editor, the newspaper industry began massive layoffs, driven by the digital revolution and a sharp economic recession. Despite overseeing massive cutbacks, Drescher labored to protect three areas that he considered the paper's franchise: watchdog reporting, government/political news, and higher education, including sports.

Although legendary investigative reporter Pat Stith retired in 2008, the paper doubled down on its investigative team. The team included at various times Andrew Curliss, Joseph Neff, Bill Krueger, Dan Kane, Mandy Locke, and researcher David Raynor.

The *News and Observer* continued its powerful watchdog role in state politics. The paper's investigations played crucial roles in House Speaker Jim Black and Agriculture Commissioner Meg Scott Phipps going to prison for accepting illegal campaign contributions. The paper also spotlighted a series of indiscretions by Governor Mike Easley—from illegal free corporate flights and accepting a beach property at a discounted rate, to getting free use of an automobile for his son and allegedly having his campaign pay for his house repairs. Easley entered an Alford plea to a single charge of accepting an illegal campaign contribution—a plea in which he did not admit guilt but by which he also became the first North Carolina ex-governor to become a felon.

Dana Cope, the director of the State Employees Association of North Carolina, went to prison after the paper reported he had spent half a million of his organization's money on personal expenses such as house improvements. The paper also forced the resignation of Secretary of State Rufus Edmisten, a former attorney general, by exposing the misuse of state employees who were doing work on his house. A series of lesser figures were indicted after the newspaper's investigations, including state representative Michael Decker, lottery commissioner Kevin Geddings, and Easley's chief aide, Ruffin Poole.

The spate of investigations, nearly all of them targeting Democrats, allowed Republicans to use the corruption issue to help fuel a Republican surge in the state. "I don't think there is any question that the *News and Observer* reporting led to the Republicans gaining control of the legislature in 2010 and [Republican governor Pat] McCrory winning the governorship in 2012," Drescher said. "We didn't have any ulterior motives but to get to the corruption." (There were other forces also at work. The year 2010 was a Republican wave election in which twenty state legislative bodies—either House or Senate—flipped from Democratic control to Republican control.)[17]

The investigations in the 1990s and the next decade policed not just politicians. There were stories in 1996 about racial profiling of Black motorists by the State Highway Patrol, which led the legislature to pass reforms and inspired the national Stanford Open Policing Project. As a result of the paper's reporting in 2009, an innocent man, Alan Gell, was freed from death row. And because of other reporting, the legislature changed laws requiring prosecutors to turn over evidence to defense attorneys.

At least one investigation by the newspaper backfired. In 2010, the paper ran a four-part series called "Agents' Secrets" that raised questions about whether a forensic analysis of a bullet fragment by Beth Desmond, a State Bureau of Investigation agent, contributed unfairly to a murder conviction in Pitt County in 2006. Desmond successfully sued, and a jury found that the *News and Observer* had acted with malice, awarding an eye-popping $9 million, later reduced to $6 million. The verdict was upheld on appeal, but the court ordered a review of the damages. The case was settled out of court for an undisclosed sum in January 2021.[18]

The jury verdict was one more blow for a newspaper in decline.

Decline

Newspapers—the printed page delivered to doorsteps—were essentially a product of the nineteenth- and twentieth-century industrial age, and they struggled to survive in the new information age. The speed of the technological revolution was breathtaking: blogs began appearing in 1997, Google was created in 1998, and Craigslist went national in 2000. Wikipedia appeared in 2001, LinkedIn and Myspace in 2003, Facebook in 2004, YouTube in 2005, Twitter in 2006, and the Apple smartphone in 2007.

In what turned out to be a disastrous bet, McClatchy newspapers in 2006 doubled down on the old media, purchasing the much larger Knight Ridder newspaper chain for $4.5 billion and assuming $2 billion in debt. It was a big fish swallowing an even larger fish. The move put the chain deeply in debt just as the industry collapsed. During the next twelve years, the chain shriveled from 15,000 employees to 3,300 as it sought to deal with the debt and declining revenues.[19]

The *News and Observer*'s honeymoon with McClatchy soon turned sour as corporate headquarters demanded more and more cuts and more centralization to finance its ill-advised purchase. Even during the honeymoon period, there was a shift in business practices. The Daniels family had been content to operate at a 20–25 percent gross profit margin, continuing to invest in the paper. But like most newspaper chains, McClatchy wanted a 30 percent return from the paper. "That is a completely different philosophy," said Frank III.[20]

Soon after Drescher became editor, newspapers went into a free fall all over the industrialized world—the result of the 2008–9 recession, the worst since the Great Depression of the 1930s. *Business Insider* declared that 2009 was "the year newspapers died."[21]

The *News and Observer* cut seventy-eight positions in March 2009, including twenty-seven full-time news jobs. Some of its most talented reporters and editors posed for a goodbye photograph on the roof of the paper's headquarters after they were axed. This was the first major layoff in the history of the paper, which under the Danielses had had a paternalistic practice of keeping staff on the payroll, years after they lost their edge. But that was just the beginning of the cuts.[22]

In June 2011, the *News and Observer* and other regional McClatchy papers consolidated their copyediting desks in Charlotte. Twenty-five staffers in Raleigh were told they could keep their jobs if they moved to Charlotte.

The Raleigh paper eliminated many specialty beats such as science, medicine, health, the environment, and religion. The features section lost most of its staff, and cultural coverage nearly disappeared. The business desk went from eleven reporters to one (later expanded to three). Gone was the theater critic, the music critic, the architecture critic, and the restaurant critic. Also cut were layers of editors who provided oversight and quality control. Once one of the nation's best, the paper's research department was largely scrapped. The Chapel Hill and Durham bureaus were closed in all but name. Metro and editorial page columnists who had been an important part of the newspaper's brand—Dennis Rogers, Jack Aulis, Ruth Sheehan, Jim Jenkins, Nicole Brodeur, and Barry Saunders—largely became a thing of the past.

The investigative team was reduced. The local editorial page staff was cut to one person—who reported to the *Charlotte Observer*, which had been purchased by McClatchy. Veteran reporters were replaced by young recent journalism school graduates, who were paid far less. The Under the Dome column—one of the paper's daily signatures since 1934—was changed from the daily source of inside political gossip to a repository for run-of-the-mill political news stories and published only intermittently.

The book page that had been carefully nurtured since the 1920s disappeared, and with it went decades of goodwill among the writer networks and readers. "They just burned the house down," said Peder Zane, the former book editor.[23]

The newsroom staff went from 260 journalists in 2002 to 69 in 2022, including staff for the *News and Observer*, the *Durham Herald Sun*, which the paper acquired, and the political news service *The Insider*. The cuts are even more stark when one includes the journalists who worked on community papers owned by the *News and Observer*.[24]

During the twenty-first century, the newspaper industry lost more jobs than coal mining.

Loss of Advertising

Newspapers live and die on their advertising, with the *News and Observer* earning four dollars in advertising for every one dollar it collected in subscriptions.[25]

Print newspaper advertising collapsed with the advent of the Internet, dropping 71 percent nationally between 2000 and 2012. Classified advertising—want ads for jobs and ads from people wanting to sell things—all but dried up. This was catastrophic for the *News and Observer* because such advertising provided up to 50 percent of its revenue. On the first Sunday of January 2000, the paper included fourteen classified advertising pages. On the same Sunday in 2020, the paper had one and a quarter pages of classified ads. Other advertising had also dropped dramatically, including ads for real estate, automobile dealers, supermarkets, and department stores.

The paper shrank from 127 pages on July 1, 2000, to 84 pages a decade later, to 24 pages in 2020. Compensating for the lost advertising revenue, the paper continually hiked subscription costs. Subscriptions rose from $2.77 per week for daily and Sunday papers in 2000 to $29.99 per week in 2024.

Newspapers hoped that their digital counterparts would attract sufficient advertising to offset their loss of print advertising. But while advertising spending rose, most was funneled into the digital duopoly of Facebook and Google, which could narrowly target consumers by using algorithms in a way that newspapers could not. The *News and Observer* earned about a dollar on digital ads for every ten dollars it made in print advertising.[26]

The *News and Observer* should have been prepared for the digital revolution. The paper was among the more tech-savvy newspapers in the country in the 1990s, serving a tech-oriented readership of the Research Triangle. But the newspaper never figured out a way to make its online operations profitable.

In hindsight, it is easy to point out mistakes. While a few newspapers such as the *Wall Street Journal* erected a paywall for its digital newspaper, McClatchy moved in the opposite direction. It offered its online papers for free, betting that attracting more readers would allow its papers to charge more for advertising. This was a dilemma that many of the nation's best newspapers wrestled with. But drawing a large free online readership was essentially meaningless, because online advertising was never very profitable. "You can't click your way to profitability," Drescher said. "The digital advertising—there is just not enough money in it."[27]

There were other missed opportunities, such as the failure of the company to move into television. Frank Jr. was reluctant to shift a significant number of journalists over to the paper's digital operation. Even the innovator had his flaws. Although Frank III was strong on ideas, colleagues describe him as weak on follow-through.

Like many news organizations, the *News and Observer* was caught in a vicious downward cycle, offering subscribers a shrinking product while charging much higher prices. Readers abandoned their print subscriptions in droves, although some continued to read the paper online. Print subscriptions dropped to 50,047 in 2021—less than a third of the 188,229 in average print subscribers in 2006. There were 22,413 digital-only subscriptions.[28]

The paper undertook a series of increasingly desperate measures. In 2017, the paper sold its building at 215 S. McDowell Street to a real estate developer for $22 million. The *News and Observer* moved to rented office space on two floors of the One City Plaza Building on Fayetteville Street. In March 2020, the paper stopped printing its Saturday edition. In 2021, the paper closed its printing plant in Garner, laying off forty-eight full-time and thirty-three part-time employees, outsourcing the printing of the paper to a Fayetteville vendor. It also dropped its subscription to the *New York Times* wire service.

The paper also began some controversial practices, such as hiring an Atlanta firm to help it set subscription prices based on demographic and geographic data. The tactic meant that next-door neighbors could pay different rates for the paper.[29]

The paper was in such financial straits that it began asking readers for donations to help fund reporting positions. The *News and Observer* also turned to several nonprofit philanthropic organizations, such as Report for America, 1Earth Fund, and Innovate Raleigh, to finance reporting positions. Additionally, it participated in a consortium of North Carolina newspapers to produce more in-depth work.[30]

The decline occurred in a fast-growing, prosperous Sunbelt market as Raleigh's population grew from 403,892 in 2010 to 474,258 in 2024. The suburbs were growing even faster, and the Raleigh-Durham metro area topped 2 million people.

It was not just Raleigh that was suffering. So were neighboring communities such as Durham and Chapel Hill and suburban communities where the *News and Observer* had purchased papers during flush times.

Durham, a neighboring city of 300,000, is a vibrant community that is part of the high-tech industry of the Research Triangle Park, home to Duke University and a sizable and influential Black community. During the first decade of this century, Durham was the subject of a newspaper war, with the *News and Observer* attempting to compete with the *Herald-Sun* in the fast-growing market.

The Raleigh paper had an 18-member bureau covering Durham, while the *Herald-Sun* had 80 people in its newsroom—or nearly 100 people dedicated to delivering print news. But it was more than just numbers. Such award-winning reporters staffed the *News and Observer*'s Durham bureau as Joe Neff, Craig Whitlock, Todd Richissin, Jane Stancill, and Nikole Hannah-Jones, who later become stars for the *New York Times*, the *Washington Post*, and the *Baltimore Sun*.

McClatchy purchased the *Herald-Sun* in 2016 from Kentucky-based Paxton Media Group for an undisclosed sum, with the Raleigh and Durham papers combining staff. As of 2021, the two combined papers had two and a half reporters assigned to cover a city with a larger population than St. Louis, Missouri. (The *News and Observer* augments its Durham coverage by contributions from Raleigh-based business, sports, and other reporters.)

Few people better understand the impact of the decline of news coverage in Durham than Steve Schewel, a former two-term mayor, former city councilman, former school board member, part-time Duke University public policy professor, and former publisher of a successful alternative weekly.

"Nobody is covering our council meetings now," said Schewel. "It is not never, but it is almost never. And nobody has been covering the county commission meetings for a long time. [The paper's] ability to cover the ongoing operations of government is just massively down from where it was, and it hurts our community because they are not informed. It leaves the information stream to people who are often saying a lot of crazy or inaccurate stuff online."[31]

The news desert—or at least a semi-arid zone—not only means that citizens have less information about the actions of their representatives. It also makes it harder for reporters to understand deeper trends and develop the sources needed to explain what is going on. Every aspect of news coverage has been badly damaged—from election news to insights from columnists such as Jim Wise and Barry Saunders, who helped Durhamites better understand their community, Schewel said. Nor has television filled the vacuum. "TV is still murders and fires," he said.

A national study by PEN America, a nonprofit organization, found that the decline of local newspapers has led to government officials conducting themselves with less integrity, efficiency, and effectiveness. Government corruption and costs have increased; salaries, taxation, and deficits have risen. Corporate misconduct, such as environmental degradation, has gone unchecked. The same study found that when newspapers disappear, civic engagement dries up: people are less likely to vote, are less politically informed, and are less likely to run for office. Another study found that the cost of municipal borrowing was higher by $650,000 per issue in communities that lost their newspapers.[32]

Beyond watchdog journalism, regions can lose their sense of identity. "It's the way a local columnist can express a community's frustration or triumph, the way the local music critic can review a concert, the deeply reported feature stories, the assessment of a new restaurant, the obituaries, the letters to the editor," wrote Margaret Sullivan, the former media columnist for the *Washington Post*. "The newspaper ties a region together, helps it make sense of itself, fosters a sense of community, serves as a village square whose boundaries transcend Facebook's filter bubble."[33]

Metro papers were not the only publications dismantled. McClatchy also killed off a string of suburban Raleigh papers it owned that once were the lifeblood of community news—from high school sports to local civic club meetings.

Some newspapers were institutions. The *Smithfield Herald* (circulation 14,200), started in 1882, provided award-winning coverage of the towns of Smithfield, Selma, Clayton, Four Oaks, Benson, Kenly, Princeton, Pine Level, Micro, and Wilson's Mills.

Cary, population 186,000, is one of the nation's fastest-growing suburbs. It now has more people than Jackson, Mississippi, or Columbia, South Carolina. But since the closing of the *Cary News*, the town has had no hometown paper.

Serving a college town, the *Chapel Hill News*, with a circulation of 25,000, had a rich history. Its longtime editor, Jim Shumaker, was immortalized in *Shoe*, a nationally syndicated cartoon strip about a motley crew of newspapermen, all of whom were birds. The strip was drawn by Pulitzer Prize–winning cartoonist Jeff MacNelly, who got his start at the paper, which once had a circulation of 25,000.

Few communities in the country were so heavily covered as Chapel Hill—a town dominated by a reading public of college faculty and wealthy retirees. Like Durham, Chapel Hill was the subject of a newspaper war in the 1990s and the next decade. Competing for readers was the *Chapel Hill News* (owned by the *News and Observer*) and the *Herald-Sun*. They put about a dozen reporters combined on the streets to cover everything from the courts and cops to the schools, city and county governments, and prep and college sports. Both newspapers were free and distributed to every household. In addition, separately, the *News and Observer* had an Orange County bureau with several reporters, which did not contribute to the *News and Observer*–owned *Chapel Hill News*.

"It was great for the community," said Ted Vaden, who was publisher of the *Chapel Hill News* for a decade after the Raleigh paper purchased it. "Everything that moved got covered."[34]

By 2023, the *Chapel Hill News* had been shuttered, and the combined bureaus for the Raleigh and Durham newspapers were manned by a single community-based reporter. One result is that many voters now go to the polls equipped with little information about the candidates.

"There is a loss of the citizens in this community having enough information to exercise their democratic responsibilities," Vaden said. "You don't get good information about the schools. You don't get good information about growth and development. You certainly don't get good information about the disenfranchised or lower-income population. There is no incentive for these publications to cover them. There is not very good coverage of the university. ... There is no awareness of crime because there are no police reporters.... If a politician were inclined to be corrupt or incompetent, they could get away with it because no one is watching the henhouse."[35]

Faced with a dearth of news, the *Daily Tar Heel*, the student newspaper of UNC Chapel Hill, has stepped up its coverage of the town, becoming a vital community news source.

The closing of the suburban papers also meant the loss of jobs—fifty at the *Smithfield Herald*, twenty-six at the *Cary News*, twenty-three at the *Chapel Hill News*.[36]

When Orage Quarles retired in 2018, he was replaced by Sara Glines, a veteran of smaller newspapers in the Gannett chain, as the paper's first woman publisher. After a little more than a year in Raleigh, she replaced Drescher as editor with Robyn Tomlin.

The new team could not halt the rapid decline; given the industry trends, probably no one could. McClatchy's new team did not last long. In 2020, Glines was laid off, and in 2021, Tomlin was promoted to a McClatchy-wide executive position. She was replaced by Bill Church, a Japanese American and a veteran newsman with Gatehouse Media, a large media company that merged with Gannett in 2019.

Tomlin has an inspiring personal story. A Texas native raised mainly in Chapel Hill, Tomlin became pregnant in high school and ignored a teacher's suggestion that she drop out of high school. Instead, she raised a child as a single mother while attending Durham Technical College and then earning a degree at UNC Chapel Hill. Tomlin spent much of her career working mostly for smaller newspapers—including as a reporter and editor at the *Asheville Citizen-Times*, editor of the *Wilmington Star-News*, editor of a short-lived Internet project based in New York, and managing editor of the *Dallas Morning News*.[37]

McClatchy increasingly relied on algorithms based on the number of times readers clicked on a story on the paper's website to turn around its declining fortunes. McClatchy began pushing reporters to generate 800,000 clicks on their stories per year. But the difficulty of that practice was demonstrated in 2017 when three reporters for the Raleigh and Charlotte papers spent nearly a year working on a three-part series outlining how low-income students with good grades were being steered away from honors or advanced placement classes. In a rare moment of bipartisanship, the high-impact series prompted the state legislature to unanimously pass a law reforming the policy. But the series garnered only 180,00 clicks. The lead reporter on the series, Neff, began looking for a new job.[38]

The paper's coverage of the 2019 Raleigh mayor's race reflected the flaws in click-counting. For the first time in eight years, there was an open race for mayor of the city of about 470,000 people. The field included three significant candidates—a former city councilwoman, a former Wake County commissioner, and a prominent African American lawyer.

The paper provided what could most charitably be described as bare-bones coverage of the race. Aside from short stories announcing their candidacies and the election results, the *News and Observer* ran four news stories about the mayoral race. The paper provided almost no information about the candidates' backgrounds, records, or past stances on issues; who was supporting them; who was financing their campaigns; or how they planned to lead a city with a larger population than Miami or Minneapolis.

It turned out to be a consequential election. Shortly after taking office, the new mayor, former city councilwoman Mary Ann Baldwin, was making important decisions regarding mask restrictions because of the COVID-19 pandemic and handling sometimes destructive street demonstrations following the death of George Floyd and the energizing of the Black Lives Matter movement.

At the same time that it virtually ignored the Raleigh mayor's race, the paper ran nine stories about the impending opening of a Wegman's grocery store. Stories about a new grocery store generated clicks—not stories about who would lead the city.

The paper boasts many talented reporters and editors who continue to do good work, including covering the COVID-19 pandemic and the national period of racial reckoning around the police killings of Black people. But the staff's inexperience, thinness, and devotion to algorithms often shows.

Consider:

- In an article about racial reckoning in 2020, the paper described the Raleigh of the 1970s as a racial backwater that gave rise to Senator Jesse Helms. No reporters or editors seemed to know that in 1973, Raleigh became the first majority-white southern city to elect a Black mayor. Or that Raleigh and Wake County merged their school systems in the 1970s to enhance racial integration. Or that Helms was to Raleigh what Donald Trump was to New York City—a place where he was from but not where he got his support. For a local newspaper to not understand the city it purports to cover is headshaking.[39]

- Also in 2020, North Carolina elected a lieutenant governor—a former factory worker who trafficked in antisemitic, anti-Muslim, antigay, and anti-transgender remarks. Mark Robinson called First Lady Michelle Obama a man and said Barack Obama was "a worthless anti-American atheist." Robinson also said much worse things. The paper included one pre-election story about his extremism, running it on page B-11 three weeks before Election Day. The paper did not disclose Robinson's four bankruptcies, his criminal conviction for writing bad checks, or the thousands of dollars he owed in unpaid taxes, rent, and car payments. Mark Robinson, an African American Republican, is the GOP nominee for governor in 2024.[40]

Shortly before he retired in 1990, Claude Sitton warned against newspapers shirking their responsibility to provide public affairs coverage. "Let us cut no slack for the imbeciles in our ranks who say that the press can reduce that coverage. Why do they think the First Amendment was adopted and ratified?" Sitton said in a speech at the University of Georgia. "If we fail to cover public affairs, we will lose not only the reason for that protection but also that protection itself."[41]

Like other corporations facing difficulties, the *News and Observer*'s top management, most notably Tomlin, declined to be interviewed for this book. Management also turned down requests from other journalists writing about the paper. When Church became editor in 2021, the paper devoted more resources to public affairs coverage than it did under Tomlin.

In February 2020, McClatchy, overwhelmed by debt and declining revenue, filed for Chapter 11 bankruptcy. The chain was purchased for $312 million by Chatham Asset Management, a New Jersey–based hedge fund that was a major lender and shareholder for the chain. The hedge fund is also the principal owner of American Media, which owns such tabloids as the *National Enquirer*. The paper showed signs of financially stabilizing under Chatham Asset Management, hiring some new reporters and offering the first pay raises in years.

But for many journalists, it was a downward slide—from family-owned newspaper to corporate ownership to being owned by a hedge fund. "To think," Drescher said, "that a hedge fund cares about the people of North Carolina is a fantasy."[42]

Conclusion

"There had been great newspapers, and there had been lousy newspapers," observed historian Jill Lepore. "But the Republic had never known a time without newspapers, and it was by no means clear that the Republic could survive without them, or at least without freedom of the press on which they were established, the floor on which civil society stands."[1]

The *News and Observer* has been both great and lousy. As the nineteenth century became the twentieth, the paper played a crucial role in disenfranchising Black voters, imposing a system of racial segregation, and keeping the Jim Crow caste system in place for several generations. Josephus Daniels, the family patriarch, is the most problematic figure. He was more than a lifelong segregationist; he was one of the architects of the Jim Crow system that did untold damage to the lives of millions of North Carolinians.

But if Josephus Daniels was a racist—and he was—he was also a more complicated person than he is sometimes portrayed.

"During his 60 years in politics, Daniels stretched the definition of 'Southern Democrat' almost to the breaking point," wrote historian Michael Kazin, a leading scholar of the Democratic Party, noting that his many roles included racist, Bryanite, navy secretary, anti-imperialist Mexican ambassador, and New Deal defender of leftist vice president Henry Wallace. "It was a career that defied conventional notions of 'right' and 'left' while making the North Carolinian useful to every successive leader of his party."[2]

Some historians—such as Sid Bedingfield and Kathy Roberts Forde—argue that Daniels was part of a southern press that, along with its political and business allies, was responsible for "effectively killing democracy in the South for nearly a century." There is merit in their assertion. Voter participation sharply dropped after the white supremacy campaigns as North Carolina

The statue of Josephus Daniels is pulled down in 2020 in the midst of a national period of racial reckoning. (Reprinted with permission of the News and Observer.)

effectively became a one-party state and most Blacks were pushed off the voting rolls. But that is not the entire story. Daniels also fought to expand democracy by supporting women's suffrage, labor democracy, and election reforms such as the direct election of US senators.[3]

Starting in the 1930s under Jonathan Daniels, the *News and Observer* became one of the leading papers in the South to push—however haltingly and incrementally—for a more racially inclusive society. It was a frustratingly slow movement at times as Jonathan's views evolved and as he weighed how much change white North Carolinians would accept.

By 1953, Jesse Helms, the leading conservative voice in the state, was denouncing the *News and Observer* for selling out the South for several generations. This was the view of many white Tar Heels, even as many Black North Carolinians thought the paper was not moving fast enough.

Until it was purchased by a California chain in 1995, the *News and Observer* was dominated by the Daniels family. They not only were proprietors but also edited the paper for most of the 101 years they owned it, setting the editorial direction of the paper. There were few papers in the country where one family played such an all-encompassing, ink-stained role.

A handful of other newspapers strongly identified with one family—the Sulzbergers of New York, the McCormicks of Chicago, the Binghams of Louisville. But they tended to be owners rather than hands-on editors.

What also set the Daniels family apart was their long history of involvement in Democratic Party politics—as advisors to presidents and governors, holding high-level government positions. Their history coincides with the twentieth-century rise of the Democratic Party in both the country and the state. They whispered in the ears of William Jennings Bryan, Woodrow Wilson, Franklin Roosevelt, Harry Truman, Adlai Stevenson, and Lyndon Johnson.

The national political connections of Josephus and Jonathan were integral to the clout of the *News and Observer* in North Carolina. The identity of Josephus and Jonathan as newspaper editors was inseparable from their roles as national party leaders. In a one-party state like North Carolina, no one was better politically connected than the Danielses, and not just for one administration but for more than half of a century.

The Raleigh paper was a powerful influence on North Carolina politics—whether exposing skullduggery or endlessly hectoring public officials from its perch in the state capital. But the *News and Observer* rarely dominated Tar Heel politics. Its views were more often to the political left of the corporate lobbyists who heavily influenced the legislature and the governor's mansion and of the social conservatism of the piney woods Baptist churches and later the megachurches of the suburbs. But it could rarely be ignored.

The Raleigh paper consistently opposed concentrations of great wealth and corporate power, championed progressive taxation, advocated for women's rights and labor, and argued for expanding educational opportunity and making health care more available. The *News and Observer* was for antitrust legislation, rural high schools, and Obamacare. It fought child labor and was a reliable ally of the University of North Carolina. It battled antisemitism, the Ku Klux Klan, Red Scare tactics, McCarthyism, and anti-immigration sentiments. Conservatives fumed that it was a left-wing newspaper with socialist, anti-business tendencies. Others saw it as arrogant, self-righteous, and highly partisan.

The paper was often shrill and had a Manichean view of the world—divided between good and evil with few gray areas. The *News and Observer* circulated (and continues to circulate) in deeply divided political terrain—a hotly contested Upper South state that voted for both George Wallace and Barack Obama. How could a liberal, brawling paper that was issued in what was once the heart of Klan country be anything but an arrogant, in-your-face publication? Just the mention of the *News and Observer* would in some circles cause jaws to tighten and eyes to narrow. It never was a beloved paper. It richly earned the nickname the "Nuisance and Disturber."

The *News and Observer*, of course, was not alone. North Carolina has long had a reputation as a strong newspaper state. At various times, the major newspapers in Charlotte, Greensboro, and Winston-Salem were also solid voices for progress—although none so consistently or fiercely as the Raleigh paper.

It is arguably not a coincidence that North Carolina moved to the political right about the same time the *News and Observer*—as well as the other major papers—began their economic decline.

The paper's leaders sometimes wondered whether the constant paddling against the tide was worth it. Despite decades of pushing progressive policies, Claude Sitton noted shortly after retiring in 1990 that pervasive poverty still plagued much of North Carolina. In a letter to Frank Jr., Sitton wrote that "for all of your best efforts and mine, as well as those of your father, your uncle and your grandfather, that state of affairs has changed but little for most North Carolinians."[4]

It is a bit of a mystery that a paper that so continually poked its fingers in the eyes of so many readers prospered for as long as it did. But arguably the paper's strong segregationist sentiments in its formative decades gave it political cover to steer to the left on other issues. When the paper began to diverge from the rigid segregation line in the 1930s by pointing out racial injustices, the *News and Observer* was already an established if not beloved institution.

The newspaper cultivated the state's cultural and intellectual life by encouraging authors, literary events, and classical concerts. And it served as a community touchstone for the eastern part of the state, providing news not only of government and politics but of the latest college basketball game, deaths and marriages, recipes for making fried chicken, the latest fashions, and how the tobacco markets were faring.

A newspaper is known by both its friends and its enemies. It was a champion for moderates and progressives such as Terry Sanford, Jim Hunt, Kerr Scott, Frank Porter Graham, and Charles Brantley Aycock (who was also a white supremacist). It made enemies of conservatives such as Jesse Helms, I. Beverly Lake Sr., Josiah Bailey, and Willis Smith.

Since at least the mid-twentieth century, North Carolina has often been regarded as among the most progressive—or at least most moderate—states in the South. It was more industrialized and had more historically Black colleges and fewer lynchings, and today its citizens have among the highest education level achievements in the South.

Numerous observers—such as W. J. Cash, V. O. Key, George Tindall, and Neil Pierce—have asserted that the Daniels family and their paper helped set the tone for the state, providing cover for political leaders to adopt more moderate policies than could be found in many other southern states.

John Gunther, probably the best journalist of mid-twentieth-century America, wrote that North Carolina was by far the most liberal state in the South, and one reason was "the influence of independent newspapers like the Raleigh *News and Observer*." More recent writers and historians have cast doubt on North Carolina's progressive reputation. There is plenty of conflicting evidence to provide ammunition for both sides of that argument.[5]

Hunt, the four-term Democratic governor, said the University of North Carolina was the most critical influence in the state. "But the Raleigh *News and Observer*, being read by the governor, being read by the Legislature, moving out into the areas in especially Eastern North Carolina where conservatism and traditionalism was the strongest, and where the *News and Observer* just, pow, hit it every day, was probably the second most important influence in the state."[6]

Having a state capital paper serve as an aggressive watchdog should not be undervalued. For decades, the paper uncovered misdeeds by public officials, dug up scandals in the sports programs of major state universities, discovered shenanigans among labor leaders, and spotlighted miscarriages of justice. The paper was often excoriated for doing so.

When asked by one of his appointees what was expected of him, Democratic governor Gregg Cherry replied, "I want you to do your job and don't do anything that you don't want to read about on the front page of the *News and Observer* the next morning."[7]

Cherry's advice could serve as the paper's epitaph.

Acknowledgments

I would like to thank the Daniels family for their cooperation on this project. Although it was not commissioned by them, Daniels family members readily agreed to sit down for interviews.

While they may disagree with the painful parts of this book, I believe the family has provided an invaluable service to North Carolina.

The Daniels family members' own writing was a treasure trove, whether it was Josephus's five-part autobiography, the twenty-one books by Jonathan, or the memoirs of Lucy Daniels. Frank Daniels Jr. commissioned a series of interviews with important individuals in connection with the University of North Carolina's oral history program, which was an important resource.

Because the Daniels family is history-minded, they left for UNC a vast collection of their letters, memos, and reports that were very valuable. There are few other instances where we have in writing key newspaper executives discussing whether to slant their coverage in favor of a particular candidate or how to deal with the complexities of race.

My manuscript was helped enormously by the generosity of several readers: Lee A. Craig, the author of an excellent biography of Josephus Daniels; Ted Vaden, the wise ombudsman and veteran editor at the *News and Observer*; and Peder Zane, the paper's erudite former book editor and author. Any mistakes or misinterpretations are, of course, my own.

I have also benefited from the scholarship of numerous authors. Lee Craig and Joseph Morrison provided excellent road maps on Josephus Daniels's life. Charles Eagles expertly documented Jonathan Daniels's tortuous path on race. David Cronon's book on Josephus Daniels's Mexican sojourn was invaluable.

I would like to thank the staff of the Southern Historical Collection at UNC, where I spent many weeks, for their unfailing helpfulness, especially during the trying times of the COVID pandemic. In particular, I would like to thank Taylor de Clerk, who was a joy to work with. But I owe my gratitude to the entire staff, headed by Jason Tomberlin, John Blythe, and, at the beginning of my research, Bob Anthony. Also helpful were the staff of the special collections at Emory University in Atlanta and Duke University in Durham.

Helping me find photos to illustrate the book were Vann Evans and Ian Dunn at State Archives, Scott Sharpe at the *News and Observer*, and Tim Hodgdon of UNC's Wilson Library.

This book could not have been published without the persistence of my editor, Lucas Church. I also owe a thank-you to a raft of professionals at UNC Press, including Alyssa Brown, Thomas Bedenbaugh, Erin Granville, Julie Bush, and others.

Most of all, I would like to thank my wife, Margot, a history widow, who has been a model of patience and encouragement throughout my ventures into history.

Notes

ABBREVIATIONS

    CCOH Columbia Center for Oral History, Columbia University, New York
    FD Sr. Frank Daniels Sr.
    FD Jr. Frank Daniels Jr.
    FD III Frank Daniels III
    JD Josephus Daniels
    JWD Jonathan Daniels
    N&O Raleigh *News and Observer*
    SHC Southern Historical Collection, University of North Carolina, Chapel Hill
    SOHP Southern Oral History Project, Southern Historical Collection, University of North Carolina, Chapel Hill
    SARL Stuart A. Rose Manuscript, Archives, and Rare Book Library, Emory University, Atlanta, GA

INTRODUCTION

1. Constance Laibe, "Statue Unveiled in Nash Square"; Melanie Sill, "Friday Recalls the Fighting Spirit of Newspaper's Founder," N&O, September 25, 1985.
2. Martha Quillin, "Daniels Family Removes Statue of Racist Ancestor," N&O, June 17, 2020.
3. T. Thomas Fortune, "Free Speech in the South," *New York Age*, reprinted in N&O on December 13, 1903, under headline "Lynchers at Trinity Find One Defender."
4. Bedingfield and Forde, "Journalism and the World It Built," 5.
5. Eleanor Roosevelt, "Josephus Daniels' Friendliness Made Him Beloved by Everyone," *St. Petersburg Times*, February 21, 1948.

6. Woodward, *Strange Career*, 91.
7. "Helms Hits Truman, *N&O*, September 18, 1953.

CHAPTER ONE

1. "Announcement," *N&O*, January 25, 1895.
2. Goodwyn, *The Populist Moment*, vii.
3. Anderson, *Race and Politics*, 114–15, 254; Craig, *Josephus Daniels*, 57–58.
4. "Butler's Work," *N&O*, August 23, 1897; "Trying to Make a Fake Issue," *North Carolinian* (Raleigh), February 17, 1898.
5. "The Frederick Douglass Disgrace," *N&O*, February 23, 1895.
6. Morrison, *Josephus Daniels Says*, 92; "Trying to Escape Responsibility," *N&O*, March 26, 1895; "Under the Dome," *N&O*, March 10, 1895.
7. Crow and Durden, *Maverick Republican*, 71–72, 110; JD, *Editor in Politics*, 204.
8. "A Warning," *Raleigh Gazette*, October 22, 1896.
9. "Post-Election Reflections," *Charlotte Observer*, November 17, 1898.
10. JD, *Editor in Politics*, 283.
11. Kazin, *Godly Hero*, 11.
12. JD, *Editor in Politics*, 295.
13. Edmonds, *Negro and Fusion Politics*, 141.
14. *N&O*, September 8, 10, 14, 23, 15, and August 9, 1898.
15. *N&O*, September 24 and November 3, 1898; JD, *Editor in Politics* 254, 288–89.
16. "The Duty of White Men To-Day," *N&O*, September 22, 1898.
17. Gilmore, "Murder, Memory," 75.
18. JD, *Editor in Politics*, 295–96.
19. "Those Who Own the Property Shall Rule," *People's Paper* (Charlotte, NC), November 4, 1898.
20. "Negro Women Active," *N&O*, November 1, 1898.
21. "The Colored Member," *N&O*, February 2, 1900.
22. Justesen, *George Henry White*, 280–83.
23. *N&O*, August 18, September 8, September 11, September 27, August 18, 1898.
24. Cartoons of the *N&O*, mid-August 1898 to November 1898; The *Homefront*, August 25, 1898.
25. Zucchino, *Wilmington's Lie*, 79.
26. JD, *Editor in Politics*, 124; Rippy, *F. M. Simmons*, 181; Umfleet, *1898 Wilmington Race Riot*, 60.
27. JD to Jennett, April 25, 1900, Norman Jennett Papers, SHC.
28. Lefler and Newsome, *North Carolina*, 518; Franklin and Moss, *From Slavery to Freedom*, 254.
29. "Two Lynchings in Two Weeks," *N&O*, November 7, 1898.
30. William Gaston, "The Whites Shall Rule," *N&O*, November 6, 1898.
31. Jeffrey J. Crow, "The N.C. Partisan Press in the 1890s" (paper presentation, University of North Carolina at Chapel Hill, November 12, 1999).
32. Author's review of *N&O* coverage from August until November 1898.
33. "Finally, Brethren," *N&O*, November 6, 1898.

34. Crow and Durden, *Maverick Republican*, 128.

35. "Whites Are Justified," *Washington Post*, reprinted in *N&O*, November 8, 1898; "Rule of the Unclean," *Baltimore Sun*, reprinted in *N&O*, November 8, 1898.

36. "Mitch Mosley Lynched," *The Semi-Weekly Citizen* (later *Asheville Citizen*), November 9, 1898.

37. "Horrible Butcheries at Wilmington," *Richmond Planet*, November 19, 1898; "A Day of Blood at Wilmington," *N&O*, November 11, 1898; H. Leon Prather, "We Have Taken a City," in Cecelski and Tyson, *Democracy Betrayed*, 16.

38. Umfleet, *1898 Wilmington Race Riot*.

39. Darity and Mullen, *From Here to Equality*, 200–201.

40. JD, *Editor in Politics*, 285.

41. "Vile and Villainous," *N&O*, August 24, 1898.

42. "Col. Waddell's Speech," *N&O*, November 6, 1898.

43. "Keynote of Exciting Campaign in North Carolina," *Washington Post*, reprinted in *N&O*, November 1, 1898; "North Carolina's Way," *N&O*, November 10, 1898.

44. "The Wilmington Trouble," *N&O*, November 11, 1898; JD, *Editor in Politics*, 335; "A Day of Blood at Wilmington," *N&O*, November 11, 1898; "Nineteen Negroes Shot to Death," *New York Times*, November 11, 1898.

45. Quoted in "Vilifiers of the South," *Washington Evening Star*, reprinted in *N&O*, November 13, 1898; *The Carolinian*, November 17, 1898.

46. "Separate Cars for the Races," *N&O*, November 19, 1898; JD, *Editor in Politics*, 331; "Three Sorts of Disenfranchisement," *N&O*, May 3, 1900; "No Negro Rule for White Men," *N&O*, June 3, 1900.

47. "Estimates of Illiteracy, by States: 1950," *Current Population Reports*, November 1959, Series P. 23, No 6, US Bureau of the Census, table "Illiteracy of the Population of the United States by Divisions and States, 1900 to 1930," https://www2.census.gov/library/publications/1959/demographics/p23-006.pdf.

48. "Why Democrats Will Vote for the Amendment," *N&O*, February 2, 1900; Raymond Gavins, "Fear, Hope, and Struggle, Recasting Black North Carolina in the Age of Jim Crow," in Cecelski and Tyson, *Democracy Betrayed*, 189.

49. *N&O*, June 17 and July 10, 1900.

50. "Breach of Faith," *N&O*, August 19, 1900.

51. Christensen, *Paradox of Tar Heel Politics*, 39; John H. Haley, "Race, Rhetoric and Revolution," in Cecelski and Tyson, *Democracy Betrayed*, 220.

52. "Breach of Faith," *N&O*, August 19, 1900.

53. T. Thomas Fortune, "The Voteless Citizen," *Voice of the Negro* 1, no. 9 (1904), republished in Alexander, *T. Thomas Fortune*, 110.

54. JD, *Editor in Politics*, 422–23.

55. "A Striking Contrast," *N&O*, February 9, 1901; "Judges Not Vindicated," *N&O*, March 29, 1901.

56. "Deserves Severe Rebuke," *N&O*, June 1, 1932; "Sowing Dragon's Teeth," *N&O*, May 29, 1932; Gershenhorn, *Louis Austin*, 48–49.

57. JD, *Editor in Politics*, 145, 422–23.

58. "All a Question of Taste," *N&O*, October 18, 1901.

59. "Is North Carolina to Imitate President Roosevelt in Social Equality?," *N&O*, August 26, 1903.

60. "Stirring Up the Fires of Race Antipathy," N&O, November 1, 1903.

61. "Bassett Committed the Unpardonable Sin," N&O, December 3, 1903.

62. JD, *Editor in Politics*, 470; Gershenhorn, *Louis Austin*, 30.

63. Cecelski and Tyson, *Democracy Betrayed*, 8.

64. JD, *Editor in Politics*, 311–12.

65. "Insanity Would Be the Only Excuse," N&O, April 28, 1899; "It Is Law and Order or Anarchy," N&O, May 2, 1899.

66. "Col. Julian Carr on Lynching," N&O, May 26, 1899; Rippy, *F. M. Simmons*, 28–29; Orr, *Charles Brantley Aycock*, 272–78; Brundage, "Press and Lynching," 104; "Col. Carr on the Race Problem," N&O, May 26, 1899.

67. "Lynchings: By State and Race, 1882–1968," Tuskegee University Archives Repository, https://archive.tuskegee.edu/repository/wp-content/uploads/2020/11/Lynchings-Stats-Year-Dates-Causes.pdf.

68. "End Such a Practice," N&O, July 9, 1913; "Relic of Barbarism," N&O, July 1, 1928.

69. JD, *Editor in Politics*, 343–50.

70. "The Watkins Verdict," N&O, September 25, 1931.

71. "The Ku Klux Klan—Then and Now," N&O, January 21, 1923; "War on the State," N&O, August 8, 1906.

72. Craig, *Josephus Daniels*, 382–83.

73. "Moton Declares Social Equality Is Ancient Myth," N&O, March 17, 1921; "Booker T. Washington Statue Unveiled at Tuskegee Institute," *New York Tribune*, April 6, 1922.

74. JD, *Wilson Era: Years of War*, 415–16; Jonathan Daniels, interview by Charles Eagles, March 9–11, 1977, SOHP, UNC.

75. "Josephus Daniels in Hot War," *New York Age*, reprinted in N&O, June 21, 1904.

76. Reynolds, *Abe*, 442.

77. Woodward, *Strange Career*, 74.

78. "Remedy Worse Than Disease," N&O, November 2, 1947.

79. John Temple Graves, "A Player of Great Parts," *Asheville Citizen-Times*, January 17, 1948.

80. FD Jr., interview by Joseph Mosnier, February 13, 2007, Raleigh, SOHP.

CHAPTER TWO

1. Craig, *Josephus Daniels*, 13.

2. JD, *Wilson Era: Years of War*, 598; Bedingfield, "Populist Insurgency," 154.

3. Webb, *Jule Carr*, 98.

4. Cooper, *Walter Hines Page*, 77.

5. JD, *Tar Heel Editor*, 380; "The Trustees College Question," *Charlotte Observer*, December 3, 1899.

6. FD Jr., "Frank Daniels, Jr.: Newspaper's Legacy," interview by Shannon Vickery, *Biographical Conversations with . . .*, UNC-TV, season 2017, episode 3, aired September 27, 2017, https://video.pbsnc.org/video/frank-daniels-jr-newspapers-legacy-fzhgjx/; JD, *Tar Heel Editor*, 346; Craig, *Josephus Daniels*, 96.

7. Craig, *Josephus Daniels*, 110; James B. Morrow, "New Navy Secretary a Fighter," *Boston Globe*, April 6, 1913.

8. JD to JWD, January 31, 1938, folder 162, JWD Papers, SHC.

9. Joseph L. Morrison, "In North Carolina—The Influence of 'That Paper in Raleigh,'" *N&O*, May 16, 1963.

10. Craig, *Josephus Daniels*, 133–38.

11. JD to supporters, July 30, 1894, JD Papers, folder 1, scan 4, SHC.

12. Craig, *Josephus Daniels*, 140; Articles of Incorporation, FD Sr. Papers, series 3, 1926, SHC.

13. Craig, *Josephus Daniels*.

14. Hofstadter, *Age of Reform*, 186–87; Kazin, *Godly Hero*, 11.

CHAPTER THREE

1. JD, *Editor in Politics*, 238.
2. Morison., *Oxford History*, 74–75; Bedingfield, "Populist Insurgency," 154.
3. JD, *Tar Heel Editor*, 389–93; JWD, *End of Innocence*, 43.
4. "Covering the Political Situation in the State," *N&O*, September 2, 1897.
5. James B. Morrow, "New Navy Secretary a Fighter," *Boston Globe*, April 6, 1913.
6. Morrison, *Josephus Daniels Says*, 25, 28.
7. JD, *Editor in Politics*, 520.
8. JD, *Editor in Politics*, 240–41.
9. "The Legislature Reviewed," *N&O*, March 14, 1897; JD, *Tar Heel Editor*, 393.
10. "Liberty of the Press Is Involved," *N&O*, June 1, 1904.
11. JD, *Editor in Politics*, 460–65.
12. JD, *Editor in Politics*, 585.
13. Noel Yancy, "As Militant as Years Ago," *Greenville (SC) News*, February 22, 1942.
14. Morrison, *Josephus Daniels Says*, 23–24.
15. "Fighting Editors," *Richmond Dispatch*, February 7, 1891; "A False Report," *Raleigh State Chronicle*, February 5, 1891.
16. "A Lively Fistfight: Senator Jones and Editor Daniels Have a Set-To Today," *Raleigh Times*, October 1, 1910.
17. Dave Jones, interview by Joseph Mosnier, November 26, December 5, and December 12, 2007, SOHP.
18. JD, *Editor in Politics*, 343–50.
19. JD, *Editor in Politics*, 143–46.
20. "Dr. Norman Gives Assault Version," *N&O*, July 23, 1925.
21. JD to FD Sr., November 16, 1936, FD Sr. Papers, series 1, November 1936, SHC.
22. Henry Reuterdahl, "Josephus Daniels, Master of Errors," *Metropolitan*, 1916, SHC.
23. JD, *Editor in Politics*, 593–94.
24. JD, *Editor in Politics*.
25. JWD, *Tar Heels*, 329.
26. Nell Battle Lewis, "Incidentally," *N&O*, January 18, 1948.

CHAPTER FOUR

1. JD, *Editor in Politics*, 50–51.
2. Kazin, *Godly Hero*, 205.
3. Kazin, *What It Took to Win*, 119.
4. Hofstadter, *Age of Reform*, 169.
5. JWD, *End of Innocence*, 38–43.
6. Kazin, *Godly Hero*, 93.
7. Quoted in Kazin, *Godly Hero*, 302.
8. Burns, *Roosevelt*, 51.
9. N&O, September 18, 1896.
10. JD, *Editor in Politics*, 191.
11. JD, *Editor in Politics*, 193–96; *Charlotte Observer*, July 7, 1900; "*New York Sun* Out for McKinley," *Chicago Chronicle*, July 1896.
12. JD, *Editor in Politics*, 199.
13. JD, *Editor in Politics*, 356, 362.
14. Kazin, *Godly Hero*, 162.
15. "All Signs of a Landslide to Bryan," N&O, November 3, 1908; "Government a Menace," N&O, November 5, 1908.
16. "Unparalleled Achievement," N&O, September 17, 1899.
17. N&O, March 3, 1912; March 23, 1914; January 2, 1929; April 30, 1933.
18. "Not Guilty," N&O, April 28, 1945.
19. Morrison, *Josephus Daniels Says*, 224.
20. "Workmen's Compensation," N&O, February 15, 1929.
21. A. J. McKelway, "Must Not Grind the Seed Corn," N&O, January 1, 1904; Claiborne, *"Charlotte Observer,"* 121; Woodward, *Origins of the New South*, 417–20.
22. "The Gulf Stream of Progress," N&O, August 3, 1911.
23. Steelman, "Progressive Democratic Convention," 102–3.
24. "Some History That Has Escaped the Record," *Greensboro (NC) Daily News*, June 21, 1914.
25. Woodward, *Origins of the New South*, 398–40; *Equal Protection of the Laws*, 30.
26. *Equal Protection of the Laws*, 30.
27. Talley, "Study of Issues and Trends," 77; "The Negro and College Education," N&O, April 15, 1909.
28. Frank Smethurst, "In My Opinion," N&O, February 29, 1936.
29. "The Question," N&O, May 22, 1908.
30. JD to Simmons, February 3, 1908, Furnifold Simmons Papers, box 1, David M. Rubenstein Rare Book and Manuscript Library, Duke University, Durham, NC.
31. Walton and Taylor, "Blacks and the Southern Prohibition Movement," 247.
32. "Editors Are Like Preachers," N&O, May 6, 1900; "Regulating Moving Pictures," N&O, February 18, 1921; "Immorality Declared Frightfully Prevalent," N&O, February 6, 1921.
33. Herbert O'Keefe, "Josephus Daniels—Navy Secretary, Ambassador, but Editor First," N&O, January 16, 1948.
34. Wylly Folk St. John, "Daniels Belied Age by Youthful Ideas," *Miami News*, January 15, 1948.

35. "A Hit," reprinted from the *Salisbury Sun* in the *N&O*, April 20, 1902; editorial, *Asheville Daily Gazette*, April 9, 1902.

CHAPTER FIVE

1. JD, *Wilson Era: Years of Peace*, 3–4.
2. Berg, *Wilson*, 168.
3. Heckscher, *Woodrow Wilson*, 241–42.
4. Morrison, *Josephus Daniels*, 47; Craig, *Josephus Daniels*, 221–22.
5. *N&O*, November 3, 1912.
6. "Theodore Roosevelt and the South," *N&O*, October 1, 1912.
7. *N&O*, November 6, 1912.
8. Berg, *Wilson*, 263; JD, *Wilson Era: Years of Peace*, 97–98.
9. Quoted in Pietrusza, *TR's Last War*, 58.
10. "Under the Big White," *Washington Evening Star*, January 18, 1914.
11. Berg, *Wilson*, 266–67.

CHAPTER SIX

1. Smith, *FDR*, 104; "Secretary Josephus Daniels Takes Up the Problem of the Enlisted Man," *Washington Evening Star*, July 6, 1913; "An Appreciation by an American Correspondent," *Times* (London), April 24, 1919.
2. "Will Daniels Get Seasick?," *Winston-Salem Journal*, March 8, 1913.
3. "Admiral Sims and Mr. Daniels," *Guardian* (UK), July 19, 1921.
4. Smith, *FDR*, 102.
5. "A Hundred Years Dry: The U.S. Navy's End of Alcohol at Sea," USNI News, US Naval Institute (website), July 1, 2014, https://news.usni.org/2014/07/01/hundred-years-dry-u-s-navys-end-alcohol-sea.
6. "Daniels Issues Lengthy Statement on Conditions, Annapolis Is Stunned and Wets Tell of Dry Visit," *Sacramento Bee*, March 7, 1918.
7. "Action of Secretary," *Raleigh State Journal*, May 30, 1913; "Blease Roasts Secretary Daniels," *Lincoln County (NC.) News*, May 30, 1913.
8. Morrison, *Josephus Daniels*, 64, 94; Michaelis, *Eleanor*, 138.
9. Sally Asher, "The Last Days of Storyville," *New Orleans Magazine*, October 2017; Morrison, *Josephus Daniels*, 95; JD, *Wilson Era: Years of War*, 198.
10. JWD, interview by Charles Eagles, March 9–11, 1977, SOHP.
11. Simkins and Roland, *History of the South*, 385.
12. Craig, *Josephus Daniels*, 377.
13. Franklin and Moss, *From Slavery to Freedom*, 293.
14. Cronon, *Cabinet Diaries*, April 11, 1913, 32–33; A. Link, *Woodrow Wilson*, 64; Tindall, *Emergence of the New South*, 144–46.
15. Franklin and Moss, *From Slavery to Freedom*, 342.
16. Yellin, *Racism in the Nation's Service*, 262–63; Franklin and Moss, *From Slavery to Freedom*, 295.

17. Yellin, *Racism in the Nation's Service*, 178; "Partiality in the Navy," *New York Age*, November 29, 1917.

18. Hales, "Josephus Daniels," 19–20.

19. Michaelis, *Eleanor*, 182.

20. McWhirter, *Red Summer*, 15; Franklin and Moss, *From Slavery to Freedom*, 313.

21. Michaelis, *Eleanor*, 186; McWhirter, *Red Summer*, 49, 109, 131, 138, 160, 195, 204.

22. McWhirter, *Red Summer*, 96–113; Cronon, *Cabinet Diaries*, July 20, 21, and 22, 1919.

23. Harry Golden, "Only Man F.D.R. Called Chief," *Los Angeles Times*, July 22, 1963; "Palestine," *Jewish Voice*, February 19, 1915; "Zionists Cheer and Weep," *Baltimore Evening Sun*, September 30, 1918.

24. "Illuminating," *N&O*, May 16, 1947; Morrison, "Southern Philo-Semite"; "Hadassah Plans Donor Luncheon," *N&O*, May 2, 1948; James Waterman Wise to JWD, May 14, 1940, box 302, JWD Papers, SHC.

25. Morrison, *Josephus Daniels*, 75; JD, *Wilson Era: Years of Peace*, 548–50; and JWD, *End of Innocence*, 194.

26. "No Aryan Doctrines at Chapel Hill," *N&O*, October 1, 1933.

27. Okrent, *Guarded Gate*, 284.

28. "Daniels on Immigration," *N&O*, January 22, 1920.

29. "Women Can't Get Degree at Cambridge," *N&O*, June 1, 1897.

30. "Women Suffrage," *N&O*, March 6, 1913; "Secretary Daniels' Address to the Women of California," *N&O*, February 3, 1915.

31. "Mrs. Daniels Makes Splendid Address," *Gastonia (NC) Gazette*, October 20, 1920; Craig, *Josephus Daniels*, 366; "Cabinet Officers Abuse the Franking Privilege," *Sacramento Bee*, August 26, 1920; Michaelis, *Eleanor*, 156.

32. Plummer, "Afro-American Response," 125; Cronon, *Josephus Daniels in Mexico*, 72.

33. Craig, *Josephus Daniels*, 276–77; Cronon, *Josephus Daniels in Mexico*, 72.

34. Craig, *Josephus Daniels*, 280

35. *New York Tribune*, December 7, 1914; *Pittsburgh Press*, November 19, 1914.

36. Robert W. Haywood to JD, August 3, 1920, folder 32, JD Papers, SHC.

37. "Navy for Defense Not for Conquest Says Mr. Daniels," *N&O*, May 25, 1913.

38. JD, *Editor in Politics*, 494; "State Opened Wider Her Arms," *Raleigh Morning Post*, October 20, 1905.

39. Pietrusza, *TR's Last War*, 58.

40. Smith, *FDR*, 666; JD, *Wilson Era: Years of Peace*, 577.

41. A. Link, *Wilson*, 2:125.

42. Morrison, *Josephus Daniels*, 68.

43. J. Cooper, *Woodrow Wilson*, 301.

44. Smith, *FDR*, 101–7.

45. Burns, *Roosevelt*, 49–50; JD, *Wilson Era: Years of Peace*, 125; Michaelis, *Eleanor*, 131.

46. Kilpatrick, *Roosevelt and Daniels*; Dallek, *Franklin D. Roosevelt*, 54–55.

47. JD, *Wilson Era: Years of Peace*, 129.

48. G. Ward, *First-Class Temperament*, 305, 350.

49. Morrison, *Josephus Daniels*, 67; Kilpatrick, *Roosevelt and Daniels*, 20.

50. G. Ward, *First-Class Temperament*, 305.

51. Smith, *FDR*, 117.
52. Michaelis, *Eleanor*, 155.
53. JWD to Joseph P. Lash, January 9, 1970, folder 1809, JWD Papers, SHC.
54. Smith, *FDR*, 666; Coletta, "Josephus Daniels."
55. AP, "Navy Not Prepared When Declaration of War Was Passed," *Reno Gazette-Journal*, February 2, 1920; G. Ward, *First-Class Temperament*, 477.
56. JD, *Wilson Era: Years of Peace*, 129.
57. "Enthroning Incompetence," *Fort Wayne (IN) Daily News*, March 3, 1917; G. Ward, *First-Class Temperament*, 322.
58. G. Ward, *First-Class Temperament*, 322.
59. "Still Attacking Daniels," *Bristol (TN) Herald Courier*, June 19, 1917.
60. JD, *Wilson Era: Years of Peace*, 139.
61. Creel, *Rebel at Large*, 149–50.
62. JD, *Wilson Era: Years of Peace*, 260.
63. Conot, *Streak of Luck*, 508; JD, *Wilson Era: Years of Peace*, 464.
64. Edison to JD, July 30, 1918, folder 31, scan 27, JD Papers, SHC.
65. "Josephus Daniels," *Atlanta Constitution*, November 14, 1916.
66. JD, *Wilson Era: Years of Peace*, 427.
67. A. Link, *Woodrow Wilson*, 183.
68. Kazin, *Godly Hero*, 206.
69. Heckscher, *Woodrow Wilson*, 437.
70. Berg, *Wilson*, 431–32; Cronon, *Cabinet Diaries*, March 20, 1917, 117–18.
71. JD to JWD, September 9, 1939, folder 270, JWD Papers, SHC.
72. Berg, *Wilson*, 440; Lepore, *These Truths*, 395.
73. Cronon, *Cabinet Diaries*, April 11, 1917, 133; Brands, *Privileged Life*, 108.
74. Cronon, *Cabinet Diaries*, April 30, 1918, 301; April 6, 1917, 130; August 17, 1917, 188.
75. Cronon, *Cabinet Diaries*, August 7, 1917, 188.
76. JD, *Wilson Era: Years of War*, 546.
77. Cronon, *Cabinet Diaries*, April 22, 1917.
78. "Views Have Moderated," *N&O*, February 8, 1920; "End the Dies Committee," *N&O*, February 16, 1942; "Guilt by Accusation," *N&O*, May 15, 1950; "Strikes Out Again," *N&O*, October 4, 1951; UP, "Evil Klan Spirit Invades Senate, Publisher Charges," *Miami Herald*, June 11, 1953.
79. UP, "Evil Klan Spirit Invades Senate, Publisher Charges," *Miami Herald*, June 11, 1953.
80. "Jewish Society to Honor WW1 Veteran," *St. Augustine Record*, February 18, 2006.
81. Cronon, *Cabinet Diaries*, April 22, 1917.
82. "The Day of Daniels," *Atlanta Constitution*, April 14, 1918.
83. JWD, *End of Innocence*, 187–88; Craig, *Josephus Daniels*, 356–59; Cronon, *Cabinet Diaries*, 405; "News of Tar Heels from Washington," *N&O*, May 4, 1919; "Josephus Daniels Abroad," *Scranton (PA) Tribune*, May 7, 1919.
84. "An Appreciation by an American Correspondent," *Times* (London), April 24, 1919.
85. JD, *Wilson Era: Years of War*, 497–502.
86. G. Ward, *First-Class Temperament*, 485–86.

87. Cooper, *Woodrow Wilson*, 568–69.
88. Smith, *FDR*, 104.
89. "Expose the Navy Scandal!," *Washington Post*, June 18, 1920.

CHAPTER SEVEN

1. "Roosevelt Calls Him Chief," *N&O*, January 11, 1942; Wylly Folk St. John, "Daniels Belied Age by Youthful Ideas," *Miami News*, January 15, 1948.
2. Richard Stradling, "The Josephus Daniels House Is Gone, but the Cannon on His Front Lawn Has a New NC Home," *N&O*, September 3, 2021.
3. Morrison, *Josephus Daniels*, 145.
4. "Daniels and the Nation," *Charlotte Observer*, February 29, 1924.
5. Morrison, *Josephus Daniels*, 153.
6. "Liberty to Think," *N&O*, February 12, 1925.
7. H. L. Mencken, "Civil War in the Confederacy," *Evening Sun* (Baltimore), July 30, 1928.
8. Morrison, *Josephus Daniels*, 159; Tony Badger to JWD, June 18, 1979, folder 1937, JWD Papers, SHC.
9. Woodward, *Origins of the New South*, 369.
10. "Open Break between Governor Morrison and Former Secretary Josephus Daniels," *Gastonia Gazette*, August 18, 1921; "Only Friendly Counsel in Interest of Democracy," *N&O*, August 18, 1921.
11. "Daniels and Morrison in Dramatic Debate at the University Finals," *Winston-Salem Journal*, June 16, 1921; "Angus W. McLean," *N&O*, June 22, 1935.
12. Morrison, *Josephus Daniels*, 144.
13. JD to JWD, April 8, 1935, April 4–8, 1935, JWD Papers, SHC.
14. JD to JWD, March 2, 1936, March 1–4, 1936, JWD Papers, SHC.
15. "No New Deal for North Carolina," *N&O*, April 15, 1933.
16. JWD to JD, December 5, 1936, folder 13, JWD Papers, SHC.
17. JWD to JD, February 11, 1937, box 151, JWD Papers, SHC; Pleasants, *Buncombe Bob*, 267.
18. Leidholdt, *Battling Nell*, 59; Nell Battle Lewis, Incidentally, *N&O*, June 13, 1948.
19. Nell Battle Lewis, Incidentally, *N&O*, September 7, 1921.
20. Leidholdt, *Battling Nell*, 298.
21. Cash, *Mind of the South*, 362.
22. Leidholdt, *Battling Nell*, 112–19.
23. Leidholdt, *Battling Nell*, 121–23.
24. Leidholdt, *Battling Nell*, 127.
25. Nell Battle Lewis, "Barbarous Gaston," Incidentally, *N&O*, May 5, 1929.
26. "Action and Quick Action," *N&O*, April 23, 1929.
27. Nell Battle Lewis, Incidentally, *N&O*, May 12, 1929.
28. Leidholdt, *Battling Nell*, 132.
29. Salmond, *Gastonia 1929*, 77–78.
30. Leidholdt, *Battling Nell*, 153; JWD to Eugene Lyons, August 19, 1940, folder 319, JWD Papers, SHC.

31. "Labor Praises *News and Observer*," *N&O*, August 26, 1930; "More Operatives Get Out of Union," *N&O*, August 29, 1930; Scales and Nickson, *Causes at Heart*, 243.

32. "How to Lose," *N&O*, July 16, 1934.

33. "Shoot to Kill," *N&O*, September 6, 1934.

34. JWD to JD, September 20, 1934, series 1.2, June–September 1934, JWD Papers, SHC.

35. JWD to Daniels, September 20, 1934, series 1.2, June–September 1934, JWD Papers, SHC.

36. JD to FDR, September 17, 1933, JD Papers, SHC.

37. Tursi, *"Winston-Salem Journal,"* 162–67; Claiborne, *"Charlotte Observer,"* 127.

38. Quoted in Lefler and Newsome, *North Carolina*, 562.

39. Leidholdt, *Battling Nell*, 204.

40. "Congratulations with a Sigh," *N&O*, September 27, 1942.

41. Neil Hester, "Dean of Telegraph Editors Looks Back on 45 Years," *N&O*, May 16, 1965.

42. Lefler and Newsome, *North Carolina*, 626.

43. Schwarz, *Speculator*, 45, 196.

44. Quoted in Morrison, "Southern Philo-Semite," 85.

45. Baruch to JWD, November 20, 1934, October–December 1934, JWD Papers, SHC; JWD to Baruch, November 22, 1934, October–December 1934, JWD Papers, SHC.

46. "What Are the Facts?," *N&O*, November 22, 1934.

47. "Unprecedented," *N&O*, March 31, 1931.

48. Cronon, "Josephus Daniels as a Reluctant Candidate," 457; Morrison, *Josephus Daniels*, 152, 161; Morrison, *Governor O*, 106.

49. JD to JWD, August 29, 1936, series 1.2, August 20–31, 1936, JWD Papers, SHC.

CHAPTER EIGHT

1. JD, *Shirt-Sleeve Diplomat*, 12–13; Cronon, *Josephus Daniels in Mexico*, 24; AP, "Josephus Daniels Begins Service at Mexico City," *N&O*, April 16, 1933.

2. JD, *Shirt-Sleeve Diplomat*, 3, 9; Cronon, *Josephus Daniels in Mexico*, 19; "Mexicans Resent Appointment of Daniels," *Los Angeles Times*, March 16, 1933.

3. Mott, *American Journalism*, 719–20.

4. JD, *Wilson Era: Years of Peace*, 131.

5. "Thomas Couldn't Find One Roosevelt Rooter," *Brooklyn Daily Eagle*, October 25, 1932.

6. Smith, *FDR*, 417.

7. Quoted in Cronon, *Josephus Daniels in Mexico*, 21–22, 29.

8. JD, *Shirt-Sleeve Diplomat*, 24; "Mahatma Gandhi," *N&O*, April 10, 1930.

9. Cronon, *Josephus Daniels in Mexico*, 87, 103–5.

10. Cronon, *Josephus Daniels in Mexico*, 90–91.

11. Cronon, *Josephus Daniels in Mexico*, 95–96.

12. JD to Sanford Martin, February 3, 1936, February 3–6, 1936, JWD Papers, SHC.

13. JD to Claude G. Bowers, May 9, 1936, May 1–10, 1936, JWD Papers, SHC.

14. Cronon, *Josephus Daniels in Mexico*, 107–9.

15. Morrison, *Josephus Daniels*, 202.
16. Quoted in Cronon, *Josephus Daniels in Mexico*, 171.
17. Quoted in Cronon, *Josephus Daniels in Mexico*, 216.
18. Cronon, *Josephus Daniels in Mexico*, 286.
19. Quoted in Cronon, *Josephus Daniels in Mexico*, 274, 279.
20. Quoted in Cronon, *Josephus Daniels in Mexico*, 275–76.

CHAPTER NINE

1. Fitzgerald, *This Side of Paradise*, 304; JWD, interview by Charles Eagles, March 9–11, 1977, SOHP.
2. James E. Wood to FD Jr., December 9, 1988, box 31, FD Jr. Papers, SHC.
3. JWD speech before the Southeastern Library Association, October 14, 1960, box 53, FD Jr. Papers, SHC.
4. Berg, *Max Perkins*, 329–30; Donald, *Look Homeward*, 412–13.
5. JWD, interview by Eagles.
6. JWD, interview by Eagles.
7. John Selby, "Scanning New Books," *Asbury Park (NJ) Press*, October 5, 1941.
8. Ritterhouse, *Discovering the South*, 29.
9. Ritterhouse, *Discovering the South*, 20; JWD, interview by Eagles.
10. Jonathan Coll, "Brilliant Satire," *Des Moines Register*, April 27, 1930; R. E. Powell, "Clash of Angels Sure to Bring Storm of Criticism," *Atlanta Constitution*, March 23, 1930.
11. L. Daniels, *With a Woman's Voice*, 7–8; Craig, *Josephus Daniels*, 394–95.
12. JD to JWD, April 5, 1932, Series 1.1, 1932, JWD Papers, SHC.
13. JWD, interview by Eagles.
14. Craig, *Josephus Daniels*, 394–95; L. Daniels, *With a Women's Voice*, 31; Lucy Daniels, interview by author, May 17, 2021, Raleigh.
15. L. Daniels, *With a Women's Voice*, 48.
16. L. Daniels, *With a Women's Voice*, 64–65.
17. Lucy Daniels, interview by author.
18. L. Daniels, *With a Women's Voice*, 83; Patsy Daniels, interview by author, June 16, 2021, Cary, NC.
19. JWD to JD, August 9, 1933, Series 1.2, March 1933, JWD Papers, SHC; *N&O* board minutes, October 30, 1971, box 5, FD Jr. Papers, SHC.
20. Eagles, *Jonathan Daniels and Race Relations*, 11; JWD, interview by Daniel Singal, March 22, 1972, Southern Intellectual Leaders Project, CCOH.
21. Eagles, *Jonathan Daniels and Race Relations*, xiv, xv.
22. "A Shocking Verdict," *N&O*, April 10, 1933.
23. Craig, *Josephus Daniels*; JWD to JD, July 11, 1933, and JD to JWD, March 22, 1935, folders 31 and 32, JWD Papers, SHC; Eagles, *Jonathan Daniels and Race Relations*, 3; JWD to JD, July 1, 1933, JD Papers, SHC.
24. *Equal Protections of the Laws*.
25. Du Bois, *Souls of Black Folk*, 106–7.
26. "Blackjacks," *N&O*, July 12, 1936; "Cruelty and Complacency," *N&O*, March 7, 1936; "Hesitation," *N&O*, May 1, 1933.

27. "Whitewash for Brutality," *N&O*, April 13, 1935.
28. Nell Battle Lewis, "What Is Torture in North Carolina?," Incidentally, *N&O*, July 21, 1935.
29. Nell Battle Lewis, Incidentally, *N&O*, March 15, 1931.
30. "Questions on a Killing," *N&O*, February 2, 1937.
31. Quoted in Leidholdt, *Battling Nell*, 221.
32. Eagles, *Jonathan Daniels and Race Relations*, 37.
33. Eagles, *Jonathan Daniels and Race Relations*, 57–58.
34. "Mob in Franklin County Lynches Negro Who Slew Farmer; Inquiry Started," *N&O*, July 31, 1935.
35. "Contagious Madness," *N&O*, July 31, 1935.
36. "Petty and Cruel," *N&O*, February 6, 1935; "No Place for Prejudice," *N&O*, August 3, 1933.
37. "Black Poverty," *N&O*, June 7, 1936.
38. "No Color Line in Safety," *N&O*, February 13, 1941.
39. "Progress," *N&O*, October 20, 1934.
40. JWD to Walter White, November 2, 1936, November 1–6, 1936, JWD Papers, SHC; Badger, *Why White Liberals Fail*, 67–70.
41. JWD to Virginius Dabney, June 12, 1941, folder 363, JWD Papers, SHC.
42. Ted Vaden, interview by author, June 18, 2021, Chapel Hill.
43. Eagles, *Jonathan Daniels and Race Relations*, 44.
44. AP, "Demands Admission to Pharmacy School," *N&O*, March 17, 1933.
45. Eagles, *Jonathan Daniels and Race Relations*, 44.
46. "What Are the Facts?," *N&O*, November 22, 1934.
47. Payne to JWD, January 2, 1936, series 1.2, January 1–6, 1936, JWD Papers, SHC.
48. JD to JWD, March 28, 1938, folder 174, JWD Papers, SHC.
49. "Individualistic Socialist," October 30, 1936, SHC.
50. W. T. Couch to JWD, October 31, 1936, and JWD to Couch, November 2, 1936, October 26–November 6, 1936, JWD Papers, SHC.
51. "A Spectacle," *N&O*, April 23, 1935.
52. Du Bois, *Souls of Black Folk*, 7.
53. "An Unfortunate Beginning," *N&O*, November 26, 1938.
54. Eagles, *Jonathan Daniels and Race Relations*, 62–63; "Negroes and Voting," *N&O*, April 1, 1940; "Experiment and Responsibility," *N&O*, March 9, 1941.
55. Eagles, *Jonathan Daniels and Race Relations*, 232.
56. Lucy Rudolph Mason to JWD, September 17, 1938, folder 212, JWD Papers, SHC.
57. Herbert O'Keefe, draft obituary for JWD, written in advance of his death, April 1978, box 20, FD Jr. Papers, SHC.
58. O'Keefe, draft obituary.
59. "Editor Pays $4.35 for Speed Lesson," *N&O*, September 29, 1936.
60. JWD, "A Hasty Retreat—with Thanks," *N&O*, March 21, 1969.
61. Herbert O'Keefe draft obituary.
62. "Contributions to the State, Nation Remembered," *N&O*, November 7, 1981.
63. Untitled article in the *Nation*, reprinted in *N&O*, February 24, 1942.
64. Quoted in Ritterhouse, *Discovering the South*, 20.
65. JWD, *Southerner Discovers the South*, 9.

66. Tindall, *Emergence of the New South*, 741.
67. Ritterhouse, *Discovering the South*, 291.
68. Egerton, *Speak Now against the Day*, 253–54.

CHAPTER TEN

1. "Snail and Buggy," *N&O*, February 12, 1937; JWD to JD, February 11, 1937, folder 151, JWD Papers, SHC; Morrison, *Josephus Daniels*, 175.
2. JWD to JD, February 11, 1937, folder 151, JWD Papers, SHC.
3. JWD to Charles Lindbergh, August 12, 1940, folder 318, JWD Papers, SHC; "The Home Cause," *N&O*, October 1, 1939; Eagles, *Jonathan Daniels and Race Relations*, 83.
4. JD to JWD, September 19 and 21, 1939, folder 271, JWD Papers, SHC.
5. JD to FDR, August 27, 1939, folders 269 and 270, JWD Papers, SHC; JD to JWD, September 1, 1939, Sept. 1–12, 1939, folder 270, JWD Papers, SHC.
6. Graham, Green, and Couch to JWD, August 7, 1940, folder 317, JWD Papers, SHC.
7. Morgan to JWD, June 10, 1940, folder 308, JWD Papers, SHC; Couch, Graham, and Green to JWD, August 7, 1940, folder 317, JWD Papers; "Action beyond Argument," *N&O*, March 17, 1941; JWD to Hauben, March 24, 1941, box 357, JWD Papers, SHC.
8. JD, *Frontier on the Potomac*, 189; Hoover to JWD, December 1, 1943, folder 449, JWD Papers, SHC; JWD FBI files, folder 2546, JWD Papers, SHC.
9. JWD to JD, undated, November 1940, folder 333, JWD Papers, SHC.
10. J. David Stern to JWD, June 11, 1936, June 11–16, 1936; JD to JWD, December 13, 1941; and JD to JWD, August 15, 1941, folders 402 and 414, JWD Papers, SHC.
11. FDR to JD, September 28, 1940, September 1940, FD Sr. Papers, SHC.
12. JD to Claude G. Bowers, May 9, 1936, May 1–10, 1936, JWD Papers, SHC.
13. Lucy Daniels, interview by author, May 17, 2021, Raleigh.
14. List for the president: a few examples of wealthy young officers, commissioned for wartime duty in Washington in October 1942; and JWD to FDR, October 14, 1942, both in folder 417, JWD Papers, SHC.
15. "Editor Bailey on Preachers and Politicians," *N&O*, July 7, 1901; JD, *Editor in Politics*, 436.
16. Eagles, *Jonathan Daniels and Race Relations*, 98–99; JWD, *Tar Heels*, 323; JWD, interview by James R. Fuchs, October 4–5, 1963, Oral History Interviews, Harry S. Truman Presidential Library and Museum, Independence, MO, https://www.trumanlibrary.gov/library/oral-histories/danielsj; JWD to JD, March 17, 1943, folder 429, JWD Papers, SHC.
17. Drew Pearson, "Washington Merry-Go-Round," *N&O*, May 23, 1943.
18. JWD, interview by Fuchs.
19. JWD to FDR, memo, November 24, 1942, folder 418, JWD Papers, SHC.
20. Leidholdt, *Battling Nell*, 219–20; Pleasants, *Home Front*, 240.
21. Gershenhorn, *Louis Austin*, 61.
22. Pleasants, *Home Front*, 240.
23. FD Sr. to JWD, August 25, 1942, folder 414, JWD Papers, SHC.
24. FD Sr. to JWD, August 16–September 11, 1942 file, folder 418, JWD Papers, SHC; "No Ostrich Philosophy," *N&O*, August 21, 1942.

25. FD Sr. to JWD, September 25, 1944, folder 480, JWD Papers, SHC.
26. JWD to Lester B. Granger, August 14, 1942, folder 415, JWD Papers, SHC.
27. JWD to Howard W. Odum, August 24, 1942, folder 418, JWD Papers, SHC.
28. JWD to JD, January 6, 1943, folder 427, JWD Papers, SHC.
29. Eagles, *Jonathan Daniels and Race Relations*, 110.
30. Hartnett, *Carolina Israelite*; Morris Milgram to JWD, November 17, 1943, folder 448, JWD Papers, SHC.
31. JWD to FDR, February 8, 1944, folder 456; JWD to Rep. William D. Hassett, memo, March 7, 1944, folder 459; JWD to FDR, September 28, 1944, folder 1847, JWD Papers, SHC.
32. Lawrence C. Cramer to JWD, May 5, 1977, folder 1910, JWD Papers, SHC; JWD, interview by Daniel Singal, March 22, 1972, Southern Intellectual Leaders Project, CCOH.
33. JWD diary, October 15, 1942, folder 2524, JWD Papers, SHC; Michaelis, *Eleanor*, 327, 339–40, 408.
34. JWD to Bernice Baumgarten, April 6, 1945, folder 501, JWD Papers, SHC.
35. AP, "Roosevelt to Speak Today on His Mission to Crimea," *N&O*, March 1, 1945; Herbert Elliston, "Candor on the President's Condition," *St. Louis Post-Dispatch*, October 27, 1955.
36. JWD, interview by Daniel Singal.
37. JWD, *Man of Independence*, 27.
38. McCullough, *Truman*, 364.
39. UP, "Editor, Governor Exchange Blasts," *N&O*, February 26, 1947.
40. L. Daniels, *With a Woman's Voice*, 69.
41. FD Sr. to JWD, April 5, 1945, folder 501, JWD Papers, SHC.
42. "Public Enemies," *N&O*, January 16, 1942.
43. Pleasants, *Home Front*, 181.
44. Statement of the Ownership, *N&O*, October 4, 1940; October 3, 1950.
45. Wylly Folk St John, "Daniels Belied Age by Youthful Ideas," *Miami Herald*, January 15, 1948.
46. "This Is Labor Day," *N&O*, September 1, 1947.
47. "Trustees of UNC Reject Clark Race Resolution," *N&O*, February 11, 1947.
48. "Must Be Remedied," *N&O*, October 9, 1946.
49. JWD to Eagles, July 17, 1972, folder 1847, JWD Papers, SHC.
50. Morrison, *Josephus Daniels*, 227–28; FDR to Daniels, September 11, 1940, September 7–12, 1940, folder 323, JWD Papers, SHC; "Construction of the Parkway," National Park Service, last updated February 2017, https://www.nps.gov/blri/learn/historyculture/construction.htm.
51. JD, *Editor in Politics*, 491–92.
52. "Man of the Courage of His Convictions," *N&O*, June 5, 1947; Scales and Nickson, *Causes at Heart*, 183.
53. Key, *Southern Politics*, 228; Gunther, *Inside U.S.A.*, 659–60, 719–20; AP, "Editors Praise Daniels as Leader in Profession," *N&O*, January 16, 1948.
54. FD Jr., speech to Family Forum Talk, August 10, 1993, box 53, FD Jr Papers, SHC; "Daniels' $344,130 Estate Is Left to His Four Sons," *N&O*, January 28, 1948; Lucy Daniels, interview by author.

55. Last will and testament, series 3, 1946, FD Sr. Papers, SHC.
56. Last will and testament, series 3, 1946, FD Sr. Papers, SHC.
57. "The State Has Lost Her Greatest Citizen," *High Point (NC) Enterprise*, January 18, 1948.

CHAPTER ELEVEN

1. "Like a Communist Bullet," *N&O*, September 11, 1948.
2. J. Ward, *Defending White Democracy*, 104–5.
3. "Daniels Tells Students to Follow Liberal Paths," *N&O*, March 3, 1948.
4. Quoted in Eagles, *Jonathan Daniels and Race Relations*, 140.
5. C. C. Stone to JWD, May 30, 1948, folder 607, JWD Papers, SHC.
6. S. Burke to JWD, May 29, 1948, folder 607, JWD Papers, SHC.
7. Egerton, *Speak Now against the Day*, 259.
8. Joseph Driscoll, "Truman's Loyal Brain Trust of Four Working Hard for Him, but He Plays His Own Tunes," *St. Louis Post-Dispatch*, October 6, 1948; Eagles, *Jonathan Daniels and Race Relations*, 141.
9. Truman to Lucy Daniels, October 5, 1948, folder 608, JWD Papers, SHC.
10. JWD, "Truman: An Appraisal of the Man," *N&O*, October 31, 1948; McCullough, *Truman*, 588.
11. Westbrook Pegler to JWD, May 26, 1954, and JWD to Pegler, May 26, 1948, folder 1016, JWD Papers, SHC.
12. JWD, interview by James R. Fuchs, October 4–5, 1963, Oral History Interviews, Harry S. Truman Presidential Library and Museum, Independence, MO.
13. JWD, interview by Fuchs; Duke Shoop, "Clash over Post," *Kansas City Times*, May 4, 1949.
14. Michael L. Hoffman, "Soviets for Inquiry on Negroes in U.S.," *New York Times*, December 3, 1947.
15. JWD, interview by Daniel Singal, March 22, 1972, Southern Intellectual Leaders Project, CCOH.
16. JD to JWD, August 29, 1935, and JD to JWD, March 5–10, 1938, folder 170, JWD Papers, SHC.
17. Lynn Nisbet, "Around Capital Square," *Statesville (NC) Daily Record*, November 7, 1949; Eula Nixon Greenwood, "Raleigh Roundup," *Robesonian* (Lumberton, NC), March 15, 1950.
18. JWD, interview by Fuchs.
19. JD to Frank Porter Graham, March 4, 1936, February 1–4, 1936, JWD Papers, SHC.
20. JWD to Eleanor Roosevelt, December 27, 1949, folder 672, JWD Papers, SHC.
21. AP, "N.C. Primary Funds Reached Kitty, Court Told," *N&O*, July 7, 1956; JWD, interview by Singal.
22. JWD to Harry Vaughan, March 3, 1950, and Vaughn to JWD, March 10, 1950, folder 690, JWD Papers, SHC.
23. Pleasants, *Buncombe Bob*, 274.
24. Pleasants and Burns, *Frank Porter Graham*, 117–18; JWD, interview by Charles Eagles, March 9–11, 1977, SOHP.

25. JWD to Truman, June 15, 1950, folder 716, JWD Papers, SHC.

26. JWD, "Sound the Tocsin," N&O, May 21, 1950.

27. Simmons Fentress, "Smith Supporters Jubilant as Run-Off Brings Victory," N&O, June 25, 1950.

28. JWD to Truman, June 26, 1950, folder 718, JWD Papers, SHC.

29. Martin, *Adlai Stevenson*, 116.

30. Drew Pearson, "Sen. George Author of Part of Loyalty Oath," *Lexington (KY) Leader*, July 26, 1952; AP, "Editor Daniels Criticizes Press Campaign Work," *Bradenton (FL) Herald*, November 2, 1952.

31. JWD to Adlai Stevenson, April 5, 1955, folder 1049, JWD Papers, SHC.

32. Mott, *American Journalism*, 859.

33. Woodrow Price, "Alton Lennon Forces Flood State with 'Phony' Race Issue Leaflets," N&O, May 28, 1954.

34. LBJ to JWD, November 24, 1954, folder 1057, JWD Papers.

35. Charles Craven, "Tar Heel Republicans Stage Rally," N&O, September 27, 1953.

36. Quoted in "More Power to 'Em," *Charlotte News*, April 10, 1952.

CHAPTER TWELVE

1. "Daniels Gives Southern View," N&O, March 17, 1954.

2. Egerton, *Speak Now against the Day*, 602.

3. "The South Never Needed Wisdom More, nor Fury Less," N&O, May 17, 1954.

4. Egerton, *Speak Now against the Day*, 354.

5. Russell Clay, "Tar Heels Reject State's Label of No. 1 for Klan," N&O, October 24, 1965.

6. Quoted in Eagles, *Jonathan Daniels and Race Relations*, 195–96.

7. JWD, "Ignorance as a Policy for the South," address to Coker College, reprinted in N&O, October 10, 1955.

8. "Would Turn Back the Clock a Century," N&O, October 15, 1955.

9. Dan Jones, letter to the editor, "Integration," and JWD's reply in an "editor's note," N&O, July 18, 1956.

10. "Good Morning," N&O, August 11, 1956.

11. Eagles, *Jonathan Daniels and Race Relations*, 185.

12. Quoted in Eagles, *Jonathan Daniels and Race Relations*, 189.

13. Eagles, *Jonathan Daniels and Race Relations*, 190; Noel Yancey, AP, "Funeral for Editor Was Not Up to Its Advertising," N&O, September 11, 1956.

14. JWD, interview by Charles Eagles, March 9–11, 1977, SOHP.

15. Leidholdt, *Battling Nell*, 292, 212, 213; Nell Battle Lewis, Incidentally, N&O, June 6, 1954; July 27, 1947.

16. "Acquittal by Prejudice," N&O, January 12, 1952; "Both Should Be Tried," N&O, March 19, 1954; "Tough on Defendant," N&O, June 12, 1954; "Substantial Justice," N&O, November 26, 1954.

17. "A Southern Tragedy," N&O, November 10, 1955.

18. "A Good Record Marred," N&O, September 14, 1957; Thomas Iverson to JWD (undated), September 1957 file, folder 1207, SHC.

19. "Complicated Custom," N&O, February 11, 1960; Eagles, *Jonathan Daniels and Race Relations*, 219.

20. FD Jr., interview by Joseph Mosnier, April 23, 2007, SOHP.

21. Charles Whaley, "We Dissent," *Louisville Courier Journal*, November 11, 1962.

22. "Time of Testing," N&O, May 10, 1963.

23. Forest P. Payne to JWD, February 16, 1960, folder 1348; Mable Pearl Lilly to JWD, May 1963, folder 1480, JWD Papers, SHC.

24. FD Jr,. interview by Mosnier.

25. "President's Address," N&O, June 14, 1963; "The Rights of All," N&O, July 15, 1963.

26. Jesse Helms, *Viewpoint*, aired April 23, 1964, on WRAL, transcript in North Carolina Collection, Wilson Library, University of North Carolina, Chapel Hill.

27. Jesse Helms, *Viewpoint*, aired May 31, 1962, on WRAL, transcript in North Carolina Collection, Wilson Library, University of North Carolina, Chapel Hill.

28. Offering Statement for Raleigh Newsweekly Publishing Company, January 3, 1979, box 18, FD Jr. Papers, SHC.

29. JWD, interview by Daniel Singal, March 22, 1972, Southern Intellectual Leaders Project, CCOH.

30. Eig, *King*, 296.

31. Eagles, *Jonathan Daniels and Race Relations*, 234.

32. Lucy Daniels Inman to JWD, September 17, 1965, folder 1552, JWD Papers, SHC.

33. Drew Pearson to JWD, April 10, 1963, folder 1484, JWD Papers, SHC.

34. "Building for What?," N&O, December 28, 1966; "Possibility for Peace," N&O, January 10, 1968.

35. JWD to Graham, May 7, 1958, and Graham to JWD, May 5, 1958, folder 1247, JWD Papers, SHC.

36. JWD to Henry Belk, October 31, 1959, folder 1283, JWD Papers, SHC.

37. Bert Bennett to JWD, July 18, 1960, and JWD to Frank Graham (undated), folder 1333, JWD Papers, SHC.

38. Chester Bowles to JWD, November 15, 1960, folder 1324, JWD Papers, SHC.

39. JWD to Arthur Schlesinger Jr., September 6, 1962, folder 1419, JWD Papers, SHC.

40. Roy Parker, interview by Joseph Mosnier, November 28 and December 13, 2007, SOHP.

41. Gene Roberts, interview by Joseph Mosnier, February 7, 2008, SOHP.

42. Rob Christensen, "Sanford Finding Few Obstacles on the Campaign Trail," N&O, April 30, 1986.

43. Gene Roberts, "Employment Problems Plentiful for Tar Heel Negro Graduates," N&O, September 3, 1961.

44. Roberts, interview by Mosnier.

45. Gary Pearce, "Roy Parker Jr.," *Talking about Politics* (blog), April 5, 2013, https://talkingaboutpolitics.com/roy-parker-jr/.

46. Steve Schewel, interview by author, January 6, 2022, Durham.

47. Roberts quoted in Guillory, "Mass Media in North Carolina Politics," 110.

48. "Poison, Mind, Body, and Heart," N&O, April 25, 1901.

49. "To Stop Smoking," N&O, March 5, 1960; "A Few Kind Words for Tobacco," N&O, December 16, 1959.

50. JWD to John W. Morris, August 19, 1964, folder 1521, JWD Papers, SHC.

51. Roberts, interview by Mosnier.

52. James L. Whitfield, "Long Hours and Many People Involved in Paper You Read Each Day," N&O, May 16, 1965.

53. AP, "Gardner Attacks Scott Appointees," *Charlotte Observer*, April 19, 1972.

54. Parker, interview by Mosnier.

55. Charles Craven, "Governor Racks 'Em Up at the Mansion," N&O, February 8, 1971.

56. Treva Jones, "Lives and Times," N&O, August 13, 1995.

57. Morrison, *Josephus Daniels Says*, 197–98.

58. Roberts, interview by Mosnier.

59. W. L., "Another American Tragedy," N&O, March 24, 1940; JWD, review of *Native Son*, folder 2496, JWD Papers, SHC.

60. Frank Smethurst, "In My Opinion," N&O, September 11, 1932; "W. E. B. DuBois Will Speak Tonight," N&O, December 7, 1926.

61. JWD to James E. Shepard, April 2, 1935, folder 1935, JWD Papers, SHC.

62. Nell Battle Lewis, Incidentally, N&O, December 2, 1923; November 9, 1924.

63. Bowling, *Sam Ragan*, xxix.

64. Bowling, *Sam Ragan*, 104–5.

65. Peder Zane, interview by author, June 9, 2021, Raleigh.

66. King, *Southern Ladies and Gentlemen*, 127–28.

67. Davenport to FD Jr., April 9, 1990, FD Jr. Papers, SHC.

CHAPTER THIRTEEN

1. L. Daniels, *With a Woman's Voice*, 31.

2. "Open House" edition of N&O and the *Raleigh Times*, box 2, FD Jr. Papers, SHC.

3. FD Sr. to Dale Plummer, August 14, 1975, box 47, FD Sr. Papers, SHC.

4. JWD, *Tar Heels*, 21; FD Jr., "Frank Daniels, Jr.: Newspaper's Legacy," interview by Shannon Vickery, *Biographical Conversations with . . .*, UNC-TV, season 2017, episode 3, aired September 27, 2017, https://video.pbsnc.org/video/frank-daniels-jr-newspapers-legacy-fzhgjx/.

5. L. Daniels, *With a Woman's Voice*, 31.

6. Misc., Corr., September 1971, and FD Sr. to E. N. Richards, August 19, 1972, July–September 1972, FD Sr. Papers, SHC.

7. FD Jr., interview by author, January 7, 2019, Raleigh; Dave Jones, interview by Joseph Mosnier, November 26, December 5, and December 12, 2007, SOHP.

8. Ted Vaden, interview by author, June 18, 2021, Chapel Hill.

9. Ferrel Guillory, interview by Joseph Mosnier, October 20, 2007, SOHP.

10. Claude Sitton, interview by Joseph Mosnier, June 12–13, 2007, SOHP; Fred Crisp, interview by author, December 29, 2021, Raleigh.

11. Sitton, interview by Mosnier; FD Jr., "Frank Daniels, Jr.: Newspaper's Legacy," interview by Shannon Vickery, *Biographical Conversations with . . .*, UNC-TV, season 2017, episode 3, aired September 27, 2017, https://video.pbsnc.org/video/frank-daniels-jr-newspapers-legacy-fzhgjx/.

12. JD to FD Sr., March 15, 1939, March–April 1939, FD Sr. Papers, SHC.

13. FD Jr., interview by author; "Radio Station WNAO Sold to New TV Interests Here," N&O, November 18, 1952.

14. FD Jr. to Brandt Ayers, January 31, 1975, box 8, and FD Jr. to board, memo, June 5, 1981, FD Jr. Papers, SHC.

15. FD Jr., interview by author.

16. FD Jr., "Frank Daniels, Jr.: Newspaper's Legacy."

17. FD Jr., interview by Mosnier, February 13, April 10, April 23, and May 3, 2007, SOHP.

18. FD Jr., interview by Mosnier.

19. Rob Waters, interview by author, December 2, 2021, Raleigh.

20. Richard Hampton Jenrette, telephone interview by Joseph Mosnier, April 11, 2008, SOHP.

21. Tifft and Jones, *The Trust*, 714.

22. Jenrette, interview by Mosnier.

23. FD Jr. to Graham, March 1, 1993 (no date on Graham note), box 37, FD Jr. Papers, SHC; Craig Whitlock, "Frank Daniels Jr. Retires, Ending an Era at the N&O," N&O, December 22, 1996.

24. Arthur Sulzberger to FD Jr., February 29, 1974, box 11, FD Jr. Papers, SHC.

25. Tifft and Jones, *The Trust*, 552; Nagourney, *The "Times,"* 119–20.

26. Tifft and Jones, *The Trust*, 551.

27. Walker Stone, "The U.S. Oil Men Rap Envoy in Mexico," *Pittsburgh Press*, December 1, 1939.

28. Daniels's sons to Frank Graham (undated but 1938), box 13, JWD Papers, SHC.

29. "Anti–Closed Shop Bill Opposed by Daniels at Senate Body Hearing," *Asheville (NC) Citizen-Times*, March 7, 1947.

30. JD to JWD, March 28, 1938, folder 174, JWD Papers, SHC.

31. FD Jr. to JWD, no date but probably April 1975, folder 31, JWD Papers, SHC.

32. Claude Sitton to JWD, August 25, 1970, folder 1819, JWD Papers, SHC.

33. Wayne Hurder, telephone interview by author, April 15, 2022.

34. Company statement, August 20, 1976, box 13, FD Jr. Papers, SHC.

35. International Typographical Union complaint against the N&O, box 13, FD Jr. Papers, SHC; Crisp, interview by author.

36. Donaldson, Lufkin, and Jenrette report on the *News and Observer*, undated but probably 1989, box 52; report to stockholders, March 29, 1985, box 51, FD Jr. Papers, SHC.

37. FD Jr. to Earle Phillips, December 3, 1979, box 16, FD Jr. Papers, SHC.

38. FD Jr., interview by Mosnier.

39. L. Daniels, *With a Woman's Voice*, 160–61.

40. Jonathan Daniels, interview by Daniel Singal, March 22, 1972, Southern Intellectual Leaders Project, CCOH.

41. Egerton, *Speak Now against the Day*, 253–54.

CHAPTER FOURTEEN

1. Lew Powell, "From N.C. Hutch, the Chief Bunny," *Charlotte Observer*, April 3, 1979, box 18, FD Jr. Papers, SHC.

2. Powell, "From N.C, Hutch, the Chief Bunny."

3. Lawrence T. Mahoney, "Knight Errant Derick Daniels," *Miami Magazine*, March 1977, box 18, FD Jr. Papers, SHC.

4. JWD to David Cooper, March 16, 1977, folder 1908, JWD Papers, SHC.

5. FD Jr., interview by Joseph Mosnier, February 13, April 10, April 23, and May 3, 2007, SOHP; Gene Roberts, interview by Joseph Mosnier, February 7, 2008, SOHP.

6. Roberts and Klibanoff, *Race Beat*, 186.

7. Claude Sitton, speech to Raleigh Executives Club, February 2, 1988, box 15, Sitton Papers, SARL.

8. Roberts and Klibanoff, *Race Beat*, 191.

9. Don Schanche Jr., Associated Press, "Claude Sitton, Fearless Civil Rights Reporter," *Boston Globe*, March 11, 2015.

10. Schanche, "Claude Sitton."

11. Branch, *Pillar of Fire*, 362.

12. Branch, *Pillar of Fire*, 364: Roberts and Klibanoff, *Race Beat*, 361; Elaine Woo, "Karl Fleming Dies at 85; *Newsweek* Reporter Chronicled Civil Rights Struggle," *Los Angeles Times*, August 12, 2012.

13. Claude Sitton, speech (undated), box 15, Sitton Papers, SARL.

14. Fleming, *Son of the Rough South*, 299–300.

15. Sitton to JWD, 1968, undated, folder 2333, JWD Papers, SHC.

16. Claude Sitton, interview by Joseph Mosnier, June 12–13, 2007, SOHP; Carroll to Sitton, March 12, 1968, box 16, Sitton Papers, SARL.

17. *Greensboro Daily News* editorial reprinted in *N&O*, May 31, 1968.

18. Willie York to JWD, February 27, 1975, folder 1882, JWD Papers, SHC.

19. Derek Daniels to FD Jr., April 15, 1968, box 17, FD Jr. Papers, SHC.

20. Gary Pearce, interview by Joseph Mosnier, December 4 and 13, 2007, SOHP.

21. Sitton to Price, memo, undated, box 1, Sitton Papers, SARL.

22. FD Jr., speech to Family Forum Talk, August 10, 1993, box 53, FD Jr. Papers, SHC; FD Jr., "Frank Daniels, Jr.: Newspaper's Legacy," interview by Shannon Vickery, *Biographical Conversations with . . .*, UNC-TV, season 2017, episode 3, aired September 27, 2017, https://video.pbsnc.org/video/frank-daniels-jr-newspapers-legacy-fzhgjx/.

23. FD Jr. to *N&O* board, May 12, 1972, box 5, and FD Jr. to John McGee, February 1, 1968, box 2, FD Jr. Papers, SHC.

24. Pearce, interview by Mosnier.

25. Pearce, interview by Mosnier.

26. Robert W. Scott, diary entry, September 21, 1972, RWS Private Papers, Robert W. Scott Family Papers, North Carolina Division of Archives and History, Raleigh.

27. Hamilton, *Democracy's Detectives*, 233.

28. Pat Stith, "The IRS Plumber," *Final Edition* (blog), December 6, 2019, https://patstith.com/index.php/2019/12/16/the-irs-plumber/; Jay Price, "Claude Sitton, Pulitzer-Winning Journalist and Former *N&O* Editor, Has Died," *N&O*, March 10, 2015.

29. Dave Jones, interview by Joseph Mosnier, November 26, December 5, and December 12, 2007, SOHP.

30. Barry Yeoman, "N.C.'s Media Monarchy," *Independent* (Durham, NC), December 3, 1987.

31. Roberts and Klibanoff, *Race Beat*. 187.

32. Sitton, speech to Wake Chapter of the American Civil Liberties Union, November 8, 1989, box 53, FD Jr. Papers, SHC.

33. FD Jr., "The N&O Family Is Proud of Editor," N&O, April 24, 1983, box 53, FD Jr. Papers, SHC.

34. Hall, "Brown-Lung Controversy."

35. James B. Hunt, interview by Joseph Mosnier, April 11, 2008, SOHP.

36. FD Jr., speech to Carteret County Chamber of Commerce, November 30, 1989, box 53, FD Jr. Papers, SHC.

37. Sitton, interview by Mosnier.

38. "The Issue of Duke," N&O, February 15, 1969.

39. "Discrediting Themselves," N&O, April 28, 1969.

40. "Boyce Changes Nothing," N&O, August 5, 1969.

41. Jesse Helms, *Viewpoint*, aired August 18, 1969, on WRAL, transcript in North Carolina Collection, Wilson Library, University of North Carolina, Chapel Hill.

42. FD Jr., interview by Mosnier.

43. Linda Williams, interview by author, May 17, 2021, Wake Forest, NC.

44. Sitton to JWD, February 24, 1970, folder 1819, JWD Papers, SHC; Sitton to Thomas F. Adams Jr., November 8, 1973, box 3, Sitton Papers, SARL.

45. JWD to Terry Sanford, folder 1889, JWD Papers, SHC.

46. Williams, interview by author.

47. Ted Vaden, interview by author, June 18, 2021, Chapel Hill.

48. JWD to Sitton, June 4, 1977, and Sitton to JWD, June 9, 1977, folder 1911, JWD Papers, SHC.

49. Pat Stith, "Soul City: A Tangled Web," N&O, March 2, 1975.

50. Claude Sitton, "Soul City's Plan or Wilkins' Way," N&O, January 19, 1969; Frederick P. Hege to FD Jr., May 27, 1971, box 2, Sitton Papers, SARL.

51. Healy, *Soul City*, 17–18, 261, 292.

52. Quoted in W. Link, *Frank Porter Graham*, 88.

53. Claude Sitton, "Crum's Case Provides Some Grubby Insights," N&O, November 22, 1987.

54. William Friday, interview by Joseph Mosnier, January 15, 2007, SOHP.

55. Bruce Poulton to FD Jr., March 12, 1985, FD Jr. Papers, SHC.

56. Jim White to Sitton, January 1, 1989, box 14, Sitton Papers, SARL.

57. Tiede to FD Jr., February 17, either 1989 or 1990, box 33, FD Jr. Papers, SHC; Jones, interview by Mosnier; FD Jr., interview by Mosnier; Sitton to W. B. Aycock, December 17, 1970, box 2, Sitton Papers, SARL.

58. Sarah Lyall, "Reporter Digging into Scandal Hits a University's Raw Nerve," *New York Times*, April 26, 2014.

59. JWD to Sitton, May 31, 1975, box 4, Sitton Papers, SARL.

60. Sitton to Irwin D. Smith, July 9, 1970, box 2, Sitton Papers, SARL.

61. FD Jr., speech to Kinston Rotary Club, July 13, 1989, box 53, FD Jr. Papers, SHC.

62. Robert D. McFadden, "Harold Evans Dies at 92; Crusading Editor with a Second Act," *New York Times*, September 24, 2020.

63. FD Jr. to John Van Pelt of Raleigh, November 8, 1988, box 31, FD Jr. Papers, SHC.

64. Fred Crisp, interview by author, December 29, 2021, Raleigh.

65. Jim Jenkins, interview by author, December 22, 2021, Raleigh.

66. Pearce, interview by Mosnier.

67. Text of Martin's letter, *N&O*, February 25, 1990.

68. FD Jr., interview by Mosnier.

69. Ferrel Guillory, interview by Joseph Mosnier, October 20, 2007, SOHP.

70. Vaden, interview by author.

71. Sitton, interview by Mosnier.

72. FD Jr., diary entry, January 22, 1981, box 53, FD Jr. Papers, SHC.

73. FD Jr., interview by author, January 7, 2019, Raleigh; Jones, interview by Mosnier; Sitton, interview by Mosnier.

74. Guillory, interview by Mosnier.

75. FD Jr., interview by author; Jones, interview by Mosnier; FD III, interview by Joseph Mosnier, October 14, 2008, SOHP.

76. Barlow Herget, interview by author, May 5, 2021, Raleigh; JWD to FD Jr., November 21, 1977, folder 1916, JWD Papers, SHC.

77. Jones, interview by Mosnier.

78. Williams, interview by author.

79. Vaden, interview by author.

80. Newsroom personnel analysis, February 25, 1975, box 8, FD Jr. Papers, SHC; Sitton, interview by Mosnier.

81. Grover C. Bailey, interview by Joseph Mosnier, July 17, 2008, SOHP.

82. Williams, interview by author.

83. FD Jr. to Ralph Campbell, November 30, 1979, box 16, FD Jr. Papers, SHC.

84. Harrill Jones to *N&O*, November 21, 1990, box 33, FD Jr. Papers, SHC; "Man Protests Minority Hiring at *N&O*," *N&O*, June 6, 1990.

85. Sitton, interview by Mosnier; Sitton to Washington Journalism Center, April 13, 1972, box 3, Sitton Papers, SARL.

86. Will Sutton, telephone interview by author, June 6, 2021.

87. Ronald Mulder, vice president, Media Studies and Consulting Division, memo, July 5, 1989, box 35; Jeff Burcham, memo, May 31, 1989, box 35, FD Jr. Papers, SHC.

88. Sitton, draft memo, May 23, 1972, box 6; and *N&O* task force memo, June 19, 1989, box 35, FD Jr. Papers, SHC.

89. Annual report, box 7, and FD Jr. report to stockholders, March 31, 1978, box 17, FD Jr. Papers, SHC; Crisp, interview by author.

90. Kay Horner to FD Jr., May 1990, box 33, FD Jr. Papers, SHC.

91. Carol Y. Henry to FD Jr., January 1991, box 34, FD Jr. Papers, SHC.

92. J. W. Taylor to FD. Jr., May 17, 1990, box 34, FD Jr. Papers, SHC.

93. June B. Long to FD Jr., May 10, 1990, box 34, FD Jr. Papers, SHC.

94. Joseph H. Thigpen to *N&O*, April 12, 1990, box 34, FD Jr. Papers, SHC.

95. Martha H. Holloman to FD Jr., April 21, 1990, box 34, FD Jr. Papers, SHC.

CHAPTER FIFTEEN

1. "Helms Hits Truman," *N&O*, September 18, 1953.

2. Helms to FD Jr., August 14, 1985, box 39, FD Jr. Papers, SHC; Jesse Helms,

Viewpoint, aired February 19, 1970, on WRAL, transcript in North Carolina Collection, Wilson Library, University of North Carolina, Chapel Hill.

3. Thrift, *Conservative Bias,* 31.

4. "Pious Incitement," *N&O,* February 1, 1958; JWD to Gerald Johnson, December 15, 1958, folder 1262, JWD Papers, SHC.

5. Quoted in Covington, *Uncommon Giving,* 92.

6. Jesse Helms, *Viewpoint,* aired November 21, 1960, on WRAL, transcript in North Carolina Collection, Wilson Library, University of North Carolina, Chapel Hill.

7. WRAL *Viewpoint* editorials 1960–72, transcripts in North Carolina Collection, Wilson Library, University of North Carolina, Chapel Hill.

8. Jonathan Daniels, "All Quiet in Orangeburg," *N&O,* February 13, 1968.

9. Jesse Helms, *Viewpoint,* aired February 16, 1968, on WRAL, transcript in North Carolina Collection, Wilson Library, University of North Carolina, Chapel Hill.

10. Claude Sitton, interview by Joseph Mosnier, June 12–13, 2007, SOHP.

11. "Liberal Press Is Enemy, Helms Says in Soliciting," Under the Dome, *N&O,* December 16, 1983.

12. David Funderburk to Claude Sitton, September 25, 1979, box 16, FD Jr. Papers, SHC.

13. FD Jr., "The *N&O* Family Is Proud of Editor," *N&O,* April 24, 1983, box 53, FD Jr. Papers, SHC.

14. Lauch Faircloth, interview by Joseph Mosnier, November 28, 2007, SOHP; Congressional Club fundraising letter in author's possession; FD Jr. to Helms for Senate, January 29, 1991, box 34, FD Jr. Papers, SHC.

15. James B. Hunt, interview by Joseph Mosnier, April 8, 2008, SOHP.

16. FD Jr., report to stockholders, March 29, 1985, box 51, FD Jr. Papers, SHC.

17. "Hate-Helms Media Humbled," AIM Report, November 1990, FD Jr. Papers, SHC.

18. Sitton, interview by Mosnier.

19. Jim Jenkins, interview by author, December 22, 2021, Raleigh.

20. Reese Hart, AP, "Hargrove: Sex Deviates Numerous," *N&O,* December 4, 1967; Judy Bolch, telephone interview by author, May 4, 2021; Pat Stith, "They Were Friends for Over Six Years," *N&O,* August 12, 1972.

21. Sitton, interview by Mosnier.

22. FD Jr., "Frank Daniels, Jr.: Newspaper's Legacy," interview by Shannon Vickery, *Biographical Conversations with . . .,* UNC-TV, season 2017, episode 3, aired September 27, 2017, https://video.pbsnc.org/video/frank-daniels-jr-newspapers-legacy-fzhgjx/.

CHAPTER SIXTEEN

1. Nagourney, *The "Times,"* 99

2. FD Jr., interview by Joseph Mosnier, February 13, April 10, April 23, and May 3, 2007, SOHP; FD III, interview by Joseph Mosnier, October 14, 2008, SOHP.

3. Lucy Daniels, interview by author, May 17, 2021, Raleigh.

4. FD Jr., speech to Family Forum Talk, August 10, 1993, FD Jr. Papers, Box 53, SHC.

5. Fred Crisp, interview by author, December 29, 2021, Raleigh.

6. FD III, interview by Mosnier.

7. FD III to FD Jr., July 23, 1978 (or 1979), box 15, FD Jr. Papers, SHC.

8. FD III, interview by author.

9. FD III, interview by Mosnier.

10. "Mandela Poses Threat," Capps's letter to the editor, *N&O*, July 15, 1990.

11. Joe Neff, "Minority Goals Encouraged, Not Enforced in NC," *N&O*, June 4, 1995.

12. FD Jr., interview by Mosnier.

13. "Bush Dines with Rich on Paleo," Under the Dome, *N&O*, May 4, 2015.

14. Judy Bolch, telephone interview by author, May 4, 2021.

15. Melanie Sill, interview by author, May 12, 2021, Raleigh.

16. N&O Publishing Co. Consolidated Statement of Assets and Liabilities for 1992 and 1994, box 40, FD Jr. Papers, SHC.

17. Quoted in Philip Meyer, "Close Gaps in Wall between Ads, Unpaid Information," *USA Today*, April 20, 2004.

18. Lany McDonald, interview by Beth Millwood, April 27, 2007, SOHP.

19. Rob Waters, interview by author, December 2, 2021, Raleigh.

20. FD III, speech, "The Self-Sufficient Newsroom: Address to Investigative Reporters and Editors," October 23, 1993, box 1, FD Jr. Papers, SHC.

21. Cleves Rich to stockholders, January 10, 1972, box 17, FD Jr. Papers, SHC.

22. Chart for stockholders, box 51, FD Jr. Papers, SHC.

23. Jack Kent Cooke to FD Jr., November 17, 1986, box 28, FD Jr. Papers, SHC; Richard Hampton Jenrette, telephone interview by Joseph Mosnier, April 11, 2008, SOHP.

24. FD Jr., interview by Mosnier.

25. Lucy Daniels, interview by author.

26. "Key Made WNC, World a Better Place," *Asheville Citizen-Times*, August 23, 2014.

27. FD Jr., speech to Family Forum Talk.

28. FD Jr., interview by Mosnier; McClatchy to FD Jr., June 19, 1991, box 40, FD Jr. Papers, SHC.

29. FD Jr., "Frank Daniels, Jr.: Newspaper's Legacy," interview by Shannon Vickery, *Biographical Conversations with . . .*, UNC-TV, season 2017, episode 3, aired September 27, 2017, https://video.pbsnc.org/video/frank-daniels-jr-newspapers-legacy-fzhgjx/; FD Jr., interview by Mosnier.

30. FD Jr., speech to Family Forum Talk; Information Statement for Class B. Shareholders of N&O, July 10, 1995, copy in author's possession.

31. Bobby Woronoff, interview by author, May 18, 2021.

32. "From Waterloo to the Future: The *N&O* Looks Ahead," box 41, FD Jr. Papers, SHC.

33. Minutes of board of directors meeting, October 29, 30, 1993, box 41, FD Jr. Papers, SHC.

34. FD III, interview by author; Erwin Potts, interview by Joseph Mosnier, February 11, 2008, SOHP.

35. FD Jr., interview by Mosnier.

36. Information Statement for the Class B. Shareholders of the *News and Observer*, July 10, 1995, copy in author's possession.

37. Burke Koonce, III, "Change Signaled by N&O Owner," *Triangle Business Journal*, September 1, 1995.

38. Jacob Feldman, "An Oral History of Quokka, the Company That (Almost) Shook Up Sports," Sportico, July 23, 2020, www.sportico.com/business/tech/2020/quokka-oral-history-dot-com-startup-sports-media-1234609714/.

CHAPTER SEVENTEEN

1. FD Jr., "Frank Daniels, Jr.: Newspaper's Legacy," interview by Shannon Vickery, *Biographical Conversations with . . .*, UNC-TV, season 2017, episode 3, aired September 27, 2017, https://video.pbsnc.org/video/frank-daniels-jr-newspapers-legacy-fzhgjx/.
2. Ted Vaden, interview by author, June 18, 2021, Chapel Hill.
3. Orage Quarles III, interview by author, May 11, 2021, Raleigh.
4. David Braun, "Rewrite Man," *Minnesota Monthly*, August 25, 2006.
5. "Newspaper Quality Rankings," Journawiki, accessed August 8, 2024, https://journalism.fandom.com/wiki/Newspaper_quality_rankings.
6. Downie and Kaiser, *News about the News*, 69, 75.
7. Downie and Kaiser, *News about the News*, 73.
8. Quoted in Rachel Smolkin, "Justice Delayed," *American Journalism Review*, August/September 2007.
9. Quoted in Smolkin, "Justice Delayed."
10. Samiha Khanna and Anne Blythe, "DNA Tests Ordered for Duke Athletes," *N&O*, March 24, 2006.
11. Reeves Wiedeman, "The Duke Lacrosse Scandal and the Birth of the Alt-Right," *New York Magazine*, April 14, 2017.
12. Joseph Neff, interview by author, May 18, 2021, Durham.
13. Joseph Neff, "Duke Lacrosse Files Show Gaps in DA's Case," *N&O*, August 6, 2007.
14. Taylor and Johnson, *Until Proven Innocent*, 259.
15. Timothy B. Tyson, "The Ghosts of 1898: Wilmington's Race Riot and the Rise of White Supremacy," *N&O*, November 17, 2006.
16. "VP of Content and Executive Editor Melanie Sill to Depart KPCC," *Inside KPCC*, January 31, 2017.
17. John Drescher, interview by author, May 6, 2021, Raleigh.
18. Richard Stradling, "Libel Suit against the *N&O*, Former Reporter Settled," *N&O*, January 27, 2021.
19. "Chatham Hedge Fund Has the Winning Bid for McClatchy Newspapers," *New York Times*, July 12, 2020.
20. FD III, interview by author, May 24, 2021, Raleigh.
21. Abramson, *Merchants of Truth*, 182.
22. "N&O to Cut 70 Jobs; Parent Chain Slashes Work Force 10%," June 17, 2008, www.wral.com/story/3051381.
23. Peder Zane, interview by author, June 9, 2021, Raleigh.
24. Hamilton, *Democracy's Detectives*, 276; Jeremy Borden, "Searching for McClatchy's North Carolina Future," *The Assembly*, June 18, 2021; Melanie Sill, "Is WUNC Ready to Turn It Up?," *The Assembly*, March 31, 2022.

25. Quarles, interview by author; Information Statement for the Class B Shareholders of N&O, July 10, 1995, copy in author's possession.

26. PEN America, *Losing the News*; Quarles, interview by author.

27. Drescher, interview by author.

28. Statement of the Ownership, N&O, 2019, 2006, and 1940.

29. Borden, "Searching for McClatchy's North Carolina Future."

30. "News and Observer Receives Grant to Bolster Coverage of Climate Change, the Environment," N&O, May 28, 2021.

31. Steve Schewel interview by author, January 6, 2022, Durham.

32. PEN America, *Losing the News*; Gao, Lee, and Murphy, *Financing Dies in Darkness*?

33. Sullivan, *Ghosting the News*, 94.

34. Vaden, interview by author.

35. Vaden, interview by author.

36. Information Statement for Class B. Shareholders of N&O, July 10, 1995, copy in author's possession.

37. Margaret Sullivan, "Once a Pregnant Teen, an Editor Takes On New Challenge," *Washington Post*, June 21, 2018.

38. Neff, interview by author; Joseph Neff, Ann Doss Helms, and David Raynor, "Smart, Low-Income Students Excluded from Gifted Classes," N&O, May 21, 2017.

39. Andrew Carter, "After Nights of Mayhem, a Movement Emerges," N&O, June 7, 2020.

40. Colin Campbell, "Lt. Governor Candidate's Derogatory Posts Draw Outrage," N&O, October 11, 2020; Will Doran, "Robinson's Financial Woes Surface Again in GOP Primary. Will NC Voters Care?," WRAL News, August 15, 2023, https://www.wral.com/story/robinson-s-financial-woes-become-central-to-gop-primary-will-nc-voters-care/21001862/.

41. Claude Sitton, speech at University of Georgia, February 16, 1990, box 15, SARL.

42. Drescher, interview by author.

CONCLUSION

1. Lepore, *These Truths*, 737.
2. Kazin, *Godly Hero*, 204.
3. Bedingfield and Forde, "Journalism and the World It Built," 2.
4. Sitton to FD Jr., undated, 1991, box 16, Sitton Papers, SARL.
5. Gunther, *Inside U.S.A.*, 719–20.
6. James B. Hunt, interview by Joseph Mosnier, April 8, 2008, SOHP.
7. Quoted in Bowling, *Sam Ragan*, 86.

Bibliography

ARCHIVES

Columbia Center for Oral History, Columbia University, New York
    Southern Intellectual Leaders Project
David M. Rubenstein Rare Book and Manuscript Library, Duke University, Durham, NC
    Furnifold Simmons Papers
Harry S. Truman Presidential Library and Museum, Independence, MO
    Oral History Interviews
North Carolina Division of Archives and History, Raleigh
    Robert W. Scott Family Papers
Stuart A. Rose Manuscript, Archives, and Rare Book Library,
       Emory University, Atlanta, GA
    Claude Sitton Papers
Wilson Library, University of North Carolina at Chapel Hill
    North Carolina Collection
    Southern Historical Collection
        Frank Daniels Jr. Papers
        Frank Daniels Sr. Papers
        Jonathan Daniels Papers
        Josephus Daniels Papers
        Norman Jennett Papers

NEWSPAPERS AND PERIODICALS

American Journalism Review
Asbury Park (NJ) Press
Asheville (NC) Citizen-Times
Asheville Daily Gazette
Assembly (NC)
Atlanta Constitution

Baltimore Sun
Boston Globe
Bradenton (FL) Herald
Bristol (TN) Herald Courier
Brooklyn Daily Eagle
Carolina Times (Durham)
Carolina Tribune (Raleigh)
Charlotte News
Charlotte Observer
Chicago Chronicle
Collier's
Columbia Journalism Review
Des Moines Register
Durham Independent
Evening Sun (Baltimore)
Fort Wayne (IN) Daily News
Gastonia (NC) Gazette
Greensboro (NC) Daily News
Greenville (SC) News
Guardian (UK)
High Point (NC) Enterprise
Homefront (Raleigh)
Jewish Voice
Kansas City Times
Lexington (KY) Leader
Lincoln County (NC) News
Los Angeles Times
Louisville Courier Journal
Metropolitan (New York)
Miami Herald
Miami Magazine
Miami News
Minnesota Monthly
New Orleans Magazine

New Republic
New York Age
New York Magazine
New York Press
New York Times
New York Tribune
North Carolinian (Raleigh)
People's Paper (Charlotte, NC)
Pittsburgh Press
Raleigh Gazette
Raleigh Morning Post
Raleigh News and Observer
Raleigh State Chronicle
Raleigh State Journal
Raleigh Times
Reno-Gazette Journal
Richmond Dispatch
Richmond Planet
Robesonian (Lumberton, NC)
Sacramento Bee
Scranton (PA) Tribune
Statesville (NC) Daily Record
St. Augustine Record
St. Louis Post-Dispatch
St. Petersburg Times
Times (London)
Triangle Business Journal
Washington Evening Standard
Washington Evening Star
Washington Post
Wilmington Daily Record
Wilmington Messenger
Winston-Salem Journal

INTERVIEWS BY AUTHOR

Robert Ashley, May 28, 2021, Durham
Judy Bolch, May 4, 2021, telephone interview from Portland, OR
Fred Crisp, December 29, 2021, Raleigh
Frank A. Daniels Jr., January 7, 2019, Raleigh
Frank A. Daniels III, May 24, 2021, Raleigh
Lucy Daniels, May 17, 2021, Raleigh
Patsy Daniels, June 16, 2021, Cary, NC
John Drescher, May 6, 2021, Raleigh

Steve Ford, May 11, 2021, Cary, NC
Anders Gyllenhaal, January 26, 2022, Raleigh
Barlow Herget, May 5, 2021, Raleigh
Wayne Hurder, April 15, 2022, telephone interview from Raleigh
Lucy Inman, December 27, 2021, Raleigh
Jim Jenkins, December 22, 2021, Raleigh
Joseph Neff, May 18, 2021, Durham
Dudley Price, December 1, 2021, Raleigh
Orage Quarles III, May 11, 2021, Raleigh
Steve Schewel, January 6, 2022, Durham
Melanie Sill, May 12, 2021, Raleigh
Will Sutton, June 6, 2021, telephone interview from New Orleans
Ted Vaden, June 18, 2021, Chapel Hill
Rob Waters, December 2, 2021, Raleigh
Linda Williams, May 17, 2021, Wake Forest, NC
Bobby Woronoff, May 18, 2021, Raleigh
David Woronoff, May 21, 2021, Pinehurst, NC
Peter Zane, June 9, 2021, Raleigh

BOOKS, ARTICLES, AND DISSERTATIONS

Abrams, Douglas Carl. "A Progressive-Conservative Duel: The 1920 Democratic Primaries in North Carolina." *North Carolina Historical Review* 55, no. 4 (October 1978): 421–43.
Abramson, Jill. *Merchants of Truth: The Business of News and the Fight for Facts*. New York: Simon and Schuster, 2019.
Alexander, Shawn Leigh, ed. *T. Thomas Fortune: The Afro-American Agitator*. Gainesville: University Press of Florida, 2008.
Anderson, Eric. *Race and Politics in North Carolina, 1872–1901: The Black Second*. Baton Rouge: Louisiana State University Press, 1981.
Ashby, Warren. *Frank Porter Graham: A Southern Liberal*. Winston-Salem: John F. Blair, 1980.
Badger, Anthony J. *Why White Liberals Fail: Race and Southern Politics from FDR to Trump*. Cambridge, MA: Harvard University Press, 2022.
Baime, A. J. *The Accidental President: Harry S. Truman and the Four Months That Changed the World*. Boston: Houghton Mifflin Harcourt, 2017.
Bedingfield, Sid. "Populist Insurgency, Alabama." In *Journalism and Jim Crow: White Supremacy and the Black Struggle for a New America*, edited by Kathy Roberts Forde and Sid Bedingfield, 135–60. Urbana: University of Illinois Press, 2021.
Bedingfield, Sid, and Kathy Roberts Forde. "Journalism and the World It Built." In *Journalism and Jim Crow: White Supremacy and the Black Struggle for a New America*, edited by Kathy Roberts Forde and Sid Bedingfield, 1–28. Urbana: University of Illinois Press, 2021.
Berg, A. Scott. *Max Perkins: Editor of Genius*. New York: E. P. Dutton, 1978.
———. *Wilson*. New York: Berkeley Books, 2013.

Blight, David W. *Frederick Douglass: Prophet of Freedom*. New York: Simon and Schuster, 2018.
Bowling, Lewis. *Sam Ragan: North Carolina's Literary Godfather*. Durham: Carolina Academic Press, 2020.
Branch, Taylor. *Parting the Waters: America in the King Years, 1954–63*. New York: Simon and Schuster, 1988.
———. *Pillar of Fire: America in the King Years, 1963–65*. New York: Simon and Schuster, 1998.
Brands, H. W. *The Privileged Life and Radical Presidency of Franklin Delano Roosevelt*. New York: Anchor Books, 2008.
Brundage, W. Fitzhugh. "The Press and Lynching." In *Journalism and Jim Crow: White Supremacy and the Black Struggle for a New America*, edited by Kathy Roberts Forde and Sid Bedingfield, 83–114. Urbana: University of Illinois Press, 2021.
Burns, James McGregor. *Roosevelt: The Lion and the Fox*. New York: Harcourt, Brace and World, 1956.
Cash, W. J. *The Mind of the South*. New York: Alfred A. Knopf, 1941.
Cecelski, David S., and Timothy B. Tyson, eds. *Democracy Betrayed: The Wilmington Race Riot of 1898 and Its Legacy*. Chapel Hill: University of North Carolina Press, 1998.
Christensen, Rob. *The Paradox of Tar Heel Politics: The Personalities, Elections, and Events That Shaped Modern North Carolina*. Chapel Hill: University of North Carolina Press, 2008.
———. *The Rise and Fall of the Branchhead Boys: North Carolina's Scott Family and the Era of Progressive Politics*. Chapel Hill: University of North Carolina Press, 2019.
Claiborne, Jack. *The "Charlotte Observer": Its Time and Place, 1869–1986*. Chapel Hill: University of North Carolina Press, 1986.
Clouse, Barbara Barksdale. *Ralph McGill: A Biography*. Macon: Mercer University Press, 1998.
Coletta, Paola E. "Josephus Daniels." In *American Secretaries of the Navy*, 530. Annapolis, MD: Naval Institute Press, 1980.
Collier, Simon. *From Cortes to Castro: An Introduction to the History of Latin America, 1492–1973*. New York: Macmillan, 1974.
Conot, Robert. *A Streak of Luck: The Outrageous and Passionate Life of Thomas Alva Edison*. New York: Bantam Books, 1979.
Cooper, John Milton, Jr. *Walter Hines Page: The Southerner as American, 1855–1918*. Chapel Hill: University of North Carolina Press, 1977.
———. *Woodrow Wilson: A Biography*. New York: Vintage Books, 2009.
Cooper, William J., Jr., and Thomas E. Terrill. *The American South: A History*. New York: Alfred A. Knopf, 1990.
Covington, Howard E., Jr. *Fire and Stone: The Making of the University of North Carolina under Presidents Edward Kidder Graham and Harry Woodburn Chase*. Chapel Hill: University of North Carolina Press, 2018.
———. *Uncommon Giving: A. J. Fletcher and a North Carolina Legacy*. Raleigh: A. J. Fletcher Foundation, 1999.
Covington, Howard E., Jr., and Marion A. Ellis. *Terry Sanford: Politics, Progress, and Outrageous Ambitions*. Durham: Duke University Press, 1999.

Craig, Lee A. *Josephus Daniels: Life and Times*. Chapel Hill: University of North Carolina Press, 2013.
Creel, George. *Rebel at Large: Recollections of Fifty Crowded Years*. New York: G. P. Putnam's Sons, 1947.
Cronon, E. David. "Josephus Daniels as a Reluctant Candidate." *North Carolina Historical Review* 33, no. 4 (October 1956): 458–82. Published by the North Carolina Office of Archives and History.
———. *Josephus Daniels in Mexico*. Madison: University of Wisconsin Press, 1960.
———, ed. *The Cabinet Diaries of Josephus Daniels, 1913–1921*. Lincoln: University of Nebraska Press, 1963.
Crow, Jeffrey J., and Robert F. Durden. *Maverick Republican in the Old North State: A Political Biography of Daniel L. Russell*. Baton Rouge: Louisiana State University Press, 1977.
Crow, Jeffrey J., Paul D. Escott, and Charles L. Flynn Jr., eds. *Race, Class, and Politics in Southern History*. Baton Rouge: Louisiana State University Press, 1989.
Culver, John C., and John Hyde. *American Dreamer: A Life of Henry Wallace*. New York: W. W. Norton, 2000.
Dallek, Robert. *Franklin D. Roosevelt: A Political Life*. New York: Viking, 2017.
Daniels, Jonathan. *The End of Innocence*. Philadelphia: J. B. Lippincott, 1954.
———. *Frontier on the Potomac*. New York: Macmillan, 1946.
———. *The Man of Independence*. Philadelphia: J. B. Lippincott, 1950.
———. *A Southerner Discovers the South*. New York: Macmillan, 1938.
———. *Tar Heels: A Portrait of North Carolina*. Westport, CT: Negro Universities Press, 1941.
———. *The Time between the Wars: Armistice to Pearl Harbor*. New York: Doubleday, 1966.
———. *White House Witness, 1942–1945*. New York: Doubleday, 1975.
Daniels, Josephus. *Editor in Politics*. Chapel Hill: University of North Carolina Press, 1941.
———. *Shirt-Sleeve Diplomat*. Chapel Hill: University of North Carolina Press, 1947.
———. *Tar Heel Editor*. Chapel Hill: University of North Carolina Press, 1939.
———. *The Wilson Era: Years of Peace, 1910–1917*. Chapel Hill: University of North Carolina Press, 1944.
———. *The Wilson Era: Years of War and After, 1917–1923*. Chapel Hill: University of North Carolina Press, 1946.
Daniels, Lucy. *With a Woman's Voice: A Writer's Struggle for Emotional Freedom*. Lanham, MD: Madison Books, 2001.
Darity, William A., Jr., and Kirsten Mullen. *From Here to Equality: Reparations for Black Americans in the Twenty-First Century*. Chapel Hill: University of North Carolina Press, 2020.
Davies, David R. *Press and Race: Mississippi Journalists Confront the Movement*. Oxford: University Press of Mississippi, 2001.
Donald, David Herbert. *Look Homeward: A Life of Thomas Wolfe*. Boston: Little, Brown, 1987.
Downie, Leonard, Jr., and Robert G. Kaiser. *The News about the News: American Journalism in Peril*. New York: Alfred A. Knopf, 2002.

Downs, Gregory P. "University Men, Social Science, and White Supremacy in North Carolina." *Journal of Southern History* 75, no. 2 (May 2009), 267–304. Published by the Southern Historical Association, http:wwwjstor.org/stable 27778937.

Du Bois, W. E. B. *The Souls of Black Folk*. New York: Dover, 1903.

Dwyer, John H. "The End of U.S. Intervention in Mexico: Franklin Roosevelt and the Expropriation of American-Owned Agricultural Property." *Presidential Studies Quarterly* 28, no. 3 (Summer 1998): 495–509. http://www.jstor.org/stable/27551897.

Dyaj, Thomas. *Walter White: The Dilemma of Black Identity in America*. Chicago: Ivan R. Dee, 2008.

Eagles, Charles W. *Jonathan Daniels and Race Relations: The Evolution of a Southern Liberal*. Knoxville: University of Tennessee Press, 1982.

———. "Two Double V's: Jonathan Daniels, FDR and Race Relations during World War II." *North Carolina Historical Review* 59, no. 3 (July 1982), 252–70.

Edmonds, Helen G. *The Negro and Fusion Politics in North Carolina, 1894–1901*. Chapel Hill: University of North Carolina Press, 1951.

Egerton, John. *Speak Now against the Day: The Generation before the Civil Rights Movement in the South*. Chapel Hill: University of North Carolina Press, 1994.

Eig, Jonathan. *King: A Life*. New York: Farrar, Straus and Giroux, 2023.

Fitzgerald, F. Scott. *This Side of Paradise*. New York: Charles Scribner's Sons, 1921.

Fleming, Karl. *Son of the Rough South: An Uncivil Memoir*. New York: Public Affairs, 2005.

Forde, Kathy Roberts, and Sid Bedingfield, eds. *Journalism and Jim Crow: White Supremacy and the Black Struggle for a New America*. Urbana: University of Illinois Press, 2021.

Franklin, John Hope, and Alfred A. Moss Jr. *From Slavery to Freedom: A History of Negro Americans*. 6th ed. New York: Alfred A. Knopf, 1988.

Gavins, Raymond. "Fear, Hope, and Struggle: Recasting Black North Carolina in the Age of Jim Crow." In *Democracy Betrayed: The Wilmington Race Riot of 1898 and Its Legacy*, edited by David S. Cecelski and Timothy B. Tyson, 185–206. Chapel Hill: University of North Carolina Press, 1998.

Gerber, Larry G. *The Limits of Liberalism: Josephus Daniels, Henry Stimson, Bernard Baruch, Donald Richberg, Felix Frankfurter, and the Development of the Modern American Political Economy*. New York: New York University Press, 1984.

Gershenhorn, Jerry. "A Courageous Voice for Black Freedom: Louis Austin and the Carolina Times in Depression Era North Carolina" *North Carolina Historical Review* 87, no. 1 (January 2010): 57–92. N.C. Office of Archives and History.

———. *Louis Austin and the Carolina Times: A Life in the Long Black Freedom Struggle*. Chapel Hill: University of North Carolina Press, 2018.

Gilmore, Glenda Elizabeth. *Gender and Jim Crow: Women and the Politics of White Supremacy in North Carolina, 1896–1920*. Chapel Hill: University of North Carolina Press, 1996.

———. "Murder, Memory and the Flight of the Incubus." In *Democracy Betrayed: The Wilmington Race Riot of 1898 and Its Legacy*, edited by David S. Cecelski and Timothy B. Tyson, 73–93. Chapel Hill: University of North Carolina Press, 1998.

Goodwyn, Lawrence. *The Populist Moment: A Short History of the Agrarian Revolt in America*. Oxford: Oxford University Press, 1978.

Guillory, Ferrel. "Mass Media in North Carolina Politics: The Watchdog Mutes Its Bark." In *The New Politics of North Carolina*, edited by Christopher A. Cooper and H. Gibbs Knots, 106–25. Chapel Hill: University of North Carolina Press, 2008.

Gunther, John. *Inside U.S.A.* New York: Harper and Brothers, 1947.

Gustafson, Kristin L. "Death of Democracy, North Carolina." In *Journalism and Jim Crow: White Supremacy and the Black Struggle for a New America*, edited by Kathy Roberts Forde and Sid Bedingfield, 187–221. Urbana: University of Illinois Press, 2021.

Hahn, Steven. *A Nation under Our Feet: Black Political Struggles in the Rural South from Slavery to the Great Migration.* Cambridge, MA: Harvard University Press, 2003.

Hales, Troy Kenneth. "Josephus Daniels and the Department of the Navy: A Southern Progressive in the National Administration." PhD diss. University of North Carolina at Chapel Hill, 1991.

Hall, Bob. "The Brown-Lung Controversy: How the Press, North and South, Handled a Story Involving the South's Largest Industry." *Columbia Journalism Review*, March–April 1978, 27–35.

Hamilton, James T. *Democracy's Detectives: The Economics of Investigative Journalism.* Cambridge, MA: Harvard University Press, 2016.

Hartnett, Kimberly Marlowe. *Carolina Israelite: How Harry Golden Made Us Care about Jews, the South, and Civil Rights.* Chapel Hill: University of North Carolina Press, 2015.

Healy, Thomas. *Soul City: Race, Equality, and the Lost Dream of an American Utopia.* New York: Metropolitan Books, 2021.

Heckscher, August. *Woodrow Wilson: A Biography.* New York: Charles Scribner's Sons, 1991.

Helms, Jesse. *Here's Where I Stand: A Memoir.* New York: Random House, 2005.

Hochschild, Adam. *American Midnight: The Great War, a Violent Peace, and Democracy's Forgotten Crisis.* New York: Mariner Books, 2022.

Hofstadter, Richard. *The Age of Reform: From Bryan to F.D.R.* New York: Alfred A. Knopf, 1989.

Hunt, James L. *Marion Butler and American Populism.* Chapel Hill: University of North Carolina Press, 2003.

Jenkins, Innis LaRoche. "Josephus Daniels and the Navy Department, 1913–1916: A Study in Military Administration." PhD diss., University of Maryland, 1960.

Justesen, Benjamin R. *George Henry White: An Even Chance in the Race of Life.* Baton Rouge: Louisiana State University Press, 2001.

Kazin, Michael. *A Godly Hero: The Life of William Jennings Bryan.* New York: Anchor Books, 2007.

———. *What It Took to Win: A History of the Democratic Party.* New York: Farrar, Straus and Giroux, 2022.

Kemeny, P. C. "Protestant Moral Reformers and the Campaign to Suppress Prostitution during World War I." *Journal of Presbyterian History* 92, no. 2 (Fall/Winter 2014): 52–72. https://www.jstor.org/stable/26452653.

Key, V. O. *Southern Politics.* New York: Vintage Books, 1949.

Kilpatrick, Carroll. *Roosevelt and Daniels: A Friendship in Politics.* Chapel Hill: University of North Carolina Press, 1952.

King, Florence. *Southern Ladies and Gentlemen*. New York: Bantam Books, 1975.
Kousser, J. Morgan. *The Shaping of Southern Politics: Suffrage Restriction and the Establishment of the One-Party South, 1880–1910*. New Haven: Yale University Press, 1974.
Lanctot, Neil. *The Approaching Storm: Roosevelt, Wilson, Addams and Their Clash over America's Future*. New York: Riverhead Books, 2021.
Lefler, Hugh Talmage, and Albert Ray Newsome. *North Carolina: The History of a Southern State*. Chapel Hill: University of North Carolina Press, 1963.
Leidholdt, Alexander S. *Battling Nell: The Life of Southern Journalist Cornelia Battle Lewis, 1893–1956*. Baton Rouge: Louisiana State University Press, 2009.
Lepore, Jill. *These Truths: A History of the United States*. New York: W. W. Norton, 2018.
Link, Arthur S. "The Progressive Movement in the South, 1870–1914." *North Carolina Historical Review* 23, no. 2 (April 1946): 172–95.
———. *Wilson*. Vol. 2, *The New Freedom*. Princeton, NJ: Princeton University Press, 1956.
———. *Woodrow Wilson and the Progressive Era, 1910–1917*. New York: Harper and Row, 1954.
Link, William A. *Frank Porter Graham: Southern Liberal, Citizen of the World*. Chapel Hill: University of North Carolina Press, 2021.
———. *Righteous Warrior: Jesse Helms and the Rise of Modern Conservatism*. New York: St. Martin's Press, 2008.
Martin, John Bartlow. *Adlai Stevenson and the World: The Life of Adlai E. Stevenson*. New York: Anchor Press/Doubleday, 1978.
McCullough, David. *Truman*. New York: Simon and Schuster, 1992.
McWhirter, Cameron. *Red Summer: The Summer of 1919 and the Awakening of Black America*. New York: St. Martin's Griffin, 2011.
Meyer, G. J. *A World Undone: The Story of the Great War, 1914–1918*. New York: Random House, 2007.
Meyer, Phillip. *The Vanishing Newspaper: Saving Journalism in the Information Age*. Columbia: University of Missouri Press, 2004.
Michaelis, David. *Eleanor*. New York: Simon and Schuster 2020.
Mobley, Joe A. *Raleigh, North Carolina: A Brief History*. Charleston, SC: History Press, 2009.
Moore, John Robert. *Senator Josiah Bailey of North Carolina: A Political Biography*. Durham: Duke University Press, 1968.
Morison, Samuel Eliot. *The Oxford History of the American People*. Vol. 3, *1869 through the Death of John F. Kennedy, 1963*. New York: Oxford University Press, 1965.
Morrison, Joseph L. *Governor O. Max Gardner: A Power in North Carolina and New Deal Washington*. Chapel Hill: University of North Carolina Press, 1971.
———. *Josephus Daniels Says . . . An Editor's Political Odyssey from Bryan to Wilson and F.D.R, 1894–1913*. Chapel Hill: University of North Carolina Press, 1962.
———. *Josephus Daniels: The Small-d Democrat*. Chapel Hill: University of North Carolina Press, 1966.
———. "A Southern Philo-Semite: Josephus Daniels of North Carolina." *Judaism: A Quarterly Journal* 12, no. 1 (Winter 1963): 77–81.
Mott, Frank Luther. *American Journalism: A History, 1690–1960*. New York: Macmillan, 1962.

Nagourney, Adam. *The "Times": How the Newspaper of Record Survived Scandal, Scorn, and the Transformation of Journalism.* New York: Crown, 2023.

Okrent, Daniel. *The Guarded Gate: Bigotry, Eugenics, and the Law That Kept Two Generations of Jews, Italians, and Other European Immigrants out of America.* New York: Scribner, 2019.

O'Reilly, Kenneth. "The Jim Crow Policies of Woodrow Wilson." *Journal of Blacks in Higher Education*, no. 17 (Autumn 1997): 117–21.

Orr, Oliver H., Jr. *Charles Brantley Aycock.* Chapel Hill: University of North Carolina Press, 1961.

Page, Walter Hines. *The Southerner, a Novel: Being the Autobiography of Nicholas Worth.* New York: Doubleday, 1904.

Peirce, Neal R. *The Border South States: People, Politics, and Power in the Five Border South States.* New York. W. W. Norton, 1975.

Pietrusza, David. *TR'S Last War: Theodore Roosevelt, the Great War, and a Journey of Triumph and Tragedy.* New York: Lyons Press, 2018.

Pleasants, Julian M. *Buncombe Bob: The Life and Times of Robert Rice Reynolds.* Chapel Hill: University of North Carolina Press, 2000.

———. *Home Front: North Carolina during World War II.* Gainesville: University of Florida Press, 2017.

———. *The Political Career of W. Kerr Scott: The Squire from Haw River.* Lexington: University of Kentucky Press, 2014.

Pleasants, Julian M., and August M. Burns III. *Frank Porter Graham and the 1950 Senate Race in North Carolina.* Chapel Hill: University of North Carolina Press, 1990.

Plummer, Brenda Gayle. "The Afro-American Response to the Occupation of Haiti, 1915–1934." *Phylon* 43, no. 2 (2nd Quarter, 1982): 125–43. Published by Clark University.

Prather, H. Leon, Jr. *We Have Taken a City: The Wilmington Racial Massacre and Coup of 1898.* Wilmington: NU World Enterprises, 1984.

Reynolds, David S. *Abe: Abraham Lincoln in His Times.* New York: Penguin, 2020.

Riding, Alan. *Distant Neighbors: A Portrait of the Mexicans.* New York: Alfred A. Knopf, 1985.

Rippy, J. Fred, ed. *F. M. Simmons, Statesman of the New South: Memoirs and Addresses.* Durham: Duke University Press, 1936.

Ritterhouse, Jennifer. *Discovering the South: One Man's Travels through a Changing America in the 1930s.* Chapel Hill: University of North Carolina Press, 2017.

Roberts, Chalmers M. *The "Washington Post": The First 100 Years.* Boston: Houghton Mifflin, 1977.

Roberts, Gene, and Hank Klibanoff. *The Race Beat: The Press, the Civil Rights Struggle, and the Awakening of a Nation.* New York: Vintage Books, 2006.

Roberts, Gene, and Thomas Kunkel. *Breach of Faith: A Crisis of Coverage in the Age of Corporate Newspapering.* Fayetteville: University of Arkansas Press, 2002.

Rusbridger, Alan. *Breaking News: The Remaking of Journalism and Why It Matters Now.* New York: Farrar, Straus and Giroux, 2018.

Salmond, John A. *Gastonia 1929: The Story of the Loray Mill Strike.* Chapel Hill: University of North Carolina Press, 1995.

Scales, Junius Irving, and Richard Nickson. *Causes at Heart: A Former Communist Remembers.* Athens: University of Georgia Press, 1987.

Schwarz, Jordan A. *The Speculator: Bernard M. Baruch in Washington, 1917–1965.* Chapel Hill: University of North Carolina Press, 1981.

Simkins, Francis Butler, and Charles Pierce Roland. *A History of the South.* 4th ed. New York: Alfred A. Knopf, 1972.

Smith, Jean Edward. *FDR.* New York: Random House, 2008.

Smyth, Daniel. "Avoiding Bloodshed? US Journalists and Censorship in Wartime, War and Society." *War and Society* 32, no. 1 (2013): 64–94. https://doi.org/10.1179/0729247312Z.00000000017.

Snider, William D. *Light on the Hill.* Chapel Hill: University of North Carolina Press, 1992.

Startt, James D. *Woodrow Wilson, the Great War, and the Fourth Estate.* College Station: Texas A&M University Press, 2017.

Steelman, Joseph F. "The Progressive Democratic Convention of 1914 in North Carolina." *North Carolina Historical Review* 46, no. 2 (April 1969): 83–104.

———. "The Progressive Era in North Carolina, 1884–1917." PhD diss., University of North Carolina, 1955.

Stem, Thad, Jr. *The Tar Heel Press.* Charlotte: Heritage Printers, 1973.

Sullivan, Margaret. *Ghosting the News: Local Journalism and the Crisis of American Democracy.* New York: Columbia Global Reports, 2020.

Swanberg, W. A. *Citizen Hearst.* New York: Charles Scribner and Sons, 1961.

Talese, Gay. *The Kingdom and the Power.* New York: Anchor Books, 1969.

Talley, Banks Cooper, Jr. "A Study of Issues and Trends in Public School Education in North Carolina from 1925 to 1950 as Reflected in the *News and Observer* and the *Raleigh Times.*" PhD diss. University of North Carolina at Chapel Hill, 1966.

Taylor, Stuart, Jr., and K. C. Johnson. *Until Proven Innocent: Political Correctness and the Shameful Injustices of the Duke Lacrosse Rape Case.* New York: Thomas Dunne Books, 2007.

Thrift, Bryan Hardin. *Conservative Bias: How Jesse Helms Pioneered the Rise of Right-Wing Media and Realigned the Republican Party.* Gainesville: University of Florida Press, 2014.

Tifft, Susan E., and Alex S. Jones. *The Patriarch: The Rise and Fall of the Bingham Dynasty.* New York: Simon and Schuster, 1991.

———. *The Trust: The Private and Powerful Family behind the "New York Times."* Boston: Little, Brown, 1999.

Tindall, George B. *The Emergence of the New South, 1913–1945.* Baton Rouge: Louisiana State University Press, 1967.

Traxel, David. *1898: The Birth of the American Century.* New York: Alfred A. Knopf, 1998.

Tursi, Frank V. *The "Winston-Salem Journal": Magnolia Trees and Pulitzer Prizes.* Winston-Salem: John F. Blair Publisher and the Winston-Salem Journal, 1996.

Tyson, Timothy B. *Radio Free Dixie: Robert F. Williams and the Roots of Black Power.* Chapel Hill: University of North Carolina Press, 1999.

Urofsky, Melvin I. "Josephus Daniels and the Armor Trust." *North Carolina Historical Review* 45, no. 3 (July 1968): 237–63. www.jstor.org/stable/23517950.

———. *Louis D. Brandeis: A Life.* New York: Pantheon Books, 2009.

Walton, Hanes, Jr., and James K. Taylor. "Blacks and the Southern Prohibition Movement." *Phylon* 32, no. 3 (3rd Quarter, 1971): 247–59.
Ward, Geoffrey C. *A First-Class Temperament: The Emergence of Franklin Roosevelt, 1905–1928*. New York: Vintage Books, 1989.
Ward, Jason Morgan. *Defending White Democracy: The Making of a Segregationist Movement and the Remaking of Racial Politics, 1936–1965*. Chapel Hill: University of North Carolina Press, 2011.
Webb, Mena. *Jule Carr: General without an Army*. Chapel Hill: University of North Carolina Press, 2011.
Wilkerson, Isabel. *Caste: The Origins of Our Discontents*. New York: Random House, 2020.
Woodward, C. Vann. *Origins of the New South, 1877–1913*. Baton Rouge: Louisiana State University Press, 1951.
———. *The Strange Career of Jim Crow*. Oxford: Oxford University Press, 1955.
Yellin, Eric S. *Racism in the Nation's Service: Government Workers and the Color Line in Woodrow Wilson's America*. Chapel Hill: University of North Carolina Press, 2013.
Zucchino, David. *Wilmington's Lie: The Murderous Coup of 1898 and the Rise of White Supremacy*. New York: Atlantic Monthly Press, 2020.

STUDIES

Abernathy, Penelope Muse. *News Deserts and Ghost Newspapers: Will Local News Survive?* Chapel Hill: The Center for Innovation and Sustainability in Local Media, Hussman School of Journalism and Media, University of North Carolina, 2020.
Equal Protection of the Laws in North Carolina. Report of the North Carolina Advisory Committee to the United States Commission on Civil Rights, 1959–62. Washington: US Government Printing Office, 1962.
Gao, Pengjie, Chang Joo Lee, and Dermot Murphy. *Financing Dies in Darkness? The Impact of Newspaper Closures on Public Finance*. Hutchins Center on Fiscal and Monetary Policy at Brookings, September 2018. https://brookings.edu/research/financing-dies-in-darkness-the-impact-of-newspaper-closure-on-public finance.
PEN America. *Losing the News: The Decimation of Local Journalism and the Search for Solutions*. PEN.org, 2019. https://pen.org/wp-content/uploads/2019/12/Losing-the-News-The-Decimation-of-Local-Journalism-and-the-Search-for-Solutions-Report.pdf.
Umfleet, LeRae, principal researcher. *1898 Wilmington Race Riot: Report of the 1898 Wilmington Race Riot Commission*. Research Branch, Office of Archives and History, North Carolina Department of Cultural Resources, 2006.

Index

Page numbers in italics indicate illustrations.

Accuracy in the Media (AIM), 232–33
African Americans. *See* Black Americans
Alamance Gleaner, 16
alcohol, prohibition of. *See* prohibition of alcohol
Alderholt, Frank, 105
Alford, Lee, 78
Allen, Gary, 176
American Media Group, 264
Andrews, Alexander, 39–40, 41
anti-immigration views, 74–75
Anti-Imperialist League, 114
antisemitism, 73–74, 267
antitrust legislation, 40, 54
Apex News (newspaper), 16
Ashe, Samuel, 35, 42–43, 50
Asheboro Courier, 16
Asheville Citizen-Times, 262
Aulis, Jack, 177, 257
"Aunt Zilphia," 34–35
Austin, Louis, 22, 24, 143
Aycock, Charles Brantley, 9, 15, 22, 25, 26, 31, 54, 56, 159, 268

Bagley, Henry, 78
Bailey, A. Purnell, 59
Bailey, Grover C., 220
Bailey, Josiah, 100, 116, 268; Daniels-Bailey feud, 141–42
Baker, Ella, 143
Baldwin, Mary Ann, 263
Barber, J. Max, 21
Barnes, Nancy, 253
Baron, David, 223
Barringer, Bugs, 177
Baruch, Bernard, 109–110
Bassett, John Spencer, 23–24, 64, 79
Beal, Fred, 105
Beale, Betty, 216
Bedingfield, Sid, 3, 39, 265
Bellamy, Willie, 26
Bennett, James, 223
Bezos, Jeff, 246
Biblical Recorder, 141
Birth of a Nation, The (film), 26, 71
Black, Jim, 254
Black Americans, 15; Democratic Party, shift to, 22–23; employed as servants, 73, 126, 130, 153, 174; funding for education, 57; "passing" as white, 130; and Republican Party, 7; stereotyped as sexual predators, 14. *See also* racial issues

Black Lives Matter movement, 153, 263
Blue Ridge Parkway, 151
Boettiger, Anna, 146
Bolch, Judy, 238–39
Bottom Rail, The (Jones), 180
Brandeis, Louis D., 74
Bridgers, Elizabeth (Daniels), 122, 155
Britton, Edward E., 78
Brodeur, Nicole, 251, 257
Brooks, Robert L., 173, 204, 205, 208, 211, 230, 234
Broughton, J. Melville, 143, 160
Brown v. Board of Education (1954), 164–65
Bryan, William Jennings, 67; anti-imperialism, 75–76; Daniels, rift with, 99; Daniels, partnership with, 47–49; on evolution, 48, 98, 99; peace initiatives, 88; presidential campaign (1896), 13, 50–51; presidential campaign (1900), 21; resignation as secretary of state, 83; support for Wilson, 62; in Wilson administration, 64–65
Bull Moose Party, 62, 85
Burden, The (Riley), 222
Burke, S., 157
Burleson, Albert, 72, 91
Business Insider, 256
Business North Carolina, 236, 237, 246
Butler, Marion, 42, 50

Caleb, My Son (Daniels), 243
Capps, Russell, 238
Cárdenas, Lázaro, 116–17
Carolina Journal, 170
Carolina Times, 22, 24, 143
Carolina Tribune, 22
Carolinian, 34, 156, 221
Carr, A. J., 215
Carr, Julian Shakespeare, 15, 25, 32, 33, 36, 54
Carroll, Wallace, 202
Carter, Jimmy, 213, 219
cartoons: color comics, 45; comics, 78; Norman E. Jennett's work, 13–15, 14, 18, 20; racist, 11
Cary, NC, 261

Cary News, 262
Cash, Wilbur J., 103, 133, 269
Cathcart, Lucy, 124
Cathcart, Noble, 121, 124
Catledge, Turner, 199
Caucasian, 50
Cecelski, David S., 25, 29
censorship, during World War I, 90–92
Chapel Hill, NC, 261
Chapel Hill News, 261, 262
Chappell, Fred, 181
Charlotte News, 205
Charlotte Observer: African American staff, 221; anti-union editorial stance, 107; editorial stance, 51, 55, 99; propaganda and hysteria, 149; Pulitzer Prize, 209; and *News and Observer*, 16, 202; state's largest conservative paper, 44–45, 108; on Supreme Court justice impeachments, 22; white supremacy campaigns, 10
Charlotte Record, 224
Chatham Asset Management, 264
Cherry, Gregg, 155, 269
Chesnutt, Charles W., 29, 180
child labor, campaign against, 54, 55
Child Labor Amendment, 55
Christensen, Rob, 231
Christian, W. E. "Billy," 43–44
Church, Bill, 262, 264
Churchill, Winston, 93, 109, 146
Civil Rights Act (1964), 169
civil rights movement, 144, 200–202; sit-ins, 168–69
Clark, David, 105, 114, 163
Clark, Walter, 33, 56
Clarke, Liz, 214
Clash of Angels (Jonathan Daniels), 123
classified advertising, 257
Cleveland, Grover, 8, 34, 62
Coble, Dorothy (Helms), 227
Columbia Journalism Review, 209, 250
comics. *See* cartoons
Committee on Civil Rights, 28
Cone Mills, Greensboro, strike, 105–6
Connor, R. D. W., 179

Conservative Manifesto (1937), 141
convict leasing system, 25–26
Cooper, David, 173
Cope, Dana, 255
Couch, William T., 131, 132, 138
Council against Intolerance, 74
Counts, Dorothy, 168
Craig, Lee, 30, 37, 71, 76–77, 124–25
Craven, Charles, 177, 194
Creel, George, 86, 90
Crisis, 179
Crisp, Fred, Jr., 187, 245, 248
Cuba, 76, 77
Curliss, Andrew, 254

Dabney, Virginius, 107, 136, 165
Daily Tar Heel (student newspaper), 121, 122, 262; and Frank Daniels Jr., 189
Daily Tribune, 41
Daniels, Adelaide "Addie" (Josephus' daughter), 34
Daniels, Adelaide Ann (Key) (Jonathan's daughter), 123, 243-44
Daniels, Adelaide Worth Bagley (Josephus's wife), 34, 35, 48, 75, 80, 92–94, 97, 118, 137, 141, 151
Daniels, Charles (Josephus's brother), 30
Daniels, Derick, 197–98, 219, 243
Daniels, Edgar, 244
Daniels, Elizabeth Bridgers, 122, 155
Daniels, Frank (Josephus's brother), 30, 54
Daniels, Frank, Jr., 1, 2, 29, 168, 188–92; anti-union stance, 194–95; *News and Observer* leadership, 218–19; *News and Observer* sports coverage, 215; political views, 216–17; sale of *News and Observer*, 244–46
Daniels, Frank, Sr. (Josephus's son), 2, 92, 120, 144, 169; McDowell Street building, 184; *News and Observer* role, 184–88
Daniels, Frank, III, 219, 235–42, *237*; after *News and Observer* sale, 246; restructuring of newspaper industry (1990s), 245–46
Daniels, Frank, IV, 236
Daniels, Jody, 30

Daniels, Joe, Jr., 120, 139
Daniels, Jonathan, 2, 44, 46, 48, 53, 71, 84, 92; alcohol, views and use of, 125–26; childhood and education, 120–22; civil rights, 164–65, 170, 211–12; *Clash of Angels*, 123–24; Democratic National Committeeman, 159–60; editor-in-training at *News and Observer*, 122–23; family life, 125; on FDR's staff, 141–42; final years and death, 195–96; foreign policies, views on, 138–39; and *Fortune*, 124; Frank Graham's senate campaign, 160–62; and Jesse Helms, 228–29; on lynching, 128–29; National Urban League address (1954), 164; *News and Observer* editorial policies, 4, 101–2, 105, 110, 124–25, 133–34; *News and Observer*, return to (1947), 148–49; New Zealand ambassadorship, 141; Office of Civilian Defense, World War II, 140–41; race relations, advisor to FDR, 143–46; racial views, evolution of, 126–33, 167–69, 170–71, 266; rebellious nature in youth, 122; social views (1960s), 171–73; Truman's presidential campaign (1948), 155–58; White House press secretary, 146–48, *147*
Daniels, Joseph (Frank III's son), 236
Daniels, Josephus, Jr., 92, 184
Daniels, Josephus, *67*
—journalism: early newspaper work, 31–32; editorial stances, strength of, 42–46; fights and altercations, 43–44; final years, 150–54; on freedom of press, 140; labor negotiations, 193; legacy of, 1–3, 265–67; moral crusades of, 58–59; *News and Observer*, purchase and early editorial work, 6–7, *7*, 35–38; *News and Observer* involvement from Mexico, 120; *News and Observer* return (1941), 137–38; *State Chronicle*, 31–34; Wilmington massacre, coverage of, 18–19; working habits of, 46
—personal life: appearance and personality, 66; autobiography, 118, 137, 150; car accident (1932), 111;

Index 315

Daniels, Josephus (continued)
—personal life (continued):
Chautauqua speaking circuit, 97–98; death and memorial, 152; estate of, 154; family background and childhood, 30–31; in final years, 150–52; financial loan (1932), 109–110; home and servants, 27; marriage and family, 34–35, 92–93; Methodist Church, 115; Mexico, embassy life, 118–19; moral and religious values, 59; mother's postmistress position, 8; prohibition of alcohol, 125–26; Wakestone (residence), 97–98, 153; Washington, DC, residence and social life, 92–94
—political influence: anti-imperialism, 75–76; William Jennings Bryant, support for, 47–49, 50–51; Democratic National Convention (1896), 49; Democratic Party, 8, 9–10, 54–55; election of 1898, 17; Franklin D. Roosevelt, relationship with, 81–85, 82; George White, treatment of, 13; governor, urged to run for, 111; Governor Morrison, criticism of, 100–102; incarceration in Yarborough House, 42; monetary policy, 48–49; political patronage, 33–34; political philosophy, 33; political power of, 3; presidential campaigns, advisor to, 50–53; presidential possibilities, 98–99; railroads, criticism of, 40; rift with Bryan, 99; white supremacy campaigns, 23; Wilson, relationship with, 80; as Wilsonian Democrat, 60–65; Wilson's reelection campaign (1916), 85–87
—public service: ambassador to Mexico, 74, 76, 112–119; Interior Department clerkship, 34–35; navy secretary, 66–71, 76–77, 85–92, 94–96; during World War I, 79–80; World War I peace negotiations, 93–94
—social issues: African Americans, relationship with, 27–28; convict leasing system, 26; Jim Crow laws, support for, 19–20, 23–24; Ku Klux Klan, opposition to, 26–27; literacy test enforcement (1903 election), 21–22; lynching, campaign against, 25; "paternalist ethos," 25, 27; prohibition of liquor, 58–59; public education reform, 56–59; racial attitudes, 3, 27–28, 73–75, 126; segregation, 8, 150–51; statue of, 1, 2, 266; suffrage for Blacks, opposition to, 20; underprivileged groups, support of, 2–3

Daniels, Julia, 238

Daniels, Kimberly, 236

Daniels, Lucy (Inman) (Jonathan's granddaughter), 223, 243

Daniels, Lucy (Inman) (Jonathan's daughter), 125, 148, 171, 183, 195–96, 235, 243

Daniels, Lucy Cathcart (Jonathan's wife), 124, 125, 157, 159, 195

Daniels, Mary Cleave, 30–31

Daniels, Worth, 92–93, 118–19, 120, 139, 197

Daniels, Worth, Jr., 244

Davison, Teresa, 236

Day, John, 214

Debnam, Betty, 219–20

Decker, Michael, 255

DeCock, Luke, 215

Democracy Betrayed (Cecelski and Tyson), 29

Democracy's Detectives (Hamilton), 206

Democratic Party, 2, 6; Black shift to, 22–23; William Jennings Bryan's influence, 48; control of newspapers, 16; Jonathan Daniels as National Committeeman, 159–60; Daniels family contributions, 267; defense of Daniels, pre–World War I, 86–87; Democratic National Convention (1896), 49; Democratic National Convention (1928), 100; Democratic National Convention (1936), 116; Democratic National Convention (1952), 162; early twenty-first century, 255; funding for *News and Observer*, 15; Ku Klux Klan, opposition to, 27; North Carolina politics, 53–56;

from populism to progressivism, 60–61; presidential campaign (1924), 98–99; presidential campaign (1948), 155–58; rooster symbol, 63; whites-only primaries, 22
Depression (1930s), 109–11
Desmond, Beth, 255
Dewey, Thomas, 155–56
Dixiecrat Party, 155–56
Dixon, Thomas, 71
Dominican Republic, 76, 77
Douglass, Frederick, 8–9
Downie, Leonard, Jr., 250
Drescher, John, 253–54, 254, 255, 256, 258, 264
Du Bois, W. E. B., 127, 133, 179
Duke, David, 233
Duke University, 210; lacrosse case, 252–53; Trinity College, 23–24, 33, 64
Durham, NC, 33, 259
Durham Herald Sun, 257
Durhams, Sharif, 222

Eagles, Charles, 126, 127, 131, 132–33, 166
Eagles, Joseph C., 167
Easley, Mike, 254–55
East, John, 230, 232
East Carolina University, 209
Edison, Thomas, 87, 90, 92
Edmisten, Rufus, 255
Edmonds, Helen G., 11, 29, 180
education: for African Americans, 129; evolution in curriculum, 58, 99; in Mexico, 115; public education reform, 56–59
Egerton, John, 136, 157, 196
Ehringhaus, J. C. B., 101–2, 129
1898 Wilmington Race Riot Report (2006), 253
Eisenhower, Dwight, 163
Elliot, Margaret "Bette," 149
Ellis, Tom, 233
End of Innocence, The (Daniels), 84
Enloe, William G., 169
Ericson, Eston Everett, 132
Ervin, Sam, Jr., 172

Espionage Act (1917), 91
Etheridge, Mark, 165
Evans, Harold, 216
Evening Visitor, 188
evolution: in school curricula, 58, 99; Scopes trial, 48

Fair Employment Practices Commission (FEPC), 145
Fairness in Media, 232
Farmers' Alliance, 6
Fayetteville Times, 174
Fentress, Simmons, 173
Field, Marshall, Jr., 148
Fields, Spurgeon, 150
Fields, Spurgeon, III, 236
Fire in Flint, The (White), 180
Fleming, Karl, 200–201
Fletcher, A. J., 226, 227–28
Fontello-Nanton, Hugo I., 22
Ford, Henry, 87, 92, 138
Ford, James W., 132
Ford, Steve, 238
Forde, Kathy Roberts, 3, 265
Fortune, 124
Fortune, T. Thomas, 3, 19, 21, 27
Franklin, John Hope, 29, 71–72, 73
Franklin, Jon, 239, 251
Freedom Riders, 170
Friday, William C., 1, 214
Frinks, Golden, 210
Frontier on the Potomac (Jonathan Daniels), 148
Funderburk, David, 231
Fusion government, 7–8, 16

Gaines, Robert "Bob," 27, 93
Galt, Edith Bolling, 80, 86
Gantt, Harvey, 232
Gardner, Ava, 152
Gardner, Jim, 177
Gardner, O. Max, 101, 103, 110, 116
Gastonia Daily Gazette, 103, 105
Gastonia textile strike, 101, 103–5
Gatehouse Media, 262
Geddings, Kevin, 255

Gell, Alan, 255
George Polk Award, 251
Gibson, Greg, 176
Gilded Age, 48
Gilmore, Glenda Elizabeth, 12
Glines, Sara, 262
Godbey, Earle, 103
Golden, Harry, 170
gold standard, 48–49
Goldwater, Barry, 163, 229, 230
Golenbock, Peter, 214
Goodnight, James, 184
Graham, Edward Kidder, 57
Graham, Frank Porter, 57–58, 74, 105, 130, 132, 138, 160–62, 172, 213, 227
Graham, Katherine "Kay," 190, 191
Graves, John Temple, 28, 165
Graves-Field House, 153–54
Green, Jimmy, 231
Green, Paul, 105, 121, 125, 138
Greensboro Daily News, 45, 103, 108, 179, 202, 232
Greensboro News, 92
Greensboro News and Record, 205
Greensboro Record, 224
Greenville Reflector, 16
Greenwood, Eula Nixon, 160
Gregg, Gail, 191
Gregory, Marion, 238, 251
Grumann, Cornelia, 251
Guggenheim, Simon, 110
Guggenheim Fellowship, 123
Guillory, Ferrel, 187, 204, 218
Gunther, John, 133, 147, 269
Gyllenhaal, Anders, 222, 238–39, 249–51, 250

Haiti, 76, 77
Hale, Peter M., 35
Hall, Jane, 149
Hamilton, James T., 206
Hannah-Jones, Nikole, 222, 251, 259
Harding, Warren G., 50, 94, 98, 99
Haywood, Robert W., 78
Healy, Thomas, 213
Hearst, William Randolph, 10, 98

Heck-Andrews House, 40
Hefner, Hugh, 197
Helms, Jesse, 4, 170, 209, 210, 263, 266; feud with *News and Observer*, 226–34, 268; *Viewpoint* (WRAL-TV), 227–28
Hemingway, Ernest, 121
Henderson, Dick, 245
Henry, Carol Y., 224
Herald-Sun, 259–60
Herbert, Dick, 177–78, 215
Hester, Neil, 108
higher education, 131. *See also* North Carolina State University; University of North Carolina
High Point Enterprise, 153, 154
Hill, Jemele, 222
Hobby, Wilbur, 194
Hocutt, Thomas R., 131
Hodges, Luther, 165, 166–67, 185
Hoey, Clyde, 50, 102, 111
Hold, Joseph Hiram, 165
Holden, William, 50
Holding, J. N., 36
Holloman, Martha H., 225
Holshouser, James, 218
homosexuality, 233
Hoover, Dan, 231
Hoover, Herbert, 24, 98, 100
Hoover, J. Edgar, 139
Hoover, Wesley, 27
Horner, Kay, 224
House, Edward, 86
House Un-American Activities Committee, 91, 139
Hughes, Charles Evan, 85, 86
Hull, Cordell, 100, 117–18
Humphries, Bill, 177
Hunt, Jim, 177, 181, 209, 217–18, 231, 232, 268, 269
Hunter, Marjorie, 149
Hurder, Wayne, 193
Hyman, Ethan, 176

Ickes, Harold, 141
immigration, views of, 74–75
Inman, Lucy Daniels, 171, 223, 243

Inman, Tom, 171, 198
Insider, 240, 246
integration: busing, 211; Pearsall Commission, 165–67; Raleigh schools, 210–11. *See also* segregation
International Typographical Union, 194
Island Packet, 195

Jacobs, Sally, 251
Jenkins, Jay, 173
Jenkins, Jim, 257
Jenkins, John, 44
Jennett, Norman E., 13–15, 20
Jenrette, Dick, 190
Jervey, Paul R., Sr., 156
Jewish Americans, discrimination against, 73–74, 267
Jewish Relief Committee, 74
Jim Crow laws, 3, 6, 72, 133; after Wilmington massacre, 19–20; Committee on Civil Rights, 156; opposition to, 23–24
John Locke Foundation, 170
Johnson, Gerald W., 103
Johnson, Guy B., 150
Johnson, Louis, 159
Johnson, Lyndon B., 2, 136, 142, 163; Great Society programs, 171
Jones, Dan H., 166
Jones, Dave, 43, 207, 215
Jones, Harrill, 221
Jones, Julia, 189
Jones, W. B., 43
Jordan, B. Everett, 172
journalism. *See* newspapers

Kaiser, Robert G., 250
Kane, Dan, 215, 251, 254
Kazin, Michael, 11, 47, 48, 49, 51, 88, 265
Kelly, Erin, 223
Kendrick, Swan, 72
Kennedy, John F., 2, 172, 200
Kennedy, Robert, 200
Kerouac, Jack, 199
Key, V. O., 269
Kilgo, John C., 24

Kilpatrick, James J., 167
King, Florence, 181
King, Martin Luther, Jr., 168, 171, 210, 227
Kinston Free Press, 16, 31
Kitchen, Claude, 84, 88
Klibanoff, Hank, 173–74, 199
Knight Commission on Intercollegiate Athletics, 214
Knight Ridder newspaper chain, 197, 202, 244, 249, 256
Krueger, Bill, 254
Ku Klux Klan, 26–27, 71, 165

labor unions, 102–9; Cone Mills, Greensboro, strike, 105–6; Gastonia textile strike, 101, 103–5; labor wars (1920s), 103–8; newspaper workers, 193–95
Lacy, Bridgett A., 222
La Follette, Robert, 55, 99
Laibe, Connie, 211
Lake, I. Beverly, Sr., 165, 167, 172, 268
Landis, James M., 140–41
Landmark Communications, 244
Larkins, John R., 131
Leidholdt, Alexander, 103
Lennon, Alton, 163, 226
Lepore, Jill, 265
letterpress printing, 208
Lewis, Nell Battle, 46, 100, 102–8, 128, 148, 161, 167, 180
Liddy, Chuck, 176
Life of Woodrow Wilson, The (Jonathan Daniels), 98
Liggett Myers Company, 101
Lilly, Mable Pearl, 169
Lindbergh, Charles, 138
linotype, 208
literacy tests for voting, 10, 20–22
Locke, Mandy, 254
Long, June B., 225
Lowenstein, Corey, 176
Lynch, Bob, 194
lynching, 15; anti-lynching laws, 128–29, 130, 156; campaign against, 25; Dillsboro (1898), 17
Lyons, Kelly Starling, 222

MacNeill, Ben Dixon, 108
Manly, Alex, 17–18, 21
Man of Independence, The (Jonathan Daniels), 159
Mapplethorpe, Robert, 233
March on Washington (1963), 170
Marlow, Gene, 194
Marrow of Truth, The (Chesnutt), 29
Marshall, Thurgood, 146
Martin, Gerald, 215
Mason, Lucy Rudolph, 133
Matthews, T. Z., 200
Mayo, Henry T., 76
McAlpin, Harry, 145
McCarthy, Joe, 91–92
McCarty, Barry, 231
McClatchy, James, 244
McClatchy Interactive, 246–47
McClatchy newspapers, 246, 248–49, 256; Chapter 11 bankruptcy, 264; decline of, 262–63
McCrory, Pat, 255
McDonald, Lany, 240–41
McDonald, Ralph, 111
McDonald, Sam R., 149
McGill, Ralph, 136, 165, 170
McKelway, A. J., 55
McKinley, William, 21, 50
McKissick, Floyd, 212
McKnight, Pete, 202, 232
McLean, Angus, 101
Media General, 244
Mencken, H. L., 100
Mercer, Lucy, 84
Meredith College, 33
Merritt, Fred, 44, 46
Mexico: Cárdenas, Lázaro, 116–17; Daniels's ambassadorship, 74, 76, 112–19; Mexico City, 114, 115
Middleton, Abe, 9
migration, 114
Miller, Mary, 251
Miller, Robert, 176
Miller, Stephen, 252
Mills, Beverly, 249
miscegenation laws, 28

monetary policy, 48–49
Moon, Owen, 170
Morgan, J. Pierpont, 39–40
Morrison, Cameron, 56, 97, 99, 100–101, 121
Moton, Robert, 27
Murphy, John, 206, 218
Murray, Pauli, 128
Murray, Steve, 176
Murrow, Edward R., 172
Myrdal, Gunnar, 133

NAACP (National Association for the Advancement of Colored People), 73, 130, 143, 166
Nando.net, 245, 246
Nando Times, 240
Nashville Argonaut, 16
Nation, 134
National Labor Committee on Child Labor, 55
National Labor Relations Board, 194
National Textile Workers Union, 103
Naval Academy, 68, 69, 70
Neff, Joseph, 252–53, 254, 259, 263
Negro and Fusion Politics in North Carolina, The (Edmonds), 29, 180
Negro State Fair (1898), 25
Neil, Dan, 240, 251
New Communities project, 212–13
New Day, The (Ragan), 181
New Deal liberalism, 60
News and Observer: advertisers, 45; anti-Fusionist stance, 8–9; children's Mini-Page, 219–20; circulation and revenue, 44–45, 52–53, 78, 108–9, 176, 185–86, 203, 224, 239, 243, 258; civil rights and racial issues, 128, 210–13; courtesy titles, 131–32; criticism for being liberal, 170; cultural affairs coverage, 178–12; Daniels family sale of (1988), 243–46; Daniels family shareholders, 243; Daniels' purchase of, 35–38; during Daniels' service in Washington, DC, 77–78; decline and advertising losses, 256–61; Democratic

stance, 171–74, 176–77; during Depression (1930s), 109–111; digital age adaptations, 240–41; Duke University lacrosse case, 252–53; *1898 Wilmington Race Riot Report,* 253; feud with Jesse Helms, 226–34, 268; Frank Daniels Jr.'s role, 190–91; Frank Daniels III's leadership, 235–42; labor negotiations, 192–95; labor union and strike coverage, 105–6; lawsuit (2010), 255; Martin Street building, 52, 53, 183–84; McClatchy era, 248–55; McDowell Street building, 183–84, 185, 258–59; minority recruitment, 220–23; New Deal, stance on, 137; during 1970s, 207–9; operating committee (1990s), 245–46; photojournalism, 176; political agenda, 54–55, 237–38; progressive views, 216; as propaganda tool, 11–12; race-baiting tactics, 11–12; racial issues, 131, 161; reorganization after Sitton's departure, 223–25; reprints from other papers, 16; reputation/legacy, 28–29, 45–46, 265–69; rural mail delivery, 45; on segregation and integration, 166; Sitton's editorship, political shifts, 215–20; sports coverage, 108, 213–15; and state politics, 254–55; support for Bryan, (1896), 50–51; technology, linotype to letterpress, 208; Under the Dome political column, 131, 174–75, 219, 223, 257; as union shop, 150; Wilson's campaign, 63; women on staff, 148–49; Women's Department, 181

Newspaper Association of America, 222

newspapers: advertising decline, 257–58; classified advertising, 257; community news, role of, 260–62; conservative political attacks on, 230–33; culture of newspapers, 208–9; decline of industry, 250, 254, 256; Democratic vs. Republican papers, 16; digital age, adaptation to, 240, 256, 258; journalistic ethics, 11, 218; labor unions for newspaper workers, 193–95; news deserts, 260; newspaper growth and influence (1920s), 108–9; newspaper industry, late nineteenth century, 38; railroads, reliance upon, 41; restructuring of newspaper industry (1990s), 244–45; role and impact of, 268–69; technology: flexographic presses, 245; Wilmington massacre, coverage of, 19; yellow journalism, 10–11. *See also names of individual newspapers*

New York Age, 27, 72

Nicaragua, 76, 77

Nifong, Mike, 252

Niolet, Benjamin, 253

Nixon, Richard, 151, 212, 216, 229

No Day of Triumph (Redding), 180

North Carolina: Black poverty, 129; cultural life, 268; Democratic Party politics, 53–56; education, 56–59; elections (1898), 15–17; financial struggles, Depression-era (1930s), 110–111; justice system, racial bias in, 127; labor wars (1920s), 103–8; newspapers, 108, 175, 268; poverty, 268; progressive movement, 100–102; Research Triangle, 181, 185, 203, 245, 258, 259; tobacco industry, 40, 101, 107, 175

North Carolina Central University, 130

North Carolina Historical Review, 179

North Carolina Peace Conference, 64–65

North Carolina Review, 178–79

North Carolina State University, 57, 180

North Carolina Supreme Court: impeachment of justices (1901), 22

Obama, Barack, 233, 264

Odum, Howard W., 130–31, 144

Office of Civilian Defense, 140

O'Hara, James, 8

O'Keefe, Herb, 134, 149, 223

Orangeburg massacre, 228–29

Our Navy at War (Daniels), 98

Overman, Lee, 84

Page, Walter Hines, 31, 32, 64

Park, John, 188

Parker, Roy, 172–73, 174

Index 321

patent medicine advertising, 45
paternalism, racial, 25, 27, 129–30, 133
Paxton Media Group, 259
Payne, Foster P., 131–32, 169
Pearce, Gary, 174, 202, 204, 217
Pearsall Commission, 165–67
Pearson, Drew, 171
Pearson, Richard, 44
Pegler, Westbrook, 4, 158
PEN America, 260
Pence, Tom, 61–62
People's Paper (Charlotte, NC), 12
Pepper, Claude, 131
Personal Fouls (Golenbock), 214
Phillips, Bruce, 215
Phipps, Meg Scott, 254
photojournalism, 176
Pierce, Neil, 240, 269
Pilot, 204, 246
Playboy Enterprises, 197
PlayMakers theater company, 121
poetry, 179
police brutality, 127–28
political patronage, 33–34
Polk, Leonidas, 33
Pollack, Lisa, 251
poll taxes, 10, 20–22, 129, 148, 156
Poole, Ruffin, 255
Pope, Art, 170
populism, 48–49. *See also* Fusion government
Populist Party, 6–7
Potts, Erwin, 244, 246
Pou, E. W., 84
Poulton, Bruce, 214–15
poverty: anti-poverty programs, 171; in North Carolina, 268
Powell, Dwane, 230
Prather, Leon, 29
Price, Woodrow, 173, 176–77, 205
prison abuses/brutality, 26, 127–28
progressive income tax, 54
prohibition of alcohol, 58–59; on naval property, 69–70; Prohibition campaign, 75, 100, 125–26
prostitution, 70

public education reform, 56–59
Pulitzer Prizes, 179, 204–5, 206, 209, 222, 235, 241, 251
Purnell, T. R., 42

Quarles, Orage, III, 222, 248–49, 262
Quokka Sports Inc., 247

Race Beat, The (Roberts and Klibanoff), 173–74, 199
racial issues: biological foundation for racism, 28; contemporary views, 153; integration on *News and Observer* staff, 220–23; Jonathan Daniels as FDR's advisor, 143–46; racial paternalism, 25, 27, 129–30, 133; terminology and wording used, 131–32; in twenty-first century, 263–64
Ragan, Sam, 161, 176, 178, 180–81, 198, 220–21
railroads: criticism of, 40; newspapers, reliance on, 41; opposition to, 40–41; power of, 39–40
Raines, Howell, 235
Raleigh, NC, 33, 37; city manager form of government, 132–33; integrated schools, 210–11; mayoral race (2019), 263; radio and television stations, 187–88
Raleigh Evening Times, 41
Raleigh Morning Post, 41
Raleigh Newsweekly, 170
Raleigh Sentinel, 35
Raleigh Times, 188, 192, 220, 223–24, 227
Raleigh Typographical Union, 193
Rankin, Jim, 149
rape: accusations of, 12, 13, 17; Black people portrayed as sexual predators, 14
Rayburn, Sam, 142
Raynor, David, 254
Reagan, Ronald, 229, 231
Redding, J. Saunders, 180
Red Scare, 91
Red Shirts, 10, 20, 84
Red Summer, 73
Republican Party, 255; Populist Party coalition, 6–7

Research Triangle, 181, 185, 203, 239, 245, 258, 259
Reynolds, Robert, 161
Rich, Cleves, 242, 243
Richissin, Todd, 251, 259
Riley, Rochelle, 222
Riley, Steve, 253
Ritterhouse, Jennifer, 135
Roberts, Gene, 173–74, 175, 176, 179, 198, 199, 239
Robinson, Mark, 264
Robinson, Russell, 244
Rocky Mount Reporter, 31
Rogers, Dennis, 177, 217, 257
Rogers, Wiley, 46
Romney, Mitt, 238
Roosevelt, Eleanor, 3, 73, 83, 125, 136, 152; racial views, 144, 146
Roosevelt, Franklin D.: appointment of Daniels as ambassador, 112–13; Child Labor Amendment, 55; foreign policy, 114, 117; Jonathan Daniels as aide, 141–46; Jonathan Daniels as press secretary, 146–47; Jonathan Daniels's correspondence with, 106–7; as Josephus Daniels's assistant, 77, 81–85, 82; Josephus Daniels's support for, 22; New Deal policies, 48, 137
Roosevelt, Theodore, 23, 62, 64, 79, 83
Rosenwald, Julius, 57
Russell, Daniel, 9, 10, 13, 218

Sanders, Charlie, 190
Sanford, Terry, 159, 166, 170, 171, 172–73, 216, 268
Sargent, Mike, 176
Saunders, Barry, 222, 257, 260
Saunders, William L., 35
Scales, Junius, 152
Schewel, Steve, 175, 260
Schlesinger, Arthur, Jr., 136, 172
Schuster, M. Lincoln, 110
Scopes trial, 48, 99
Scott, Bob, 176, 177, 181, 205–6
Scott, W. Kerr, 159, 160, 163, 166, 172, 177, 205, 268

Scottsboro Boys, 126–27
Sedition Act (1918), 91
segregation, 8, 126, 150–51; culture of, in the South, 28; and Democratic Party (1890s), 19–20; Dixiecrat Party, 155–56; end of, 164; Frank Daniels Sr.'s support for, 144; *News and Observer* support for, 4; Southern Manifesto, 167. *See also* integration
Sharpe, Scott, 176
Shaw University, 169
Sheehan, Ruth, 251, 257
Shepard, James E., 130, 180
Sherwood, Ben, 223
Shipp, Bill, 200
Shoemaker, Don, 198
Shumaker, Jim, 261
Sill, Melanie, 28, 239, 241, 251–53
Simmons, Furnifold, 9, 10, 20, 22, 25, 33, 49, 53, 54–55, 56, 74–75, 84, 100
Simmons, Tim, 250–51
Simmons Machine, 53, 100
Sims, William, 94–95
Sitton, Claude, 173, 187, 193, 198–207, 203, 209, 213–14, 264, 268; civil rights activism, coverage of, 210–13; editorial role, 218–19; and Jesse Helms, 229–33; *News and Observer* political shifts, 215–20
Skube, Michael, 179, 251
Smethurst, Frank, 58, 102, 108, 124, 226
Smith, Al, 100, 103
Smith, Hoke, 34
Smith, Jean Edward, 84, 95–96
Smith, Lee, 181
Smith, Willis, 161–62, 226, 227, 268
Smithfield Herald, 261, 262
Snider, Bill, 232
Snow, A. C., 223
Sosna, Morton, 133
Soul City development, 212–13
Sousa, John Philip, 92
Southern Conference on Human Welfare, 133
Southerner Discovers New England, A (Jonathan Daniels), 136

Southerner Discovers the South, A (Jonathan Daniels), 135–36
Southern Manifesto, 167
Spanish-American War, 10, 75
Spencer, Richard, 252
Squire, Elizabeth Daniels, 243–44
Stancill, Jane, 259
State Chronicle, 31–34
Steptoe, Easy, 201
Stevenson, Adlai, 2, 136, 162–63
Stith, Pat, 205–7, 212, 240–41, 241, 251, 254
Stone, C. C., 156–57
Strange Career of Jim Crow, The (Woodward), 4
Sullivan, Margaret, 260
Sulzberger, Arthur Ochs, Jr., 191–92
Sulzberger, Arthur "Punch," 191
Sutton, Will, 222
Svrluga, Barry, 215
Swann v. Charlotte-Mecklenburg Board of Education, 211

Taft, William Howard, 51, 62
Taft-Hartley Act, 193
Talmadge, Eugene, 162, 199
Tar Heels (Jonathan Daniels), 136
tariffs, 54
Taylor, J. W., 224–25
Taylor, Mary-Jeanette, 197
Taylor, Stuart, Jr., 253
Textile Bulletin, 105, 114, 163
textile industry, 55, 103; Cone Mills, Greensboro, 105–6; Gastonia strike, 101, 103–5
Thigpen, Joseph H., 225
Thomas, Norman, 106, 113
Tiede, Joe, 215
Tillman, Benjamin, 72, 84
Time between the Wars, The (Daniels), 84
Tindall, George B., 133, 135, 269
tobacco industry, 40, 101, 175; R. J. Reynolds strike (1947), 107
Tocsin, 193
Tomlin, Robyn, 262, 264
Trinity College (Duke University), 23–24, 33, 64

Truman, Harry, 2, 28, 48, 136, 151, 152; Jonathan Daniels as press secretary, 147–48; presidential campaign (1948), 155–58
Truman, Margaret, 159
Trump, Donald, 222, 230, 263
Tudor, Caulton, 215
Tuskegee Institute, 27
Tyson, Timothy B., 25, 28, 29, 253

Umfleet, LeRae, 29
Umstead, William, 165
University of North Carolina, 57–58, 78, 99, 100, 150; *Daily Tar Heel*, 121, 122, 189, 262; funding for, 10; Jonathan Daniels' attendance, 121; sports programs, 213–15
USS *Addie Bagley Daniels*, 151
USS *Dolphin*, 67–68
USS *Josephus Daniels*, 172
Uzzle, Burk, 176

Vaden, Ted, 218, 220, 261–62
Valvano, Jim, 213, 214–15
Vietnam War, 171
vigilante groups: Ku Klux Klan, 26–27, 71, 165; Red Shirts, 10, 20, 84
Vital Source Technologies Inc., 247
voting rights: poll taxes and literacy tests, 10, 20–22, 129, 148, 156; voter registration efforts, 22; women's suffrage, 75
Voting Rights Act (1965), 169

Waddell, Alfred, 18
Wakestone (residence), 97–98, 153
Wall, Julia, 176
Wallace, George, 200, 216, 230
Wallace, Henry, 3, 116, 151–52, 155, 265
Ward, Govan "Sweat," 128–29
Warrick, Joby, 241, 251
Washington, Booker T., 23–24, 27
Washington, DC, 71–72
Watauga Club, 33
Waters, Rob, 190, 242
Watts, A. D., 101
Wayne, Leslie, 204

324   *Index*

We Have Taken a City (Prather), 29
Wells, Ida B., 21
White, George, 12–13
White, Jim, 215
White, Walter F., 130, 180
white supremacy: *News and Observer*'s editorial stance, 11–12; white supremacy campaigns, 3, 9–10, 16–17, 51, 153, 253, 265–66
Whitlock, Craig, 251, 259
Wiggins, Ella Mae, 105
Willett, Robert, 176
Williams, Linda, 210, 220, 221, 222
Williams, Robert E. "Fleet," 104, 108
Wilmington Messenger, 16, 18–19
Wilmington massacre, 17–19, 28–29, 253
Wilmington's Lie (Zucchino), 29
Wilmington Star, 16
Wilmington Star-News, 224, 262
Wilmington Ten, 211–12
Wilson, Woodrow, 2, 48, 55, 60–65, 67; Daniels, relationship with, 80; racial views, 72; reelection campaign (1916), 85–87; World War I, 88–89
Wilson Advance, 31
Winston Free Press, 16
Winston Journal, 16
Winston-Salem Journal, 45, 107, 202
Wise, Jim, 260

WNAO (television station), 188
WNAO/WKIX (radio station), 187–88
Wofford, Lawrence, 176
Wolfe, Thomas, 121–22, 136, 196
women's rights, 75
Wood, James L., 45
Woodward, C. Vann, 4, 28, 56, 100
World War I, 78–80, 83, 85, 87–90; censorship, 90–92
World War II, 89, 138–39, 149
Woronoff, Bobby, 236, 245
Woronoff, David, 236, 246
Woronoff, Patsy, 244
Worth, Jonathan, 34
WRAL-TV, 227

xenophobia, 74

Yalta Conference, 146
Yarborough, Wilson F., 167
Yates, E. Y., 84
yellow journalism, 10–11
Yeoman, Barry, 208
Yopp, Mike, 192
Young, James, 9, 13–14

Zane, J. Peder, 179, 181, 257
Zucchino, David, 14, 29, 204